RUSSIA AND THE WESTI
FAR RIGHT

The growing influence on the Western far right has been much discussed in the media recently. This book is the first detailed inquiry into what has been a neglected but critically important trend: the growing links between Russian actors and Western far-right activists, publicists, ideologues and politicians. The author uses a range of sources including interviews, video footage, leaked communications, official statements and press coverage in order to discuss both historical and contemporary Russia in terms of its relationship with the Western far right.

Initial contacts between Russian political actors and Western far-right activists were established in the early 1990s, but these contacts were low profile. As Moscow has become more anti-Western, these contacts have become more intense and have operated at a higher level. The book shows that the Russian establishment was first interested in using the Western far right to legitimise Moscow's politics and actions both domestically and internationally, but more recently Moscow has begun to support particular far right political forces to gain leverage on European politics and undermine the liberal-democratic consensus in the West.

Contributing to ongoing scholarly debates about Russia's role in the world, its strategies aimed at securing legitimation of Putin's regime both internationally and domestically, modern information warfare and propaganda, far-right politics and activism in the West, this book draws on theories and methods from history, political science, area studies, and media studies and will be of interest to students, scholars, activists and practitioners in these areas.

Anton Shekhovtsov is Visiting Fellow at the Institute for Human Sciences, Austria.

Routledge Studies in Fascism and the Far Right

Series editors: Nigel Copsey, *Teesside University*, and
Graham Macklin, *Teesside University*

This new book series focuses upon fascist, far-right and right-wing politics primarily within a historical context but also drawing on insights from other disciplinary perspectives. Its scope also includes radical-right populism, cultural manifestations of the far right and points of convergence and exchange with the mainstream and traditional right.

Titles include:

RUSSIA AND THE WESTERN FAR RIGHT

Tango Noir

Anton Shekhovtsov

Routledge
Taylor & Francis Group

LONDON AND NEW YORK

First published 2018
by Routledge
2 Park Square, Milton Park, Abingdon, Oxon OX14 4RN

and by Routledge
711 Third Avenue, New York, NY 10017

Routledge is an imprint of the Taylor & Francis Group, an informa business

British Library Cataloguing in Publication Data
A catalogue record for this book is available from the British Library

Library of Congress Cataloging-in-Publication Data
A catalog record has been requested for this book

ISBN: 978-1-138-65863-9 (hbk)
ISBN: 978-1-138-65864-6 (pbk)
ISBN: 978-1-315-56099-1 (ebk)

Typeset in Bembo and Stone Sans
by Florence Production Ltd, Stoodleigh, Devon, UK

Printed and bound by CPI Group (UK) Ltd, Croydon, CR0 4YY

To the memory of my mother,
Lyudmila Shekhovtsova
(2 December 1950–28 June 2015)

'Anton Shekhovtsov is the world's leading expert on Russian political warfare against the West. His book is a masterly investigation of the Kremlin's tactics and strategy, highlighting both successes – and failures. It is essential reading for anyone who wants to defend our freedom from our most formidable adversaries: Russia's crony-capitalist ex-KGB regime.'

Edward Lucas, Senior Editor, The Economist

'Events in Ukraine, Syria, and the US elections have thrust Putin's foreign policies to the centre of the attention of the Western media. Meanwhile, the growing nexus of informal contacts between his government and the far right, both inside and outside Russia, has been practically ignored. Shekhovtsov has deployed his rare combination of expertise in fascist studies and fluency in the relevant languages and cultures to good effect, filling in with meticulous scholarship what turns out to be a disturbingly large gap in the conventional understanding of Putinism. The result is a book relevant not just to observers of right-wing extremism and Russia-watchers everywhere, but to anyone prepared to be even more concerned about the new Cold War, where firewalls, encryption, and maskirovka have replaced watchposts, spies, and Pravda.'

Roger Griffin, Author of Modernism and Fascism

CONTENTS

TABLE

ACKNOWLEDGEMENTS

This book is a result of a two-year-and-a-half research project conducted, for the most part, during my two postdoctoral fellowships in the vibrant intellectual atmosphere of the Vienna-based Institute for Human Sciences (Institut für die Wissenschaften vom Menschen, IWM), which is famous for its support of research on human rights, and democratic transitions and transformations.

I am grateful to all staff members of the IWM, and especially to the rector of the Institute Shalini Randeria and the fellowship programme coordinator Mary Kemle-Gussing, for making my stay at the Institute the best and most productive experience I ever had. I am grateful to permanent fellows of the IWM Ivan Krastev, Klaus Nellen and Timothy Snyder, as well as the director of several fellowship programmes Tetiana Zhurzhenko, for their overwhelming and enthusiastic support of my research.

During my stay at the IWM, I was privileged to discuss various aspects of this book with Russian colleagues who visited the Institute through the 'Russia in Global Dialogue' programme, in particular Irina Borogan, Masha Gessen, Vladislav Inozemtsev, Alexander Morozov and Andrei Soldatov – I cannot thank them enough for sharing their ideas with me.

I wish to express my deepest gratitude to people who provided moral support during my work on this book: my family and friends, Devin Ackles, Anne Applebaum, Gerry Gable, Sonia Gable, Paul Goble, Roger Griffin, Stefan Klatev, Péter Krekó, Marlène Laruelle, Edward Lucas, Peter Pomerantsev and Andrew Wilson.

I would like to thank dozens of followers of my blog, Facebook and Twitter accounts – the majority of them will remain unnamed for various reasons – who ensured that I was informed of the most recent developments related to the subject of my book. I am also grateful for useful information, important sources and valuable advice provided by Jeffrey Bale, Dimitar Bechev, Robert Beckhusen, Denis

Bohush, Olga Bronnikova, Jean-Yves Camus, Paula Chertok, Fabio D'Aleo, Herwig Höller, Robert Horvath, Mathias Huter, Victor Ilie, Sanita Jemberga, Gregory Kalyniuk, Nicolas Lebourg, Marian Madeła, Magdalena Marsovszky, Bernhard Odehnal, Marcin Rey, Uwe Sailer, Giovanni Savino, Anya Stroganova, Raphaël Tresanini, Joris Van Bladel, Alexander Verkhovsky, Oleh Vernik and Jakub Woroncow.

I also wish to thank the editors of the Routledge book series 'Fascism and the Far Right' Nigel Copsey and Graham Macklin, Routledge's senior publisher for politics and international studies Craig Fowlie, as well as anonymous reviewers of the first draft of this book for their helpful and thoughtful comments.

Finally, for long-standing and continuous support, I am indebted to Andreas Umland who not only helped me through numerous difficult moments during this research, but also edited this manuscript and provided insightful suggestions as to how to improve it.

Anton Shekhovtsov
5 June 2017
Vienna

ABBREVIATIONS

AAFER	Association Alliance France-Europe Russie (Association France-Europe-Russia Alliance)	France
ACLR	Associazione Culturale Lombardia Russia (Lombardy-Russia Cultural Association)	Italy
ADFR	Association Dialogue Franco-Russe (French-Russian Dialogue Association)	France
AfD	Alternative für Deutschland (Alternative for Germany)	Germany
ALDE/ADLE	Alliance of Liberals and Democrats for Europe Group	European Union
BfV	Bundesamt für Verfassungsschutz (Federal Office for the Protection of the Constitution)	Germany
BIB	Bundesinstitut für internationalen Bildungs- und Technologietransfer (Federal Institute for International Education and Technology Transfer)	Austria
BNP	British National Party	United Kingdom
BRICS	Brazil, Russia, India, China and South Africa	International
BZÖ	Bündnis Zukunft Österreich (Alliance for the Future of Austria)	Austria
CDU	Christlich Demokratische Union Deutschlands (Christian Democratic Union of Germany)	Germany
CEDADE	Circulo Espanol de Amigos de Europa (Spanish Circle of Friends of Europe)	Spain
CEO	Chief executive officer	International

CFR	Collectif France-Russie (France-Russia Collective)	France
CIA	Central Intelligence Agency	United States of America
CIS	Commonwealth of the Independent States	International
CIS-EMO	Commonwealth of the Independent States – Election Monitoring Organisation	Russia
CoE	Council of Europe	International
CPE	Coordinamento Progetto Eurasia (Eurasia Coordination Project)	Italy
DF	Dansk Folkeparti (Danish People's Party)	Denmark
DNR	'Donetsk People's Republic'	Ukraine
DRP	Deutsche Reichspartei (German Imperial Party)	West Germany
DVU	Deutsche Volksunion (German People's Union)	Germany
ECAG	Europejskie Centrum Analiz Geopolitycznych (European Centre of Geopolitical Analysis)	Poland
ECR	European Conservatives and Reformists	European Union
EEC	European Economic Community	International
EEU	Eurasian Economic Union	International
EFD	Europe of Freedom and Democracy	European Union
EFDD	Europe of Freedom and Direct Democracy	European Union
ELF	European Liberation Front	United Kingdom, international
EODE	Eurasian Observatory for Democracy & Elections	Belgium
EPP	European People's Party	European Union
ESM	Evraziyskiy soyuz molodezhi (Eurasian Youth Union)	Russia
EU	European Union	International
FBI	Federal Bureau of Investigation	United States of America
FCRB	First Czech-Russian Bank	Russia
FeS	Führungsring ehemaliger Soldaten (Leadership Committee for Former Soldiers)	East Germany
FN	Front National (National Front)	France
FPÖ	Freiheitliche Partei Österreichs (Freedom Party of Austria)	Austria

FRM	Fond 'Russkiy Mir' (Russian World Foundation)	Russia
FSB	Federal'naya sluzhba bezopasnosti (Federal Security Department)	Russia
GRECE	Groupement de recherche et d'études pour la civilisation européenne (Research and Study Group for European Civilisation)	France
Greens/EFA	The Greens – European Free Alliance	European Union
GRU	Glavnoe Razvedyvatel'noe Upravleniye (Main Intelligence Directorate)	Russia
GSN	Gruppe Sozialrevolutionärer Nationalisten (Group of Social Revolutionary Nationalists)	German Empire
GUD	Groupe Union Défense (Defence Union Group)	France
GUE-NGL	United Left/Nordic Green Left	European Union
IDC	Institute of Democracy and Cooperation	Russia
IPA CIS	Interparliamentary Assembly of the CIS Member Nations	Russia
IsAG	Istituto di Alti Studi in Geopolitica e Scienze Ausiliarie (Institute of Advanced Studies in Geopolitics and Auxiliary Sciences)	Italy
JAfD	Junge Alternative für Deutschland (Young Alternative for Germany)	Germany
KGB	Komitet gosudarstvennoy bezopasnosti (Committee for State Security)	Soviet Union
KPD	Kommunistische Partei Deutschlands (Communist Party of Germany)	German Empire
KPÖ	Kommunistische Partei Österreichs (Communist Party of Austria)	Austria
KPRF	Kommunisticheskaya partiya Rossiyskoy Federatsii (Communist Party of the Russian Federation)	Russia
LAOS	Laikós Orthódoxos Synagermós (Popular Orthodox Rally)	Greece
LDPR	Liberal'no-demokraticheskaya partiya Rossii (Liberal-Democratic Party of Russia)	Russia
LN	Lega Nord (Northern League)	Italy
LNR	'Luhansk People's Republic'	Ukraine
LPR	Liga Polskich Rodzin (League of Polish Families)	Poland
MAC	Mouvement d'Action Civique (Civic Action Movement)	Belgium

MED	Mezhdunarodnoe evraziyskoe dvizhenie (International Eurasianist Movement)	Russia
MEP	Member of the European Parliament	European Union
MFA	Ministry of Foreign Affairs	International
MNA	Magyar Nemzeti Arcvonal (Hungarian National Front)	Hungary
MP	Member of Parliament	International
MSI	Movimento Sociale Italiano (Italian Social Movement)	Italy
NA	Nacionālā apvienība (National Alliance)	Latvia
NATO	North Atlantic Treaty Organisation	International
NBP	Natsional-bol'shevistskaya partiya (National-Bolshevik Party)	Russia
NDI	National Democratic Institute	United States of America
NDPD	Nationaldemokratische Partei Deutschlands (National-Democratic Party of Germany)	East Germany
NDV	Nationaldemokratischen Verband (National Democratic Union)	Austria
NI	Non-Inscrits (independent MEPs)	European Union
NL	Nationale Liga (National League)	Austria
NPD	Nationaldemokratische Partei Deutschlands (National-Democratic Party of Germany)	West Germany/ Germany
NRP	National Renaissance Party	United States of America
NSDAP	Nationalsozialistische Deutsche Arbeiterpartei (National Socialist German Workers' Party)	Third Reich
OAS	Organisation de l'armée secrete (Organisation of the Secret Army)	France
ODIHR	Office for Democratic Institutions and Human Rights	International
ORFG	Österreichisch-Russische Freundschaftsgesellschaft (Society of Austrian-Russian Friendship)	Austria
OSCE	Organisation for Security and Cooperation in Europe	International
ÖVP	Österreichische Volkspartei (Austrian People's Party)	Austria
PACE	Parliamentary Assembly of the Council of Europe	International

PCE	Parti Communautaire Européen (European Communitarian Party)	Belgium
PCN	Parti Communautaire National-Européen (Communitarian National-European Party)	Belgium
PCS/ML	Parti communiste suisse/marxiste-léniniste (Swiss Communist Party/Marxist-Leninist)	Switzerland
PDF	Parti de la France (Party of France)	France
PRM	Partidului România Mare (Greater Romania Party)	Romania
PS	Perussuomalaiset (The Finns)	Finland
PVV	Partij voor de Vrijheid (Party for Freedom)	Netherlands
RBM	Rassemblement bleu Marine (Marine Blue Gathering)	France
REKOS	Die Reformkonservativen (Reform Conservatives)	Austria
RIM	Rossiysko-Ital'yanskaya molodyozh (Russian Italian Youth)	Italy/Russia
RNE	Russkoe natsional'noe edinstvo (Russian National Unity)	Russia
S&D	Progressive Alliance of Socialists and Democrats	European Union
SA	Sturmabteilung (Storm Detachment)	Third Reich
SD	Sverigedemokraterna (Sweden Democrats)	Sweden
SMA	Soviet Military Administration	East Germany
SNS	Slovenská národná strana (Slovak National Party)	Slovakia
SPD	Sozialdemokratische Partei Deutschlands (Social Democratic Party of Germany)	West Germany/ Germany
SPÖ	Sozialdemokratische Partei Österreichs (Social Democratic Party of Austria)	Austria
SRP	Sozialistische Reichspartei (Socialist Reich Party)	West Germany
SRS	Srpska Radikalna Stranka (Serbian Radical Party)	Serbia
SS	Schutzstaffel (Protection Squadron)	Third Reich
TT	Tvarka ir teisingumas (Order and Justice)	Lithuania
UK	United Kingdom of Great Britain and Northern Ireland	
UKIP	UK Independence Party	United Kingdom
UM	Union Movement	United Kingdom
UN	United Nations	International

US	United States	
USA	United States of America	
USAID	United States Agency for International Development	United States of America
USSR	Union of Soviet Socialist Republics	
VB	Vlaams Belang (Flemish Interest)	Belgium
VdU	Verband der Unabhängigen (Federation of Independents)	Austria
VoR	Voice of Russia	Russia
WCF	World Congress of Families	International
XA	Laïkós Sýndesmos – Chrysí Avgí (Popular Association – Golden Dawn)	Greece

INTRODUCTION

In the recent few years, there has been a growing concern in the West about the convergence or, at least, marriage of convenience between Vladimir Putin's Russia and far-right forces in the West, most notably in Europe. Indeed, we have witnessed the increasing number of far-right politicians' statements praising Putin's Russia and contacts between the Western far right and Russian officials and other actors.

Concerns about these developments seem to be even more pronounced given the present condition of the West characterised – among many other ills – by the threat of terrorist attacks, migration and refugee crises, austerity policies, the Eurozone crisis and perceived lack of effective leadership. Moscow's apparent cooperation with the far right, which blame liberal-democratic governments for the West's woes, is often interpreted, especially in the Western mainstream media, as an attempt to weaken the West even further and undermine liberal democracy internationally. For example, an article in *Foreign Policy* argues that 'Russian support of the far right in Europe has [to do] with [Putin's] desire to destabilize European governments, prevent EU expansion, and help bring to power European governments that are friendly to Russia'.[1] An article in *The Economist* presumes that the rise of the far right 'is more likely to influence national politics and to push governments into more Eurosceptic positions' and this will make it harder 'for the Europeans to come up with a firm and united response to Mr Putin's military challenge to the post-war order in Europe'.[2]

Are these fears and anxieties regarding Moscow's intentions or expectations justified? Does Putin's Russia – by cooperating with illiberal and isolationist politicians and activists in the West – pursue policies seeking to undermine Western liberal-democratic governments and weaken Western unity? At the same time, why has Putin's Russia recently become a focal point for many Western far-right parties and organisations and what do they expect from cooperation with

Russia? These questions constitute some of the main issues addressed in this book. However, they cannot be pursued out of a more general context. Thus, before I proceed with a discussion of the existing literature on the subject and outline the main hypotheses and structure of the book, I will provide this general context by giving a brief overview of Russia's contemporary relations with the West, on the one hand, and surveying the contemporary far-right milieu, on the other, as well as explaining major concepts and terms used throughout the book.

Re-emergence of the Russian challenge

After the demise of the Soviet Union in 1991, the West welcomed Russia as a democratising state and embraced its apparent desire to integrate into the Western markets and political institutions. As a legal successor of the Soviet Union, post-Soviet Russia assumed the Union's seat in the United Nations (UN), including the permanent seat in the UN Security Council, thus retaining the powerful instrument of exerting international influence. The European Economic Community and, later, the European Union (EU) became Russia's main trading partner; Russia joined the Council of Europe (CoE) in 1996 and was admitted into the Group of Seven (better known as G7), the elite club of major industrialised countries that, consequently, became G8 in 1997. The same year, the NATO-Russia Permanent Joint Council was created and then replaced, in 2002, by the NATO-Russia Council, 'a mechanism for consultation, consensus building, cooperation, joint decision and joint action, in which the individual NATO member states and Russia work as equal partners on a wide spectrum of security issues of common interest'.[3] It appeared that – recalling the intellectual movements in the Russian Empire in the nineteenth century – the Russian Westernisers (*zapadniki*) eventually won over the Slavophiles (*slavophily*), the adherents of Russia's authoritarian 'special path'.

In reality, however, the relations between the West and Russia already in the 1990s were a cynical case of (self-)deception. While presenting itself as a striving liberal democracy, Russia occupied part of post-Soviet Moldova and backed the creation of an unrecognised state of Transnistria in 1992. In 1994–1996, Russian armed forces ruthlessly suppressed the Chechen separatists during the First Chechen War. None of these developments hampered Russia's joining the CoE. Perhaps predictably, Russia has failed to honour some of the most important obligations and commitments that it undertook when it joined the CoE: it has not ratified Protocol No. 6 to the European Convention on Human Rights concerning the abolition of the death penalty; neither has Russia denounced the concept of 'near abroad' that effectively identified the other former Soviet republics as Russia's zone of special influence; nor has Russia withdrawn its troops from Transnistria although it officially agreed to do it first by 1998 and, later, by the end of 2002. The CoE would repeatedly reprimand the Russian authorities over the non-fulfilment of their obligations and commitments, but Russia ignored the appeals and went unpunished.

Western liberal progressivists assumed that it was necessary to be patient with Russia: its pace of reforms might not be as fast as that of Poland or Hungary, but Russia's integration into the capitalist market and international institutions would put the country firmly on the track democratising political reforms. This assumption failed miserably.

In the 1990s, Russia's transition from a socialist planned economy to a capitalist market economy turned into a catastrophe for the Russian society. As David Satter put it, the course of reforms in Russia was shaped by a set of attitudes that included 'social darwinism, economic determinism and a tolerant attitude toward crime'.[4] While the population became impoverished, money was concentrated 'in the hands of gangsters, corrupt former members of the Soviet nomenklatura,[5] and veterans of the underground economy. Resources were controlled by government officials'.[6]

The Russian state itself turned into what can – in an exaggerated form – be called 'a mafia state'. Ironically, the first noteworthy assessment of Russia as a mafia state originated from Russia's first president Bons Yeltsin himself: in 1994, he publicly described his own country as the 'biggest mafia state in the world' and the 'superpower of crime'.[7] Behind these sensationalist terms was the fact that:

> Corruption in Russia has penetrated the political, economic, judicial and social systems so thoroughly that has ceased to be a deviation from the norm and has become *the norm itself*. By pursuing poorly thought-out actions during its transition to a market economy [in the 1990s], *the state became a generator of crime*; in other words, *the authorities became criminal-based institutions* generating a social behaviour.[8]

All-permeating corruption became a major foundation of the 'virtuality' of Russia as a democratic state. This 'virtuality' was further advanced by the development of a new class of people who helped the ruling elites run the country, namely political technologists, 'ultra-cynical political manipulators who created a fake democracy because Yeltsin couldn't build a real one, and who distracted the population with carefully scripted drama because the energy wealth had temporarily stopped flowing'.[9] In a sense, political technology in Yeltsin's Russia became a substitute for efficient political institutions, just as corruption was a substitute for working economic institutions that Yeltsin failed to build after the demise of the Soviet Union.

The West played a detrimental role in this process: not only did Western capitals ignore the negative developments in Russia, 'the Western community [also] allowed the Russian elite to turn its banks and business structures into machines for laundering Russian dirty money. And the West's political and business circles understood perfectly what was going on'.[10]

Western governments did heavily criticise the Russian authorities over their actions during the Second Chechen War that started in 1999. There were strong statements and speculations about Western economic sanctions against Russia. US President Bill Clinton threatened that Russia would 'pay a heavy price' for its actions,[11] while UK Foreign Secretary Robin Cook compared Russia's tactics in Chechnya to those of Yugoslavia's President Slobodan Milošević in Kosovo[12] – this was a menacing statement considering that NATO allies had bombed Milošević's Yugoslavia for the persecution of the Albanian population in Kosovo. However, no matter how strong the words of Western leaders were, none of their statements was accompanied by any policy initiative. The head of the Organisation for Security and Cooperation in Europe (OSCE) acknowledged there was little that the organisation could do 'beyond attempting to put moral pressure on Moscow'.[13] The Parliamentary Assembly of the CoE (PACE) suspended Russia in 2000 because of the human rights violations in Chechnya, but reinstated it within less than a year, despite the fact that Russia continued to violate human rights in the insurgent region.

After Putin replaced Yeltsin as Russian president, the situation gradually worsened. Not only did Russia maintain military presence in Moldova's Transnistria in violation of its commitments and invade Georgia in 2008 without any consequences from the West, but Putin's regime became also increasingly right-wing, authoritarian, patrimonial and anti-Western.[14]

To thwart the attempts of some countries in the 'near abroad', in particular Georgia, Moldova and Ukraine, to move closer to the West, Moscow drew upon the Soviet experience of so-called active measures (*aktivnye meropriyatiya*). According to one Soviet top-secret counterintelligence dictionary, active measures are 'actions of counterintelligence that allow it to gain an insight into an enemy's intentions, forewarn his undesirable moves, mislead the enemy, take the lead from him, disrupt his subversive actions'.[15] Active measures are implemented through 'actions aimed at creating agent positions in the enemy camp and its environment, playing operational games with the enemy directed at disinforming, discrediting and corrupting enemy forces'.[16] Oleg Kalugin, former Major General of the Komitet gosudarstvennoy bezopasnosti (Committee for State Security, KGB), described active measures as 'the heart and soul of the Soviet intelligence':

> Not intelligence collection, but subversion: active measures to weaken the West, to drive wedges in the Western community alliances of all sorts, particularly NATO, to sow discord among allies, to weaken the United States in the eyes of the people of Europe, Asia, Africa, Latin America, and thus to prepare ground in case the war really occurs. To make America more vulnerable to the anger and distrust of other peoples.[17]

From a practical perspective, according to Richard Shultz and Roy Godson, active measures could be 'conducted overtly through officially sponsored foreign propaganda channels, diplomatic relations and cultural diplomacy', while covert political techniques included 'the use of covert propaganda, oral and written disinformation, agents of influence, clandestine radios, and international front organizations'.[18] Scientific progress and subsequent technological innovations since the Cold War have obviously contributed to the enhancement of both overt and covert political techniques.

Until 2014, the extent of Russia's active measures in the West – perhaps with the exception of the Baltic states[19] – was limited. Russian authorities preferred to use their personal contacts with Western leaders and economic cooperation to advance their interests in the West. Given the domination of postmodern *Realpolitik* in the West, the Kremlin was largely successful in its endeavours, while Putin's apparently friendly relations with Silvio Berlusconi (Prime Minister of Italy in 1994–1995, 2001–2006 and 2008–2011), Gerhard Schröder (Chancellor of Germany in 1998–2005) and, to a lesser extent, Nicolas Sarkozy (President of France in 2007–2012) allowed Moscow and Western capitals to 'smooth away' their differences to the disadvantage of human rights and political freedoms in Russia, as well as national security of the countries in the 'near abroad'. In 2009, even the Obama administration, following the Russian invasion of Georgia, attempted to improve relations with Russia with the help of a so-called 'reset',[20] although it did not collaborate as closely.

After Russia had occupied and then annexed Ukraine's Autonomous Republic of Crimea and invaded Eastern Ukraine in 2014,[21] some Western leaders belatedly realised – often without admitting their own complacency – that Putin's regime became too assertive and defiant, as well as directly threatening European security and challenging the post-war order. Russia was suspended from the PACE and G8, while the EU, United States, Canada, Norway, Switzerland and some other nations imposed political and economic sanctions on Russia and its officials over the aggression against Ukraine.

Not only did Moscow respond with anti-Western sanctions, but also Russian state-controlled structures as well as groups loyal to the Kremlin dramatically stepped up active measures and other subversive activities inside the West.[22] According to a report by the Chatham House, Putin's Russia has used 'a wide range of hostile measures' including 'energy cut-offs and trade embargoes, . . . subversive use of Russian minorities, malicious cyber activity of various forms, and the co-option of business and political elites'.[23] A report by the Center for European Policy and Analysis argues that, in the West, the Kremlin 'promotes conspiratorial discourse and uses disinformation to pollute the information space, increase polarization and undermine democratic debate. Russia's actions accelerate the declining confidence in international alliances and organizations, public institutions and mainstream media'.[24] Moreover, Russia 'exploits ethnic, linguistic, regional, social and historical tensions, and promotes anti-systemic causes, extending their reach and giving them a spurious appearance of legitimacy'.[25]

To a certain extent, today's cooperation between various Russian pro-Kremlin actors and Western far-right politicians may be seen as an integral part of Moscow's active measures in the West. However, it seems to be oversimplification to limit the relations between Russia and the Western far right to the Kremlin's active measures, at least because such an assumption would reduce the agency of the other major element of this relationship, namely the far right itself.

European far-right milieu

The term 'far right' is used here as an umbrella term that refers to a broad range of ideologues, groups, movements and political parties to the right of the centre right.[26] It is probably impossible to define an umbrella term such as 'far right' as anything less vague than a range of political ideas that imbue a nation (interpreted in various ways) with a value that surpasses the value of human rights and fundamental freedoms. Thus, the concept of a nation is central to all manifestations of the far right, but they differ in the ways they imagine the 'handling' of a nation.

The exponents of fascism, which was the very first far-right ideology to have acquired worldwide significance, offered arguably the most radical approach to 'handling' a nation. According to Roger Griffin, fascism can be defined as

> a revolutionary species of political modernism originating in the early twentieth century whose mission is to combat the allegedly degenerative forces of contemporary history (decadence) by bringing about an alternative modernity and temporality (a 'new order' and a 'new era') based on the rebirth, or palingenesis, of the nation. Fascists conceive the nation as an organism shaped by historic, cultural, and in some cases, ethnic and hereditary factors, a mythic construct incompatible with liberal, conservative, and communist theories of society. The health of this organism they see undermined as much by the principles of institutional and cultural pluralism, individualism, and globalized consumerism promoted by liberalism as by the global regime of social justice and human equality identified by socialism in theory as the ultimate goal of history, or by the conservative defence of 'tradition'.[27]

In the two twentieth-century European regimes, which successfully implemented essential tenets of fascism on the state level, namely Benito Mussolini's Italy and Adolf Hitler's Third Reich, fascisms differed largely in that Italian Fascists conceived the nation in ethnic terms, while the German National Socialists articulated their idea of the nation in racial terms, or to be more precise, in terms of the *Volk*, a metaphysical notion incorporating the concepts of race, German history and culture. The difference in these interpretations of the nation as the core concept for the definition of fascism allows for distinguishing a very specific form of fascism, namely National Socialism or Nazism, that emphasises a specifically racist or *völkische* interpretation of one's own nation.

After the military defeat of the Third Reich in 1945, fascism was forced to evolve into three major forms. Organisations that still wanted to participate in the political process had to dampen their revolutionary ardour rather dramatically and translate it 'as far as possible into the language of liberal democracy'.[28] This strategy gave birth to the non-fascist phenomenon of radical right-wing political parties.[29] Revolutionary ultranationalists, on the other hand, retreated to the fringes of socio-political life in the West. As they still remained true to the idea of an alternative totalitarian modernity underpinned by the palingenesis of the nation – however unrealistic its implementation was in the post-war period – their ideas and doctrines were termed as neo-fascist (but sometimes simply fascist) or neo-Nazi. The third form of post-war fascism appeared only at the end of the 1960s and was associated, first, with the French New Right (or *Nouvelle Droite*) and, later, with the European New Right.[30] This is a movement that consists of clusters of think-tanks, conferences, journals, institutes and publishing houses that try to modify the dominant liberal-democratic political culture and make it more susceptible to a non-democratic mode of politics. Importantly, the European New Right has focused almost exclusively on the battle for hearts and minds rather than for immediate political power. As biological racism became totally discredited in the post-war period, the European New Right came up with the idea of ethno-pluralism arguing that peoples differed not in biological or ethnic terms but rather in terms of culture.

Naturally, the above-mentioned forms of the far right thought need to be treated as 'ideal types' in the Weberian sense of the term. The boundaries between them are often blurred, while their various permutations – including those adopting elements of other, non-nationalist ideologies – embodied in the plethora of groups, movements and organisations have acquired new names such as national-revolutionary and national anarchist movements, racial separatism, Radical Traditionalism, national communism, Identitarian Movement, Third Position, neo-Eurasianism, etc.

Radical right-wing political parties are arguably the most widespread form of far-right politics today. Michael Minkenberg defines right-wing radicalism as 'a political ideology, whose core element is a myth of a homogeneous nation, a romantic and populist ultranationalism directed against the concept of liberal and pluralistic democracy and its underlying principles of individualism and universalism'.[31] He argues that 'the nationalistic myth' of right-wing radicalism 'is characterized by the effort to construct an idea of nation and national belonging by radicalizing ethnic, religious, cultural, and political criteria of exclusion and to condense the idea of nation into an image of extreme collective homogeneity'.[32]

Cas Mudde provides yet another insightful interpretation of what he calls 'radical right-wing populism' suggesting that it can be defined as a 'combination of three core ideological features: nativism, authoritarianism, and populism'.[33] As Mudde argues, nativism 'holds that states should be inhabited exclusively by members of the native group ("the nation") and that non-native elements (persons and ideas) are fundamentally threatening to the homogenous nation-state'; authoritarianism implies 'the belief in a strictly ordered society, in which infringements of authority are to be punished severely'; and populism 'is understood as a thin-centred ideology that considers society to be ultimately separated into two homogeneous and antagonistic groups, "the pure people" versus "the corrupt elite"'.[34]

There is less academic consensus on the differences between the radical right and the extreme right, and, for example, French and German scholars of far-right politics use the terms like *droite radicale* or *Rechtsradikalismus* less often than the terms *extrême droite* or *Rechtsextremismus* when they refer to the political phenomena that, especially in the Anglo-Saxon academic world, would generally be distinguished between right-wing radicalism (or radical right-wing populism) and right-wing extremism. In this book, this distinction exists and implies that the difference between radical right-wing and extreme right-wing movements and parties is their attitude towards violence as an instrument of achieving political goals: the former reject it, while the latter tolerate or even embrace it.

The blurring of the boundaries between various forms of far-right politics is also reflected in the ideological heterogeneity of the electorally most successful far-right parties of today, namely the radical right-wing populist parties. Many of these parties have long political histories, and, over the years, they have integrated many activists coming from the movements and organisations of varying degrees of radicalism or extremism. Activists who have fascist, neo-Nazi or extreme-right background may and usually do moderate under the pressure of the party leadership who – for political or tactical reasons – believe that extremist ideas and rhetoric will be harmful for electoral success.

Indeed, the deradicalisation process has become a common stage for the most successful European far-right parties today. The Norwegian Fremskrittspartiet (Progress Party), which was considered a radical right-wing party in the past,[35] has gradually removed or toned down most of its hardliners and now perhaps cannot be even considered a far-right party anymore. In the European Parliament, the Dansk Folkeparti (Danish People's Party) and Perussuomalaiset (The Finns) prefer to cooperate with conservative parties such as the UK's Conservative Party and Poland's Prawo i Sprawiedliwość (Law and Justice), rather than with the radical right-wing populists represented, for example, by France's Front National (National Front, FN),[36] Austria's Freiheitliche Partei Österreichs (Freedom Party of Austria, FPÖ)[37] or Italy's Lega Nord (Northern League, LN).[38] However, the FN, FPÖ and LN have taken steps to moderate too. Under the leadership of Marine Le Pen, the FN even expelled her father and the FN's long-time President Jean-Marie Le Pen for his radicalism. In the recent years, Hungary's radical right-wing Jobbik party,[39] too, has considerably toned down its anti-Semitic and anti-Roma rhetoric, and the deradicalisation strategy has proved to be relatively successful: at the time of the writing, Jobbik is the second most popular party in Hungary.

There is a historical precedent for this process: the most notable early example of deradicalisation of the far-right is the refashioning of the fascist Movimento Sociale Italiano (Italian Social Movement) into a 'post-fascist' party in the late 1980s and early 1990s. This was followed by the expulsion of right-wing extremists and transformation into the national-conservative Alleanza Nazionale (National Alliance) in 1995, and, eventually, the merger of the Alleanza Nazionale into Silvio Berlusconi's now defunct centre-right Popolo della Libertà (People of Freedom) in 2009.

Deradicalisation has contributed to the growing popular support for the 'moderated' radical right-wing parties, allowing them to enter sectors of the political spectrum that mainstream parties have long abandoned. Compared to the 1990s, the 'moderate' radical right now have even more appeal to liberal voters concerned about identity issues, to the working class on labour and immigration issues, and to conservative voters anxious to preserve so-called traditional values.

Doubtlessly, deradicalisation is not a mandatory condition for the electoral success of the far right, which is corroborated by the electoral fortunes of the Greek neo-Nazi Laïkós Sýndesmos – Chrysí Avgí (Popular Association – Golden Dawn, XA)[40] at the parliamentary elections in 2015 or the Slovak extreme-right Kotleba – Ľudová strana Naše Slovensko (Kotleba – People's Party Our Slovakia)[41] at the parliamentary elections in 2016. However, in general, the more extreme the far-right parties are, the less electoral support they have, and vice versa.[42] Some of the more extreme far-right parties of today, for example, the British National Party (BNP),[43] Italian Forza Nuova (New Force),[44] Nationaldemokratische Partei Deutschlands (National-Democratic Party of Germany, NPD) or Svenskarnas parti (Party of the Swedes) have rarely had any tangible electoral successes. Even if many citizens of Western countries are seeking existential refuge in national identities, they are predominantly repulsed by blatant right-wing extremism and racist rhetoric. Some elements of the electorate of radical right-wing populist parties may clearly be driven by more extreme views than those espoused by their political favourites, but the majority of the voters do not seem to be racists or ultranationalists. Elaborating on the observation made by Laurent Fabius, France's Socialist Prime Minister (1984–1986), who said in 1984 that the FN's Jean-Marie Le Pen asked the right questions but came up with the wrong answers, one can suggest that the greater part of the electorate of radical right-wing parties make their electoral decisions because they are tempted by the right questions that the more moderate far-right politicians ask – about the efficiency of the liberal-democratic establishment, economic inequalities, job security, social cohesion, immigration, religious traditions and identity. Not that the far right give smart answers, but their defiant readiness to pose questions, some of which very few mainstream politicians would dare to address or even ask, bolsters their support.

The more support the radical right-wing populists have, the more opportunities they have to promote their visions and utopias in the socio-political environment in which political postmodernists are crushing despondent liberal progressivists, while disgruntled Western citizens are increasingly disaffected with the mainstream political class as a whole.

Research background

Until 2014, apart from occasional references to pro-Russian statements of some European far-right leaders, few scholars and experts observed a growing rapprochement between the Western far right and Putin's Russia. Arguably the first investigation that reported on this development was a report titled 'Russia's Far-Right Friends' and published in 2009 by the Hungary-based Political Capital Institute.[45] On the basis of their research, its authors argued that 'far-right parties in several eastern European countries [had] become prominent supporters of Russian interests and admirers of the Russian political-economic model' and that, for Russia, 'forming partnerships with ultranationalists could facilitate its efforts to influence these countries' domestic politics . . . until Moscow finds an even more influential ally elsewhere on the political spectrum'.[46]

In 2010, Angelos-Stylianos Chryssogelos analysed the foreign policy positions of the radical right-wing FN and FPÖ, as well as of the German left-wing populist Die Linke (The Left), and specifically focused on their attitudes towards the United States, transatlantic relations, NATO and Russia. He concluded that these parties were united in their aversion of NATO and American influence in Europe, but, at the same time, they looked favourably at Putin's Russia. According to Chryssogelos, 'populist parties see Russia as a source of energy and military clout as well as an attractive partner with similar cultural traits as Europe has', while by discarding 'issues of human rights and democracy in their relations with Russia', these 'populists reinforce their vision of sovereign nation states furthering their interests without reference to universal values or prior institutional commitments'.[47] The author, however, did not elaborate on the Russian agenda behind the cooperation with the European far right.

The international expert and academic community in general started to pay attention to the relations between Russia and the Western far right in 2013–2014. For example, Marcel Van Herpen noted that West European far-right parties were moving away from 'their traditional anti-communist and anti-Russia ideologies, with many expressing admiration – and even outright support' – for Putin's regime.[48] Van Herpen asserted that, since Putin's regime did not 'openly reject democracy or explicitly advocate a one-party state', it might serve as a model for the far-right parties, which could not 'openly advocate an authoritarian regime or a one-party system'.[49] Moreover, through its specific policies and practices, Putin's regime was able to demonstrate to the illiberal European political forces 'how to manipulate the rules of parliamentary democracy . . . to serve authoritarian objectives'.[50]

The Political Capital Institute continued working on the phenomenon of 'Russian influence in the affairs of the far right' seen as 'a key risk for Euro-Atlantic integration at both the national and the [European] Union level'.[51] The Institute's 2014 report distinguished – in the context of their views on Russia – between 'committed', 'open' and 'hostile' European far-right parties. The 'committed' category would include parties that openly professed their sympathy for Russia. The 'open' category would refer to parties that could either 'show sympathy based simply on considerations in relation to foreign and economic policy and realpolitik, without regard to Putin's economic and social regime as a model', or 'in most cases display a negative or neutral attitude toward Russia', but at the same time would 'support the Russian position [on some important issues] even in the absence of genuine motivation'.[52] Finally, the 'hostile' category would include far-right parties coming 'primarily from countries in conflict with Russia'.[53] In 2015, the Political Capital Institute also published four collaborative country-specific reports on the relations between various Russian stakeholders and the far right in Hungary,[54] Greece,[55] France[56] and Slovakia.[57] Marlène Laruelle, who co-authored the France-related report, edited an insightful collection of chapters that looked at the relations between Russia and the far right through the perspective of the spread of the ideology of Russian neo-Eurasianism, as well as focusing, in particular, on the cases of France, Italy, Spain, Hungary and Greece.[58]

Aims and structure of the book

Despite the rising number of journalistic investigations, expert analyses and academic studies of the phenomenon, we still lack a general picture of the relations between Russia and the Western far right, and this book is set to address considerable gaps in our understanding of this under-researched yet important aspect of international relations.

Relations between Russia and the Western far right are a complex and multi-layered phenomenon which cannot be explained by any single causal factor. The overarching hypothesis of this book is that each side of this relationship is driven by evolving and, at times, circumstantial political and pragmatic considerations that involve, on the one hand, the need to attain or restore declining or deficient domestic and international legitimacy and, on the other hand, the ambition to reshape the apparently hostile domestic and international environments in accordance with one's own interests. Putin's corrupt and authoritarian regime enjoyed, especially during his first presidential term (2000–2004) domestic and international legitimacy, but started to feel increasingly threatened by the processes of democratisation in Russia's immediate neighbourhood as it perceived these processes as a Western attempt to bring about a regime change in Russia. These assumptions on the part of the Russian ruling elites led to their gradual opening to Western far-right politicians who had tried to court Putin's regime even before Russian pro-Kremlin actors decided to turn to them to use them, first, as one of the sources of political legitimacy in the domestic environment and, thus, consolidation of the regime, then as tools of Moscow's foreign policy in the Russian neighbourhood, and, eventually, as an instrument of destabilisation of Western societies. In the latter case, Moscow's intentions are, to a certain degree, underpinned by the understanding that the far right are more potent today than they have ever been before in the post-war era and are posing a growing threat to Western liberal democracy. Moreover, radical right-wing parties no longer need to vindicate themselves and be at pains over proving political eligibility of their ideas. Today, they refer to Putin's Russia as the model of an alternative political order opposing liberal democracy. By expressing their ideological kinship with contemporary Russia, which is far from being a fringe country, and winning different forms of support from Moscow, radical right-wing parties may claim *alternative* political legitimacy and represent themselves not simply as the opposition to the mainstream parties, but essentially as the *alternative* mainstream.

This book aims to explore relations between various Russian actors and the far right in all their complexity by scrutinising their most important aspects. The fact that some initial analyses of the pro-Russian sentiments of the contemporary Western far right started to appear only in 2009–2010 does not imply that these sentiments did not exist before, and it is almost impossible to understand them without examining their nature and historical manifestations. Thus, Chapter 1 goes back as far as the interwar period to show that, even then, particular elements of the far right sided with Russia, and then explores how the far-right pro-Russian attitudes developed in the West during the Cold War, as well as pointing out that Soviet Russia was often prone to use the Western far right for its own political benefits. Chapter 2 discusses the active cooperation, as well as the motivations behind this cooperation, between Russian and Western far-right politicians after the fall of the Soviet Union; while their attempts at building more structured relationships largely failed at that time, they facilitated and contributed to the deepening of the relations between Russian pro-Kremlin actors and the Western far right when more favourable conditions arose in the second half of the 2000s. The emergence of these conditions was determined by the internal evolution of Putin's regime from an authoritarian kleptocracy into an anti-Western right-wing authoritarian kleptocracy in the second half of the 2000s, and Chapter 3 discusses this evolution and demonstrates how particular elements of the Western far right embraced it. Chapters 4 and 5 consider two areas of dynamic cooperation between various Russian actors and Western far-right politicians and organisations aimed at supporting and consolidating alternative institutions that aspire to challenge and undermine liberal-democratic practices and traditions: electoral monitoring and the media. Chapter 6 looks at openly pro-Russian activities that European far-right movements and organisations have carried out in their national contexts, and identifies several types of structures and individuals who furthered cooperation between the European far right and the Russian actors linked to the Kremlin. Finally, Chapter 6 explores the performance of European far-right politicians on high-profile discussion platforms in Moscow and at sessions of the European Parliament in Strasbourg and Brussels, and analyses the narratives that they promote within these settings.

This book not only aims to provide deeper insights into the cooperation between Putin's Russia and representatives of the Western far right, but will also inspire further, more narrow research into this phenomenon and its particular aspects. The urgency of these endeavours cannot be overstated. The Western liberal-democratic order, being challenged by destructive developments from outside and inside Western societies themselves, faces hard times. The Western world, to be sure, is strong enough to resist the challenges of either the far right or Putin's regime. Individually, neither of these forces can bring about the collapse of the West as we know it. But we witness today that Putin's Russia gradually joins forces with the far right against liberal democracy; they reinforce each other, and their coalition may be able to weaken and destabilise the West and, especially, the EU.

Notes

1   Mitchell A. Orenstein, "Putin's Western Allies", *Foreign Affairs*, 25 March (2014), https://foreignaffairs.com/articles/russia-fsu/2014-03-25/putins-western-allies

2   "Russia's Friends in Black", *The Economist*, 19 April (2014), http://economist.com/news/europe/21601004-why-europes-populists-and-radicals-admire-vladimir-putin-russias-friends-black. See also Katerina Safarikova, "Putin and the European Right: A Love Story", *Transitions Online*, 16 April (2014), http://tol.org/client/article/24262-putin-and-the-european-right-a-love-story.html; Benjamin Bidder, Gregor Peter Schmitz, "Putins rechte Freunde", *Spiegel Online*, 2 May (2014), http://spiegel.de/politik/ausland/putin-in-ukraine-krise-rechtspopulisten-in-europa-stuetzen-russland-a-967155.html

3   "NATO-Russia Council", *NATO*, http://nato.int/nrc-website/EN/about/index.html

4   David Satter, *Darkness at Dawn: The Rise of the Russian Criminal State* (New Haven: Yale University Press, 2003), p. 38.

5   *Nomenklatura* is an umbrella term for the Soviet ruling elites that included party and government officials, senior army officers, top bureaucrats, senior managers, etc.

6   Satter, *Darkness at Dawn*, p. 38.

7   Quoted in Marina Martynova, *Politicheskaya elita Rossii na rubezhe XXI veka* (Arkhangelsk: Pomorskiy gosudarstvenny universitet, 2001), p. 169.

8   Serguei Cheloukhine, Maria R. Haberfeld, *Russian Organized Corruption Networks and Their International Trajectories* (New York: Springer, 2010), p. 53. My emphasis.

9   Andrew Wilson, *Ukraine Crisis: What It Means for the West* (New Haven: Yale University Press, 2014), p. 19. See also Andrew Wilson, *Virtual Politics: Faking Democracy in the Post-Soviet World* (New Haven: Yale University Press, 2005).

10 Lilia Shevtsova, *Odinokaya derzhava. Pochemu Rossiya ne stala Zapadom i pochemu Rossii trudno s Zapadom* (Moscow: ROSSPEN, 2010), p. 43.

11 "Russia Will Pay for Chechnya", *BBC*, 7 December (1999), http://news.bbc.co.uk/2/hi/europe/553304.stm

12 "UK Condemns Chechnya Ultimatum", *BBC*, 7 December (1999), http://news.bbc.co.uk/2/hi/uk_news/politics/554075.stm

13 "Putin Rebuffs Chechnya Warnings", *BBC*, 7 December (1999), http://news.bbc.co.uk/2/hi/europe/554019.stm

14 Chapter 3 looks at this process in more detail.

15 *Kontrazvedyvatel'ny slovar'* (Moscow: Nauchno-izdatel'skiy otdel, 1972), p. 161.

16 *Kontrazvedyvatel'ny slovar'*, ibid., p. 162.

17 "Inside the KGB: An Interview with Retired KGB Maj. Gen. Oleg Kalugin", *CNN* (1998), http://web.archive.org/web/20070627183623/http://www3.cnn.com/SPECIALS/cold.war/episodes/21/interviews/kalugin/

18 Richard H. Shultz, Roy Godson, *Dezinformatsia: Active Measures in Soviet Strategy* (Washington: Pergamon-Brassey's, 1984), p. 2. Arguably the most prominent among many other front organisations aimed at achieving Soviet foreign policy objectives was the World Peace Council founded in 1948, see János Radványi, *Psychological Operations and Political Warfare in Long-term Strategic Planning* (New York: Praeger, 1990), p. 43. The World Peace Council operated through smaller "peace-loving" front organisations – some of them were based in the West – to discredit the "warmongering" US and Western countries in general.

19 See, for example, Nerijus Maliukevičius, "Russia's Information Policy in Lithuania: The Spread of Soft Power or Information Geopolitics?", *Baltic Security & Defence Review*, Vol. 9 (2007), pp. 150–170; Stephen Herzog, "Revisiting the Estonian Cyber Attacks: Digital Threats and Multinational Responses", *Journal of Strategic Security*, Vol. 4, No. 2 (2011), pp. 49–60.

20 Stephen Blank, "Beyond the Reset Policy: Current Dilemmas of U.S.–Russia Relations", *Comparative Strategy*, Vol. 29, No. 4 (2010), pp. 333–367.

21 See András Rácz, *Russia's Hybrid War in Ukraine: Breaking the Enemy's Ability to Resist* (Helsinki: The Finnish Institute of International Affairs, 2015); Nikolay Mitrokhin, "Infiltration, Instruction, Invasion: Russia's War in the Donbass", *Journal of Soviet and*

Post-Soviet Politics and Society, Vol. 1 (2015), pp. 219–249; James Miller, Pierre Vaux, Catherine A. Fitzpatrick, Michael Weiss, *An Invasion by Any Other Name: The Kremlin's Dirty War in Ukraine* (New York: The Institute of Modern Russia, 2015), http://interpretermag.com/wp-content/uploads/2015/09/IMR_Invasion_By_Any_Other_Name.pdf; Maksymilian Czuperski, John Herbst, Eliot Higgins, Alina Polyakova, Damon Wilson, *Hiding in Plain Sight: Putin's War in Ukraine* (Washington: Atlantic Council, 2015), http://atlanticcouncil.org/images/publications/Hiding_in_Plain_Sight/HPS_English.pdf

22 Andrew Wilson, "Russian Active Measures: A Modernised Tradition", *The Institute for Statecraft*, 1 March (2016), http://statecraft.org.uk/research/russian-active-measures-modernised-tradition; Martin Kragh, Sebastian Åsberg, "Russia's Strategy for Influence through Public Diplomacy and Active Measures: The Swedish Case", *Journal of Strategic Studies*, 5 January (2017), pp. 1–44.

23 Keir Giles, Philip Hanson, Roderic Lyne, James Nixey, James Sherr, Andrew Wood, *The Russian Challenge* (London: Chatham House, 2015), p. vii. See also Keir Giles, *Russia's "New" Tools for Confronting the West: Continuity and Innovation in Moscow's Exercise of Power* (London: Chatham House, 2016); Orysia Lutsevych, *Agents of the Russian World: Proxy Groups in the Contested Neighbourhood* (London: Chatham House, 2016), p. 10.

24 Edward Lucas, Peter Pomerantsev, *Winning the Information War: Techniques and Counter-strategies to Russian Propaganda in Central and Eastern Europe* (Washington: Center for European Policy Analysis, 2016), p. 1.

25 Ibid., p. 2.

26 Islamism, too, could be included in the "far right" category taking into consideration Jeffrey Bale's definition of Islamism as "an extreme right-wing, theocratic, totalitarian, and Islamic supremacist political ideology based upon an exceptionally strict, literalist, and puritanical interpretation of core Islamic religious and legal doctrines". (This is a revised definition of Islamism originally published in Jeffrey M. Bale, "Denying the Link between Islamist Ideology and Jihadist Terrorism: 'Political Correctness' and the Undermining of Counterterrorism", *Perspectives on Terrorism*, Vol. 7, No. 5 (2013), pp. 5–46 (13). This revised definition was provided to the author via e-mail exchange with Bale.) However, since this book does not deal with Islamism, it is excluded here from the "far right" category to avoid any misunderstanding.

27 Roger Griffin, *Modernism and Fascism: The Sense of a Beginning under Mussolini and Hitler* (Basingstoke: Palgrave Macmillan, 2007), p. 181.

28 Roger Griffin, "From Slime Mould to Rhizome: An Introduction to the Groupuscular Right", *Patterns of Prejudice*, Vol. 37, No. 1 (2003), pp. 27–50 (38).

29 On radical right-wing parties see, in particular, Hans-Georg Betz, *Radical Right-Wing Populism in Western Europe* (New York: St. Martins Press, 1994); Herbert Kitschelt with Anthony J. McGann, *The Radical Right in Western Europe: A Comparative Analysis* (Ann Arbor, University of Michigan Press, 1995); Elizabeth L. Carter, *The Extreme Right in Western Europe: Success or Failure?* (Manchester: Manchester University Press, 2005); Terri E. Givens, *Voting Radical Right in Western Europe* (New York: Cambridge University Press, 2005); Pippa Norris, *Radical Right: Voters and Parties in the Electoral Market* (New York: Cambridge University Press, 2005); Cas Mudde, *Populist Radical Right Parties in Europe* (Cambridge: Cambridge University Press, 2007); David Art, *Inside the Radical Right: The Development of Anti-Immigrant Parties in Western Europe* (New York: Cambridge University Press, 2011).

30 On the New Right see Pierre-André Taguieff, "From Race to Culture: The New Right's View of European Identity", *Telos*, Nos. 98–99 (1993–1994), pp. 99–125; Roger Griffin, "Interregnum or Endgame? The Radical Right in the 'Post-Fascist' Era", *Journal of Political Ideologies*, Vol. 5, No. 2 (2000), pp. 163–178; Roger Griffin, "Between Metapolitics and Apoliteia: The Nouvelle Droite's Strategy for Conserving the Fascist Vision in the 'Interregnum'", *Modern & Contemporary France*, Vol. 8, No. 1 (2000), pp. 35–53; Alberto Spektorowski, "The New Right: Ethno-regionalism,

Ethno-pluralism and the Emergence of a Neo-fascist 'Third Way' ", *Journal of Political Ideologies*, Vol. 8, No. 1 (2003), pp. 111–130; Tamir Bar-On, *Where Have All the Fascists Gone?* (Aldershot: Ashgate, 2007).

31 Michael Minkenberg, "The Radical Right in Postsocialist Central and Eastern Europe: Comparative Observations and Interpretations", *East European Politics and Societies*, Vol. 16, No. 2 (2002), pp. 335–362 (337).

32 Ibid.

33 Mudde, *Populist Radical Right Parties in Europe*, p. 22.

34 Ibid., pp. 22–23.

35 Anders Widfeldt, *Extreme Right Parties in Scandinavia* (Milton Park: Routledge, 2015), p. 83.

36 On the FN see, in particular, Peter Davies, *The National Front in France: Ideology, Discourse and Power* (London and New York: Routledge, 1999); James G. Shields, *The Extreme Right in France: From Pétain to Le Pen* (London and New York: Routledge, 2007).

37 On the FPÖ see Hella Pick, *Guilty Victim: Austria from the Holocaust to Haider* (London and New York: I.B. Tauris, 2000); Ruth Wodak, Anton Pelinka (eds), *The Haider Phenomenon in Austria* (New Brunswick: Transaction, 2002); Göran Adamson, *Populist Parties and the Failure of the Political Elites: The Rise of the Austrian Freedom Party (FPÖ)* (Frankfurt: Peter Lang, 2016).

38 On the LN see Anna Cento Bull, Mark Gilbert, *The Lega Nord and the Northern Question in Italian Politics* (Basingstoke: Palgrave Macmillan, 2001); Andrej Zaslove, *The Re-invention of the European Radical Right: Populism, Regionalism, and the Italian Lega Nord* (Montréal: McGill-Queen's University Press, 2011).

39 On Jobbik see Miroslav Mareš, Vratislav Havlík, "Jobbik's Successes: An Analysis of Its Success in the Comparative Context of the V4 Countries", *Communist and Post-Communist Studies*, Vol. 49, No. 4 (2016), pp. 323–333; Péter Krekó, Attila Juhász, *The Hungarian Far Right: Social Demand, Political Supply, and International Context* (Stuttgart, Germany: *ibidem*-Verlag, 2017).

40 On the XA see Antonis A. Ellinas, "The Rise of Golden Dawn: The New Face of the Far Right in Greece", *South European Society and Politics*, Vol. 18, No. 4 (2013), pp. 543–565; Antonis A. Ellinas, "Neo-Nazism in an Established Democracy: The Persistence of Golden Dawn in Greece", *South European Society and Politics*, Vol. 20, No. 1 (2015), pp. 1–20.

41 On the Slovak far right in general and Kotleba in particular see Alena Kluknavská, Josef Smolík, "We Hate Them All? Issue Adaptation of Extreme Right Parties in Slovakia 1993–2016", *Communist and Post-Communist Studies*, Vol. 49, No. 4 (2016), pp. 335–344.

42 Elizabeth L. Carter, *The Extreme Right in Western Europe: Success or Failure?* (Manchester: Manchester University Press, 2005), p. 203.

43 On the BNP see, in particular, Nigel Copsey, *Contemporary British Fascism* (Basingstoke: Palgrave Macmillan, 2004); Matthew J. Goodwin, *New British Fascism: Rise of the British National Party* (Abingdon: Routledge, 2011).

44 On Forza Nuova see Giovanna Campani, "Neo-fascism from the Twentieth Century to the Third Millennium: The Case of Italy", in Gabriella Lazaridis, Giovanna Campani, Annie Benveniste (eds), *The Rise of the Far Right in Europe: Populist Shifts and "Othering"* (London: Palgrave Macmillan, 2016), pp. 25–54.

45 Péter Krekó, Krisztián Szabados, "Russia's Far-Right Friends", *Political Capital*, 3 December (2009), http://riskandforecast.com/post/in-depth-analysis/russia-s-far-right-friends_349.html

46 Ibid.

47 Angelos-Stylianos Chryssogelos, "Undermining the West from Within: European Populists, the US and Russia", *European View*, Vol. 9, No. 2 (2010), pp. 267–277 (273).

48 Marcel H. Van Herpen, "Putinism's Authoritarian Allure", *Project Syndicate*, 15 March (2013), https://project-syndicate.org/commentary/putinism-as-a-model-for-western-europe-s-extreme-right-by-marcel-h--van-herpen

49   Ibid.
50   Ibid.
51   Political Capital, "The Russian Connection: The Spread of Pro-Russian Policies on the European Far Right", *Political Capital Institute*, 14 March (2014), www.riskandfore cast.com/useruploads/files/pc_flash_report_russian_connection.pdf
52   Ibid.
53   Ibid.
54   Attila Juhász, Lóránt Győri, Péter Krekó, András Dezső, *"I Am Eurasian": The Kremlin Connections of the Hungarian Far-Right* (Budapest: Political Capital Kft./Social Development Institute Kft., 2015).
55   Lóránt Győri, Péter Krekó, Angelos Chryssogelos, Paris Ayiomamitis, Judit Takács, *"Natural Allies": The Kremlin Connections of the Greek Far-Right* (Budapest: Political Capital Kft., 2015).
56   Marlène Laruelle, Lóránt Győri, Péter Krekó, Dóra Haller, Rudy Reichstadt, *"From Paris to Vladivostok": The Kremlin Connections of the French Far-Right* (Budapest: Political Capital Kft., 2015).
57   Péter Krekó, Lóránt Győri, Daniel Milo, Juraj Marušiak, János Széky, Anita Lencsés, *Marching towards Eurasia: The Kremlin Connections of the Slovak Far-Right* (Budapest: Political Capital Kft./Social Development Institute Kft., 2016).
58   Marlène Laruelle (ed.), *Eurasianism and the European Far Right: Reshaping the Europe-Russia Relationship* (Lanham: Lexington Books, 2015).

1

SOVIET RUSSIA IN THE WESTERN FAR-RIGHT PERSPECTIVE

Ideology, collaboration, active measures

Introduction

To properly understand the contemporary relations between the Western far right and various Russian actors, it is essential to place them in a historical perspective and examine how far-right authors, movements and parties perceived Soviet Russia before the demise of the USSR.

Even raising this question could to someone appear a dishonest intellectual exercise. The invasion, in 1941, of the Soviet Union by the Axis powers led by the Third Reich seems to provide an ultimate, self-explanatory reply to this question: Western far-right regimes and movements wanted to destroy Soviet Russia. The will to destroy Soviet Russia was driven by ideological and political motives that revealed the alleged irreconcilability between ultranationalism that underpinned the Axis powers and the declared internationalism of the Soviets. Anti-Russian and anti-Soviet attitudes were inherent ideological characteristics of all the major fascist and ultranationalist regimes and movements in Europe in the interwar period and during the Second World War. In 1920, Adolf Hitler might still be talking about Bolshevism being no more than 'a cloak for the creation of a great Russian empire',[1] but, already in 1922, 'the identification of Russia with Bolshevism and the Jews in Adolf Hitler's mind was completed',[2] while his *Mein Kampf* (My Struggle) published in 1925 explicitly stated that the Russians were racially inferior to the Aryan Germans and that Germany needed Russian territories. Hitler and the leaders of other far-right regimes and movements saw the Soviet Union as controlled by 'Judeo-Bolsheviks', and no rapprochement was deemed viable.

However, the general animosity to Soviet Russia on the part of the Western far right notwithstanding, there was a limited space where ideological and political confluence was indeed possible, and where various ideas about rapprochement between the Soviets and the far right thrived as a complex and heterogeneous minority faith.

Two major, largely overlapping factors enabled the existence of this space. The first factor is that fascism and communism are revolutionary and totalitarian ideologies. As defined by Emilio Gentile, totalitarianism is:

> an *experiment in political domination* implemented by a *revolutionary movement* that has been organized by a party with military discipline and an *all-absorbing concept of politics* aimed at the *monopoly of power*, which on taking power by legal or illegal means destroys or transforms the previous regime and builds a new state founded on a *single-party regime* with the principal objective of *conquering society*, that is, the subjugation, integration, and homogenization of the ruled on the basis of the *totally political nature of existence*, whether individual or collective, as interpreted by the categories, myths, and values of an institutionalized ideology in the form of a *political religion*, with the intention of molding individuals and masses through an *anthropological revolution*, in order to regenerate the essence of humanity and create a *new man* devoted body and soul to the realization of the revolutionary and imperialist projects of the totalitarian party, and thus a *new civilization* of a supranational nature.[3]

The fact that both fascism and communism are revolutionary and totalitarian ideologies does not mean that they are identical. Their core myths and values, at least on the theoretical level, are drastically different, and this difference has always been so significant that it largely precluded any rapprochement between the Western far right and Soviet Russia. The central myth of fascism is that of a rebirth of a nation;[4] fascism sacralises a nation (or race in the case of Nazism) as the highest form of human existence and conceives it 'as an organism shaped by historic, cultural, and in some cases, ethnic and hereditary factors, a mythic construct incompatible with liberal, conservative, and communist theories of society'.[5] Communism is internationalist, while its core myth is a classless society that implements collective control over the means of production. Therefore, even if fascism and communism aspire towards a monopoly of power and a totalitarian regime in order to carry out an anthropological revolution, the prospective utopian societies of fascism and communism are different.

However, it is the palingenetic thrust towards a new society, social regeneration and, ultimately, a new civilisation that characterises both fascism and communism, and this 'spiritual' concurrence is one of the two major factors that enable the existence of space where fascism and communism may converge.

The second factor is that fascism and communism envision two particular modernities, which – while dissenting from each other – concurrently challenge yet another modernity, the one that is represented by liberalism. Thus, political confluence between fascism and communism is possible if particular exponents of both ideologies feel that the spread of 'decadent and degenerate' liberalism poses an existential threat to them, and they decide to join forces against it. What results from an alliance of fascism and communism against liberalism is a political discourse that attacks capitalism and 'Western imperialism'. Naturally, other combinations are possible too: before the Second World War, many Western liberal democrats praised the Fascist regime in Italy for its anti-communism, while the war was won by the joint forces of liberal democracy and communism.

Anti-capitalism and anti-liberalism constituted ideological foundations of the Molotov-Ribbentrop Pact, the secret protocols to which divided North-Eastern and Central-Eastern Europe into the spheres of influence of the Third Reich and Soviet Union. However, the ideological element of the Pact was only a minor component of the otherwise non-ideological agreement. In the late 1930s, the Nazis understood that they had to obtain access to Russian resources such as oil, metal ores and food to fight their expansionist war. Moreover, both countries – the Third Reich and Soviet Union – wanted to secure that the other party would not build an alliance with the United Kingdom and France, and, for Joseph Stalin, the Pact with Adolf Hitler seemed more sensible, as he could not imagine that the Third Reich would risk a war on two fronts. In June 1941, on the eve of the invasion of the Soviet Union, Hitler confessed to Benito Mussolini that 'the partnership with the Soviet Union' was 'often very irksome' to him, as it seemed to be 'a break with [his] whole origin, [his] concepts, and [his] former obligations'.[6] Mussolini initially welcomed the Molotov-Ribbentrop Pact, which he saw as 'a convenient means of preventing alliance between Russia and the West',[7] but urged Hitler to refrain from deepening the collaboration with the Soviets because it 'would have catastrophic repercussions in Italy, where anti-Bolshevist unanimity, especially among the Fascist masses, [was] absolute, *granitico*, indivisible'.[8] For both fascist regimes, as well as the overwhelming majority of fascist and far-right movements and parties in the interwar period and during the Second World War, it was clear that pragmatic considerations could not transcend the difference between the core myths of fascism and communism.

This chapter does not focus on the dominant faith of the Western far right that considered communism and Soviet Russia as implacable enemies. Rather, it explores how particular Western far-right activists and ideologues experimented with the two above-mentioned factors mixing revolutionary, palingenetic, nationalist, totalitarian, modernist and socialist narratives in the ideological and political space that, in their view, enabled cooperation with Soviet Russia. First, the chapter looks into the phenomenon of National-Bolshevism that emerged in interwar Germany. Second, it discusses the pro-Russian activities of far-right neutralist groups in post-war West Germany and Austria, and how the Soviet and socialist counterintelligence services exploited the Western far right in these countries. Finally, the chapter analyses the writings and activities of Francis Parker Yockey and Jean Thiriart, who were arguably the most important post-war Western far-right ideologues calling for an alliance with Soviet Russia. The ideas produced by National-Bolsheviks, far-right 'neutralists', Yockey and Thiriart might seem bizarre in their times, but they have exerted considerable influence on the ideological rationale of the pro-Russian arguments and activities of Western far-right political activists today, and, therefore, require close attention.

National-Bolshevism: The pro-Russian far right in interwar Germany

'National Bolshevism' is the name of one of the most paradoxical and ambiguous phenomena in the history of the twentieth century. In relation to the German interwar manifestation of National Bolshevism, it is possible to distinguish two major contrasting interpretations of the phenomenon. One interpretation, which can be considered restrictive, is suggested by Erik Van Ree, who – following the arguments presented by Louis Dupeux[9] – defines it as 'that radical tendency which combines a commitment to class struggle and total nationalization of the means of production with extreme state chauvinism'.[10] The second, inclusive interpretation employs the term 'National Bolshevism' to refer to various currents in the political thought of (1) German interwar ultranationalists who favoured the rapprochement with Soviet Russia and particular elements of socialism, and/or (2) German communists who embraced ultranationalism.[11]

This section briefly discusses the trends, and ideas behind them, in interwar Germany that can be described as National Bolshevik according to both interpretations, as well as suggesting that the second interpretation allows for distinguishing a manipulative form of National Bolshevism that today's social scientists would likely define as a political technology or political manipulation.

Historical literature usually identifies three periods in interwar Germany when different actors attempted to 'launch' National Bolshevism – in 1919, 1923 and 1930.[12] In 1919, a member of the national-conservative Deutschnationale Volkspartei (German National People's Party) Paul Eltzbacher published an essay titled 'Bolshevism and the German Future'.[13] Evidently devastated by the dire economic situation, in this essay he argued for the adoption of Bolshevism which 'compel[ed] the individual to subordinate his interests to those of the community',[14] and the creation of the Russo-German alliance. Soviet Russia, in his view, would not try to dominate Germany; on the contrary, the introduction of Bolshevism and the alliance with Russia would ensure that 'Germany [would] be ruled by Germans. Who would not prefer to submit to the dictation of his German brothers rather than let himself be enslaved and exploited by cold-blooded Englishmen and vengeful Frenchmen?'[15]

The same year, two dissident militant leaders of the Hamburg office of the Kommunistische Partei Deutschlands (Communist Party of Germany, KPD), Heinrich Laufenberg and Fritz Wolffheim, made their own contribution to the National Bolshevik theory. Laufenberg and Wolffheim rebelled against the Treaty of Versailles, turned to the 'stab in the back' mythology accusing the Social Democrats of national treason, and called for a war against the Entente's 'merciless imperialists' to restore the greatness of the German fatherland.[16] To achieve the victory of the German 'proletarian nation' against 'Western imperialism', Germany needed an alliance with Soviet Russia. 'Such collaboration they considered eminently feasible, since Russia needed German technical skills to establish socialism fully.'[17] Laufenberg and Wolffheim put forward this theory to Karl Radek, a Soviet expert on Germany and future Secretary of the Comintern, but he rejected it, as he believed that a joint German-Soviet war effort against the Entente powers would endanger Soviet Russia. Soviet leader Vladimir Lenin himself renounced 'the crying absurdities of "National Bolshevism"' of 'Laufenberg and others'.[18] Nevertheless, Radek accepted the idea of National Bolshevism 'as a possible means to pierce the admitted isolation of Soviet Russia by capitalist powers'.[19] Already then, Radek's conceptualisation of National Bolshevism implied manipulation to the benefit of the Soviets. However, the original National Bolsheviks, including Eltzbacher, Laufenberg and Wolffheim, had almost no followers, and the first attempt to launch the National Bolshevik movement failed.

In 1923, the French and Belgian troops started the military occupation of the Ruhr valley, an important industrial region of Germany, to force the country to continue paying the reparations. The occupation resulted in the radicalisation of German patriotism and ultranationalism, in particular, among the workers. The KPD feared that they would lose support among the working class and could no longer ignore the increased nationalist sentiment in the society. *Die Internationale*, the theoretical publication of the KPD, asserted: 'It is essential that we exploit this sentiment to avoid it being used against us.'[20] In their turn, the Soviets were concerned that the 'Western imperialists' would take Germany under total control.

Furthermore, the Ruhr occupation seemed to undermine the plans of the presumed German-Soviet attack on Poland. Already in 1922, Germany and Soviet Russia signed the Treaty of Rapallo – a proposal for the Treaty came from Hans von Seeckt, chief of staff of the Reichswehr – that laid the foundations of the cooperation between the two countries. This Treaty did not mention any military collaboration, but the latter was laid down in a secret Soviet-German Military Pact, and Gordon H. Mueller argued that this Pact had been motivated by Germany's wish to secretly rearm in violation of the Treaty of Versailles and to build an alliance with the Soviets against Poland.[21] However, even the Soviet-German Military Pact was only a formal, albeit secret, acknowledgement of the military collaboration between Germany and Soviet Russia that had started before the signing of the Pact. In particular, the so-called Schwarze Reichswehr (Black Imperial Army), the Reichswehr's underground section consisting primarily of ultranationalist volunteers (Freikorps among them), had been granted training facilities in Soviet Russia.[22]

The increased radical nationalism that followed the Ruhr occupation prompted the Soviets and Comintern to advance the links between the KPD and German ultranationalists. Radek, then Secretary of the Comintern, was a key politician who was assigned to help the process. In 1923, he delivered a speech to the Enlarged Executive of the Comintern in Moscow that heralded the second National Bolshevik initiative in interwar Germany. Radek devoted his speech to a far-right Freikorps member Albert Leo Schlageter whom the occupiers of Ruhr had executed for the sabotage operations. He called Schlageter, who also became one of the first Nazi martyrs, 'a courageous soldier of the counter-revolution' who deserved 'to be sincerely honoured by us, the soldiers of the revolution'.[23] The Secretary of Comintern maintained that Schlageter, as a far-right activist, deluded himself, as he believed that the revolutionary working class, rather than German capital, was the internal enemy. However, his patriotism was sincere, and real German patriots did not need to repeat his fate. 'If those circles of German fascists, who honestly wanted to serve the German people, failed to understand the significance of Schlageter's fate, Schlageter died in vain.'[24] The solution was to join forces with Soviet Russia against the capitalists.

> Against whom do the German people wish to fight: against the Entente capital or against the Russian people? With whom do they wish to ally themselves: with the Russian workers and peasants in order to throw off the yoke of Entente capital together, or with the Entente capital for the enslavement of the German and Russian peoples?[25]

Radek's speech drew a positive response from particular left-wing and right-wing circles. 'Young Communists, young nationalists, officers, nationalist philosophers, literati, all began to discuss "the Schlageter line"'.[26] A special issue of the KPD's daily *Rote Fahne* (Red Flag) discussed 'the Schlageter line' and featured essays written by *völkische* intellectuals Ernst Graf zu Reventlow and Arthur Moeller van den Bruck, a leading figure of the Conservative Revolution. Although Reventlow and Moeller were critical of Radek's idea, they argued that 'both *Völkische* and Communists put their trust in Russia, which, as an oppressed and "proletarian nation", was the natural ally of "proletarian Germany" against the West and all it stood for'.[27] At the same time, in a later work, Moeller argued that *völkische* socialism could only be realised 'with the elimination of all Jewish influence, a step that the Communists, both in Germany and in Russia, would have to take to prove themselves acceptable allies'.[28]

Although the National Bolshevik trend was more dynamic in 1923 than in 1919, it suffered the same fate, which can be explained, at least partially, by the advent of the Golden Twenties, a period of the economic growth in Germany in 1924–1929. Only after the Wall Street Crash of 1929 that resulted in large-scale unemployment in Germany and social instability, did some left-wing and right-wing circles return to National Bolshevism. For the KPD, yet again, National Bolshevism was a tactical manoeuvre, rather than a genuine belief, as they considered it important to employ ultranationalist rhetoric to woo the working-class nationalists who increasingly supported the Nationalsozialistische Deutsche Arbeiterpartei (National Socialist German Workers' Party, NSDAP). Particular right-wing circles, however, demonstrated the authentic full or partial adoption of socialism.

Former Social Democrat Ernst Niekisch became the most prominent representative of National Bolshevism of the third wave. Already in the second half of the 1920s, he founded the Widerstandsbewegung (Resistance Movement) for which he chose the slogan 'Sparta – Potsdam – Moscow' and the emblem that featured a Prussian eagle, a hammer, a sword and a sickle.[29] In 1930, he published a pamphlet titled *Entscheidung* (Decision) in which he argued for the creation of a

Prussian-inspired 'Germanic-Slavonic bloc' from Vladivostok to Vlissingen.[30] According to Niekisch, Russia discovered a national form of the class struggle, and the German working class had to follow the example of the Russians in order to learn how to think nationally and develop the German form of the class struggle. Furthermore, the German people had to 'promote the global political Russian-Asian advance on Europe and become part of this thrust (because Germany can regain itself only against Europe)' and 'destroy all things Western in its borders and approve of everything that the West abhorred: anti-liberalism, anti-individualism, autocracy, and open commitment to violence'.[31]

Niekisch was serious about the cooperation with Soviet Russia, and joined – together with Reventlow – the ARPLAN (Consortium for the Study of the Soviet Planned Economy) that was founded in 1931 and aimed at investigating 'modes of viable economic relations between Germany and the Soviet Union'.[32]

Niekisch's National Bolshevik ideas exerted particular influence on Ernst Jünger, a major far-right writer and intellectual, and a member of ARPLAN. In his famous *Der Arbeiter* (The Worker),[33] Jünger praised the 'total mobilisation' in Soviet Russia, as well as the Soviet practice of regulating and militarising labour.

Both Niekisch and Jünger influenced Karl Otto Paetel who founded, in 1930, the emphatically National Bolshevik Gruppe Sozialrevolutionärer Nationalisten (Group of Social Revolutionary Nationalists, GSN). The GSN 'stood for overthrow of the Versailles Treaty, repudiation of foreign economic and financial controls, alliance with Soviet Russia, and prosecution of the class struggle against international capitalism and imperialism'.[34] Like Niekisch's Widerstandsbewegung, the GSN was also ardently anti-Western, as they saw the West as 'corrupting and ruining Germany' through urbanism, liberalism, and parliamentarism.[35] As one of the top members of the GSN Georg Osten argued, the Germans had to smash the capitalist order in order to free themselves from the foreign domination. After the victory over capitalism, 'a socialist Germany would sever all ties with the West, support the liberation movements of oppressed colonial peoples, and join Soviet Russia in its war for survival against the imperialist powers'.[36]

The National Bolsheviks of the third wave were generally in opposition to Adolf Hitler and the NSDAP, and Niekisch was even imprisoned for life for his radical anti-Nazi positions (he was released in 1945 and worked in the German Democratic Republic). Nevertheless, some members of the GSN were also members of the NSDAP and belonged to the party's radically anti-capitalist group that represented the original revolutionary socialist hard core of the NSDAP. This group was formed around two influential left-wing Nazis Otto and Gregor Strasser who were deeply devoted to the idea of a revolution that would be national and socialist at the same time. For his socialist positions, Otto Strasser was expelled from the NSDAP in 1930, formed the Schwarze Front (Black Front), and, during that year, was close to the GSN. However, in contrast to the GSN, Otto Strasser rejected any collaboration with the KPD, and the GSN and Schwarze Front parted ways. Also in contrast to the GSN, the Strasser brothers did not favour Soviet Russia. Gregor Strasser resigned from the NSDAP in 1933 over the persistent conflicts with Hitler, and was killed during the Night of the Long Knives in 1934, along with his associate Ernst Röhm, the leader of the Sturmabteilung (Storm Detachment, SA), the paramilitary wing of the NSDAP. With the death of the prominent left-wing Nazi Gregor Strasser and the consolidation of the Nazi regime, any further development of National Bolshevism in interwar Germany became impossible, and it was marginalised.

According to Erik Van Ree's restrictive definition, of all the activists and authors mentioned in this section, only Paul Eltzbacher, Heinrich Laufenberg, Fritz Wolffheim, Ernst Niekisch and the GSN can be considered genuine National Bolsheviks, as they promoted the combination of the intransigent class struggle, total nationalisation, and ultranationalism. Other far-right activists and writers discussed above accepted only particular elements of socialism. For the KPD, flirtation with ultranationalism was a tactical move – a political technology aimed at wooing German ultranationalists and countering the rise of the NSDAP.

In general terms, National Bolshevism in interwar Germany rejected the treaty of Versailles and associated it with international capitalism and Western domination over Germany. National Bolsheviks considered the abolition of capitalism in Germany as an opportunity not only to strengthen the organic German *Volk*, but also to weed out all Western influence seen as alien to Germany. For National Bolshevism, Germany was a 'proletarian nation', but so was Soviet Russia, and National Bolsheviks believed that an alliance with the Soviets would reinforce Germany in its fight against the West. The fascination with Soviet Russia did not imply the acceptance of Soviet control over Germany. Rather, National Bolsheviks were enraptured by the modernising, revolutionary force of Russia's thrust towards a new society, and aspired to adopt certain Soviet practices, which arose from this thrust, to develop their own form of socialism imbued with the authentically *völkische* ethos.

Reviving the Tauroggen myth: The rise of far-right neutralism in West Germany and Austria

The defeat of fascism's war machine crushed in 1945 by the joint forces of the Western liberal democracies and the totalitarian Soviet Union dismayed Western fascists. It led many of them, who remained faithful to the visions of ultranationalist palingenesis, to revise their strategy in the post-war period. As the winners effectively divided Europe in two – the division was institutionalised in 1949 and 1955 with the creation of NATO and the Warsaw Pact respectively – the far right felt that they found themselves between the liberal Scylla and the communist Charybdis, even more acutely than in the interwar period.

However, these geopolitical concerns did not impede the re-appearance of pro-Russian and pro-Soviet sentiments among particular Western fascist circles. In post-war Europe, these sentiments had two major, sometimes interconnected, sources. One was the legacy of National Bolshevism; the other was the rise of internationalist, pan-European fascism, or Eurofascism.

The legacy of National Bolshevism was especially evident in the ideology of the Bruderschaft (Brotherhood), a semi-secret extreme-right group formed in the British occupation zone of West Germany in 1949. Its main ideologue and a co-chair was Alfred Franke-Gricksch, a former close associate of Otto Strasser and, later, an SS-Obersturmbannführer (a senior storm unit leader of the Schutzstaffel (Protection Squadron, SS)). The other co-chair was Helmut Beck-Broichsitter, a former officer of the Panzer Grenadier Division Großdeutschland (Tank Division Greater Germany). Although the founding members of the Bruderschaft renewed the secret oaths of loyalty to the NSDAP at their inaugural meeting,[37] they understood that the official relaunch of the Nazi party was hardly possible, and decided to concentrate on winning 'the key positions in all areas of public life' and infiltrating 'the major political parties and movements through civil service posts'.[38] The Bruderschaft also advocated the rehabilitation of German soldiers and officers, as well as the release of former Wehrmacht officers charged with war crimes – these issues were politically topical in post-war Germany.

Originally critical of both the United States and the Soviet Union, the Bruderschaft envisaged the revival of Germany and its restoration as a dominant power within 'Nation Europa'[39] – a united Europe free of any foreign occupation. According to the Central Intelligence Agency (CIA), which kept the Bruderschaft under close observation, this Europe 'would withdraw from close political and military cooperation with the US and, although opposing international Bolshevism and Soviet interference in European affairs, could take a neutral position between the US and USSR or even enter as an equal partner into alliance with the USSR'.[40]

In the beginning of the Cold War, neutralism became a major topic in the foreign policy debates in West Germany.[41] Pro-Western Chancellor Konrad Adenauer, the leader of the Christlich Demokratische Union Deutschlands (Christian Democratic Union of Germany, CDU), ardently promoted the idea of the rearmament of Germany and its membership in NATO. The Sozialdemokratische Partei Deutschlands (Social Democratic Party of Germany, SPD) was critical of Adenauer's foreign policy, arguing that West Germany's neutralism would open the path to the restoration of a unified and independent Germany that would position itself not in the West or the East, but between the two geopolitical poles. The SPD called for the creation of the collective European security system, and hoped that 'such a system could both reunite Germany and protect it against Soviet domination. Disarmament and détente could reduce the acute danger facing Europe and could also improve the superpowers' relationship'.[42] Neutralist arguments could be found not only in the rhetoric of the SPD, but also across other major parties, including the CDU.[43]

The Soviet Union supported the idea of a neutralist West Germany and opposed its membership in NATO. The KGB was heavily involved in undermining pro-NATO ambitions and pro-American sentiments in West Germany through various active measures.

Many West German right-wing extremists sided with the neutralists. The slogan of far-right neutralists was 'Ohne mich!' ('Count me out!') – a phrase popularised by Otto Ernst Remer, a former Wehrmacht officer and the leader of the short-lived post-war Sozialistische Reichspartei (Socialist Reich Party, SRP). The perceived trauma of fascism's defeat in the war rendered the imperialist arguments about *Lebensraum* inappropriate – a more pressing and eminently fundamental issue was a problem of two Germanies divided by the Elbe. Most of the post-war far-right neutralists opposed the rearmament of West Germany and its membership in NATO, because they believed that these steps would deepen and, eventually, fix the division of Germany. As German nationalists, they could hardly tolerate such a development and, on the contrary, strove to restore Germany to its 1937 borders. This implied a fundamental revision of the Potsdam and Yalta agreements that extended western borders of Poland at the expense of Germany.

A certain ambivalence of the Bruderschaft's geopolitical attitudes registered by the CIA reflected a conflict between Franke and Beck who expressed contrasting views on international relations. Kurt Tauber, in his monumental study of the post-war German far right, epitomised this conflict as follows:

> Franke – Russophile in foreign-policy orientation, national-Bolshevik in ideology, opportunist in his desire for Eastern reinsurance in facing the hated West – had suggested the Russo–German alliance as part of the matrix within which Germany's rebirth must be effected. Part of this policy was the permanent weakening of the defensive power of the West. Beck, on the other hand, was clearly an attentist in his approach to the problem of German rebirth. Probably no less anti-Western in his resentments than Franke, his primary goal was not so much the permanent weakening of the West as the enforcing of conditions which would make West German rearmament possible only after the rehabilitation, and with the well-rewarded assistance, of the National [i.e. far right] Opposition.[44]

In the course of time, the divisions between Franke's and Beck's lines became even more distinct. Franke, who called himself 'Chancellor of the European Brotherhood of the German Nation', radically rejected all Western defence structures and advocated the development and signing of a pact with the Soviet Union along the lines of the Treaty of Rapallo. Conjuring up the language of National Bolshevism of the 1920–1930s, Franke argued that:

> The torch of racial and cultural rebirth has fallen from the enervated hands of once proud peoples and has been retrieved by the sinewy young Slavs and Germans, who have become the real founders of a revolutionary order. The Prussian eagle and the Russian bear are the symbols of a new synthesis in which German idealism and Slavic materialism will be raised to a new dialectical level.[45]

In his turn, Beck adopted a more favourable position towards the Western Allies and was not that uncompromisingly opposed to Germany's rearmament, possibly under the pressure from the former Wehrmacht officers who hoped for re-employment in the military.[46]

There are, however, two important caveats to these observations. First, there was evidence that Franke tried to use his apparent pro-Soviet position to gain leverage on the Western Allies. According to Franke, 'Germany should pretend to collaborate with the East until certain concessions are granted by the West, then shift toward the West to gain concessions from the East'.[47] Second, Beck's cautiously pro-Western position could have been determined by his collaboration with the Bundesamt für Verfassungsschutz (Federal Office for the Protection of the Constitution, BfV), a domestic intelligence agency that was originally concerned with the neo-Nazi and communist threats. Collaboration charges against Beck eventually led to the split of the Bruderschaft in 1951.

Whether Franke and Beck were honest or dishonest in their geopolitical views, both tried to establish contacts, according to Tauber, with the representatives of the Soviet authorities in East Germany.[48] To date, however, it is still not clear who attempted to manipulate whom. Following his attentist, 'wait-and-see' strategy, Beck tried to establish relations with the Soviets and the Americans simultaneously. A CIA officer James Critchfield suggested that the Bruderschaft 'had been penetrated and controlled by the East German communists as an "active measure" to attract public and international interest and opposition to German remilitarization – a high priority of the Soviet KGB'.[49] At the same time, Richard Breitman and Norman Goda, who worked in the CIA archives, reveal that the Bruderschaft was heavily infiltrated by the US Army Counterintelligence Corps and CIA.[50] Franke was eventually lured into East Germany by a 'far-right' front organisation in 1951, brought to Moscow, charged with the 'creation of a counter-revolutionary organisation and espionage', executed in 1952, and rehabilitated by Russia's Chief Military Prosecutor's Office as a 'victim of political repressions' (!) in 1995.[51]

It seems that the Bruderschaft was infiltrated by all the parties involved in the Cold War. In either case, when Franke started to gain an upper hand in the leadership of the Bruderschaft, his rhetoric – permeated by such phrases as 'American imperialism', 'the process of social rebirth in the Soviet Union', 'the peoples of Asia are fighting for their freedom', etc.[52] – clearly demonstrated the impact of the arguments of the Soviet and East Germany's authorities.

The Bruderschaft ceased to exist in 1951, but a wider far-right neutralist movement had already come into existence by that time.

One of the leaders of this wider movement was Wolf Schenke, a former editor of Hitlerjugend's (Hitler Youth) *Wille und Macht* (Will and Power) and Far East correspondent for the NSDAP's *Völkischer Beobachter* (People's Observer).[53] In 1950, he founded the Dritte Front (Third Front), an emphatically nationalist-neutralist organisation that hosted some other former Hitlerjugend's officials such as Wilhelm Jurzek, Siegfried Zantke and Johann M.G. Schmitz. For Schenke, the main characteristic of the post-war period was not the West-East opposition, but rather – and there one could detect traces of National Bolshevik Third-Worldism and a narrative about 'proletarian nations' – 'the anti-colonialist and anti-imperialist struggle of the peoples of the Third World against the imperialist industrialised nations'.[54]

In terms of the immediate strategy, the Dritte Front favoured contacts with the Soviet occupation zone, and Jurzek visited East Berlin in 1951 to hold private talks with the leader of East Germany's official socialist youth movement Freie Deutsche Jugend (Free German Youth)[55] that was a member organisation of the Nationale Front (National Front), the ruling political alliance in East Germany. Upon his return to West Germany, the Dritte Front launched the newspaper *Deutscher Beobachter* (German Observer; the name suggested a reference to *Völkischer Beobachter*) that revealed strong affinities with the agenda of the Nationale Front.[56] Because of these overt affinities, however, the newspaper suspended publication. The Dritte Front continued the attempts to build the neutralist movement and, in 1951, contributed to organising – together with Rudolf Jungnickel, the Conservative Revolutionary leader of the apparently pro-Soviet front organisation Friedenskorps West (Peace Corps West) – the German Congress that hosted 130 West German neutralists of different ideological creeds.[57]

Yet another prominent far-right neutralist organisation was Otto Ernst Remer's SRP that 'propagated a typically Nazi doctrine of the Reich as a kind of mystical blood union of the German people, openly expressed their admiration for Hitler and his regime, and violently attacked the leaders of the West German government'.[58]

Although the SRP was neutralist, Remer, like many other West German neutralists, was more inclined to embrace the Soviets, rather than the Americans. He even suggested posting 'ourselves as traffic policemen, spreading our arms so that the Russians [could] find their way through Germany as quickly as possible ... [and] pick the [British and American] lords and ladies out of their silken beds!'.[59] It was hardly surprising that the SRP presumably received financial support from the Soviets.[60]

The SRP was founded in 1949 and even had some electoral success, but the West German authorities considered the SRP too extreme and outlawed it in 1952. Remer would flee to Egypt and Syria where he became involved in arms sales to Arab customers including the Algerian nationalists who fought for independence from France.[61] During the Cuban crisis in the 1960s, Remer and another former SRP member Ernst Wilhelm Springer would also try to purchase Belgian weapons for the regime of Fidel Castro who, at that time, recruited former Waffen-SS officers to instruct the Cuban military.[62]

After the destruction of the SRP, many of its former members joined the Deutsche Reichspartei (German Imperial Party, DRP) that was chaired by a former Hitlerjugend leader Herbert Freiberger and urged West Germany to withdraw from NATO and the European Common Market.[63]

During the 1950s, there were many conferences and meetings that aimed at uniting West German neutralists from the far right, far left and centre, but none of the attempts produced any lasting result. Apart from the ideological differences between the neutralists and continuous conflicts over leadership, one factor that impeded the creation of a unified neutralist front was a persistent suspicion of the Soviet or communist money involved in all these initiatives. As they 'were fighting hard to prevent the Federal Republic's alignment with the Western bloc',[64] the Soviets encouraged all neutralist activities in West Germany even if the groups and organisations involved in them did not favour the Soviet Union. As Ladislav Bittman, a former agent of the Czechoslovak security services and expert in disinformation campaigns, observed:

> In early Soviet disinformation campaigns, KGB operatives were somewhat hesitant to use slogans and propagandists evidence that did not *directly* support Soviet policies. They found later that they could be more effective by hiding behind any kind of political mask, including left-wing organizations or even neo-fascist movements, as long as they served Soviet interests.[65]

This was precisely the case with West German neutralists of any political stance. While it would be too far-fetched to argue that all neutralist groups in West Germany were paid stooges of the Soviet Union, the suspicion that there was indeed Communist money involved even in the workings of the far-right neutralist groups was not ungrounded as the examples below evidently indicate.

In 1950, the Nationaldemokratische Partei Deutschlands (National-Democratic Party of Germany, NDPD),[66] a Communist-controlled party in East Germany created to reintegrate former members of the NSDAP and Wehrmacht into the socialist society, appealed to all former supporters of the Third Reich to oppose the continued partition of Germany.[67] While Moscow and the Nationale Front created various front organisations pretending to be 'peace', 'women's organisations', 'youth', 'sports' and 'cultural groups' in West Germany,[68] the NDPD helped form, during the 1950s, 'numerous pressure groups, newspapers, and "study circles" for former officers'[69] through its West German contacts among former Nazis and Wehrmacht officers. For these purposes, the NDPD received 700,000 East German Marks a month from a Soviet bank.[70]

One of the joint initiatives of the NDPD and its contacts in West Germany was the creation of the extreme-right, anti-Semitic Führungsring ehemaliger Soldaten (Leadership Committee for Former Soldiers, FeS) in 1951. In geopolitical terms, as their leaders argued, the FeS was anti-Western, anti-Eastern, German, pro-European, friendly to Russia 'regardless of her inner political orientation', insofar as Russia did not interfere in the affairs of Germany.[71] However, the rhetoric of their publication, *Rundbrief* (Circular Letter), was pro-Eastern rather than equally anti-Western *and* anti-Eastern. As some leaders of the FeS argued, 'the so-called dangers from the East, against which West German rearmament was to guard, were little more than hobgoblins of the overheated imagination of Western [Hans

Joachim] Morgenthau boys.[72] On the contrary, the East . . . was more than willing to arrive at an understanding'.[73] During their meetings, their political position generously sponsored by the Soviets was even clearer: 'The Soviet Government managed to rouse the youth to its banner. If there should be a war, I'd rather go to the enthusiastic youth of the East who surely will win if pitted against the lame West. The youth of the East Zone still believe that they have something worth defending.'[74]

Yet another example of the involvement of the East in funding of the far-right neutralist initiatives in West Germany was provided by the activities of Rudolf Steidl, a dedicated Nazi and a regular contributor to the FeS' *Rundbrief*. In 1955, he revealed that a Communist official approached him in 1951 with a proposal to start publishing an information bulletin that would promote extreme-right and anti-Western neutralist ideas. For his activities, Steidl obtained 2,363,000 Deutschmarks in the period 1951–1954.[75] He used these funds for publication of the *Internationale Militärkorrespondenz* (International Military Correspondence; 1952), *Militärpolitische Forum* (Military Political Forum; 1952), *Deutsche National-Zeitung* (German National Newspaper; 1953) and *Die Nation* (The Nation; 1954).

The contents of these publications were similar to the production of other West German far-right philo-Soviet neutralists who drew on the legacy of National Bolshevism, Conservative Revolution and/or left-wing Nazism of the Strassers, as well as criticising the policies of Adenauer and calling for a new Tauroggen.[76] The *Internationale Militärkorrespondenz* concussed that 'a German contribution to the Western "defensive posture" was not only futile but highly dangerous', and 'that the military interests of Germany demanded now, as they had constantly done since the time of Frederick the Great, an agreement with the East'.[77] The *Deutsche National-Zeitung* wrote about the 'continued efforts of the Soviet Union to come into a conversation with the Western powers'.[78]

Despite all the neutralist initiatives – whether genuine or Soviet-sponsored, coming from the far right, left or centre – West Germany joined NATO in 1955. Conferences and meetings of West German neutralists continued until the end of the 1950s, but they became increasingly irrelevant. However, the tradition of far-right – and often philo-Soviet – neutralism exerted important ideological influence on many successive far-right movements across the West.

With neutralism failing and West Germany joining NATO, the Soviets changed their tactics at the end of the 1950s: rather than promoting neutralism, the Soviet-controlled secret services mainly attempted to discredit West Germany. The KGB and its counterparts in the countries of the Warsaw Pact kept on infiltrating neo-Nazi organisations in West Germany and some other Western countries, but then with a different aim, namely to goad them into extremist activities, only to accuse Western countries of the alleged resurgence of Nazism afterwards. One example of such initiatives was the 'swastika graffiti operation' devised by Soviet KGB General Ivan Agayants, who at that time headed the KGB Department D (disinformation), and carried out in 1959–1960 in West Germany.[79] In that period, KGB agents painted swastikas and anti-Semitic slogans on synagogues, tombstones and Jewish-owned shops. Jewish families received anonymous hate mail and threatening phone calls. The initial KGB operation would stir up residual anti-Semitic sentiments in the West German society and, consequently, produce a snowball effect where troublemakers would carry out anti-Semitic activities on their own.[80]

The 'swastika graffiti operation' in West Germany caused considerable damage to the reputation of the country in the West: its diplomats were ostracised, West German products boycotted, Bonn assailed for the alleged inability to deal with Nazism and questions raised about the credibility of the country as a member of NATO.[81] However, there was yet another effect of the operation. As Michael Scholz argues, 'the fabricated Swastika graffiti enabled [East Germany's] foreign country propaganda to point out a concrete danger, which came from the alleged aggressive, imperialistic and revanchist policy of the Bonn government'.[82] By doing so, the authorities of East Germany attempted to raise its 'international reputation', and 'to strengthen and broaden its "international positions"'.[83] Thus, the KGB-inspired 'swastika graffiti operation' against West Germany helped East Germany legitimise itself as a peace loving, antifascist state.

In the beginning of the 1950s, a far-right neutralist movement also existed in Austria that, at that time, was under the Allied occupation, albeit this movement was not as significant as in West Germany.

The emergence of the Austrian far-right neutralist phenomenon was underpinned by a combination of domestic and international politics. On the one hand, the Sozialdemokratische Partei Österreichs (Social Democratic Party of Austria, SPÖ) was fighting against its primary rival, the Österreichische Volkspartei (Austrian People's Party, ÖVP), and, to undermine its electoral base, welcomed the creation of the far-right Verband der Unabhängigen (Federation of Independents, VdU) that appealed to the nationalist voters and former Nazis, and clearly siphoned votes from the ÖVP. On the other hand, the Soviets and the Soviet-controlled Kommunistische Partei Österreichs (Communist Party of Austria, KPÖ) feared that the 'bourgeois parties', that is, the SPÖ, ÖVP and VdU, would come to dominate the Austrian politics leaving no political space for the pro-Soviet forces, and, therefore, attempted to make inroads in the far-right camp. For the Soviets, the political situation in Austria became especially problematic after the 1949 parliamentary elections in which the far right and pro-Western VdU obtained 11.67 per cent of the votes and became the country's third largest party, while the KPÖ secured only 5.08 per cent of the votes.

To undermine support for the VdU, the communists followed the same line they adopted in West Germany with the creation of the NDPD. The first attempt at this endeavour was associated with Josef Heger, a former regional chairman of the VdU who was expelled from the party 'for fraudulent claims to the title of engineer and high military rank and decorations'.[84] According to a declassified confidential despatch of the CIA, Heger 'had passed through a Soviet indoctrination camp after his capture on the Russian front',[85] and thus his membership in the VdU could be an element of the Soviet infiltration effort. In 1950, Heger founded the far-right Nationaldemokratischen Verband (National Democratic Union, NDV) that, unlike the VdU, promoted the neutralist agenda, and was 'composed mostly of former SS officers who mingled a fanatical German nationalism with totalitarian communism'.[86] As the leader of the NDV, Heger was reported to regularly meet with the Soviet High Commissioner of Austria Vladimir Sviridov and the Soviet political representative in Austria Mikhail Koptelov. According to the CIA files,

> Heger was even to have obtained Soviet approval of a secret ten point platform which included: (1) An attempt to split the VdU; (2) advocacy of a radical social program; (3) the use of radical tactics to instigate and promote strikes; (4) opposition to US influence and the MARSHALL Plan; (5) denunciations of Allied dismantling in Germany and Western intelligence activities in Germany and Austria.[87]

The NDV, however, turned out to be unsuccessful and soon disappeared from the Austrian political landscape.

The second attempt at building the far-right neutralist movement in Austria was associated with Adolf Slavik, a former Hitlerjugend organiser and SS-Obersturmführer. Because of the de-Nazification laws, he could not officially lead any organisation, yet he was the unofficial founder and leader of the far-right Nationale Liga (National League, NL) that was established in 1950 and whose rhetoric was characterised by 'a crude mixture of pro-Soviet and neo-Nazi propaganda'.[88] Similar to both the VdU and NDV, former Nazis constituted the organisational core of the NL.

The NL's manifesto titled 'What Does the National League Want?' appeared relatively moderate. It demanded 'the establishment of a socialist community', 'absolute equality of rights between our people and all other nations', 'equal rights, socially and economically, for women and generous state support for newly married couples'. Its neutralist position manifested itself in the demands for 'the national characteristics and the sovereignty of all peoples' to be respected, 'the neutrality of Austria and a policy of true agreement *also* with the Eastern countries', and 'a planned economy which will serve only the national interests of our national economy'. At the same time, the NL professed what it called 'German national ways', regarded 'the restoration of German unity as an essential prerequisite to the recovery of Europe', and demanded 'immediate naturalization of all Volksdeutsche willing to work, but eviction of all alien parasites'.[89]

The NL's newspaper, *Österreichische Beobachter* (Austrian Observer; its name was a reference to the NSDAP's *Völkischer Beobachter*, similar to the Dritte Front's *Deutscher Beobachter*) was less moderate, and frequently published openly Nazi and pan-German texts. The office of the *Österreichische Beobachter* was located in the Soviet sector in Vienna and in the same building that also hosted the office of the KPÖ-associated newspaper *Tagebuch* (Diary).[90] In December 1950, *Österreichische*

Beobachter was banned for 2 months, and during this period was published under the title *Österreichische National-Zeitung* (Austrian National Newspaper). The Western occupation authorities protested the publication of this 'new' newspaper, but the Soviet authorities disagreed with the Western allies, and the publication of *Österreichische National-Zeitung* continued.[91]

Slavik also tried to develop contacts with West German far-right neutralists: in November 1950, in Salzburg, he met with Alfred Franke-Gricksch, one of the leaders the Bruderschaft. However, Slavik's main contacts seemed to be Soviet officials. According to an informant of a CIA agent in Austria, Slavik contacted Soviet occupation forces not through the KPÖ but directly, while the funding for the NL came from the Administration for Soviet Property in Austria.[92] Furthermore, Slavik claimed that he had managed to secure leading positions in the Administration for Soviet Property for 30 former SS chiefs.[93] The CIA believed that Slavik also travelled 'through West Germany, ostensibly on official business for the Administration of Soviet Property in Austria, but actually to establish an intelligence network "on behalf of an eastern service"'.[94]

While the Soviet authorities in Austria never admitted that the NL was a Soviet front organisation, they described it the following way:

> The National League is a new democratic organisation that features representatives of the Austrian intelligentsia, workers and civil servants, petite bourgeoisie dissatisfied with the policies of the Austrian government [and] the reactionary parties (ÖVP, SPÖ and VdU). A significant element of the supporters of the National League comprises of former National Socialists dissatisfied with the pro-American policies of the Austrian government and aspiring to establish friendly relations with the Soviet Union and countries of popular democracy.[95]

Because of the NL's strong links to the Soviets, Austrian media often attacked it referring to the organisation as 'Kommunazi' and 'National Bolsheviks'. In May 1950, the Austrian newspaper *Weltpresse* (World Press) published an article on the NL that argued: 'The Russian occupation authorities use former SS officer Adolf Slavik for recruiting former frontline officers and National Socialists who would take part in the struggle for the National-Bolshevik ideals in Austria'.[96]

The NL existed for a longer period than the NDV, but it ceased to exist by 1955. According to the declassified secret CIA report, Slavik would later travel to Casablanca where he helped arrange for the delivery of 'a large shipmemt of Soviet sponsored arms' to the Algerian nationalists.[97] In the second half of the 1960s, Slavik was arrested in Istanbul and sentenced to 12 years of imprisonment on the espionage charges. The Austrian newspaper *Express* reported that, during the trial, Slavik told the Istanbul Military Court that he was a KGB agent running the Middle-East espionage network.[98] Slavik was apparently exchanged for a Turkish spy by socialist Bulgaria in the early 1970s.

Towards the European Imperium: The case of Francis Parker Yockey

National Bolshevism and left-wing Nazism were primary ideological sources of pro-Russian attitudes within the Western far-right neutralist movements, but pro-Soviet tendencies appeared in yet another post-war movement, namely pan-European fascism.

Internationalist trends in European fascism emerged already in the interwar period. As Roger Griffin argues, 'certain strands of interwar fascism', albeit marginal at that time, 'were actively concerned with resolving the decadence brought about by the status quo as a whole, not just in a particular nation, and thus thought of rebirth in pan-European or even Western terms'.[99] However, the concern of pan-European fascists in interwar Europe was *both* American liberalism and Soviet Bolshevism. It was equally true for the first post-war pan-European fascists: unlike the majority of West German far-right neutralists who might officially condemn both the Americans and the Soviets, but then evidently side with the latter, the first pan-European fascists were predominantly and sincerely critical of the two global forces, and were intrinsically more neutralist than the self-styled neutralists themselves. Major pan-European fascists imagined Europe as a 'Third Force':

> This federated Europe, having achieved the power to extricate itself from the grip or influence of both the United States and the Soviet Union would – under the slogan, 'Europe for the Europeans' – represent a Third Force of absolute neutrality between the alien and inimical Powers in the East and the West.[100]

One of the most important publications of pan-European fascists was *Nation Europa – Monatsschrift im Dienste der europäischen Neuordnung* (Nation Europe – Monthly in the Service of the European New Order) launched in 1951 by former SS officer Arthur Ehrhardt and former SA officer Herbert Böhme. Since then, *Nation Europa* published writings of important ideologues of the post-war and contemporary far right including Julius Evola, Oswald Mosley, Armin Mohler, Alain de Benoist, Jean-Marie Le Pen, Yvan Blot, Bruno Mégret, Filip Dewinter, and Andreas Mölzer.

Given the critical approach that the first proponents of Nation Europa took towards both the United States and Soviet Union, it is a historical irony that one of the key ideological attempts at building a pan-European fascist movement not only originated in the United States, but also welcomed, although only at a later stage, the involvement of the Soviet Union. This attempt was associated with the works and activities of Francis Parker Yockey, an American political philosopher and one of the most intriguing, enigmatic and prominent exponents of post-war pan-European fascism. Yockey extensively travelled all over the world after the Second World War and established a vast network of contacts with fascist and extreme-right activists to promote his pan-European cause, most of which are thoroughly documented in Kevin Coogan's biography of Yockey, *Dreamer of the Day*.[101]

Yockey's *magnum opus* was *Imperium: The Philosophy of History and Politics*, a fundamental exposition of pan-European fascism written and published in 1948.[102] In *Imperium*, Yockey asserted that the meaning of the word 'Europe' was no longer limited to the geographical Europe, but implied the entire Western Civilisation. 'Former nations' such as Spain, Italy, France, England and Germany were dead: 'the era of political nationalism' passed in the process of 'the *organic* advance of the History of the West'.[103] It was imperative for Europe to unite, and to take 'the form of unity of People, Race, Nation, State, Society, Will – and naturally also – economy'. Yockey presented *Imperium* as a declaration of war on 'the financial trickery of retarders, the petty-stateism of party-politicians, and the occupying armies of extra-European forces'.[104]

Imperium was critical of Russia and clearly associated it, along with the United States, with the 'extra-European forces' threatening Europe. Nevertheless, Yockey distinguished between two Russias: one was 'the true Russia' and the other – the Bolshevik Russia. In his view,

> the true, spiritual, Russia, is *primitive* and *religious*. It detests Western Culture, Civilization, nations, arts, State-forms, Ideas, religions, cities, technology. This hatred is natural, and organic, for this population lies outside the Western organism, and everything Western is therefore hostile and deadly to the Russian soul.[105]

Bolshevik Russia, on the other hand, welcomed Western technology and economic models, but was still hostile to Europe. Yockey believed that it was erroneous to assume that Bolshevik Russia – in its approach to the West – was either willing to reform the society along the preferences of one particular class or to reorganise the world in accordance with the political and socio-economic conditions in Russia. The only mission that Russia had was to destroy the West, and to implement that mission Russia would exploit 'any inner agitation within the West' itself: 'class-war, race-war, social degeneration, crazy art, decadent films, wild theories and philosophies of all kinds'.[106] Yockey saw Russia as 'the bearer of no Utopian hopes for the West' and stated that anyone, who would believe it was, was 'a Cultural idiot'.[107]

With Europe largely ruined by the war, America, according to Yockey, was the only remaining rival of Russia, and both prepared for the Third World War. At the same time, however, Yockey considered Russia less dangerous for Europe than America, because although Russia tried to split Europe, it could eventually only unite it, while the effect of the 'American occupation' was exactly the fragmentation of Europe through appeals 'to the sub-Europeans, the Retarders, ... the money-worshipers, the lazy and the stupid, and to the worst instincts in every European'.[108] Nevertheless, Russia, 'by virtue of its physical situation', would and should always 'remain the enemy of the West, as long as these populations' were organised 'as a political unit'.[109]

Shortly before writing *Imperium*, Yockey met with Oswald Mosley, the former leader of the British Union of Fascists who was interned for his Nazi sympathies during most of the Second World War. After his imprisonment, Mosley 'abandoned "Britain First" fascism in favour of a regenerative pan-European fascist vision – "Europe-a-Nation" '.[110] In 1948, he formed the Union Movement (UM) ideologically underpinned by Mosley's own magnum opus *The Alternative* that proclaimed pan-European fascism opposing both America and Russia.[111] Yockey became a paid member of the UM,[112] as well as contributing to the publications of the organisation. However, although both Yockey and Mosley were pan-Europeanists, they did differ in their geopolitical views. Yockey and Mosley condemned the United States and the Soviet Union, but Yockey's attitude towards America was more critical than to Russia, while it was the opposite case for Mosley. In one of his works, still referring to the United States and the Soviet Union as 'occupying powers', Mosley wrote: 'Under Russia, European freedom is killed, and under America, European freedom can still exist and even grow'.[113] Coogan suggests that the 'American question' was one of the issues that eventually forced Yockey and Mosley to part ways.[114]

Around the time Yockey established contacts with Mosley, he also met Alfred Franke-Gricksch, one of the leaders of the Bruderschaft, and introduced him to Mosley. Franke was briefly 'the chief German advisor' to the UM,[115] but Franke and Mosley also broke up due to the differences in their geopolitical views.

Together with a few renegades from the UM, Yockey founded, in 1948–1949, the European Liberation Front (ELF) set to free Europe from its enemies and to fly 'the European banner' over Europe's 'own soil from Galway to Memelland and from North Cape to Gibraltar'.[116] Already during the formation of the ELF, Yockey suggested, in a private conversation, helping 'organize secret partisans in Western Germany who would be prepared to collaborate with the Soviet military authorities in action against the Western occupying powers'.[117] After its establishment, the ELF also attempted to recruit to its subversive anti-Western cause other British fascists, by infiltrating and hijacking the extreme-right organisations. According to the far-right groupuscule Nationalist Information Bureau (better known as NATINFORM), one ELF's leading functionary, Guy Chesham, approached their member and offered collaboration with Yockey's organisation. Inter alia, Chesham 'suggested that forces could be raised in England for direct action against American military bases in England'.[118] Furthermore, Chesham argued that, since the Communist Party of Great Britain was 'making no progress' – apparently in terms of subversive activities – 'it would be possible to obtain financial support from the Soviet Embassy in London', if the British fascists organised 'successfully an anti-American front with popular support'.[119] Whether the ELF was successful in obtaining funding from the Soviet Embassy in London is unknown, but, in his book on American neo-Nazism, William Goring speculated that the ELF had been 'secretly encouraged and, possibly, financed in part by the Soviet Union'.[120]

However, officially, the ELF refrained from voicing straightforwardly pro-Soviet positions. *The Proclamation of London*, the ELF's manifesto written by Yockey, makes only a slight shift – in comparison to Yockey's previous works – towards reconciliation with Russia. The manifesto still assailed the country as 'one of the leaders of the coloured revolt against the European race', but it also pointed to the conflict 'between the Western elements of Russia and the Asiatic will-to-destruction', as well as identifying 'the Asiatic elements' and the Jews as a source of Russia's re-orientation against Europe. Importantly, however, the manifesto argued that 'European possibilities still exist[ed] within Russia, because in certain strata of the population adherence to the great organism of the Western Culture [was] an instinct, an Idea, and no material force [could] ever wipe it out, even though it [might] be temporarily repressed and driven under'.[121]

The acknowledgement of Russia's 'European possibilities' and the identification of particular 'anti-European' elements of contemporary Russia clearly represented a change in Yockey's official position towards Russia. This shift was reminiscent of Moeller's reservations about National Bolshevism and his argument that a viable alliance of Germany and Russia required the preliminary 'elimination of all Jewish influence' in both countries.

The link between Russia's 'European possibilities' and 'Jewish influence' was an ideological framework within which Yockey interpreted specific developments in socialist Europe in the beginning of the 1950s – the developments that prompted Yockey to revise further his public views on Russia. In 1952, Yockey closely followed the Slánský trial in Czechoslovakia – a show trial against 14 top officials (11 of them of Jewish origin) of the Komunistická strana Československa (Communist Party of Czechoslovakia), including General Secretary of the party Rudolf Slánský.[122] The Kremlin-backed Czechoslovak authorities charged them with high treason, sabotage, spying, conspiracy and harbouring Zionist sentiments, and executed 11 of them. The Slánský trial was strongly anti-Semitic in character. It was preceded by the Night of the Murdered Poets – an execution of 15 Soviet Jews, including 5 poets[123] – and was followed by the notorious Doctors' Plot in 1953 when a group of prominent Soviet doctors, predominantly of Jewish origin, were accused of conspiring to murder Kremlin leaders.[124] Stalin saw Jews in the Soviet Union and its satellites in Europe as potential traitors and Western agents, and the anti-Semitic trials aimed at purging the Soviet and socialist political elites of the Jewish presence.

Yockey considered the Slánský trial a turning point, a sign that the 'Western elements' were prevailing over the 'Jewish influence' in Soviet Russia. In 1952, he anonymously published an essay 'What is behind the hanging of the eleven Jews in Prague?' where he wrote that the trial in Prague was a testimony to the fact that the Russian leadership was 'killing Jews for treason to Russia, for service to the Jewish entity', and that it was 'a war-declaration by Russia on the Jewish-American leadership'.[125] By 'playing off Russia against the Jewish-American leadership', Europe could 'bring about its Liberation' and put an end to 'the American hegemony of Europe'.[126]

In his *Der Feind Europas* (The Enemy of Europe) published in 1953 in German language, Yockey came out as a dedicated proponent of pan-Europeanist anti-Americanism: *the* Enemy of Europe was the United States.[127] Although neither America, nor Russia belonged to the 'Western Civilisation', while Russian Empire was, for Yockey, 'only a formless grouping of barbaric tribes with a purely negative mission',[128] he acknowledged that, as long as the 'Russian Soul' existed 'within the sphere of influence of a Western organism', there remained 'in Russia a powerful urge towards reunion with the West'.[129] Europe could take advantage of Russia's conflict with America, as well as the combination of Russia's barbarian will to destroy the West and the inferior nature of Russia's character. Yockey referred to the 'Barbarian Invasion of Rome', and argued that, because the barbarians were spiritually weaker than the Romans, the invasion failed to destroy 'the body of the Culture' and, eventually, the barbarians were absorbed into the 'Culture-body'.[130]

His discussion of Russia's 'barbarianism' developed along similar lines, and Yockey even seemed to *welcome* a specific form of the Russian occupation of Europe:

> A Russian occupation would develop along one or the other of two lines. The first possibility is an endless series of European uprisings against Russia that could result only in the expulsion of the demoralised barbarians. The second possibility would result from Russia's introducing a clever regime and according Europe extensive autonomy and magnanimous treatment. Within a few decades, this Europe would naturally aim at infiltrating horizontally the whole Russian seat of origin, its technical, economic, social, and, finally, military and political life. Instead of the Russification of Europe, . . . would result [in] the Europeanisation of Russia once again, and this time in far stronger degree. . . . An attempt by Russia to integrate Europe into its power-accumulation peacefully would eventually result in the rise of a new Symbiosis: Europe-Russia. *Its final form would be that of a European Imperium.*[131]

None of the previous pan-European fascists or interwar National Bolsheviks had ever gone as far as Yockey did in his geopolitical envisioning of the Europe-centred regeneration of the world with the aim of creating 'the Culture-State-Nation-Imperium of the West'.[132] Despite the fact that Yockey previously discussed, in private conversations, prospective anti-American subversive actions that could be carried out in a joint effort with the Soviet military, his officially voiced suggestion that the occupation of Europe by 'Russian barbarians' could be beneficial was as revolutionary as it was bizarre at that time – at the time of his writing, nobody was prepared to introduce it to a doctrine of any political movement.

In his concluding essay, 'An Estimate of the World Situation',[133] Yockey elaborated on two important themes as parts of his far-right geopolitical analysis: neutralism and Third-Worldism. The essay generally focused on the anticipated Third World War between the United States and the Soviet Union. Yockey's position on the war was clear and concise: 'Victory means, in the Third World War, not annihilation of the opponent, but conclusion of peace on one's own terms. Speaking thus of political victory, it is clear that America-Jewry – under the conditions of 1960 – must lose, and Russia must win'.[134] In this context, two developments seemed important to him. First, Europe had to adopt an anti-American neutralist position. Second, Third-World countries were no longer outside the geopolitical struggle, and the rise of 'nationalist, neutralist regimes' in the Third World was beneficial to Europe. For him, European neutralism and Third-World countries could potentially even prevent the war: 'The growing tide of neutralism in the world, is due to the political incapacity of the leadership corps of America-Jewry. If this tide rises in Europe, America-Jewry would be defeated before the war.'[135] There is little doubt that Yockey adopted the notion of neutralism from the West German far-right neutralists, some of whom he met personally.

Yockey's tactical embrace of Soviet Russia, socialist countries in Central and Eastern Europe, and the Third World had a practical angle too, transcending private theoretical discussions about carrying out anti-American subversive actions. According to a prominent American fascist and Yockey's close associate Harold Keith Thompson, Yockey did 'a brief courier job' for the Czechoslovak intelligence in the 1950s.[136] In 1953, Yockey also met in Cairo with the future Egyptian President Gamal Abdel Nasser, under whom Egypt adopted a neutralist position.[137] Shortly before his death in 1960, Yockey visited Cuba where he tried, yet failed, to arrange a meeting with contemporary Prime Minister Fidel Castro.

Yockey disappeared for some time in 1955; there were rumours among his American fascist counterparts that he visited East Germany and/or the Soviet Union, while the Federal Bureau of Investigation (FBI) alleged that he had contacts with the Soviet authorities.[138] Furthermore, one anonymous source suggested, in a mid-1970 interview, that Yockey could be involved in the dubious Soviet-coordinated activities in West Germany: 'I think [Yockey] was a coordinator of some sort. I think the Russians, particularly in [Western] Germany, were encouraging some of those radical rightist groups and parties, for their own purposes.'[139] If this assessment of Yockey's activities is correct, he might have participated in the West German neutralist movement or the Soviet attempts to discredit West Germany after the failure of the neutralists. According to the FBI, Yockey cooperated with Remer's SRP, and was even registered as a foreign agent for the SRP with the US Department of Justice.[140] After the SRP was banned by the West German authorities, its hard core joined the DRP, and these were its active members who were arrested for smearing swastikas on the synagogue in Cologne in 1959,[141] that is, during the KGB-inspired 'swastika graffiti operation'. However, none of Yockey's alleged Soviet contacts has been conclusively proven so far.

Yockey's pro-Soviet attitudes apparently exerted influence even on particular fascist circles in the United States. For example, the largely anti-Semitic *National Renaissance Bulletin* of the first US neo-Nazi organisation, the National Renaissance Party (NRP), was often sympathetic towards the Soviet Union. Arguably under the impact of Yockey's arguments, the 'rationale for this was that the Soviet Union was anti-Jewish and the Jews were trying to destroy that nation, hence it couldn't be all bad'.[142] James Hartung Madole, the founder of the NRP, 'retained a strong interest in events in Europe, as well as the emerging Third World liberation struggles'.[143] As the leader of the party, which John George and Laird Wilcox described as 'a bunch of fanatics, adventurers and informants',[144] Madole also developed contacts with the Soviet consulate in New York in the late 1950s, and was particularly close to one Soviet press officer to whom he submitted a plan 'meant to interest the Russians in backing an anti-Communist and anti-Jewish group'.[145] Harold Keith Thompson maintained contacts with the Soviet diplomatic corps in the United States, especially with Soviet diplomat Valerian Zorin who was a permanent representative of the USSR at the UN Security Council in 1952–1953 and 1956–1965. Thompson, who was introduced to Zorin in 1961, 'traded favors with the Russians to encourage the release of high-ranking Nazis still held by them'.[146]

As Coogan put it, the 'nagging suspicion that Yockey was working with *both* the Nazis and the Communists to encourage the spread of anti-American sentiment in Europe and the Third World is what led Washington to become so concerned with him'.[147] The FBI was trying to apprehend him for about a decade, but Yockey kept on avoiding arrest with the help of multiple fake identities and passports, as well as extensive travelling and going underground. The FBI eventually arrested him in 1960, and, shortly afterwards, he committed suicide in custody by taking a cyanide pill. On the night before his suicide, he told his cellmate that 'he had knowledge of people he loved and thought he'd be forced to reveal it'.[148]

During Yockey's lifetime, his ideas about anti-American pan-Europeanism, the tactical alliance with the Soviet Union, and geopolitical focus on the Third World remained marginal and failed to convince the majority of his far-right contemporaries. However, certain Western far-right movements rediscovered Yockey's ideas a few decades after his death. He was then retrospectively hailed as a 'Spenglerian visionary' and 'the prophet of the Imperium'.[149]

Jean Thiriart: Towards the Euro-Soviet Empire from Vladivostok to Dublin

Preceded by a number of meetings and conferences, pan-European fascism became a dominant trend in the European far-right circles by the beginning of the 1960s. In 1962, the major Italian post-war fascist party, Movimento Sociale Italiano (Italian Social Movement, MSI), convened – on the initiative of Mosley's UM – a meeting in Venice to found the National Party of Europe.

The final document of the convention was the 'Declaration of Venice'. It declared a 'European communion of blood and of spirit' and announced the birth of 'Europe a Nation'. Europe would 'have a common government for purposes of foreign policy, defence, economic policy, finance and scientific development', while 'national parliaments in each member country of Europe a Nation [would] have full power over all social and cultural problems, subject only to the overriding power of European Government in finance and its other defined spheres, in particular the duty of economic leadership'.[150] The Declaration also promoted the idea of armed neutralism and stated: 'With the creation of Europe a Nation as a third power strong enough to maintain peace, a primary object of the European government will be to secure the immediate and simultaneous withdrawal of both Russian and American forces from the occupied territories and military bases of Europe.'[151]

The 'Declaration of Venice' was signed by Mosley, the MSI's Giovanni Lanfre, the DRP's contemporary leader Adolf von Thadden, and convicted Belgian collaborator Jean Thiriart who represented the Mouvement d'Action Civique (Civic Action Movement, MAC).[152]

The Venice initiative suffered the same fate that befell all the previous attempts at creating a viable pan-European fascist movement. Yet the fates of the four signatories of the Declaration of Venice were different. Mosley's political career ended after 1966. Adolf von Thadden went on to co-found the NPD, the most significant German post-war neo-Nazi party that, for some reason, was named after the Communist-controlled, East German party that operated as a socialist front organisation. Giovanni Lanfre became a relatively successful politician and a one-time member of the Senate. Jean Thiriart failed as a politician, but became one of the most important ideologues of pan-European fascism who eventually embraced the Soviet Union.

Thiriart was arrested, for a few months, by the Belgian authorities immediately after his return from Venice to Brussels, apparently for his involvement in the French Organisation de l'armée secrete (Organisation of the Secret Army, OAS). The OAS was a clandestine right-wing terrorist group that resisted the liberation of Algeria from the French rule and was involved in assassination attempts on President Charles de Gaulle who supported the independence of Algeria. According to Daniele Ganser, the OAS was infiltrated by soldiers of the NATO stay-behind[153] originally aimed at resisting the Soviet military in case the Soviets invaded a West European country or preventing a communist party from coming to power in the West. The NATO involvement in the OAS has not been unambiguously proven so far, but after Algeria declared independence in 1962, Thiriart preferred to distance himself from one of the branches of the OAS, namely the Armée nationale secrète (Secret National Army), as he believed it was pro-American and pro-NATO.[154]

Already in 1961, Thiriart founded, in France, the organisation Jeune Europe (Young Europe) named after the title of *La Jeune Europe*, a journal published by Nazi Germany in 1942–1945. The MAC then became a branch of Jeune Europe in Belgium that mainly promoted the agenda of the OAS. Jeune Europe, as well as the MAC and OAS, was initially pro-colonial and supported European domination over a number of African countries – Thiriart explicated these ideas in his *Le Manifeste à la nation européenne* (the Manifesto for the European nation).[155] Because of the originally pro-colonial nature of the ideology of Jeune Europe, it was able to secure financial support from the Portuguese government, enterprises such as the Belgian mining company Union Minière du Haut Katanga, and Dutch and West German financial groups and agricultural companies that had business interests in the African colonies.[156]

After his release from prison, Thiriart abandoned the MAC as an organisational initiative and focused exclusively on Jeune Europe; its branches were established in Italy, Spain, Portugal, France, Austria and the Netherlands. In Spain, members of Joven Europa (Young Europe) would establish – officially in 1966 – the Circulo Español de Amigos de Europa (Spanish Circle of Friends of Europe, widely known by its Spanish acronym CEDADE). CEDADE outlived Joven Europa and became a significant Spanish neo-Nazi association that 'set up a wide network of international relations with associations, parties and even governments of non-democratic states', as well as founding 'several publishing houses and bookshops that acted as centres of dissemination for neo-Nazi propaganda'.[157]

While still in prison, Thiriart started writing his major work, *Un Empire de 400 millions d'hommes* (An Empire of 400 million people),[158] that was published in 1964. Elaborating on some of the ideas exposed in *Le Manifeste à la nation européenne*, Thiriart condemned 'superficial and ill-informed or morbid defeatists [who had] cultivated the legend of a "small" Europe crushed between the two "greats" the USA and the USSR'.[159] The 'European state', Thiriart wrote, extended from Brest to Bucharest, and after the liberation of Eastern Europe, then 'enslaved by the communist dictatorship and foreign occupation', its total population would amount to 414 million people – more than the populations of the United States and the Soviet Union combined.[160]

Similar to Yockey, Thiriart assailed with criticism the concept of 'Europe of the fatherlands' (*Europe des Patries*) arguing that 'small cramped nationalisms [possessed] no other sign of life than a hatred of their neighbours either real or imagined'. 'Private patriotisms' were only 'suitable to tired old reactionaries'. 'Narrow, paltry nationalisms [had to] subliminate themselves to serve the greater conception of Europe.' 'To face Russian and American imperialistic nationalism', national patriotisms had to give way to 'European nationalism'.[161]

Thiriart called for the reunification of Germany and for European 'vigilant and armed' neutrality, for a European army with nuclear weapons, yet outside NATO and any American control over the European defence structures. United Europe would not undertake 'crusades outside its territory', but post-war frontiers might be questioned, and Thiriart suggested returning to 'the 1938 frontiers between Europe and the USSR that [had] preceeded the Stalin conquests'.[162]

Like the majority of far-right neutralists before him, Thiriart sympathised with the Third World. He proposed symbiosis between Europe and Africa, because he considered the latter to be 'the natural extension of Europe'. Thiriart insisted that Europe could not 'permit the installation of a non-African power in Africa thus threatening [the] Southern flank' of Europe,[163] yet his pro-colonial attitudes were obvious, as he defended France in Algeria, Belgium in Congo, and Portugal in Angola.[164] Latin America fought against 'American Imperialism' and 'communist subversion'; therefore, Latin America and Europe had common enemies, and seeking an alliance between them was only natural. To the Arab world, Thiriart proposed friendship; the unity of the Arab world would 'bar communism from Africa' and 'eliminate pretexts for American intervention in the Eastern Mediterranean'.[165]

Then a stark anti-communist, Thiriart argued that 'United Europe [would] not tolerate communism internally under the naive and suicidal idea that it [was] an opinion "just like any other" '.[166] Furthermore, Thiriart considered communism as 'no more than an agent of Pan-Russian politics' and 'an instrument of nationalist and expansionist Russian policies . . . designed to mask the traditional imperialist appetites of the Kremlin'.[167] In Western Europe, communist parties would be banned 'as undisguised agents of treason' and tools of 'idealistic espionage'.[168] The destruction of communism in Western Europe would be a prerequisite for any fair and balanced negotiations with Moscow: retaining the possibility of unleashing revolutions in Western Europe through their communist agents of influence, the Soviets would only talk to Western Europe from a position of strength.

At the time of the writing of *Un Empire de 400 millions d'hommes*, Thiriart's main slogan was 'Neither Moscow nor Washington', and his demand from both was liberation of Europe from their political domination. After this, Europe would co-exist peacefully with Russia and build 'relations based on equality' with the United States. Thiriart, however, provided a theoretical opening towards Russia and even a possible embrace of it – at the same time denying this to the United States.

The idea that Europe could embrace Russia was already evident in the first manifesto of Jeune Europe, *La révolution nationale-Européenne* (The national-European revolution), written apparently by the organisation's chief ideologue Emile Lecerf and published in 1962.[169] This manifesto was characterised by 'the virtual disappearance of the anti-Soviet discourse in favour of the total stigmatisation of the USA'.[170] Breaking free from 'American imperialism' would allow Western Europe to take shape, and then it would 'extend its hand to its Eastern sister, so that she can shake off the Communist yoke, and in turn draw Russia to the European revolution'.[171]

Thiriart's *Un Empire de 400 millions d'hommes* provided an insight into a similar idea, which he alluded to already in 1962 in his article on a 'new Treaty of Rapallo'[172] and which he further elaborated at a later stage of his career as a far-right ideologue, – the idea that the liberation of Eastern Europe and consolidation of the European state from Brest to Bucharest would allow for extending Europe as far as to Vladivostok:

> Politics consists of treating certain enemies as if they would become allies next day and vice versa. That is why we should not hope for the total destruction of Russia but only a weakening that would force the return of East Europe. . . .
>
> The first phase of Europe's anti-Russian policy could even be pro-Chinese until the Dniester frontier is recovered. Once these territories are recovered a 'volte-face' will occur and coexistence will replace implacable hostility.
>
> In the short period we must hope for an anti-Russian thrust by the Chinese and in the long period do everything to help the Russians contain the Asian flood. We must weaken Russia but not conquer it. . . . Siberia occupied by an overwhelming majority of whites from European Russia will, in future, constitute the embankment of Europe.[173]

Thiriart's tactical, initially theoretical resort to China for its help in weakening the Soviet Union was soon followed by an ideological transformation that was most evident in the doctrine of the Parti Communautaire Européen (European Communitarian Party, PCE) that substituted Jeune Europe in 1965 as Thiriart's major organisational initiative. The ideology that Thiriart started to profess was 'national-European communism'; the Celtic cross, a symbol of white supremacy adopted by Jeune Europe, disappeared from a cover of Thiriart's new journal, *La Nation européenne*, along with the pro-colonial rhetoric – from Thiriart's articles.[174]

In *La Nation européenne*, Thiriart also started to praise 'national-communist' regimes in Josip Broz Tito's Yugoslavia, Nicolae Ceaușescu's Romania, and Ho Chi Minh's Democratic Republic of Vietnam.

The PCE offered logistical support to the Brussels-based Chinese secret services, who were interested in gathering intelligence on the NATO Supreme Headquarters Allied Powers Europe located in the Belgian town of Mons, but Thiriart broke off the collaboration.[175] As he complained, the Chinese services revealed 'total political and psychological incomprehension of Europe'. The Chinese seemed to be interested only in having China-controlled militants in Europe.[176] However, he had further contacts with the Chinese. In 1966, Thiriart travelled to Romania and met with Ceaușescu, who then contributed an article to *La Nation européenne*. Through Ceaușescu, Thiriart also met, while in Bucharest, with Zhou Enlai, the first Premier of the People's Republic of China under Mao Zedong.[177] During the conversation with Enlai, Thiriart asked for money that would be spent on publications and for a 'sanctuary for the organisation' that would be used for 'the preparation and building of the political-military apparatus of the European revolution'. Enlai referred him to the Chinese services, but the collaboration with the Chinese apparently never materialised.[178]

Despite the rupture with the Chinese, the PCE and European branches of Jeune Europe collaborated with the Maoists at the end of the 1960s. Thiriart acted as a liaison between the Chinese Embassy, the Parti communiste suisse/marxiste-léniniste (Swiss Communist Party/Marxist-Leninist (PCS/ML)) and the Portugal-based Aginter Press. The latter was a press agency founded by former members of the OAS and used as a cover for a number of clandestine operations such as 'an espionage office' most probably linked to several Western security services; a unit for 'recruiting and training mercenaries'; a strategic centre involved in 'coordin-ating "subversion and intoxication operations" that worked in conjunction with reactionary regimes';[179] and a rallying centre for a number of extreme-right organisations including the Ordine Nuovo (New Order) and Avanguardia Nazionale (National Vanguard).[180] One of the political aims of the Aginter Press was infiltrating communist and Maoist groups, and the PCS/ML was one of the organisations that the Aginter Press apparently infiltrated. Moreover, Claudio Mutti, a leading figure in Giovane Europa (Young Europe), the Italian branch of the Jeune Europe, joined the 'Nazi-Maoist' Organizzazione Lotta di Popolo (Organisation of People's Struggle) established in 1969 by Serafino Di Luia, a member of the Avanguardia Nazionale connected to the Aginter Press and influenced by Thiriart's ideas.

Thiriart's argument about a 'sanctuary for the organisation' articulated during his conversation with Enlai was a reference to the important concept that Thiriart developed in the second half of the 1960s, namely the 'outside lung' (*poumon extérieur*) or 'outside springboard' (*tremplin extérieur*). As he explained, all revolutionary actions required 'local and national fertile soil' and they rarely could 'succeed without an outside lung', or a 'springboard', that played 'a critical role in any subversive action' against the American presence or influence in Europe. Thiriart was convinced that 'the European Revolution' could 'begin on the ground only when it [found] a sanctuary for its logistical bases, not before'.[181]

In other words, an 'outside lung' implied a country run by an anti-American regime that would provide financial and logistic support for the European national-revolutionaries, and serve as 'a refuge from repression in the militants' native country' or 'a training ground for future "direct action"' in Europe.[182]

Yet another important concept that Thiriart elaborated alongside the notion of 'outside lung' was that of 'European brigades'. European national-revolutionaries would organise themselves in 'European brigades' and participate in armed conflicts in Third-World countries to receive real-life training and, thus, form 'the political and military avant-garde of the European revolution'.[183]

None of these concepts was entirely original. In the interwar period, officers and soldiers of the Schwarze Reichswehr, who were unable to conduct military exercises on the German soil due to the conditions of the Treaty of Versailles, used the territory of the Soviet Union as a training ground, and, therefore, the Soviet Union was an 'outside lung' for the German armed forces in their fight against France and Belgium. The militants of the OAS fought against Algerian nationalists, then returned to France and attempted to stage a revolution against de Gaulle – thus, Algeria would be an 'outside springboard' for the revolutionaries of the OAS operating in France. The notion of 'European brigades' seemed to originate from the involvement of various international brigades in the Spanish Civil War. Despite the fact that the practical implementation of 'outside lung' and 'European brigades' was not new, Thiriart was the first to theorise these notions and make them an integral part of a possible revolutionary strategy.

China was not the only country that the PCE considered an 'outside lung' for the European revolution. In 1967, Thiriart wrote: 'We, nationalists, we, European revolutionaries, need to go and form in Africa the cadres of a future political and military force that, after serving in the Mediterranean and the Near East, will one day fight in Europe and do away with the collaborators of Washington.'[184] Gérard Bordes, director of *La Nation européenne*, went to Algeria in 1967 and held talks with the officials of the National Liberation Front, the main nationalist movement during the Algerian War (1954–1962), but no tangible cooperation was established.

In 1968, Thiriart toured the Middle East, and met with Egyptian President Gamal Abdel Nasser in Cairo, as well as the leadership of the Ba'ath Party, including the future President of Iraq Saddam Hussein, – in Baghdad.

Uncompromisingly hostile to Israel, 'a pawn of American imperialism', Thiriart also established relations with George Habash, the founder of the Popular Front for the Liberation of Palestine, who then provided financial assistance to the publication of *La Nation européenne*.[185] The PCE's journal, in its turn, advertised anti-Zionist literature produced by a Beirut-based 'research centre' attached to the Palestine Liberation Organisation.[186] Thiriart explicitly called upon European national-revolutionaries to take part in the armed struggle against Israel on the Palestinian side:

> Participation [of pan-European nationalists] in military action and liberation of Palestine would . . . provide material and moral support to the Arabs; that would also be an opportunity for us to establish an armed formation of intervention that would later – after the Palestinian campaign – serve on other battle grounds.[187]

There might be a limited number of Belgian national-revolutionaries who volunteered to join the Palestinian fight against Israel. *La Nation européenne* ran a piece praising Roger Coudroy, 'the first European to die for the Palestinian cause'. According to the journal, Coudroy was killed by the Israeli forces when he tried to enter Palestine as a member of the Fatah commando. However, no credible evidence exists as to the circumstances of Coudroy's death – *La Nation européenne* might have mythologised it for propaganda purposes.[188]

Thiriart's efforts to secure an efficient 'outside lung' or build a 'European brigade' never came to fruition. Crushed by the failure, he almost completely withdrew from politics in 1969 and largely focused on his professional activities as an optometrist for the next 10 years.

Thiriart returned to the far-right circles in the beginning of the 1980s, and introduced a new concept: the Euro-Soviet Empire from Vladivostok to Dublin. In 1981, he declared that he would publish a book titled *L'empire Euro-Sovietique de Vladivostock a Dublin*, but it never appeared. In 1984, Thiriart's disciple Luc Michel edited and published a volume under this title,[189] but it was only a collection of Thiriart's essays and pretentious publishing plans.[190] Michel used the publication of this volume, in particular, to promote his newly established party called Parti communautaire national-européen (Communitarian National-European Party) that succeeded Thiriart's PCE.

Despite the fact that Thiriart failed to publish his book, he elaborated on the concept of 'Euro-Soviet Empire', 'a hyper-nation-state equipped with a de-Marxified hyper-communism',[191] in a number of articles and interviews. For Thiriart, the Soviet Union was 'historically and geopolitically a European power in essence': 'the last independent state in Europe',[192] 'a "Eurasian" Europe, a Very Great Europe, the New Rome'.[193] Alluding to himself as 'a pan-European National Bolshevik',[194] Thiriart praised the Molotov-Ribbentrop Pact, and argued that the Soviet Union was, 'geopolitically speaking, the heir of the Third Reich. The enemies of Hitler's Third Reich became the enemies of the USSR'.[195] He insisted on the withdrawal of NATO from Western Europe, and warned that an armed conflict between Western Europe and the Soviet Union would be 'a civil war of tomorrow', similar to the Second World War, 'a civil war of yesterday'.

The concept of 'Euro-Soviet Empire' revealed a significant and radical departure from Thiriart's 'geopolitical treatise' of the 1960s, and this departure was symbolically reflected in the reversal of the direction of prospective European unification. In *Un Empire de 400 millions d'hommes*, Thiriart speculated about a Europe from Brest *to Vladivostok*, while, in the 1980s, he talked about a Europe *from Vladivostok* to Dublin, similar to National Bolshevik Ernst Niekisch who wrote about a 'Germanic-Slavonic bloc' *from Vladivostok* to Vlissingen.

> My thinking has evolved since 1964 when I envisaged a Europe deriving its momentum from the West and spreading eastward, while all the time maintaining good, close relationships with the USSR. Now, in 1987, I have changed my perspective in favour of an east to west dynamic. . . .
>
> In my view, it is imperative that [Eastern European nations] never again be allowed to look at the 21st century with any hope of real independence whatsoever. This would be a negation of European unification. Historically speaking, even if the Soviet occupation from Warsaw to Sofia is a cruel thing in terms of current, day-to-day living, it is a good and positive thing for the formation of Europe.[196]

The change in perspective implied that Thiriart discussed the unification of Europe largely through the lens of potential benefits to the Soviets which was a clear deviation from the ideology of Jeune Europe and the PCE. Thus, in the 1980s, he was concerned that, without the building of a 'Soviet Europe', the USSR would be 'completely unable to contain China in 2025' and would be 'sandwiched between the Chinese and American giants'.[197] He also saw the USSR as unable to properly exploit and develop Siberia, as it lacked necessary means. 'Western provinces of Europe', however, possessed those industrial, economic and financial means; therefore, were the Euro-Soviet Empire to be actualised, Siberia would 'develop five times faster than today'.[198] Thiriart was also concerned that the Soviet Union had to spend extensive resources on defence, as 'NATO in Europe and the Sixth Fleet in the Mediterranean' were 'a real nightmare for the Soviets', 'an awful position of weakness'. At the same time, 'the fusion of the USSR with Western Europe would release huge numbers of armed forces (currently defending the plain from Lubeck to Sofia) that could be used elsewhere.' By using the Soviet armed forces 'elsewhere', Thiriart implied reclaiming control over the territories in Africa lost by France, Belgium, Portugal and Spain in 1955–1965.[199]

Thiriart envisaged 'a Europe made by the USSR', but he uncompromisingly rejected the Russification of Europe:

> If Moscow wants to make Europe Russian, I will be the first to recommend armed resistance to the occupier. If Moscow wants to make Europe

European, I preach total collaboration with the Soviet enterprise. I will then be the first to put a red star on my cap. Soviet Europe, yes, without reservations.[200]

Thiriart in the 1980s arrived at almost the same conclusions that Niekisch and Yockey, whose works Thiriart knew well, did in the 1930s and 1950s correspondingly: Niekisch argued that National Bolsheviks should 'promote the global political Russian-Asian advance on Europe', while Yockey defended the idea of a 'clever regime' of the Russian occupation of Europe that 'would eventually result in the rise of a new Symbiosis: Europe-Russia', 'a European Imperium'.[201]

The collapse of the Soviet Union seemed to distress Thiriart, and he wrote that 'political and military partition of the USSR' was and would always remain 'an unforgivable historical mistake'. In his view, after the demise of the Soviet Union, the 'great Russia' no longer had any chance of being a great power. 'Russia only', that is, the Russian Federation without its former colonies and satellites, was 'a country without a future', 'a Brazil with snow'. Washington was to blame, and the United States had enough weapons at its disposal not only to complete 'the partition of the USSR', but to partition Russia itself.[202] This despondence notwithstanding, Thiriart visited Moscow shortly before his death in 1992 and spent a few months there meeting with the leaders of the opposition to President Boris Yeltsin and participating in various conferences.[203]

Conclusion

Russophile and pro-Soviet attitudes were a minority faith among the Western far right. Especially in the interwar period and during the Second World War, they existed only on the margins of the fascist and far-right politics. However, proponents of the far-right alliance with Soviet Russia offered a number of peculiar combinations of nationalist, revolutionary, socialist and palingenetic narratives that provided ideological and political justification for the cooperation with the Soviets.

National Bolshevism in interwar Germany was arguably the first significant movement that conceived Germany and Soviet Russia as natural allies in their struggle against international capitalism and 'Western imperialism'. The Germans and the Soviets were 'young proletarian nations' that suffered under the yoke of the 'predatory West' at that time mainly represented by Britain and France. German National Bolsheviks did not support the idea of the Russification of Germany, but were eager to use the Soviet military force to liberate Germany from the capitalist oppressors.

Pro-Soviet sentiments on the part of the Western far right in the post-war period originated from the legacy of National Bolshevism, Conservative Revolution, left-wing Nazism of the Strasser brothers, and pan-European fascism. In West Germany, philo-Soviet attitudes could be found in the far-right neutralist movement that originally protested against the influence of both the Americans and the Soviets, but increasingly shifted towards the pro-Soviet positions. As several examples revealed, the Soviets encouraged and often sponsored the pro-Soviet shift of West German far-right neutralists in the 1950s mainly to prevent West Germany from joining NATO, as well as supporting far-right neutralists in Austria to damage the pro-American far right.

Pan-European fascism, albeit strictly neutralist at an early stage of its development, gave rise to two most influential post-war exponents of rapprochement between European fascism and the Soviet Union, namely Francis Parker Yockey and Jean Thiriart. Although the start of the most active part of Thiriart's political career largely coincided with the death of Yockey, their ideological trajectories revealed striking similarities. Originally critical of both the United States and Soviet Union, they gradually adopted more sympathetic attitudes towards Soviet Russia and, eventually, brought forward the idea of building the anti-American, anti-liberal geopolitical alliance in cooperation with the Soviets: European Imperium (Yockey) or Euro-Soviet Empire (Thiriart). Furthermore, much like particular National Bosheviks and post-war West German far-right neutralists, Yockey and Thiriart praised the anti-American struggle in every part of the world and considered authoritarian Third-World regimes as important allies in the revolutionary struggle for the reborn Europe.

While various Soviet politicians and counterintelligence services sometimes exploited pro-Soviet and pro-Russian attitudes of particular far-right forces as part of the Soviet active measures against the West, it is important to stress that these attitudes emerged independently of the direct Soviet influence. They were products of ideological discussions about the geopolitical positioning of European nations or Europe as a whole, and imagined an alternative Europe that would be radically different from all the liberal-democratic European projects. The far-right Europe would be illiberal, cleansed of the influence of the United States, and, instead, aligned with the totalitarian Soviet Union.

The concepts, arguments and narratives that National Bolsheviks, far-right neutralists and pan-European fascists had developed since the 1920s until 1980s, comprised a set of powerful ideological tools that have been employed by contemporary Western far-right activists and ideologues to ideologically justify their cooperation with the Russian ultranationalists after the demise of the Soviet Union and, eventually, with Putin's regime.

The next chapter focuses on the determinants, nature and scope of the first direct contacts between Russian and Western far-right politicians in the period between the end of Perestroika and the end of Putin's first presidential term.

Notes

1 Hitler's speech quoted in Geoffrey Stoakes, "The Evolution of Hitler's Ideas on Foreign Policy, 1919–1925", in Peter D. Stachura (ed.), *The Shaping of the Nazi State* (London: Croom Helm, 1978), pp. 22–47 (24).

2 Aristotle A. Kallis, *Fascist Ideology: Territory and Expansionism in Italy and Germany, 1922–1945* (London: Routledge, 2000), p. 55.

3   Emilio Gentile, *Politics as Religion* (Princeton: Princeton University Press, 2006), p. 46. Emphasis in the original.

4   See Roger Griffin, *The Nature of Fascism* (New York: St. Martin's Press, 1991); Griffin, *Modernism and Fascism*.

5   Ibid., p. 181.

6   "Letter from Hitler to Mussolini, June 21, 1941", in Raymond James Sontag, James Stuart Beddie (eds.), *Nazi-Soviet Relations, 1939–1941: Documents from the Archives of the German Foreign Office* (Washington: Department of State, 1948), pp. 349–353 (353).

7   MacGregor Knox, *Mussolini Unleashed, 1939–1941: Politics and Strategy in Fascist Italy's Last War* (Cambridge: Cambridge University Press, 1982), p. 63.

8   Quoted in Knox, *Mussolini Unleashed*, p. 68.

9   Louis Dupeux, *National bolchevisme: stratégie communiste et dynamique conservatrice* (Paris: H. Champion, 1979).

10   Erik Van Ree, "The Concept of 'National Bolshevism': An Interpretative Essay", *Journal of Political Ideologies*, Vol. 6, No. 3 (2001), pp. 289–307 (289).

11   Klemens von Klemperer, "Towards a Fourth Reich? The History of National Bolshevism in Germany", *The Review of Politics*, Vol. 13, No. 2 (1951), pp. 191–210; Abraham Ascher, Guenter Lewy, "National Bolshevism in Weimar Germany – Alliance of Political Extremes against Democracy", *Social Research: An International Quarterly*, Vol. 23, No. 4 (1956), pp. 450–480; Walter Laqueur, *Young Germany: A History of the German Youth Movement* (New Brunswick: Transaction Books, 1984), pp. 179–187.

12   See, for example, Klemperer, "Towards a Fourth Reich?"; Ascher, Lewy, "National Bolshevism in Weimar Germany".

13   Paul Eltzbacher, *Der Bolschewismus und die deutsche Zukunft* (Jena: E. Diederichs, 1919).

14   Ibid., p. 38.

15   Ibid., p. 28.

16   Ruth Fischer, *Stalin and German Communism: A Study in the Origins of the State Party* (Cambridge: Harvard University Press, 1948), p. 92; Chris Harman, *The Lost Revolution: Germany, 1918 to 1923* (London: Bookmarks, 1982), p. 193.

17   Ascher, Lewy, "National Bolshevism in Weimar Germany", p. 452.

18   Quoted in Fischer, *Stalin and German Communism*, pp. 94–95.

19   Klemperer, "Towards a Fourth Reich?", p. 200.

20   Quoted in Ascher, Lewy, "National Bolshevism in Weimar Germany", p. 457.

21   Gordon H. Mueller, "Rapallo Reexamined: A New Look at Germany's Secret Military Collaboration with Russia in 1922", *Military Affairs*, Vol. 40, No. 3 (1976), pp. 109–117.

22   William L. Shirer, *The Rise and Fall of the Third Reich: A History of Nazi Germany* (New York: Simon & Schuster, 2011), p. 150; Eric D. Weitz, *Weimar Germany: Promise and Tragedy* (Princeton: Princeton University Press, 2013), p. 115.

23   Karl Radek, "Leo Schlageter, der Wanderer ins Nichts", *Marxists.org*, www.marxists.org/deutsch/archiv/radek/1923/06/schlageter.html

24   Ibid.

25   Ibid.

26   Fischer, *Stalin and German Communism*, p. 282.

27   Ascher, Lewy, "National Bolshevism in Weimar Germany", p. 466.

28   Ibid.

29   Klemperer, "Towards a Fourth Reich?", p. 200.

30   Ernst Niekisch, *Entscheidung* (Berlin: Widerstands-Verlag, 1930).

31   Hans Buchheim, "Ernst Niekischs Ideologie des Widerstands", *Vierteljahrshefte für Zeitgeschichte*, Vol. 5, No. 4 (1957), pp. 334–361 (346).

32   Corina L. Petrescu, *Against All Odds: Models of Subversive Spaces in National Socialist Germany* (New York: Peter Lang, 2010), p. 193.

33   Ernst Jünger, *Der Arbeiter, Herrschaft und Gestalt* (Hamburg: Hanseatische Verlagsanstalt, 1932).
34   James J. Ward, "Pipe Dreams or Revolutionary Politics? The Group of Social Revolutionary Nationalists in the Weimar Republic", *Journal of Contemporary History*, Vol. 15, No. 3 (1980), pp. 513–532 (518).
35   Ascher, Lewy, "National Bolshevism in Weimar Germany", p. 475.
36   Ward, "Pipe Dreams or Revolutionary Politics?", p. 520.
37   Beate Baldow, *Episode oder Gefahr? Die Naumann-Affäre*. Dissertation zur Erlangung des Doktorgrades (Berlin: Fachbereich Geschichts- und Kulturwissenschaften der Freien Universität Berlin, 2012), p. 35.
38   Ibid., p. 36.
39   The concept of Nation Europe originates from the writings of British fascist Oswald Mosley, see below.
40   Quoted in Richard Breitman, Norman J.W. Goda, *Nazi War Criminals, U.S. Intelligence, and the Cold War* (Washington: National Archives, 2010), p. 57.
41   Rainer Dohse, *Der dritte Weg. Neutralitätsbestrebungen in Westdeutschland zwischen 1945 und 1955* (Hamburg: Holsten, 1974); Alexander Gallus, *Die Neutralisten: Verfechter eines vereinten Deutschland zwischen Ost und West 1945–1990* (Düsseldorf: Droste, 2001); Christian Bailey, *Between Yesterday and Tomorrow: German Visions of Europe, 1926–1950* (New York: Berghahn, 2013).
42   Alice Holmes Cooper, *Paradoxes of Peace: German Peace Movements since 1945* (Ann Arbor: University of Michigan Press, 1996), p. 61.
43   Alexander Gallus, "Für ein vereintes Deutschland zwischen Ost und West: Neutralisierter Protest in der Bundesrepublik Deutschland", in Dominik Geppert, Udo Wengst (eds), *Neutralität – Chance oder Chimäre? Konzepte des Dritten Weges für Deutschland und die Welt 1945–1990* (Munich: R. Oldenbourg Verlag, 2005), pp. 59–78 (70).
44   Kurt P. Tauber, *Beyond Eagle and Swastika: German Nationalism since 1945*. Vol. 1 (Middletown: Wesleyan University Press, 1967), p. 166.
45   Ibid., p. 167.
46   Ibid., pp. 167, 169.
47   Quoted in Breitman, Goda, *Nazi War Criminals*, p. 58.
48   Tauber, *Beyond Eagle and Swastika*, p. 163. Tauber wrote that they attempted to establish relations with the Soviet Military Administration (SMA) in 1950, which was hardly possible as the SMA ceased to exist in 1949, with the creation of the German Democratic Republic. In 1949, the SMA was replaced by the Soviet Control Commission that existed until 1953, and that was probably what Tauber meant.
49   James H. Critchfield, *Partners at the Creation: The Men Behind Postwar Germany's Defense and Intelligence Establishments* (Annapolis: Naval Institute Press, 2003), p. 121.
50   Breitman, Goda, *Nazi War Criminals*, pp. 53–59.
51   "Franke-Griksh Al'fred", *Martirolog rasstrelyannykh v Moskve i Moskovskoy oblasti*, http://sakharov-center.ru/asfcd/martirolog/?t=page&id=25755
52   Tauber, *Beyond Eagle and Swastika*, p. 168.
53   Ibid., p. 171.
54   Richard Stöss, *Vom Nationalismus zum Umweltschutz – Die Deutsche Gemeinschaft/ Aktionsgemeinschaft Unabhängiger Deutscher im Parteiensystem der Bundesrepublik* (Opladen: Westdeutscher Verlag, 1980), pp. 145–146.
55   Tauber, *Beyond Eagle and Swastika*, p. 172.
56   "Propaganda", *Der Spiegel*, No. 26 (1951), p. 4.
57   "Ist jemand Kommunist? ", *Der Spiegel*, No. 13 (1951), p. 5.
58   Richard S. Cromwell, "Rightist Extremism in Postwar West Germany", *The Western Political Quarterly*, Vol. 17, No. 2 (1964), pp. 284–293 (286).
59   Quoted in Tete H. Tetens, *The New Germany and the Old Nazis* (New York: Random House, 1961), p. 78.

60   Martin Lee, *The Beast Reawakens* (Boston: Little, Brown and Co., 1997), p. 74.
61   Ibid., p. 139.
62   Sven Felix Kellerhoff, "Als Castro sich für die Waffen-SS interessierte", *Die Welt*, 12 October (2012), http://welt.de/kultur/history/article109800039/Als-Castro-sich-fuer-die-Waffen-SS-interessierte.html
63   Cromwell, "Rightist Extremism in Postwar West Germany", p. 288.
64   Ibid., p. 291.
65   Ladislav Bittman, *The KGB and Soviet Disinformation: An Insider's View* (Washington: Pergamon-Brassey's, 1985), p. 77.
66   The NDPD is not to be confused with the neo-Nazi Nationaldemokratische Partei Deutschlands (NPD) founded in 1964 in West Germany.
67   Tauber, *Beyond Eagle and Swastika*, p. 192.
68   K. W., "Rot und Schwarz-Weiß-Rot", *Die Zeit*, No. 48 (1955), http://zeit.de/1955/48/rot-und-schwarz-weiss-rot
69   Cromwell, "Rightist Extremism in Postwar West Germany", pp. 291–292.
70   H. Berlin, "Infiltration der Soldatenbünde", *Die Zeit*, No. 48 (1953), http://zeit.de/1953/48/infiltration-der-soldatenbuende
71   Tauber, *Beyond Eagle and Swastika*, pp. 193–194.
72   Hans Joachim Morgenthau was a German liberal, pro-Western scholar of international politics.
73   Tauber, *Beyond Eagle and Swastika*, p. 193.
74   Ibid., p. 194.
75   Stöss, *Vom Nationalismus zum Umweltschutz*, p. 166.
76   The Convention of Tauroggen was an armistice signed in 1812 between a Prussian army corps and the Imperial Russian Army that resulted in Prussia falling away from Napoleon's France and aligning itself with Russia against France.
77   Tauber, *Beyond Eagle and Swastika*, p. 196.
78   Berlin, "Infiltration der Soldatenbünde".
79   John Barron, *KGB: The Secret Work of Soviet Secret Agents* (London: Hodder and Stoughton, 1974), pp. 172–174.
80   The KGB first tested this operation in Russia itself: "Agayants sent a group of his officers to a village about fifty miles from Moscow with instructions to daub swastikas, paint anti-Jewish slogans, and kick over tombstones under cover of darkness. KGB informers in the village reported that though the incident alarmed most inhabitants, a small anti-Semitic minority had been inspired to imitate the KGB provocation and commit anti-Jewish acts of their own", see Christopher Andrew, Oleg Gordievsky, *KGB: The Inside Story* (New York: HarperCollins, 1990), p. 463.
81   A former KGB Major General Oleg Kalugin wrote in his memoir of a similar KGB operation in the US: "Attempting to show that America was inhospitable to Jews, we wrote anti-Semitic letters to American Jewish leaders. My fellow officers paid American agents to paint swastikas on synagogues in New York and Washington. Our New York station even hired people to desecrate Jewish cemeteries". See Oleg Kalugin, *Spymaster: My Thirty-two Years in Intelligence and Espionage against the West* (New York: Basic Books, 2009), p. 54.
82   Michael F. Scholz, "Active Measures and Disinformation as Part of East Germany's Propaganda War, 1953–1972", in Thomas Wegener Friis, Kristie Macrakis, Helmut Müller-Enbergs (eds.), *East German Foreign Intelligence: Myth, Reality and Controversy* (London: Routledge, 2010), pp. 113–133 (115).
83   Ibid., p. 115.
84   "Subject: The National League – An Impotent Communist Front of Ex-Nazis", *Central Intelligence Agency*, 2? April (1954), p. 2, http://foia.cia.gov/sites/default/files/document_conversions/1705143/SLAVIK,%20ADOLF_0031.pdf
85   Ibid., p. 3.

86 Charles W. Martin, *The Nihilism of Thomas Bernhard: The Portrayal of Existential and Social Problems in His Prose Works* (Amsterdam: Rodopi, 1995), p. 218.

87 "Subject: The National League", p. 3.

88 Wolfgang Mueller, *Die sowjetische Besatzung in Österreich 1945–1955 und ihre politische Mission* (Vienna: Böhlau Verlag, 2005), p. 214. On the Nationale Liga see also Fritz Keller, "Stalinistischer Populismus – Die Nationale Liga", in Anton Pelinka (ed.), *Populismus in Österreich* (Vienna: Junius, 1987), pp. 110–122.

89 "English Translation of Platform of the National League" as a supplement to the CIA's confidential despatch "Subject: The National League", pp. 1–3.

90 Mueller, *Die sowjetische Besatzung in Österreich*, p. 216.

91 "Subject: The National League", p. 6.

92 "Re: Dr. Slavik about the Early History and Aims of His Movement. 11 October 1950", in the CIA's report "Activities of Dr Adolf Slavik, Austrian National League Leader, in 1950–1953 (Excerpts)", *Central Intelligence Agency*, http://foia.cia.gov/sites/default/files/document_conversions/1705143/SLAVIK,%20ADOLF_0001.pdf

93 "Re: Slavik Manages to Get USIA Positions for Incriminated National Socialists. 9 October 1950", in the CIA's report "Activities of Dr Adolf Slavik, Austrian National League Leader, in 1950–1953 (Excerpts)".

94 "Adolf Slavik", *Central Intelligence Agency*, 23 February (1968), p. 2, http://foia.cia.gov/sites/default/files/document_conversions/1705143/SLAVIK,%20ADOLF_0111.pdf

95 "Spravka Otdela propagandy SChSK po Avstrii 'Natsional'naya liga'. 4 avgusta 1950 g.", in Gennadiy Bordyugov, Wolfgang Mueller, Norman M. Naimark, Arnold Suppan (eds.), *Sovetskaya politika v Avstrii. 1945–1955 gg. Sbornik dokumentov* (Moscow: AIRO-XXI, 2006), pp. 379–390 (389).

96 Quoted in "Spravka Otdela propagandy SChSK po Avstrii", p. 389.

97 "Adolf Slavik", p. 2.

98 Quoted in a CIA's secret report from Vienna, 20 February (1968), http://foia.cia.gov/sites/default/files/document_conversions/1705143/SLAVIK,%20ADOLF_0113.pdf

99 Roger Griffin, "Europe for the Europeans: Fascist Myths of the European New Order, 1922–1992". In Roger Griffin, *A Fascist Century* (Basingstoke: Palgrave Macmillan, 2008), pp. 132–180 (135).

100 Kurt P. Tauber, "German Nationalists and European Union", *Political Science Quarterly*, Vol. 74, No. 4 (1959), pp. 564–589 (576).

101 Kevin Coogan, *Dreamer of the Day: Francis Parker Yockey and the Postwar Fascist International* (Brooklyn: Autonomedia, 1999).

102 Ulick Varange [Francis Parker Yockey], *Imperium: The Philosophy of History and Politics* (London: Westropa Press, 1948). Henceforth, however, all the citations are from a different edition of the book: Francis Parker Yockey, *Imperium: The Philosophy of History and Politics* (New York: The Truth Seeker, 1962).

103 Ibid., p. xlvi. Emphasis in the original.

104 Ibid., p. xlvii.

105 Ibid., pp. 578–579. Emphasis in the original.

106 Ibid., pp. 582–583.

107 Ibid., p. 586.

108 Ibid., p. 595.

109 Ibid., p. 586.

110 Graham Macklin, *Very Deeply Dyed in Black: Sir Oswald Mosley and the Resurrection of British Fascism after 1945* (London: I.B. Tauris, 2007), p. 4.

111 Oswald Mosley, *The Alternative* (Ramsbury: Mosley Publications, 1947).

112 Lloyd O. Bogstad, "Francis Parker Yockey", pp. 1–25 (11). This FBI report dated 8 July 1954 can be found in Federal Bureau of Investigation, "Subject: Francis Parker Yockey. File number: 105–8229 Section 2", https://archive.org/details/foia_Yockey_Francis_P.-HQ-2

113 Oswald Mosley, *The European Situation: The Third Force* (Ramsbury: Mosley Publications, 1950), p. 9.
114 Coogan, *Dreamer of the Day*, p. 171.
115 Bogstad, "Francis Parker Yockey", p. 11.
116 Francis Parker Yockey, *The Proclamation of London of the European Liberation Front* (London: Westropa Press, 1949), https://archive.org/details/TheProclamationOf London_284
117 Bogstad, "Francis Parker Yockey", pp. 11–12.
118 NATINFORM report quoted in Coogan, *Dreamer of the Day*, pp. 174.
119 Ibid.
120 See William Goring, *The National Renaissance Party: History and Analysis of an American Neo-Nazi Party* (Springfield: National Information Center, 1970).
121 Yockey, *The Proclamation of London*.
122 Igor Lukes, "The Rudolf Slánský Affair: New Evidence", *Slavic Review*, Vol. 58, No. 1 (1999), pp. 160–187.
123 Joshua Rubenstein, Vladimir P. Naumov (eds), *Stalin's Secret Pogrom: The Postwar Inquisition of the Jewish Anti-Fascist Committee* (New Haven: Yale University Press in association with the United States Holocaust Memorial Museum, 2001).
124 Jonathan Brent, Vladimir P. Naumov, *Stalin's Last Crime: The Plot against the Jewish Doctors, 1948–1953* (New York: HarperCollins, 2003).
125 [Francis Parker Yockey], "What Is behind the Hanging of the Eleven Jews in Prague?", *National Renaissance Bulletin* (1952), https://archive.org/details/CollectedWorksOf FrancisParkerYockey
126 [Yockey], "What Is behind the Hanging".
127 Ulik Varange [Francis Parker Yockey], *Der Feind Europas* (1953). Henceforth, all the citations are from an English edition of the book: Francis Parker Yockey, *The Enemy of Europe* (York: Liberty Bell Publications, 1981).
128 Ibid., p. 33.
129 Ibid., p. 60.
130 Ibid., pp. 80–81.
131 Ibid., p. 82. My emphasis.
132 Ibid., p. 93.
133 Yockey's associates published this essay after his death as a pamphlet: Ulick Varage [Francis Parker Yockey], *The World in Flames* (New York: Le Blanc Publications, 1961), https://archive.org/details/TheWorldInFlames
134 Ibid.
135 Ibid.
136 Coogan, *Dreamer of the Day*, pp. 264–265; Lee, *The Beast Reawakens*, p. 107.
137 Coogan, *Dreamer of the Day*, p. 17.
138 Ibid., pp. 438–439.
139 John George, Laird Wilcox, *Nazis, Communists, Klansmen, and Others on the Fringe: Political Extremism in America* (Buffalo: Prometheus Books, 1992), p. 254.
140 Bogstad, "Francis Parker Yockey", pp. 11, 13.
141 Cromwell, "Rightist Extremism in Postwar West Germany", p. 288.
142 George, Wilcox, *Nazis, Communists, Klansmen*, p. 353.
143 Jeffrey Kaplan, "The Post-war Paths of Occult National Socialism: From Rockwell and Madole to Manson", *Patterns of Prejudice*, Vol. 35, No. 3 (2001), pp. 41–67 (46).
144 George, Laird Wilcox, *Nazis, Communists*, p. 352.
145 Coogan, *Dreamer of the Day*, p. 458.
146 Ibid., pp. 441–442.
147 Ibid., p. 17. Emphasis in the original.
148 Ibid., p. 38.
149 Théodore J. O'Keefe, "The Tragic Life of a Spenglerian Visionary", *The Occidental Quarterly*, Vol. 1, No. 2 (2002), https://web.archive.org/web/20060614084128/

http://theoccidentalquarterly.com/vol1no2/to-coogan.html; *Le prophète de l'Imperium: Francis Parker Yockey* (Paris: Avatar Éditions, 2004).

150 Oswald Mosley, *My Life* (London: Black House Publishing, 2012), pp. 459–460.

151 Mosley, *My Life*, p. 461.

152 "Von Thadden's Foreign Contacts", *Patterns of Prejudice*, Vol. 1, No. 1 (1967), pp. 7–8.

153 Daniele Ganser, *NATO's Secret Armies: Operation Gladio and Terrorism in Western Europe* (London: Frank Cass, 2005), p. 97.

154 Coogan, *Dreamer of the Day*, p. 542.

155 *Le Manifeste à la Nation Européenne*; this manifesto was apparently published as a special issue of *Nation-Belgique*, No. 59 (1961).

156 Frédéric Laurent, in collaboration with Nina Sutton, *L'Orchestre noir* (Paris: Stock, 1978), pp. 101–102.

157 José L. Rodríguez Jiménez, "The Spanish Extreme Right: From Neo-Francoism to Xenophobic Discourse", in Andrea Mammone, Emmanuel Godin, Brian Jenkins (eds), *Mapping the Extreme Right in Contemporary Europe: From Local to Transnational* (London: Routledge, 2012), pp. 109–123 (116).

158 Jean Thiriart, *Un Empire de 400 millions d'hommes: l'Europe* (Brussels: [self-published], 1964). Henceforth, all the citations are from an English edition of the book: Jean Thiriart, *Europe, an Empire of 400 Million People: A Nation Built from a Historic Party* (Brussels: [n.a.], 1964).

159 Ibid., p. 1.

160 Ibid.

161 Ibid., p. 13.

162 Ibid., p. 13.

163 Ibid., p. 2.

164 Ibid., p. 5.

165 Ibid., p. 2.

166 Ibid., p. 4. This was also the case of West German far right neutralists in the 1950s. Tauber wrote: "the [far right neutralists] are neither Communists nor, in most cases, friendly to Communism. The nationalists, especially 'Tauroggeners' and conservatives, may well – and do – insist on maintaining that foreign political collaboration with the Soviet Union must never lead to tolerance of Communism within Germany". See Tauber, *Beyond Eagle and Swastika*, p. 202.

167 Thiriart, *Europe*, p. 4.

168 Ibid., p. 25.

169 *La révolution nationale-Européenne* (Nantes: Ars Magna, 1962).

170 Nicolas Lebourg, *Les Nationalismes-révolutionnaires en mouvements: idéologies, propagandes et influences (France; 1962–2002)*, These pour obtenir le grade de Docteur de l'Université de Perpignan, discipline: Histoire, présentée et soutenue publiquement par Nicolas Lebourg Le 11 mars 2005 (Perpignan: Université de Perpignan, 2005), p. 167.

171 Ibid., p. 167.

172 Tisch [Jean Thiriart], "L'Europe et l'URSS, un Rapallo européen: pourquoi pas?", *Nation Belgique*, No. 85 (1962).

173 Thiriart, *Europe*, p. 5.

174 Lee, *The Beast Reawakens*, p. 174.

175 Patrice Chairoff, *Dossier néo-nazisme* (Paris: Ramsay, 1977), p. 445.

176 Thiriart quoted in *De Jeune Europe aux Brigades rouges: anti-americanisme et logique de l'engagement revolutionnaire* (Nantes: Ars, 1986 [?]).

177 Lee, *The Beast Reawakens*, p. 175.

178 Thiriart quoted in *De Jeune Europe aux Brigades rouges*.

179 Jeffrey M. Bale, "Right-Wing Terrorists and the Extraparliamentary Left in Post-World War II Europe: Collusion or Manipulation?", *Berkeley Journal of Sociology*, Vol. 32 (1987), pp. 193–236 (203). It is unclear whether Thiriart was aware of the involvement of the (pro-)American secret services in the workings of the Aginter Press.

180 Franco Ferraresi, *Threats to Democracy: The Radical Right in Italy after the War* (Princeton: Princeton University Press, 1996), p. 62.
181 See Jean Thiriart, "Inventaire de l'anti-americanisme", *La Nation Européenne*, No. 23 (1967), pp. 12–18.
182 Jean-Yves Camus, "A Long-Lasting Friendship: Alexander Dugin and the French Radical Right", in Laruelle (ed.), *Eurasianism and the European Far Right*, pp. 79–96 (83).
183 See Jean Thiriart, "USA: le declin d'une hegemonie", *La Nation Européenne*, No. 18 (1967), pp. 4–8; Jean Thiriart, "Les Arabes et l'Europe", *La Nation Européenne*, No. 29 (1968), pp. 10–13.
184 Jean Thiriart, "USA: un empire de mercantis", *La Nation Européenne*, No. 21 (1967), pp. 4–7 (7).
185 Lee, *The Beast Reawakens*, p. 181.
186 "'Palestine Liberation' Literature. Beirut 'Research Centres' Output", *Patterns of Prejudice*, Vol. 1, No. 6 (1967), pp. 29–30 (30).
187 Thiriart, "Les Arabes et l'Europe".
188 Giorgio Ballario, "Anniversari. Roger Coudroy primo europeo a morire per la causa palestinese", *Barbadillo*, 3 June (2013), http://barbadillo.it/7208-anniversari-roger-coudroy-primo-europeo-a-morire-per-la-causa-palestinese/
189 *L'empire Euro-Sovietique de Vladivostock a Dublin l'aprés-Yalta: la mutation du communisme: essai sur le totalitarisme éclairé* (Charleroi: Edition Machiavel, 1984).
190 None of those publishing plans has ever been realised.
191 Thiriart quoted in Edouard Rix, "Jean Thiriart: The Machiavelli of United Europe", in Greg Johnson (ed.), *North American New Right*. Vol. 1 (San Francisco: Counter-Currents Publishing, 2012), pp. 262–269 (268).
192 Jean Thiriart, "L'empire Euro-Sovietique de Vladivostock a Dublin", in *L'empire Euro-Sovietique de Vladivostock a Dublin l'aprés-Yalta*, pp. 2–10 (3).
193 "Jean Thiriart: Responses to 14 Questions. Submitted by Gene H. Hogberg", *Geopolitika*, http://geopolitika.org/jean-thiriart-responses-to-14-questions/. On the basis of Thiriart's responses, we can assume that he replied to the questions in 1987.
194 Ibid.
195 Thiriart quoted in Coogan, *Dreamer of the Day*, p. 546.
196 "Jean Thiriart: Responses to 14 Questions".
197 Thiriart, "L'empire Euro-Sovietique de Vladivostock a Dublin", p. 4.
198 Ibid., p. 4; "Jean Thiriart: Responses to 14 Questions".
199 Ibid.
200 Thiriart quoted in Coogan, *Dreamer of the Day*, p. 546; and Rix, "Jean Thiriart", p. 268.
201 Yockey, *The Enemy of Europe*, p. 82.
202 Jean Thiriart, "L'Europe jusqu'à Vladivostok", *Nationalisme & Republique*, No. 9 (1992), http://voxnr.com/cc/d_thiriart/EpApFFluyyzgDwlWdS.shtml
203 See Chapter 2 for more information on Thiriart's activities in Moscow.

2
RUSSIA'S OPENING TO THE WESTERN FAR RIGHT

Introduction

Contacts between the Soviet Union and the Western far right were officially unimaginable after the end of the Second World War. The reason was obvious: prevailing anti-communism of the Western far right clashed with the official communist ideology of the Soviet Union despite particular ultranationalist trends in the ruling Communist party.[1] However, as the previous chapter demonstrated, the unofficial contacts between the Soviets and Western far right were far from non-existent, as the Soviet Union was interested in manipulating the Western far right for propaganda, intelligence and subversion purposes.

During the Cold War, there were also limited individual contacts between Russian ultranationalists and European far-right activists. Russian nationalist painter Ilya Glazunov visited Paris in 1968 and met with Jean-Marie Le Pen, the future founder of the FN. At that time, Glazunov belonged to an anti-communist, nationalist group close to the All-Union Leninist Young Communist League (widely known as Komsomol),[2] and was considered to be a KGB informant, *inter alia*, by now late American journalist John Barron.[3] French investigative journalist Vincent Jauvert claims that Glazunov was in Paris 'on a mission' – he had to paint portraits of top French politicians that the Kremlin wanted to entice.[4] The encounter with Le Pen, however, did not seem to be originally connected with Glazunov's presumed 'mission' – at that time, Le Pen was an insignificant politician who sold vinyl records featuring Nazi marches – and was apparently accidental. Nevertheless, the encounter resulted in a long-lasting friendship between the Russian and French ultranationalists; Glazunov even painted a portrait of Le Pen who has been keeping it in his home ever since.

The Soviet intelligence naturally continued recruiting agents among fascists. For example, one investigation asserts that Russia's future President Vladimir Putin, when based in Dresden in the 1980s as a KGB agent, collaborated with a neo-Nazi Rainer Sonntag and used him 'to expand the agent network with people [Sonntag knew] such as members of the neo-Nazi movement'.[5] A native of Dresden, Sonntag was allowed to immigrate in 1987 to West Germany where he established close relations with one of the leaders of the neo-Nazi movement Michael Kühnen (see on him below) and became an 'agent in the field of operations'. While in West Germany, Sonntag kept in contact with Putin's agents back in Dresden but returned there shortly before the reunification of Germany. In Dresden, Sonntag founded the neo-Nazi group Nationaler Widerstand Dresden (National Resistance Dresden) whose militants terrorised foreigners, 'raided the city's left-alternative cafes and ransacked the cardboard booths of Vietnamese street merchants'.[6] The police never took any interest in Sonntag, most likely due to the protection he enjoyed.

Despite the history of collaboration with fascists and far-right activists, however, the Soviets seemed to become suspicious of their informal and situational associates already since the 1960s, even if they had pro-Soviet or pro-Russian sympathies.[7] Thus, apart from manipulating particular individuals for intelligence purposes, Soviet authorities refrained from developing any deeper links to the Western far right like they did in the 1920–1930s or 1950s. After all, those were communist and socialist parties, as well as various 'peace movements', rather than ultra-nationalists, that were major agents of influence of the Soviet Union in the West during the Cold War.

It was not until the later period of Mikhail Gorbachev's Perestroika, and the Soviet Union's relative political liberalisation and consequent opening to the West, that the Russians started building close ties with their Western counterparts. In the course of Russia's first post-Soviet President Boris Yeltsin's rule, these contacts were further intensified.

The first international contacts on the part of Russia were established by Russian ultranationalists who were opposed to Yeltsin, and this chapter explores the nature, scope and development of the relations with Western far-right activists, authors and organisations forged by three Russian far-right politicians, namely Aleksandr Dugin, Vladimir Zhirinovsky and Sergey Glazyev, during the Yeltsin era. These international contacts were by no means limited to those established by the above-mentioned politicians. The focus on these particular figures is determined by the intensity of their international relations and the influence they gained in the Putin era. Then the chapter discusses the first initiatives to connect the interests of the Russian state to the developments in the European far-right milieu during Vladimir Putin's first presidential term. Finally, the chapter looks at how the contacts with the European far right were instrumentalised by Russian ultranationalist politician Sergey Baburin for his own political ends.

Aleksandr Dugin and the 'red-brown' alliance

The first substantial contacts between the Western far right and their Russian counterparts in the Yeltsin era were apparently established by Russian fascist

Aleksandr Dugin who started cooperating with representatives of the European far right even before the demise of the Soviet Union.[8]

During the 1990s, Dugin elaborated the ideology that became known as neo-Eurasianism. This ideology portrays Russia as a central power of the Eurasian continent that is 'organically' opposed to the Atlanticist world represented by the United States and its allies such as the United Kingdom. For neo-Eurasianism, Eurasia and the Atlanticist world are not simply geography-inspired concepts. In Dugin's view, Eurasia is associated with 'a plurality of value systems', 'tradition', 'the rights of nations', 'ethnicities as the primary value and the subjects of history', and 'social fairness and human solidarity'.[9] At the same time, neo-Eurasianism associates the Atlanticist world with 'conventional and obligatory domination of a single ideology (American liberal democracy first and foremost)', 'the suppression of cultures, their dogmas and the wisdom of traditional society', 'the "golden billion" and the neo-colonial hegemony of the "rich North" ', 'homogenization of peoples, which are to be imprisoned within artificial social constructions', and 'exploitation and the humiliation of man by man'.[10] Thus, neo-Eurasianism positions itself as the main opponent of American-style liberalism, globalisation and the 'New World Order'. Neo-Eurasianism, according to Dugin, is also a global revolutionary concept aiming to act as an ideological tool for uniting various forces against the United States and liberal democracy. Dugin's ideology of neo-Eurasianism can be defined as a form of a fascist ideology centred on the idea of revolutionising the Russian society and building a totalitarian, Russia-dominated Eurasian Empire that would challenge and eventually defeat its eternal adversary represented by the United States and its Atlanticist allies, thus bringing about a new 'golden age' of global political and cultural illiberalism.

The first Russian political movement that Dugin joined, in 1987, was the Natsional'no-patrioticheskiy front 'Pamyat' (National-Patriotic Front 'Memory'), the most significant anti-Semitic organisation during Perestroika. William Korrey identified the roots of Pamyat's ideology tracing back 'to the tsarist Black Hundreds in the early part of the twentieth century, to certain aspects of later Stalinism and, most especially, to a virulent official Judeophobic propaganda campaign, masquerading as anti-Zionism, from 1967 to 1986'.[11] The reason for Dugin's joining of Pamyat, however, was not so much its anti-Semitism but the organisation's significance in that period. Young Dugin, who was fascinated with European esotericism, fascist mysticism and the works of René Guénon[12] and Julius Evola,[13] was seen as an ideological competitor by 'a group of hardline ethnic nationalists led by Alexander Barkashov'[14] who eventually succeeded in expelling Dugin and his associate Geydar Dzhemal from Pamyat.

After his expulsion from Pamyat, Dugin travelled to Madrid to take part in a seminar dedicated to the works of Miguel Serrano, a prominent Chilean neo-Nazi who became notorious for promoting the idea of the extra-terrestrial origin of the Aryan race that descended from the mythical Hyperborean people.[15] The seminar was organised by Isidro J. Palacios and Francesc Sánchez-Bas, former members of

CEDADE, a Spanish neo-Nazi association founded in the mid-1960s by the activists of the Spanish branch of Jean Thiriart's Jeune Europe.

Palacios and Sánchez-Bas left CEDADE at the end of the 1980s and formed the Society of the Thule Group. They also launched a journal *Hiperbórea*, aimed at contributing to the 'restoration of the essential concepts that unify our . . . tradition with the land . . . [of] our ancestors and with the blood that runs through our veins: Tradition, Land and Ethnicity'.[16] As the Thule Group had contacts with international extreme-right groups, national versions of *Hiperbórea* were published in other European countries. Dugin became the Russian publisher of this Spanish neo-Nazi journal, but only one issue was published in 1991, under the title *Giperboreya*.

In 1993, Dugin took part in the international seminar 'Tradición, Tierra y Etnia' (Tradition, Land and Ethnos) in Spain organised by the Thule Group and former editors of *Hiperbórea* which was discontinued in 1992. This seminar – also attended by Serrano – was the last more or less significant meeting of 'esoteric Hitlerists' from the Thule Group.[17] Dugin's cooperation with this organisation proved to be short-lived, because at the same time he started forging links with the European New Right, and the Thule Group, as well as the journals they and Dugin published, appeared too extreme compared to the doctrine of the European New Right.

Dugin's fruitful and sustained contacts with the European New Right apparently began in 1990 with meeting the important far-right intellectual and publisher Claudio Mutti,[18] a prominent Italian disciple of Jean Thiriart. Nicholas Goodrick-Clark also described Mutti as a self-styled 'Nazi-Maoist', an 'admirer of Islamic fundamentalism and Franco Freda's[19] brand of armed right-wing terrorism to provoke revolution', 'a Muslim convert and Third Positionist' who combined 'anti-Semitism with virulent anti-Westernism'.[20] One of the outcomes of Dugin's meeting with Mutti was that, in 1991, Mutti's Parma-based Edizioni All'insegna del Veltro published Dugin's book *Continente Russia*.[21] The same year, Mutti also published a book on the 'mondialist conspiracy' against Russia by a Russian anti-Semite Igor Shafarevich.[22]

As Jean-Yves Camus suggests, it is through Mutti that Dugin met Alain de Benoist, the head of the major French New Right think-tank Groupement de recherche et d'études pour la civilisation européenne (Research and Study Group for European Civilisation, GRECE), in June 1990 in Paris.[23] In the same period, Dugin apparently met Belgian New Right author and translator Robert Steuckers.[24] Steuckers was, at times, close to the extreme-right Front nouveau de Belgique (New Belgian Front) and Vlaams Blok (Flemish Block), and founded, in 1981, the group Études, recherches et orientations européennes (European Studies, Research and Orientations) modelled on GRECE.

As it becomes clear from one of Dugin's interviews,[25] it was Steuckers who introduced the concept of National Bolshevism to Dugin but the latter did not embrace it until after the collapse of the Soviet Union in 1991. Furthermore, it was presumably Steuckers too, who introduced geopolitics to Dugin: of all Dugin's early West European contacts, Steuckers was the only one who wrote on geopolitics.

The year 1991 also saw Dugin participating in two important conferences which exerted notable influence on his further activities. First of all, Dugin took part, in March 1991, in the XXIVth Colloquium of GRECE in Paris where he presented a paper titled 'The Soviet Empire and Nationalisms in the Perestroika Era'.[26] This Colloquium was also attended by three leading figures of GRECE, namely de Benoist, Jacques Marlaud and Charles Champetier, as well as Roger Garaudy, a former French communist author and then a Muslim convert, and Luc Pauwels, the founder of the publishing house Deltastichting and editor of the Belgian New Right journal *Teksten, Kommentaren en Studies* (Texts, Commentaries and Studies), also known as *TeKoS*.

During or after another conference that Dugin attended in Paris in 1991 – 'Le complot' (The conspiracy) held by the Ecole pratique des hautes etudes at the Sorbonne – Dugin met Jean Parvulesco. The latter was a French author of Romanian origin and was known for his obsession with conspiracy theories. Dugin claimed that Parvulesco, in 1991, provided him with a copy of the 'semi-secret report' *The GRU Galaxy. The Secret Mission of Mikhail Gorbachev, the USSR and the Future of the Great Eurasian Continent.*[27] Parvulesco allegedly presented this report to the administration of the conspiratorial 'Institute of Special Metastrategic Studies "Atlantis"', and, according to Dugin, this very report formed the basis of his own seminal essay *Velikaya voyna kontinentov* (The great war of the continents).[28] Along with Steuckers's articles on geopolitics, Parvulesco's conspiracy theories on the forthcoming 'final war' (*Endkampf*) between the 'Eurasian' and 'Atlanticist orders' had shaped Dugin's perspective on geopolitics before he took an interest in the works of Russian Eurasianists.[29]

In April 1992, Dugin invited de Benoist and Steuckers to Moscow. They took part in a panel discussion at the office of the newspaper *Den'* (Day, later renamed into *Zavtra* (Tomorrow)). Dugin worked as a journalist at *Den'*, a self-styled 'Organ of the Spiritual Opposition' edited by Alexander Prokhanov, a writer and ideologist of the Russian extreme right.[30] Also present at the panel discussion were: Dugin, Prokhanov and the leader of the Kommunisticheskaya partiya Rossiyskoy Federatsii (Communist Party of the Russian Federation, KPRF) Gennadiy Zyuganov.[31] They discussed the problems of 'social and national justice', liberalism, capitalism, the 'cultural aggression of the United States', 'Russian patriotism and metaphysics' and other issues.[32]

The second meeting took place at the General Staff Academy of the Armed Forces of Russia, where Dugin taught as a guest lecturer.[33] The roundtable, which discussed 'European security issues and possible ways of Russia's and Europe's development', was attended by de Benoist and seven top military officials of the Academy, including General-Lieutenant Nikolay Klokotov.

Recalling his experience in Russia, de Benoist said, in one of the interviews, that he was 'disturbed by the crude imperialism and Jacobinism of the vast majority of the so-called [Russian] "patriots"'. According to de Benoist, since then he had not had 'any contact with Dugin (or with any other group in Russia)'.[34]

Despite the rupture between de Benoist and Dugin, the latter managed to maintain relations with Steuckers and Mutti – the latter visited Moscow in June

1992[35] – and to establish new contacts with more radical West European groups and intellectuals.

In August 1992, Dugin met, in Moscow, with the Belgian 'pan-European National Bolshevik' Jean Thiriart. In the 1980s, as the previous chapter argued, Thiriart was obsessed with the idea of creating the Euro-Soviet Empire from Vladivostok to Dublin – a project that would liberate Europe from the US influence. In his view, the creation of this 'Empire' could only be possible with the active participation of the Soviet Union that would 'fuse' with Europe and make it European again. Thiriart was distressed by the demise of the Soviet Union, but appeared to be willing to try his luck with post-Soviet Russia as a prospective 'liberator' of Europe. Therefore, he was interested in establishing relations with the anti-liberal and anti-American opposition to Yeltsin – commonly named as the 'red-brown' due to the collusion of Russian national-communists and fascists – that he hoped could come to power in Russia and implement Thiriart's project.

In 1991, Thiriart joined the European Liberation Front (ELF) – a national-revolutionary group named after the organisational initiative of Francis Parker Yockey and founded by a French far-right author Christian Bouchet, also the leader of the French National Bolshevik organisation Nouvelle Résistance (New Resistance) and editor of the journal *Lutte du peuple* (People's struggle). To promote the ideas of the new ELF and build contacts with the Russian 'red-brown' groups, Thiriart went to Moscow in August 1992. For his Moscow trip, he was joined by Michel Schneider, former adviser to the FN's contemporary leader Jean-Marie Le Pen, and editor of the far-right journal *Nationalisme et République* (Nationalism and Republic). Other representatives of the ELF delegation to Moscow included Italian New Right activists Carlo Terracciano, a member of the groupuscule Movimento Antagonista (Antagonistic Movement), and Marco Battarra, editor of the far-right journal *Orion*.

Thiriart's activities in Moscow were intense: he participated in various roundtables and discussions, did interviews and presentations. Apart from Dugin, Thiriart and his colleagues met with Prokhanov, the KPRF's Zyuganov and Yegor Ligachyov, the leaders of the ultranationalist Rossiyskiy obshchenarodny soyuz (Russian All-People Union) Sergey Baburin, Viktor Alksnis and Nikolay Pavlov, and other representatives of the 'red-brown' opposition.[36] Thiriart's visit to Russia turned out to be his last attempt at building a Russian-European National Bolshevik alliance: he died in November 1992, shortly after his return to Belgium from Russia, and Dugin wrote a long obituary praising Thiriart as 'the Last Hero of Europe'.[37]

Russian national-communists were apparently fascinated with the National-Bolshevik 'European alliance'. In March 1993, Zyuganov, Prokhanov and the main coordinator of the Russian 'red-brown' opposition Eduard Volodin wrote a letter to the editors of *Orion*. In this letter, 'the leaders of the Russian political opposition', as they called themselves, affirmed that Italian politicians such as Battara, Terracciano, Mutti and Maurizio Murelli, the founder of *Orion* (as well as convicted fascist bomb-thrower), contributed 'to the mutual understanding between the

Russian and Italian peoples on the political and cultural levels'.[38] The letter continued:

> We find *Orion*'s activity particularly important and positive in terms of converging political formations of allegedly 'opposite' orientations: left-wing forces upholding the principles of social justice and national movements insisting on adherence to national justice. This kind of synthesis has been implemented in the Russian opposition, where the 'Left' and 'Right' form one and the same formation fighting against the pro-American, cosmopolitan, anti-Rusian government and comprador neo-capitalism.[39]

Also in March 1993, Mutti, Battarra and Terracciano visited Moscow again and took part in the roundtable 'dedicated to the oppressed peoples of the New World Order' chaired by Dugin, as well as other events involving many of those who were present at meetings with Thiriart in August 1992.[40] Christian Bouchet also visited Moscow that year.

Already as a leader and the main ideologue of the Natsional-bol'shevistskaya partiya (National-Bolshevik Party, NBP) that he co-founded with Eduard Limonov,[41] Dugin visited Spain in June 1994 and signed the 'National-Bolshevik Act' with the Spanish member of the ELF, the political association Alternativa Europea (European Alternative) led by José Antonio Llopart.[42] José L. Rodríguez described the ideology of Alternativa Europea as a mixture of Thiriart's pan-European fascism, Conservative Revolution and Spanish national syndicalism of Ramiro Ledesma.[43]

After June 1994 and until the beginning of the 2000s, Dugin had scarce contacts with European far-right activists and organisations. To a varying degree, these were one-sided relationships, as it was Dugin who was influenced by theories, practices and experiences of the European New Right rather than the other way round. Through them, Dugin was introduced to, or reinforced his interest in, National Bolshevism, geopolitics, conspiracy theories and Integral Traditionalism. Moreover, following the example of his West European colleagues, Dugin started publishing a number of journals and established a publishing house Arctogaia.

Dugin originally built the above-mentioned relations in order to satisfy his interest in the contemporary interpretations of René Guénon and Julius Evola, but then he used his contacts to consolidate and strengthen his position in Russian ultranationalist and mainstream circles. In his autobiography, Eduard Limonov recollected that, in 1992, Dugin 'unwarrantedly usurped the contacts between the patriotic opposition with the Western right wing'.[44]

Despite the fact that it was Dugin who benefited the most from the relationships with the European New Right, there was still a degree of reciprocity in these relationships. European New Right activists were interested in Dugin because he was apparently the first representative of the Russian far right who spoke the same language with them – both literally[45] and intellectually – and could not only enlighten them on Russian phenomena from a native's point of view, but also disseminate their own ideas in Russia. Moreover, in 1992–1993, the West European far right – especially the 'philo-Soviet' groups – supported the Russian 'red-brown' alliance, as they were increasingly interested in political developments in Russia that could – rather feasibly – lead to a much-hoped right-wing revolution and, as the likes of Thiriart hoped, contribute to the 'liberation' of Europe.

Particular representatives of the more radical strands of the Western New Right cooperated with a group of Russian racists outside Dugin's circles and even the 'red-brown' opposition. This group coalesced around the far-right journal *Nasledie predkov* (Ancestral heritage)[46] co-edited by Anatoliy Ivanov, Pavel Tulaev and Vladimir Avdeev.[47] In spring 1996, now late Gilbert Sincyr, President of the New Right association Synergies européennes (European Synergies), which he co-founded with Robert Steuckers in 1994, visited Moscow and entitled Ivanov, Tulaev and Avdeev to establish a Russian branch of Synergies européennes. The 'Russian branch', which, in reality, was only a regional Moscow social organisation, was registered in 1997.[48] In the second half of the 1990s, this Russian group also established contacts with Steuckers, Michel Schneider of *Nationalisme et République*, now deceased German neo-Nazi Jürgen Rieger, and some other far-right publicists and activists. However, this group's influence on the far-right discourse in Russia, let alone Russian politics, remained limited due to their overt racism. The 'Russian branch' of Synergies européennes did contribute to the development of the cooperation between far-right groups and individuals in Russia and Europe, but this circle ultimately failed to extend beyond the fringes of the Russian socio-political life.

Vladimir Zhirinovsky and money politics

Dugin, as Limonov put it, might have, to a certain degree, 'usurped' the contacts of the Russian ultranationalist camp with the Western far right, but Vladimir Zhirinovsky, the leader of the misleadingly named far-right Liberal'no-demokraticheskaya partiya Rossii (Liberal-Democratic Party of Russia, LDPR),[49] also tried to forge relationships with European radical right-wing parties.

During the Soviet times, Zhirinovsky was apparently a KGB informant,[50] while many former Soviet high-ranking officials directly linked the creation of Zhirinovsky's ultranationalist party to the Soviet 'political technology'. When the USSR under Gorbachev started relative liberalisation of the Soviet political space, the Central Committee of the Communist Party of the Soviet Union and the KGB decided to create a pseudo-party that would differ from the Communist Party – and thus contribute to the alleged emergence of the multi-party system in the Soviet Union – but would still be controlled by the Communist Party.[51]

The LDPR's ideology is a mixture of ultranationalist and imperialist ideas. In his arguably major political work, *The Last Dash to the South* (published in 1993), Zhirinovsky argued that Russia should restore the empire and, to prevent instability presumably spreading from the southern countries to Russia, make the 'last dash to the South' occupying and incorporating Turkey, Afghanistan and Iran into Russia.

Russia, as Zhirinovsky wrote, was part of the world's North that also included Western states. This theoretically allowed Russia to avoid confrontation with the West, and later Zhirinovsky even suggested to create the Russian-Western-Japanese alliance that would divide the world into the spheres of influence, but his anti-Westernism radicalised dramatically in the 2000s.

In the 1990s, however, Zhirinovsky was still trying to build alliances with the Western far right. Eduard Limonov, while living in France, introduced Zhirinovsky to Jean-Marie Le Pen in autumn 1992.[52] Their meeting turned out to be beneficial to Zhirinovsky, as later the FN 'provided logistical support [to the LDPR], including computers and fax machines, in short supply in Moscow at that time'.[53]

Already during his first meeting with Le Pen, Zhirinovsky suggested establishing the International Centre of Right-Wing Parties in Moscow and invited Le Pen to Russia's capital. Le Pen, according to Limonov, 'confined himself to commending the project'.[54] In 1996, when Le Pen eventually visited Moscow and took part in a press conference with Zhirinovsky, the latter spoke of founding a pan-European far-right alliance again, under the name 'Union of Right-wing Forces of Europe'. Zhirinovsky also argued that 'a new political union' should be formed in Europe – otherwise, a war between Russia and the West was inevitable.[55] At that time, Zhirinovsky's project of a pan-European far-right alliance was not implemented, but he revived – and, to some extent, materialised – this idea after Putin became Russian President.

Zhirinovsky's other major foreign contact in the Yeltsin era was the far-right Deutsche Volksunion (German People's Union, DVU) led by now late Gerhard Frey, 'the multi-millionaire media czar' who owned and published several newspapers,[56] as well as being the main sponsor of his party. As Andreas Umland argues, the relations between Frey and Zhirinovsky 'began apparently in April 1992 when Frey's son was an official guest of the Third LDPR Congress',[57] and, later, Zhirinovsky and Frey spoke at each other's party conventions.[58] Moreover, following his staggering victory in the 1993 elections to the State Duma (Russian parliament) – the LDPR obtained 22.92 per cent of the votes – Zhirinovsky met with Frey again in Munich on his way to Austria where the leader of the LDPR spent a few days in the company of Edwin Neuwirth, 'a local industrialist, Holocaust denier and proud former member of the Waffen SS'.[59] In 1994, the LDPR and DVU signed a friendship accord.[60]

According to Russian journalist Leonid Mlechin who spoke to one of the heads of the anti-extremist department of the BfV, Frey provided financial support to the LDPR 'in exchange for the promise to return the Kaliningrad region to Germany after Zhirinovsky became president of Russia'.[61] Frey himself wrote that 'if Mr. Zhirinovsky came to power in Russia he would negotiate with Germany about the return of the lost province of East Prussia'.[62] Indeed, in his book *The Last Thrust to the South*, Zhirinovsky suggested restoring Germany to its 1937 borders.[63] Zhirinovsky's readiness to part with the Kaliningrad region seemed important to the DVU that insisted that Pomerania, Silesia and East Prussia should be returned to Germany.

Zhirinovsky's anti-Polish revisionism did not deter Janusz Bryczkowski, the leader of the neo-Nazi Polski Front Narodowy (Polish National Front), from inviting Zhirinovsky to the first congress in 1994. At the congress, Zhirinovsky obviously refrained from talking about 'returning' Western Polish lands to Germany, but turned to generally anti-Western and anti-NATO rhetoric, stating that the Poles were lured into joining NATO in order to turn people and territories of Eastern Europe into 'cannon fodder' and 'battlefields'.[64]

Some limited cooperation existed between Frey and other Russian ultra-nationalists too. For example, Frey published, in his *Deutsche National-Zeitung*, interviews with, among others, Stanislav Terekhov, leader of the extreme-right and Stalinist Soyuz ofitserov (Officers Union); Viktor Ilyukhin of the KPRF; Sergey Baburin; and Sergey Glazyev and Dmitry Rogozin of the ultranationalist Kongress russkikh obshchin (Congress of Russian Communities).[65] However, of all the Russian ultranationalists of that period, it was Zhirinovsky who developed almost exclusive relations with Frey.

Zhirinovsky also had contacts with a circle of convicted unrepentant Holocaust-deniers led by a Toronto-based publisher Ernst Zündel who published, in particular, one of the most infamous Holocaust-denial pamphlets *Did Six Million Really Die?*.[66] Zündel sponsored, in 1992 and 1993, two visits to Moscow of his German associate, Bela Ewald Althans, 'a roving ambassador for the neo-Nazi cause', who was particularly interested in developing international links and had managed to establish contacts, in particular, with the FN's Yvan Blot and the leaders of CEDADE.[67] Zhirinovsky's LDPR was hardly the main target for Althans; rather, he tried to probe all available Russian far-right activists and organisations. For instance, Althans contacted Aleksandr Barkashov's Russkoe natsional'noe edinstvo (Russian National Unity, RNE), the major fascist organisation in Russia at that time.[68] Apparently, Zhirinovsky looked more credible and politically significant to Althans, and both Zündel and Althans were invited by Zhirinovsky to visit Russia in 1994. However, while Zhirinovsky was their most important contact, they had extensive meetings with other Russian far-right activists, including Aleksandr Sterligov, retired KGB Major General and a leader of the ultranationalist Russkiy natsional'ny sobor (Russian National Rally).

Reflecting on his visit to Russia later, Zündel argued that Russia would not 'adopt an economic system with the dog-eat-dog-style capitalism of the United States', but would rather opt for 'a system that [had] worked eminently well in Europe during the 1930s, something like the National Socialist regime'. Zündel even suggested that his fellow revisionists could help the Russians build a society that would be 'compatible with their own traditions', as the revisionists supposedly could 'have an influence on developments' in Russia, 'an impact far out of proportion to [their] numbers'.[69]

While Zündel's and Althans' histories of relentless neo-Nazi and revisionist activism are unquestionable, both were involved in the activities that might suggest a double play. Already in May 1992, Althans issued a press release offering to sell, for $5,000, over 100 photos documenting 'neo-Nazi volunteers fighting in Yugoslavia on behalf of Croatian forces as well as neo-Nazi involvement in Iraq'. Moreover, Althans offered 'the names of those involved and background information about them, and contacts with some of the neo-Nazis in the photographs for interviews'.[70] The telephone and fax numbers on Althans' press release belonged to Zündel's company Samisdat Publishers in Toronto. Given the bitterly conflictual nature of neo-Nazi movements, it might well be the case that, by selling the photos and names of the neo-Nazis, Zündel and Althans were trying to wreak vengeance upon their enemies in the extreme-right milieu. However, other explanations are possible too. After being arrested in December 1994 and accused of the Holocaust denial and distribution of neo-Nazi propaganda, Althans claimed that he had stopped being a neo-Nazi several years before the arrest and that he was an informant for the BfV. To prove that he had no longer neo-Nazi views, he even called upon his Munich friends to confirm the rumours that he was bisexual – a German magazine 'outed' him in 1992. An article in *Der Spiegel* supported Althans' story arguing that he passed information to the BfV from 1990 to 1994 when the security services stopped cooperating with him because of his 'lack of honesty'.[71] Gerhard Forster, President of the Bavarian branch of the BfV, rejected Althans' and *Der Spiegel*'s claims, noting that Althans was simply offering to sell to the security services 5,000 addresses of extreme-right activists for 360,000 Deutschmarks (€184,065). According to Forster, the security services rejected the offer, but acknowledged that he had 'a very good knowledge of the international relations of neo-Nazis'.[72] At the moment, it is almost impossible to corroborate either Althans' or – given the proven history of the collaboration between the German security services and neo-Nazis[73] – Forster's story. However, one can cautiously assume that, apart from their genuinely neo-Nazi and revisionist activities, Zündel and Althans were collecting information on European far-right groups including the Russian ones, to sell or pass it to third parties.

Neither were Zhirinovsky's international relationships exclusively ideological, as they had a considerable element of financial interest. For example, in 1994, German authorities investigated whether Zhirinovsky was financed by the money of the defunct East German regime through his German contact Werner Girke who handled foreign financial holdings for the East German communists and was believed to have helped them covertly invest those funds in Western companies.[74] In 1996, Italian police suspected Zhirinovsky of the involvement in the trade of nuclear materials that also involved Licio Gelli,[75] a prominent fascist activist since the 1930s, Grand Master of the Masonic lodge Propaganda Due (better known as P2) and one of the key players in the Italian Gladio network.[76]

Zhirinovsky's other far-right contacts in the Yeltsin era included Zmago Jelinčič, the leader of the Slovenska Nacionalna Stranka (Slovenian National Party),[77] and Vojislav Šešelj, the founder and leader of the Srpska Radikalna Stranka (Serbian Radical Party, SRS).[78] Furthermore, in 1997, Zhirinovsky supported the separatist move of Umberto Bossi's LN that attempted to create a state called

'Padania' in Northern Italy. Bossi was excited about the support for his secessionist project received from 'the third political force of the Russian parliament', while Zhirinovsky took part in the opening sitting of the Padanian 'parliament' and stated that, were he Russian president, he would recognise the independence of Padania.[79]

Sergey Glazyev and the economic doomsayers

Another important Russian political figure who established links with the Western far right already in the 1990s was Sergey Glazyev, who, at the time of writing, has been a presidential aide on the issues of regional economic integration. In 1992–1993, he was Minister of External Economic Relations of the Russian Federation, but resigned in protest over the President Yeltsin's decision to dissolve the Supreme Soviet (Russian parliament in 1991–1993) – the decision that resulted in the unsuccessful coup attempt staged by Vice President Aleksandr Rutskoy and Chairman of the Parliament Ruslan Khasbulatov in October 1993 in Moscow. Glazyev was elected to the State Duma in 1994 and became the Chairman of the parliamentary Economic Affairs Committee.

Around this time, Glazyev forged relationships with Lyndon LaRouche, a US-based political activist and founder of a movement that is now known as the 'LaRouche movement'. Chip Berlet and Matthew Nemiroff Lyons describe LaRouche and his movement as follows:

> Though often dismissed as a bizarre political cult, the LaRouche organization and its various front groups are a fascist movement whose pronouncements echo elements of Nazi ideology. . . . [The LaRouchites] advocated a dictatorship in which a 'humanist' elite would rule on behalf of industrial capitalists. They developed an idiosyncratic, coded variation on the Illuminati Freemason and Jewish banker conspiracy theories.[80]

As Leonard Weinberg argued, LaRouche's ideology involved 'a theory according to which a global Anglo-Jewish conspiracy exists to weaken Western society, in the face of Soviet subversion, and makes possible its control by international bankers, drug merchants, and Zionists'.[81] In the 1970–1980s, the LaRouchites were highly critical of the Soviet Union and believed that it was controlled by the 'British oligarchs' – LaRouche's euphemism for the alleged British-Jewish conspiracy.[82] Indeed, the LaRouchites often vilified Britain; in particular, they claimed that 'British royal family (including the Queen) controlled global drug running',[83] while the 'British oligarchy' was preparing to balkanise the United States.[84]

They attacked the Soviet Union too, accusing it of dictatorial and imperialist practices, and specifically focused on the Russian Orthodox Church that the LaRouchites condemned for helping the Kremlin leadership in building the 'worldwide imperial hegemony, the "Third and Final Rome"'.[85] In 1986, LaRouche wrote about the 'decisive cultural inferiority' of the Russians and warned about 'barbarians overrunning Western Europe from the East' as 'part of the enemy's stock-in-trade in ancient and medieval times, as well as in the instance of the Holy Alliance's adoption of Russian hordes as the "policeman of Europe" '.[86] When LaRouche ran his presidential primary campaign in 1988, he stressed that Russia was dreaming of 'the world conquest' and was preparing for 'an all-out, surprise attack on the United States some time during the 1990s'.[87] His views on the Russians were blatantly racist, and he described 'a typical Russian' as 'a lazy, drunken, superstitious, immoral beast'.[88]

With the demise of the Soviet Union, however, the LaRouchites' attitude towards Russia gradually changed and LaRouche became genuinely interested in Russia and its economy, arguing against adoption of Western liberal economic models. In 1992, the Schiller Institute for Science and Culture was established in Moscow as a Russian branch of the LaRouchite international Schiller Institute and started publishing Russian translations of LaRouche's essays.

Glazyev and LaRouche most likely met in person for the first time in April 1994, when LaRouche – shortly after his release from prison where he had served 5 years for mail fraud – and his wife and associate Helga Zepp-LaRouche travelled to Russia and addressed a number of workshops at various venues including the Russian Academy of Sciences in Moscow.[89] Glazyev's senior colleague, late Russian economist Dmitry Lvov who was in contact with LaRouche too, was a full member of the Russian Academy of Sciences and might be one of the people who officially invited LaRouche to Moscow. Late Taras Muranivsky, professor at the Russian State University for the Humanities and president of the Russian branch of the Schiller Institute, might also be involved in organising LaRouche's visit to Moscow.

LaRouche's contacts in Russian academia and the Moscow-based Schiller Institute for Science and Culture actively promoted his ideas in Russia, and, since 1995, he was trying to exert direct influence on Russian policy making in the economic sphere. Representatives of the Schiller Institute for Science and Culture presented LaRouche's memorandum 'Prospects for Russian Economic Revival' at the State Duma in 1995, while later that year LaRouche himself appeared in the Russian parliament to present his report 'The World Financial System and Problems of Economic Growth'.[90] His conspiracy-driven economic theories that denounced free trade and commended protectionism, as well as attacking the workings of the International Monetary Fund, struck a chord with many a member of the Duma largely dominated by the anti-liberal forces such as the KPRF, LDPR and other ultranationalists.

During the 1990s, the LaRouchites praised Glazyev as 'a leading economist of the opposition to Boris Yeltsin's regime' and published Glazyev's interviews and articles in their weekly *Executive Intelligence Review*. In 1999, LaRouche published an English translation of Glazyev's book *Genocide: Russia and the New World Order* in which the author exposed his conspiracy theories about 'the world oligarchy' using 'depopulation techniques developed by the fascists' 'to cleanse the economic space of Russia for international capital'.[91] According to Glazyev, the United States – under the guidance of 'the world oligarchy' – is implementing 'anti-Russian policies' aimed at preventing 'the reunification of the Russian people', provoking 'further dismemberment of Russia' and undermining 'integration processes within the territory of the CIS [i.e. the Commonwealth of the Independent States]'.[92]

On the part of LaRouche, his interest in Russia and cooperation with Glazyev seemed to be driven by practical considerations. LaRouche's grand idea in relation to Russia was that of a 'Eurasian land-bridge' between Western and Eastern parts of Eurasia, a project that, according to LaRouche, the United States would be interested in and to which Russia would 'supply a crucial contributing role'.[93] While LaRouche's Russian associates might not share his views on the national interests of the United States in the framework of the 'Eurasian land-bridge' concept, they embraced his populist interpretation of the economic situation in Russia that he described as one that was characterised by a conflict between

> the imported liberalism of those 'chop-shop entrepreneurs' who stuff their own purse with money from foreign sales of national assets at stolen-goods prices, and Russians of more patriotic inclinations, notably those whose overriding commitment, as professionals, is to filling the barren, physical-economic market-baskets of their perilously hungered countrymen.[94]

The relations between LaRouche and Glazyev continued in the 2000s, the Putin era. In particular, LaRouche and Helga Zepp-LaRouche took part in the Duma hearing 'On measures to ensure the development of the Russian economy under conditions of a destabilisation of the world financial system' held in June 2001 at the initiative of Glazyev who was then Chairman of the Duma Committee on Economic Policy and Entrepreneurship. The same year LaRouches visited Russia again and met with a number of Russian academic and politicians including then Mayor of Moscow Yuriy Luzhkov. Glazyev's promotion of LaRouche and his ideas resulted in the latter's growth in popularity as an opinion maker and commentator on political and economic issues in Russia – a status that LaRouche could not enjoy in his home country where he has remained a fringe political figure.

'The Patriotic International': Lobbying for Iraq and Russia

In the course of the 1990s, Dugin, Zhirinovsky and Glazyev occupied different positions in the Russian political system. Dugin was a fringe politician yet an influential ideologue of neo-Eurasianism and National Bolshevism who was engaged in metapolitical, rather than political, struggle against liberal democracy. Zhirinovsky was the leader of the LDPR – a party that emerged as the strongest political force after the 1993 parliamentary elections and as the second strongest – after the 1995 parliamentary elections. Glazyev was, for a short period of time, Minister of Russia's External Economic Relations, then an MP and, later, head of the analytical department of the Federation Council of Russia. The three of them never cooperated with each other to any significant degree, but they shared similar views underpinned by Russian ultranationalism and aversion to liberal democracy. Furthermore, Dugin and Glazyev were in the opposition to President Yeltsin and, hence, to the contemporary regime in Russia. Zhirinovsky also claimed to be in the opposition to Yeltsin, and, formally, his party indeed was critical of some of his policies, but it essentially supported the regime on the crucial issues.[95] For example, Zhirinovsky supported Yeltsin's decision to dissolve the Supreme Soviet in 1993 that resulted in Vice President Rutskoy's unsuccessful coup, as well as backing up Yeltsin in 1998 amid the preparations for the (eventually failed) impeachment of Yeltsin initiated by the KPRF.

While Dugin, Zhirinovsky and Glazyev were apparently interested in implementing some of the ideas of their Western far-right associates in Russia, they seemed to understand that those ideas clashed with Yeltsin's regime, and they were too far removed from the state power to either associate themselves with the state or act on its behalf or instrumentalise the Western far right against the perceived *external* adversaries of the Russian state. For Dugin, Zhirinovsky and Glazyev, the immediate enemy was still *inside* Russia, so at that time they could only use their Western far-right contacts to strengthen their own positions inside the country.

This situation started to gradually change after Putin became President, and Zhirinovsky was arguably the first Russian politician who attempted to connect the interests of the Russian state to the developments in the far-right milieu in Europe, by reviving his idea of creating a Moscow-based far-right international movement that he had proposed to Le Pen already in 1992 and 1996.

On 14 September 2002, following his visit to Baghdad amid international discussions of the possible US-led military action against Iraq, Zhirinovsky, then Deputy Chairman of the State Duma, convened a meeting of the representatives of 'patriotic parties'. This meeting hosted Zhirinovsky's old friend Gerhard Frey, now late Vice President of the FN Dominique Chaboche,[96] the LN's contemporary Deputy Chairman Francesco Speroni, Mitsuhiro Kimura of the Japanese far-right Issuikai group, and a number of other far-right activists, as well as journalists and envoys from Iraq, Iran, Libya, North Korea, India and Afghanistan.[97] The meeting had two aims: to declare support for Iraq and launch the World Congress of Patriotic Parties to take place in Moscow the following year.

The Iraq connection was anything but accidental. As Umland noted, the cooperation between Zhirinovsky and Saddam Hussein apparently started already in 1992; Zhirinovsky regularly travelled to Iraq, and there were reasonable suspicions that Hussein provided financial assistance to the LDPR.[98] Hussein, who had been increasingly isolated due to Iraq's aggressive international behaviour and repressive domestic policies, needed support from sympathetic politicians outside the country and was ready to pay for such a support. Zhirinovsky and high-ranking members of the LDPR were essentially Iraqi lobbyists in Russia; moreover, Zhirinovsky 'regularly led delegations of Russian businessmen to Baghdad to arrange lucrative deals'.[99] Zhirinovsky did not deny that Hussein financially supported the LDPR, while Zhirinovsky's contemporary deputy, Aleksey Mitrofanov, admitted that the party had also 'received money from Russian companies that got contracts in Iraq thanks to Zhirinovsky's help'.[100] Furthermore, the CIA's *Duelfer Report* argued,

> Iraqi attempts to use oil gifts to influence Russian policy makers [to gain support for lifting the sanctions in the UN Security Council[101]] were on a lavish and almost indiscriminate scale. Oil voucher gifts were directed across the political spectrum targeting the new oligarch class, Russian political parties and officials. . . . The Liberal Democratic Party leader Zhirinovsky was a recipient, as was the Russian Communist party [i.e. KPRF] and the Foreign Ministry itself, according to Iraqi documents.[102]

A report of the Independent Inquiry Committee, which was appointed in 2004 by UN Secretary General Kofi Annan to look into alleged corruption in the UN's 'Oil-for-Food Programme' in Iraq, also documented Zhirnovsky's links to Hussein's regime and argued that, 'according to Iraqi officials and Iraqi Ministry of Oil records', Zhirinovsky was allocated 73 million barrels of oil 'because it was believed that he would advocate for political positions favorable to Iraq'.[103]

It was, therefore, hardly a coincidence that Zhirinovsky eventually decided to revive and materialise his idea of an explicitly pro-Iraqi far-right international against the backdrop of the growing pressure on Hussein's regime and the latter's consequently increased need for outside support. By the time of the Moscow meeting of far-right forces in September 2002, Zhirinovsky travelled to Baghdad three times that year, and it is conceivable that he secured financial backing of, if not directly coordinated with Hussein's regime, his far-right international initiative.

Zhirinovsky was far from being the first far-right politician who cooperated with Hussein. As noted in the previous chapter, Thiriart had met with Hussein already in 1968 with a view of securing the territory of Iraq as an 'outside springboard' for a fascist revolution in Europe. In the beginning of the 1990s, and especially during the Gulf War, praise for Hussein and his authoritarian anti-Western regime became an evident trend among the European far right. Gerhard Frey launched a 'phoney anti-war campaign, branding the United States and its allies as criminal for waging war on Saddam Hussein';[104] 'all members of the [French] radical right were unanimous in defending Saddam Hussein and lauding the heroism of Arab soldiers waging a desperate struggle against the [Zionist] "lobbies"'.[105] At one point, it seemed that Thiriart's dream of a fascist 'European brigade' receiving real-life training in armed conflicts in Third-World countries eventually came true: one of the leaders of the German neo-Nazi movement Michael Kühnen 'offered himself to the Iraqis as self-styled commander of a so-called international "Freedom Corps"', consisting – as he claimed – of 'over 500 volunteers from several countries, including Germany, the USA, the Netherlands, Austria and France'.[106] Kühnen even drafted an agreement between the government of Iraq and the projected 'Anti-Zionist Legion' under the command of Kühnen himself stipulating the conditions of the neo-Nazi militants' service to Hussein's regime.[107] It remains unknown whether the agreement was ever signed by the Iraqi authorities, but since German neo-Nazi Bela Ewald Althans had photographs documenting 'neo-Nazi involvement in Iraq', it is possible that at least some neo-Nazis travelled to Iraq and spent some time there.[108] However, already in the beginning of the 1990s, the assumed cooperation between the European far right and Hussen's regime had not only an ideological, but a practical angle too. As *Searchlight* argued, 'far right leaders internationally [had] been popping backwards and forwards to Baghdad, clearly more interested in getting financial support from Saddam Hussein's regime than in giving any real political commitment to it'.[109]

In the beginning of the 2000s, many Western far-right politicians also cooperated with Iraqi authorities. In particular, Jean-Marie Le Pen, Mitsuhiro Kimura, Jörg Haider in his capacity as one of the leaders of the FPÖ,[110] Vadim Tudor of the Partidului România Mare (Greater Romania Party, PRM) and Vojislav Šešelj of the SRS had relations with Hussein, while some of them, for example Le Pen, Haider, Šešelj and Kimura, visited Baghdad to meet Hussein personally.

The details about their dealings with Hussein are scarce, but, at least in particular cases, they seem to be similar to those between Zhirinovsky and Hussein. Some information is available on the relations between the FPÖ and Hussein. Like Zhirinovsky, Haider travelled to Baghdad three times in 2002. He actively remonstrated against Washington's sanctions against Baghdad and apparently organised humanitarian medical aid to Iraq, while another member of the FPÖ, Ewald Stadler, founded the Austrian-Iraqi Society. Documents found in Baghdad after the demise of Hussein's regime have revealed that Haider and Stadler, during their visit to Baghdad in May 2002, signed an agreement with the Iraqi authorities. According to that agreement, Haider and Stadler would act as Hussein's lobbyists in Europe and receive $5 million for their services ($1,250,000 for Haider and $3,750,000 for Stadler).[111] The relations between Le Pen and Hussein, however, remain a more obscure case. Le Pen had criticised the imposition of the sanctions by the UN Security Council since 1990, while his wife Jany Le Pen had been presiding, since 1995, over the non-transparent non-governmental organisation (NGO) 'SOS Enfants d'Irak' (SOS Iraq's Children) that allegedly supplied medical aid to Iraqi children as well as protesting against the sanctions against Iraq.[112] Already at the end of the 1990s, Jean-Marie Le Pen's interest in the developments around Iraq was 'widely speculated to include acting as a go-between on Iraqi oil deals'.[113]

The First World Congress of Patriotic Parties took place in Moscow on 18 January 2003, and hosted 44 representatives of 'patriotic' organisations from Europe, Asia and Africa. They adopted a resolution that stressed the need 'to defend the interests of [their] countries and peoples, their national and cultural distinctive character, spiritual values', 'to render every assistance to each other', and 'to express solidarity with the people of Iraq in its aspiration to defend its independence'.[114] The resolution was signed, inter alia, by Zhirinovsky himself; FN's Dominique Chaboche; DVU's Liane Hasselbarth; Mitsuhiro Kimura; Makis Voridis, the contemporary leader of the Greek far-right Ellinikó Métopo (Hellenic Front); Matti Järviharju, the contemporary leader of the Finnish ultranationalist Isänmaallinen Kansanliike (Patriotic People's Movement); Miroslav Sládek, the leader of the Czech far-right

Republikáni Miroslava Sládka (Republicans of Miroslav Sládek); and representatives of pro-Russian and/or anti-US organisations from Armenia, Belarus, Ukraine, Uzbekistan, Turkey, Georgia, South African Republic, Tajikistan, Transnistria, and some other countries and territories.

An important development related to the World Congress of Patriotic Parties that made it different from Zhirinovsky's earlier contacts with the European far right was that, already at the meeting in September 2002, he stressed that he greeted the delegates as Deputy Chairman of the State Duma, rather than the leader of the LDPR.[115] Zhirinovsky positioned himself as no longer just a party leader, but as a statesman who spoke in the name of the Russian state. The significance of this change in rhetoric was reinforced on the eve of the First World Congress of Patriotic Parties when Zhirinovsky, appealing to the state, declared:

> the new union of patriotic parties will do everything for the normalisation of international relations.
>
> I believe that, today, Moscow – through the workings of the First World Congress of Patriotic Parties – can have leverage in world politics in the interests of all the people on the planet.[116]

The logic behind Zhirinovsky's argument – that Russia could influence international political processes through far-right parties – was apparently informed by Zhirinovsky's own role as a Russian ultranationalist lobbyist for Hussein's regime. As the fate of Hussein and his regime showed, however, neither Zhirinovsky nor his West European counterparts were particularly successful in defending Iraq on the international stage due to their limited political significance, but the process itself was apparently profitable for those engaged in it. By suggesting an idea of instrumentalising the far right to the benefit of Russian foreign policy, Zhirinovsky might have hoped to become a paid mediator between the Kremlin and European far-right politicians, yet, at that time, there was no indication that the Russian authorities were interested in his initiative.

The lack of political support from the Kremlin, as well as the fall of Hussein's regime in 2003, possibly determined the marginalisation Zhirinovsky's 'patriotic international' enterprise over the following years. Few far-right activists went to the Second World Congress of Patriotic Parties that took place on 21 February 2004 – Zhirinovsky apparently had neither funding nor appeal to lure major far-right politicians to Moscow again. The overwhelming majority of the participants were representatives of pro-Russian parties and organisations from the former Soviet states and Asian anti-US organisations. On 24 April 2006, the third meeting hosted representatives of only two European far-right parties, namely the SRS and the Belgian Front National. At the Congress in 2006, Gordana Pop-Lazić of the SRS praised the authoritarian regime of Alexander Lukashenko and urged the International Criminal Tribunal for the Former Yugoslavia to release Vojislav Šešelj who was then in custody by the International Criminal Tribunal for the Former Yugoslavia.[117] In his turn, the founder and contemporary leader of the Belgian

Front National Daniel Féret promoted the ideas of Eurosiberia from Brest to Vladivostok.[118] The Fourth World Congress of Patriotic Parties took place on 20 May 2010 and was as marginal as the previous one. It was apparently humiliating for Zhirinovsky that, in August that year, Mitsuhiro Kimura, regular participant of Zhirinovsky's conferences, managed to convene a week-long international far-right conference in Tokyo in cooperation with the Alliance of European National Movements that sent around 20 delegates who represented parties such as the FN, BNP, FPÖ, Jobbik, Vlaams Belang (Flemish Interest, VB) and some others.[119]

Zhirinovsky's initiative of creating a functional far-right international, through which the Russian authorities would be able to influence the West, seems to have failed for one major reason which is bad timing. Zhirinovsky explicitly articulated this idea in 2003, but, at that time, the Kremlin was still largely interested in cooperating with Western mainstream actors, such as Italian Prime Minister Silvio Berlusconi or German Chancellor Gerhard Schröder, rather than the far right. In 2002, Le Pen expressed his desire to meet with Putin, as he understood the political irrelevance of Zhirinovsky, but that was not possible.[120] When the Russian authorities could have been theoretically interested in supporting Zhirinovsky's idea, that is after 2005 (see Chapter 3), the World Congress of Patriotic Parties had become a marginal project that failed to attract major European far-right politicians.

Sergey Baburin: Hiring the far-right celebrities

Zhirinovsky was perhaps the first Russian politician who attempted to woo Jean-Marie Le Pen, but he was not the only one. Le Pen became especially prominent after spring 2002 when he took the second place in the presidential election in France and faced Jacques Chirac in the second ballot. Although Chirac won a landslide victory over Le Pen – 82.21 per cent of the voters supported Chirac and 17.79 per cent voted for Le Pen – the mere fact that a far-right candidate managed to enter a second round of a presidential election in a West European country dramatically raised Le Pen's standing among the European far-right parties. Unsurprisingly, other Russian ultranationalist politicians wanted to use Le Pen for their own political ends too.

This was the case of Sergey Baburin who wanted to instrumentalise the success of Le Pen in the run-up to the 2003 parliamentary elections in Russia. In contrast to Zhirinovsky who had long-standing relations with Le Pen – even if it was Zhirinovsky who sought 'friendship' with Le Pen rather than the other way around – and other European far-right politicians, Baburin had very limited contacts with the European far right in general, but this did not prevent him from inviting Le Pen to the Second Congress of the Partiya natsional'nogo vozrozhdeniya 'Narodnaya Volya' (Party of National Revival 'People's Will'), into which Baburin's previous party, the Rossiyskiy obshchenarodny soyuz, merged in 2001. The Congress took place on 22–23 February 2003, and, apart from Le Pen, hosted foreign guests such as now late Borislav Milošević, the elder brother of former Serbian ultranationalist President Slobodan Milošević; Natalya Vitrenko, the leader of the pro-Russian, misleadingly named Prohresyvna sotsialistychna partiya Ukrainy (Progressive Socialist Party of Ukraine); and a minor official from the Embassy of Iraq in Moscow.

In his speech, Le Pen talked about the successes of the Front National, the threat of mass immigration from 'the South' into the space from Vladivostok to San-Francisco, the 'unfairness' of the looming war on Iraq.[121]

Le Pen also invited Baburin to the FN's 12th party convention that took place on 19–21 April 2003 in Nice and celebrated the FN's 30th anniversary. The FN's 12th party convention hosted hundreds of domestic delegates and representatives of European far-right parties such as the DVU, PRM, Vlaams Blok, Ellinikó Métopo, Sverigedemokraterna (Sweden Democrats, SD), Nationaldemokraterna (National Democrats) and many others. The Narodnaya Volya's party press boasted that Baburin and Le Pen were 'uniting European patriotic parties', and that the attendees of the convention unanimously supported Baburin's 'Declaration "On the unity and cooperation of national and patriotic parties"'.[122] However, the attendance of Baburin, whom other participants of the FN's convention hardly knew, seemed to be low-profile and insignificant, and he failed to develop any further international contacts. For Baburin, the 'international cooperation' was a narrative for domestic consumption, and although it is difficult to say whether the 'friendship' with Le Pen had indeed contributed to raising Baburin's standing among Russian ultranationalists, it certainly did not hurt.

In September 2003, Baburin's Narodnaya Volya, together with two other Russian 'patriotic' parties, formed the electoral bloc 'Rodina' (Motherland) led by Dmitry Rogozin and Sergey Glazyev. The 'Rodina' bloc, which was politically nationalist and economically socialist, was widely believed to be a political technology project of the Kremlin aiming at drawing votes away from the KPRF that still had the largest parliamentary group in the Duma.[123] Baburin was placed fifth on the list of 'Rodina' for the 2003 parliamentary elections and, as 'Rodina' secured 9.02 per cent of the vote, became an MP.

The success of 'Rodina' apparently gave Glazyev confidence that he could play a political role independent of the Kremlin, and he decided, with Baburin's support, to run in the 2004 presidential election. This created a tension in 'Rodina', because Rogozin, who was seen as a Kremlin's mole in the party, suggested supporting Putin in the presidential election. Glazyev left 'Rodina' and ran, unsuccessfully, for president, but Baburin stayed in the bloc and even replaced Rogozin as Deputy Chairman of the State Duma. Rogozin, at the same time, became the Chairman of the 'Rodina' parliamentary group. The initial split between the supporters of Glazyev and Rogozin was followed by another split in 2004–2005. As Marlène Laruelle insightfully noted, Baburin 'sought to strengthen his power by relying on his past as a "true" nationalist to attract the most radical voters, who were dissatisfied with Rogozin's image as a Kremlin submissive'.[124]

It was, arguably, the domestic struggle for the image of a 'true nationalist' that prompted Baburin to appeal to his alleged friendship with Jean-Marie Le Pen for the second time. Baburin invited Le Pen, as well as Bruno Gollnisch, one of the

FN's high-ranking officials, to Moscow to take a part in a meeting in the State Duma in June 2005. Rogozin apparently perceived Baburin's move as a direct claim for leadership over 'true nationalists', and expelled Baburin from the 'Rodina' parliamentary group the next day after the visit of the FN's delegation to the Duma. The media reported that Baburin had been expelled for 'divisive activities and undermining the prestige of the faction';[125] commenting on those developments in 2014, Baburin said that 'the official motivation' behind the decision to expel him from the 'Rodina' group was that he had invited Jean-Marie Le Pen to the State Duma.[126] Hardly being the main reason for the expulsion, Baburin's invitation to Le Pen was, however, most likely the last straw for Rogozin in his ongoing conflict with Baburin.

Baburin instrumentalised his relations with Le Pen in order to boost his own profile in the Russian ultranationalist milieu, and, hence, these relations were similar to those that Dugin, Glazyev and Zhirinovsky established in the 1990s as a means to strengthen their positions in Russia. However, Le Pen's visit to Moscow in 2005 also revealed the growing acceptance of the European far right in the Russian establishment. Symbolically, *Rossiyskaya Gazeta* (Russian Newspaper), an official Russian government daily newspaper, devoted two moderately sympathetic articles to cover Le Pen's visit to Moscow, although it had never covered the FN's previous visits to Russia.[127] *Rossiyskaya Gazeta* reported that Le Pen proposed – apparently following Thiriart's arguments – the creation of a continental union from Brest to Vladivostok that would replace the EU, and that his party 'rejected the policies that led to the weakening of Russia', as well as being against 'the globalist designs harboured under the supervision of one state'.[128] In 2005, similar ideas permeated the Russian mainstream, and it seemed natural that the Russian political establishment increasingly perceived the European far right as Russia's legitimate allies.

Conclusion

After the Second World War, the Soviets covertly collaborated with individual Western fascists for the purposes of intelligence gathering, as well as undermining and discrediting West European societies, but it was not until Perestroika and the opening to the West that the Russians started to openly cooperate with far-right politicians and organisations in the West. The first contacts with the far right in France, Italy, Spain, Germany, Belgium, the United States and some other countries were established by Russian ultranationalists Aleksandr Dugin, Vladimir Zhirinovsky and Sergey Glazyev. These three Russian politicians introduced European and American far-right publicists and activists into the Russian radical right-wing milieu, as well as turning them into a factor of Russian far-right politics: contacts with international counterparts increased the perceived political significance of these Russian ultranationalists.

For Western far-right activists such as Gerhard Frey or Lyndon LaRouche, cooperation with the Russians apparently promised domestic gains: Frey was deceived by Zhirinovsky's promises to 'return' the Kaliningrad region to Germany, while LaRouche assumed that Russia as the 'Eurasian land-bridge' would be useful to the US national interests. In general, however, Western far-right activists were interested in developing their Russian contacts as many of them believed that the fall of communism and the demise of the Soviet Union offered an opportunity of joining forces with the Russians against the United States. For European far-right activists such as Jean Thiriart, Alain de Benoist, Jean-Marie Le Pen and many others, the strategic cooperation with Russia was underpinned by theoretical considerations about the need for engaging Russia in the fight against liberal democracy – the considerations that gained currency in Third Positionist, National Bolshevik, New Right and other far-right circles after the Second World War.

Apart from these, as well as ideological, reasons, the cooperation between the Russian and European far right was sometimes also driven by purely pragmatic considerations – this was the case of Vladimir Zhirinovsky who apparently received money from his Western associates. Yet of all the Russian relatively important and successful far-right politicians, it was Zhirinovsky who was the first to offer an idea of using the Western far right as a tool of promoting Russian foreign policy in the West. With his experience as a paid lobbyist for Saddam Hussein's regime, Zhirinovsky implicitly suggested that Putin's regime could use Hussein's tactic and try to legitimise Russian politics on the international level through the far right. At the time when Zhirinovsky came up with this idea, that is during Putin's first presidential term, it was not supported by the Kremlin, but representatives of the Russian establishment started implementing it several years later.

The next chapter discusses the nature of Putin's regime and demonstrates that these were changes inside the regime that allowed it to claim political legitimacy from Western illiberal political forces, to lay groundwork for future cooperation with the Western far right, and to position Putin's Russia as a 'beacon of hope' of the far right's fight against liberal democracy.

Notes

1 See Nikolay Mitrokhin, *Russkaya partiya: Dvizhenie russkikh natsionalistov v SSSR, 1953–1985 gody* (Moscow: Novoe literaturnoe obozrenie, 2003).
2 Ibid., p. 242.
3 Barron, KGB, p. 104.
4 Vincent Jauvert, "Poutine et le FN: révélations sur les réseaux russes des Le Pen", *L'OBS*, 27 November (2014), http://tempsreel.nouvelobs.com/politique/20141024. OBS3131/poutine-et-le-fn-revelations-sur-les-reseaux-russes-des-le-pen.html
5 David Crawford, Marcus Bensmann, "Putin's Early Years", *CORRECT!V*, 30 July (2015), https://correctiv.org/en/investigations/system-putin/article/2015/07/30/putins-early-years/
6 Paul Hockenos, *Free to Hate: The Rise of the Right in Post-Communist Eastern Europe* (London: Routledge, 2013), p. 62.
7 On the collaboration between the East German state security services (Stasi) and right-wing extremists see Michael Wolffsohn, *Die Deutschland-Akte. Tatsachen und Legenden* (Munich: Edition Ferenczy bei Bruckmann, 1995).
8 See more on the early contacts between Dugin and the West European far right in Anton Shekhovtsov, "Alexander Dugin and the West European New Right,

1989–1994", in Laruelle (ed.), *Eurasianism and the European Far Right*, pp. 35–53. On Dugin and his ideology of neo-Eurasianism see Marlène Laruelle, Aleksandr Dugin: *A Russian Version of the European Radical Right?* (Washington: Woodrow Wilson International Center for Scholars, 2006); Anton Shekhovtsov, "The Palingenetic Thrust of Russian Neo-Eurasianism: Ideas of Rebirth in Aleksandr Dugin's Worldview", *Totalitarian Movements and Political Religions*, Vol. 9, No. 4 (2008), pp. 491–506; Andreas Umland, "Aleksandr Dugin's Transformation from a Lunatic Fringe Figure into a Mainstream Political Publicist, 1980–1998: A Case Study in the Rise of Late and Post-Soviet Russian Fascism", *Journal of Eurasian Studies*, Vol. 1, No. 2 (2010), pp. 144–152; Charles Clover, Black Wind, White Snow: *The Rise of Russia's New Nationalism* (New Haven: Yale University Press, 2016).

9 Alexander [Aleksandr] Dugin, *Eurasian Mission: An Introduction to Neo-Eurasianism* (London: Arktos, 2014), p. 54.

10 Ibid.

11 William Korey, *Russian Antisemitism, Pamyat, and the Demonology of Zionism* (London: Routledge, 2013), p. ix.

12 On René Guénon see Robin E. Waterfield, *René Guénon and the Future of the West: The Life and Writings of a 20th-Century Metaphysician* (Wellingborough: Crucible, 1987); Paul Chacornac, *The Simple Life of René Guénon* (Ghent: Sophia Perennis, 2001).

13 On Julius Evola see Paul Furlong, *Social and Political Thought of Julius Evola* (Abingdon: Routledge, 2011).

14 Clover, Black Wind, p. 167.

15 Xavier Casals, *Neonazis en España: de las audiciones wagnerianas a los skinheads* (1966–1995) (Barcelona: Grijalbo, 1995), p. 260. More on Serrano see chapter "Miguel Serrano and Esoteric Hitlerism", in Nicholas Goodrick-Clarke, *Black Sun: Aryan Cults, Esoteric Nazism, and the Politics of Identity* (New York: New York University Press, 2002), pp. 173–192.

16 Cited in Casals, *Neonazis en España*, p. 262.

17 Ibid.

18 Stéphane François, *Tradition, écologie et identité. Études sur la Nouvelle Droite et ses dissidences*, forthcoming.

19 Franko Freda has been a follower of Julius Evola and one of the most notorious Italian fascist terrorists who was involved in the Piazza Fontana bombing in 1969. See also Furlong, *Social and Political Thought of Julius Evola*, pp. 16, 100–101. Dugin described Freda as "a renowned Italian Traditionalist", who "served an absurd and unjust sentence" for his dissent, see "Professor-mudzhahid", *Mily Angel*, No. 1 (1991), http://angel.org.ru/1/mutipred.html.

20 Goodrick-Clarke, *Black Sun*, p. 105. Apparently, Mutti converted to Islam following the example of Guénon.

21 Aleksandr Dughin [Aleksandr Dugin], *Continente Russia* (Parma: Edizioni All'insegna del Veltro, 1991). In his biography, Dugin incorrectly wrote that this book had been published in 1990.

22 Igor' Safarevic [Igor Shafarevich], *La setta mondialista contro la Russia* (Parma: Edizioni All'insegna del Veltro, 1991). On Shafarevich see Krista Berglund, *The Vexing Case of Igor Shafarevich, a Russian Political Thinker* (Basel: Birkhäuser, 2012).

23 Camus, "A Long-Lasting Friendship", pp. 79–96 (85).

24 " 'Entretien avec Alexandre Douguine, éditeur traditionaliste à Moscou'. Propos recueillis par Robert Steuckers et Arnaud Dubreuil", *Vouloir*, Nos. 71–72 (janvier–février 1991), pp. 15–18 (15).

25 "Dugin Aleksandr Gel'yevich (r. 1962)", Pravaya.ru, 22 February (2006), www. pravaya.ru/ludi/451/6742.

26 Alexandre Douguine [Aleksandr Dugin], "L'empire soviétique et les nationalismes à l'époque de la perestroika", in *Nation et Empire. Histoire et concept. Actes du XXIVe colloque national du GRECE*, Paris, 24 mars 1991 (Paris: GRECE, 1991).

27 "GRU" stands for Glavnoe Razvedyvatel'noe Upravleniye (Main Intelligence Directorate), the Soviet and, later, Russian foreign military intelligence of the armed forces.

28 Aleksandr Dugin, "Vozvraschayas' k 'Velikoy voyne kontinentov'", Elementy, No. 3 (1993), p. 43. "Velikaya voyna kontinentov" was published in Dugin's book on conspiracy theories, see Aleksandr Dugin, Konspirologiya (Moscow: Arktogeya, 1993).

29 On Russian Eurasianism see Dmitry Shlapentokh (ed.), Russia between East and West: Scholarly Debates on Eurasianism (Boston: Brill, 2007); Marlène Laruelle, Russian Eurasianism: An Ideology of Empire (Baltimore: Johns Hopkins University Press, 2008).

30 Umland, "Aleksandr Dugin's Transformation from a Lunatic Fringe Figure into a Mainstream Political Publicist, 1980–1998", p. 147.

31 Despite the name of the party, the ideology of the Communist Party of the Russian Federation can be interpreted as right-wing extremist, see Andreas Umland, "Toward an Uncivil Society? Contextualizing the Decline of Post-Soviet Russian Parties of the Extreme Right Wing", Demokratizatsiya, Vol. 10, No. 3 (2002), pp. 362–391.

32 "Natsional'noe i sotsial'noe (Krugly stol v gazete 'Den')", Arktogeya, http://arcto.ru/article/1343

33 Clover, Black Wind, p. 201. According to Clover, Dugin's teaching materials then formed the basis of his seminal work Osnovy geopolitiki (The Foundations of Geopolitics), see Aleksandr Dugin, Osnovy geopolitiki. Geopoliticheskoe buduschee Rossii (Moscow: Arktogeya, 1997).

34 "Three Interviews with Alain de Benoist", Telos, No. 98–99 (1993), pp. 173–207. De Benoist's unwillingness to pursue relations with Dugin was reinforced in summer 1993, when the editorial in Le Monde condemned de Benoist for cooperating with the Russian "red-brown" groups, because the alliance between militant Communists and neo-fascists benefited the chaos that reigned in Russia, see Roger-Pol Droit, "La confusion des idées", Le Monde, 13 juillet (1993) pp. 1, 9. Le Monde's editorial appeared in support of "The Appeal to Vigilance" signed by forty intellectuals who accused "writers, publishers and managers of the print and audio-visual media" of being not sufficiently suspicious about – and, hence, legitimising – the far right views which they transmitted, see "L'appel à la vigilance lancé par quarante intellectuels", Le Monde, 13 juillet (1993), p. 8. However, de Benoist and Dugin re-established cooperation around 2005.

35 Claudio Mutti, "The Struggle of Jean Thiriart", Eurasia: Rivista di studi geopolitici, 23 February (2012), www.eurasia-rivista.org/the-struggle-of-jean-thiriart/13850/.

36 Ibid.

37 Aleksandr Dugin, "Sumerki geroyev", in Aleksandr Dugin, Konservativnaya Revolyutsiya (Moscow: Arktogeya, 1994), http://arcto.ru/article/24

38 A copy of the letter was reproduced in Marco Montanari, "Il rosso e il nero: Zjuganov tra i nazisti e Huntington", Limes: Rivista italiana di geopolitica, No. 4 (1998), pp. 157–168 (165).

39 Ibid., p. 165.

40 Marco Battarra, "Una visita a Mosca", Aurora, No. 5 (1993), http://aurora.altervista.org/05battarra.htm

41 On the NBP see Stephen D. Shenfield, Russian Fascism: Traditions, Tendencies, Movements (New York: M.E. Sharpe, 2001), especially the chapter "Dugin, Limonov, and the National-Bolshevik Party", pp.190–219; Markus Mathyl, "The National-Bolshevik Party and Arctogaia: Two Neo-Fascist Groupuscules in the Post-Soviet Political Space", Patterns of Prejudice, Vol. 36, No. 3 (2002), pp. 62–76.

42 Xavier Casals, "La ultraderecha española: ¿Una modernización imposible?", in Manuel Pérez Ledesma (ed.), Los riesgos para la democracia. Fascismo y neofascismo (Madrid: Iglesias, 1997), p. 192 (171–194); "Rusia. Declaración de la oposición revolucionaria", Tribuna de Europa, No. 7 (1994), pp. 6–7.

43 Rodríguez Jiménez, "Antisemitism and the Extreme Right in Spain". See also a comparison of the NBP and Alternativa Europea in Anna Bebenina, "New Extreme Rightist Doctrines in Post-Cold War Western Europe and Russia: The Paradox of Similarity", in Dave Carter (ed.), *Future in the Making: Opportunities . . . Choices . . . Consequences . . .* (Budapest: Civic Education Project, 2001), pp. 88–99.

44 Eduard Limonov, *Moya politicheskaya biografiya* (Saint-Petersburg: Amfora, 2002), p. 25.

45 Dugin speaks several European languages, including French, English, German and Italian.

46 The name of the journal seems to be a clear reference to Ahnenerbe (Ancestral heritage), an institute in Nazi Germany that focused on the history of the Aryan race.

47 On this group see Victor Shnirelman, " 'Tsepnoy pes rasy': divannaya rasologiya kak zashchitnitsa 'belogo cheloveka' ", in Aleksandr Verkhovsky (ed.), *Verkhi i nizy russkogo natsionalizma* (Moscow: Tsentr Sova, 2007), pp. 188–208; Aleksandr Kuzmin, " 'Novye pravye' v sovremennoy Rossii: na primere zhurnala Ateney", *Forum noveyshey vostochnoevropeyskoy istorii i kultury*, No. 2 (2010), pp. 115–135. www1.ku-eichstaett. de/ZIMOS/forum/docs/forumruss14/5Kuzmin.pdf; Richard Arnold, Ekaterina Romanova, "The 'White World's Future?': An Analysis of the Russian Far Right", *Journal for the Study of Radicalism*, Vol. 7, No. 1 (2013), pp. 79–107.

48 " 'Nasledie predkov' v Gosudarstvennoy Dume", *Nasledie predkov*, No. 5 (1998), pp. 4–6 (5).

49 On Zhirinovsky and his party see Shenfield, *Russian Fascism*, especially the chapter "Zhirinovsky and the Liberal-Democratic Party of Russia", pp. 85–112; Andreas Umland, *Vladimir Zhirinovskii in Russian Politics: Three Approaches to the Emergence of the Liberal-Democratic Party of Russia 1990–1993*, Dissertation, Promotionsausschuß FB Geschichtswissenschaft (Berlin: Freie Universität Berlin, 1997); Alan J. Koman, "The Last Surge to the South: The New Enemies of Russia in the Rhetoric of Zhirinovsky", *Studies in Conflict & Terrorism*, Vol. 19, No. 3 (1996), pp. 279–327; Anton Shekhovtsov, Andreas Umland, "Vladimir Zhirinovsky and the LDPR", *Russian Analytical Digest*, No. 102 (2011), pp. 14–16.

50 Umland, *Vladimir Zhirinovskii in Russian Politics*, pp. 97–103.

51 See Eduard Makarevich, "Filipp Bobkov – professional 'kholodnoy voyny' na vnutrennem fronte' ", in Eduard Makarevich, *Politicheskiy sysk: Ofitsery i dzhentel'meny: Istoriya, sud'by, versii* (Moscow: Algoritm, 2002), pp. 173–227; Aleksandr Yakovlev, *Sumerki* (Moscow: Materik, 2003).

52 Limonov details Zhirinovsky's meeting with Le Pen, whom Limonov himself had not met before, in Eduard Limonov, *Limonov protiv Zhirinovskogo* (Moscow: Konets veka, 1994), pp. 134–139.

53 Victor Parfenov, Marina Sergeeva, "Sowing Nationalist Grapes of Wrath", *Russia Today*, 7 August (1998), www.tol.org/client/article/5275-russia-sowing-nationalist-grapes-of-wrath.html

54 Limonov, *Limonov protiv Zhirinovskogo*, p. 138.

55 Danila Dubshin, "U nikh uzhe sto millionov polozhili", *Limonka*, No. 33 (1996), http://limonka.nbp-info.com/033_article_1226837526.html.

56 Cas Mudde, *The Ideology of the Extreme Right* (Manchester: Manchester University Press, 2000), p. 60.

57 Umland, *Vladimir Zhirinovskii in Russian Politics*, p. 201.

58 Gerhard Hertel, *Die DVU – Gefahr von Rechtsaußen* (Munich: Hanns-Seidel-Stiftung e.V., 1998), p. 27; Vadim Rossman, *Russian Intellectual Antisemitism in the Post-Communist Era* (Lincoln: University of Nebraska Press for the Vidal Sassoon International Center for the Study of Antisemitism, 2002), p. 20.

59 "Austrian Police Seek More Nazis for Bombings", *Searchlight*, No. 224 (1994), p. 15.

60 "Zhirinovsky's Party and German People's Union Sign Friendship Accord", *BBC Summary of World Broadcasts*, 10 August (1994).

61 Leonid Mlechin, "Vechernie posidelki v nemetskoy kontrrazvedke", *Izvestiya*, No. 235, 10 December (1995). The claim that the LDPR was provided financial assistance by Frey is supported by other sources, see Umland, *Vladimir Zhirinovskii in Russian Politics*, pp. 202–203; Michi Ebata, "The Internationalization of the Extreme Right", in Aurel Braun, Stephen Scheinberg (eds.), *The Extreme Right: Freedom and Security at Risk* (Boulder: Westview Press, 1997), pp. 220–249 (225).

62 Quoted in Craig R. Whitney, "Russian Nationalist Stirs Up a Storm in Germany", *The New York Times*, 23 December (1993), www.nytimes.com/1993/12/23/world/russian-nationalist-stirs-up-a-storm-in-germany.html

63 Vladimir Zhirinovsky, *Posledniy brosok na Yug* (Moscow: Izdanie Liberal'no-demokraticheskoy partii Rossii, 2007), p. 42. The book was originally published in 1993.

64 "Przyjazd Władimira Żyrinowskiego na I Kongres Polskiego Frontu Narodowego", *Kronika RP* (1994), www.kronikarp.pl/szukaj,3444,tag-690583,strona-1

65 Umland, *Vladimir Zhirinovskii in Russian Politics*, pp. 202–203.

66 Richard E. Harwood, *Did Six Million Really Die? The True at Last* (Richmand: Historical Review Press, 1974).

67 Lee, *The Beast Reawakens*, p. 261.

68 Ibid., p. 310.

69 Ernst Zündel, "My Impressions of the New Russia: Is a 'National Socialist' Russia Emerging?", *The Journal of Historical Review*, Vol. 15, No. 5 (1995), pp. 2–8 (7–8).

70 "Germany's Secret Balkans Plan", *Searchlight*, No. 205 (1992), pp. 12–16 (14).

71 "Nebenberuf V-Mann", *Der Spiegel*, No. 28 (1995), www.spiegel.de/spiegel/print/d-9201977.html

72 Sigrid Averesch, "Angeklagter Althans war kein V-Mann", *Berliner Zeitung*, 2 August (1995), www.berliner-zeitung.de/archiv/bayerischer-verfassungsschuetzer-als-zeuge-vor-gericht-angeklagter-althans-war-kein-v-mann,10810590,8983656.html

73 Already at the time of Althans' trial, former BfV agents in the German neo-Nazi movement claimed that as many as 10 per cent of all German neo-Nazi activists were state informants, see "German Magazine Names Althans as Spook", *Searchlight*, No. 242 (1995), p. 17.

74 Andreas Förster, "Ein SED-Vermögensverwalter findet zu den Nationalisten Schirinowski – Suche nach Finanziers und Partnern im Parlament: 'Verschweizertes' Geld aus dunklen Kanälen", *Berliner Zeitung*, 6 January (1994). See more on the relations between Werner Girke and the LDPR in Umland, *Vladimir Zhirinovskii in Russian Politics*, pp. 204–205.

75 Andrew Gumbel, "Zhirinovsky Link in Arms Racket", *The Independent*, 2 June (1996), www.independent.co.uk/news/zhirinovsky-link-in-arms-racket-1335019.html

76 Ganser, NATO's Secret Armies, pp. 73–75.

77 Rudolf M. Rizman, "Radical Right Politics in Slovenia", in Sabrina P. Ramet (ed.), *The Radical Right in Central and Eastern Europe since 1989* (University Park: Pennsylvania State University Press, 1999), pp. 147–170 (152).

78 Ognjen Pribićević, "Changing Fortunes of the Serbian Radical Right", in Ramet (ed.), *The Radical Right in Central and Eastern Europe since 1989*, pp. 193–211 (208).

79 Pavel Negoitsa, "Bossi v vostorge ot Zhirinovskogo", *Trud*, No. 210, 12 November (1997); Bull, Gilbert, *The Lega Nord and the Northern Question in Italian Politics*, p. 112.

80 Chip Berlet, Matthew Nemiroff Lyons, *Right-wing Populism in America: Too Close for Comfort* (New York: Guilford Press, 2000), p. 273.

81 Leonard Weinberg, "The American Radical Right: Exit, Voice and Violence", in Peter H. Merkl, Leonard Weinberg (eds.), *Encounters with the Radical Right* (Boulder: Westview, 1993), pp. 185–203 (198).

82 I am grateful to Timothy Snyder for pointing this out to me.

83 Chip Berlet, "The United States: Messianism, Apocalypticism, and Political Religion", in Roger Griffin, Robert Mallett, John Tortorice (eds.), *The Sacred in Twentieth-Century Politics: Essays in Honour of Professor Stanley G. Payne* (Basingstoke: Palgrave Macmillan, 2008), pp. 221–257 (231).

84 Webster G. Tarpley, "Is the British Oligarchy Preparing to Balkanize the US?", *Executive Intelligence Review*, Vol. 17, No. 18 (1990), pp. 20–27.

85 See, for example, Criton Zoakos, "The Surfacing of Holy Mother Rus: The Russian Orthodox Church", *Executive Intelligence Review*, Vol. 10, No. 37 (1983), pp. 18–9.

86 Lyndon LaRouche, "Dealing with the Russians' Decisive Cultural Inferiority", *Executive Intelligence Review*, Vol. 13, No. 39 (1986), pp. 36–47 (44).

87 "Test of Fire", CBS, 12 April (1988), www.youtube.com/watch?v=FXOncp24Ofk

88 "The Power of Reason", 1989, YouTube, www.youtube.com/watch?v=FXOncp 24Ofk

89 From 1989 until early 1994, LaRouche was imprisoned for mail fraud conspiracy, so his trip to Russia was one of the first foreign visits after five years in prison.

90 "LaRouche's 40-Year Record: A New International Economic Order", The Lyndon LaRouche Political Action Committee, http://larouchepac.com/new-economic-order

91 Sergei [Sergey] Glazyev, *Genocide: Russia and the New World Order* (Washington: Executive Intelligence Review, 1999), pp. 24, 85.

92 Ibid., p. 129.

93 Lyndon H. LaRouche, "Russia is Eurasia's Keystone Economy", *Executive Intelligence Review*, Vol. 25, No. 13 (1998), pp. 36–52 (43). See also The Eurasian Land-Bridge: Locomotive for World Development. EIR Special Report (Washington: EIR News Service, 1997).

94 LaRouche, "Russia is Eurasia's Keystone Economy", p. 44.

95 Galina Kozhevnikova, Anton Shekhovtsov et al. *Radikal'ny russkiy natsionalizm: struktury, idei, litsa* (Moscow: Tsentr "Sova"), p. 264.

96 Apart from the LDPR, Chaboche also kept contacts with Russian neo-Nazis from the RNE, see Daniel Schweizer (dir.), *White Terror* (Zürich: Pelicanfilms, 2006).

97 Valeriy Panyushkin, "Natsionalisticheskiy internatsional sozdan v Moskve", *Kommersant-Daily*, No. 166, 16 September (2002), p. 4; "Treffen in Moskau", *Antifaschistische Nachrichten*, No. 23, 7 November (2002), p. 2.

98 Umland, *Vladimir Zhirinovskii in Russian Politics*, pp. 196–198.

99 Peter Baker, Susan Glasser, *Kremlin Rising: Vladimir Putin's Russia and the End of Revolution* (New York: Scribner, 2005), p. 219. See also Ariel Cohen, "Russia, Islam, and the War on Terrorism: An Uneasy Future", *Demokratizatsiya*, Vol. 10, No. 4 (2002), pp. 556–567 (563).

100 Baker, Glasser, Kremlin Rising, p. 219.

101 The United Nations Security Council imposed economic sanctions against Iraq on 6 August 1990 after Iraq's failed attempt to annex Kuwait. The sanctions were largely lifted in 2003 after the fall of Hussein's regime.

102 *Comprehensive Report of the Special Advisor to the DCI on Iraq's WMD, with Addendums (Duelfer Report)*. Vol. 1 (Washington: Central Intelligence Agency, 2005), p. 39.

103 Independent Inquiry Committee into the United Nations Oil-for-Food Programme [Paul A. Volcker, Richard J. Goldstone, Mark Pieth], *Manipulation of the Oil-for-Food Programme by the Iraqi Regime*, https://web.archive.org/web/2005110101 2944/www.iic-offp.org/documents/IIC%20Final%20Report%2027Oct2005.pdf, pp. 29–30.

104 "Neo-Nazi Mercenaries Sign on for Desert War", *Searchlight*, No. 189 (1991), pp. 5–6 (5).

105 Pierre Birnbaum, "The French Radical Right: From Anti-Semitic Zionism to Anti-Semitic Anti-Zionism", *Journal of Israeli History: Politics, Society, Culture*, Vol. 25, No. 1 (2006), pp. 161–174 (169).

106 "Neo-Nazi Mercenaries Sign on for Desert War", p. 5.
107 "Exposed – Nazis' 'Foreign Legion' Deal with Saddam", *Searchlight*, No. 195 (1991), pp. 3, 7.
108 It should be noted that Kühnen had AIDS – he died a few months after the Gulf War – and was hardly capable of taking part in the fighting. Thus, as a self-styled commander of the "Anti-Zionist Legion", he would only receive money as a mediator.
109 "Editorial: Out of Control", *Searchlight*, No. 188 (1991), p. 2.
110 Haider was a chairman of the FPÖ in 1986–2000.
111 Michael Nikbakhsh, Ulla Kramar-Schmid, "Jörg Haiders geheime Geldgeschäfte mit dem irakischen Diktator Saddam Hussein", *Profil*, 7 August (2010), www.profil.at/home/joerg-haiders-geldgeschaefte-diktator-saddam-hussein-274862
112 "SOS Enfants d'Irak", *Index des ONG*, https://web.archive.org/web/20110827112629/http://observatoire-humanitaire.org/fusion.php?l=FR&id=28
113 Mark Hunter, "Nationalism Unleashed", *Transitions*, No. 5 (1998), pp. 18–28.
114 "Patrioty vsekh stran ob'yedinyayutsya", *LDPR*, No. 2 (2003), p. 3.
115 Panyushkin, "Natsionalisticheskiy internatsional sozdan v Moskve", p. 4.
116 "V. Zhirinovsky: Vsemirny Kongress patriotov – eto rychag vliyaniya Moskvy na mirovuyu politiku", *Tsentrazia*, 18 January (2003), www.centrasia.ru/newsA.php?st=1042901340
117 Viktoriya Sokolova, "Zhirinovsky verbuet inostrannykh patriotov", *Izvestiya*, No. 73, 25 April (2006), p. 4.
118 Igor Dmitriev, "Zhire krug", *Nasha versiya*, No. 17, 1 May (2006), p. 5.
119 José Pedro Zúquete, "The New Frontlines of Right-Wing Nationalism", *Journal of Political Ideologies*, Vol. 20, No. 1 (2015), pp. 69–85 (74).
120 Dzhin Vronskaya, "Le Pen: 'Ya khotel by vstretit'sya s Putinym' ", *Sovershenno sekretno*, No. 11/162, 1 November (2002), www.sovsekretno.ru/articles/id/916/
121 "Zhan-Mari Le Pen, Predsedatel' Natsional'nogo Fronta Frantsii", *Vremya*, No. 9, 6 March (2003), http://vremyababurin.narod.ru/Num9_2003/Num9_2003.html#9
122 "Sergey Baburin i Zh.-M. Le Pen ob'yedinyayut patrioticheskie partii Evropy", *Vremya,* No. 20, 15 May (2003), http://vremyababurin.narod.ru/Num20_2003/Num20_2003.html#1
123 Wilson, *Virtual Politics*, p. 112; Yury Korgunyuk, "Rossiyskie politicheskie partii zimoy-vesnoy 2004 goda", *Politiya*, No. 1 (2004), pp. 243–278 (254–255).
124 Marlène Laruelle, *In the Name of the Nation: Nationalism and Politics in Contemporary Russia* (New York: Palgrave Macmillan, 2009), p. 103.
125 Elena Bekhchanova, "Sergeya Baburina lishili 'Rodiny' ", *Izvestiya*, No. 109, 29 June (2005), p. 3.
126 Sergey Ryazanov, "Nashi storonniki v Evrope", *Svobodnaya pressa*, 17 May (2014), http://svpressa.ru/society/article/87614/
127 Tamara Shkel', "Dumskie patrioty priglasili Le Pena", *Rossiyskaya Gazeta*, No. 137, 28 June (2005), p. 9; Yevgeniy Shestakov, "Chelovek, kotory ne vnikaet v nyuansy", *Rossiyskaya Gazeta*, No. 139, 30 June (2005), p. 8.
128 Shkel', "Dumskie patrioty priglasili Le Pena", p. 9.

3

PUTIN'S RUSSIA, AN AUTHORITARIAN KLEPTOCRACY WITH A TWIST

Introduction

In the context of our discussion of the relations between Russia and the Western far right, the previous two chapters portrayed two contrasting realities. One reality is that of particular far-right groups embracing the Soviet Union that, in its turn, sometimes covertly exploits them for various pragmatic purposes. The second reality is that of Western far-right activists openly cooperating with the post-Soviet 'red-brown' opposition to Russia's President Boris Yeltsin. If one had to choose pictures to describe the two realities, they might want to choose a picture of smoke and mirrors for the first reality, and that of men dreaming of a world conquest sitting in a poorly kept room – for the second. How does then one understand a picture depicting a third reality, a Western far-right politician publicly shaking hands with a head of the Russian state?

Such a picture, let alone the reality behind it, was unimaginable during the Cold War or even 10 years before the leader of the Italian far-right LN's Matteo Salvini and Russia's President Vladimir Putin talked during a break at the Asia-Europe summit in Milan on 17 October 2014 and then – both smiling – posed for photos.

What has changed in these 10 years? The two previous chapters demonstrated that particular elements of the Western far right have always favoured Russia – whether Soviet or post-Soviet – so the 'variable' of the Western far right has remained relatively constant. Hence, one can suggest that it is Russia that has changed over the 10 years, or, more precisely, Putin's regime has.

One explanation of the change is that there is nothing unnatural in the contemporary relations between Putin's Russia and the Western far right, because the former is allegedly a fascist or, at least, a radical right regime. Zbigniew Brzezinski was arguably the first prominent commentator who compared Putin to Benito Mussolini as early as 2004:

The Fascist regime evoked national greatness, discipline, and exalted myths of an allegedly glorious past. Similarly, Putin is trying to blend the traditions of the Cheka[1] (Lenin's Gestapo, where his own grandfather started his career), with Stalin's wartime leadership, with Russian Orthodoxy's claims to the status of the Third Rome, with Slavophile dreams of a single large Slavic state ruled from the Kremlin.[2]

A number of other commentators and officials echoed Brzezinski's argument. For example, claiming that Putin was 'a Russified Pinochet or Franco', Nicholas Kristof maintained that Putin was 'not guiding Russia toward free-market democracy, but into fascism'.[3] Former CIA Director James Woolsey, in a 2005 interview, said that 'the Russian administration under Putin' was 'generally behaving more and more like a fascist government'.[4] In a similar manner, Putin's Russia is fascist or fascistoid according to Alexander Motyl whose own peculiar definition of fascist states is 'authoritarian states that glorify strength and vigor in the ruling elites and whose subject populations also glorify strength and vigor in the ruling elites'.[5]

Marcel van Herpen has taken a more balanced approach to defining Putin's regime and argued that Putinism 'could certainly not be subsumed under existing categories' and 'seemed to present a system of its kind, a totally new political formation that challenged existing political models'.[6] Still, van Herpen defined Putinism with a reference to the largely historical phenomena as 'a right-wing radical system' and 'a hybrid mixture of Mussolinian Fascism, Bonapartism, and Berlusconism'.[7]

It seems, however, misleading and unhelpful to define Putin's regime as fascist or even radical right-wing. First, the current system in Moscow does not qualify as fascist in the academic sense. Commenting on the application of the term 'fascism' to Putin's Russia, Roger Griffin, who posits fascist ideology as a form of revolutionary ultranationalism, argues:

> From the perspective of comparative fascist studies Putin's Russia is not fascist. By this, I mean it is not officially or even practically a single party state using mass organizations to create a New Russian man, and it does not use state power to engineer an alternative form of modernity on the basis of a revolutionary ideology of racist ultranationalism. Putin is a pragmatist, a master of *Realpolitik* without a utopian vision of a new type of modern state. He shows no interest in using the power he has accumulated to erect a modernist totalitarian state devoted to carrying out an anthropological and temporal revolution. Hence, Putin is not technically a fascist. There are many ways human rights and democracy can be undermined and assaulted, not just by fascism. So can we just leave fascism out of the discussion and concentrate on the uniqueness of the contemporary Russian state's corruption of democracy and the dangers it poses to world peace with its expansionism and alliances?[8]

Andreas Umland has criticised Motyl's notion of 'Putin's fascist Russia' from the perspective of conceptual pragmatism and terminological consistency stating that the issue with Motyl's interpretation is that ' "fascism" is conceptualized in a way that would lead to a general augmentation of "fascisms" in contemporary history, and thus to a loss of the heuristic, classificatory and communicative value of the term'.[9]

Moreover, the application of the terms 'fascism' or 'far right' to Putin's regime is ineffective for understanding the growing relations between Russia and the Western far right. If 'Putin's fascist Russia' is an explanation for this type of relations, then how does one explain the Kremlin's cooperation with Western left-wing or liberal-democratic political parties and politicians?

While the right-wing consolidation of Putin's regime in the recent years cannot be ignored, one of the essential arguments of this book proceeds from the underlying premise that Putin's ultimate aim is not the revival of Russia, restoration of the Russian empire, or the well-being of the Russian nation, but rather the preservation of the existing patrimonial regime at any cost. Putin's Russia is intrinsically an authoritarian kleptocracy that nevertheless seeks to be considered a peculiarly Russian form of democracy in order to gain internal and external legitimacy. The Kremlin's violent crackdown on the political opposition at home and aggressive foreign policy often expressed in military action against neighbouring states – rather than being attributes of a fascist, imperialist system – are instead results of Moscow's increasing inability to secure socio-economically based legitimacy and preserve the regime by any other means, either through soft power, diplomacy or even soft coercion.[10]

This chapter discusses the nature of Putin's regime and argues that, since the end of Putin's first presidential term, he started to feel that his authority incurred a deficit of international and domestic legitimacy. The resulting feeling of unsustainability eventually locked Moscow in a spiral of self-fulfilling prophecies: the more repressive Putin's corrupt regime became against the largely imaginary threats, the less legitimacy it enjoyed internationally, the more threatened Putin felt. This chapter also shows that, since Putin's second term, Moscow increasingly positioned itself as a power whose legitimacy derived from *alternative*, illiberal political ideas, some of which clearly originate from the far right. Finally, this chapter 'gives floor' to Western far-right activists and ideologues, and looks at their perceptions of Putin's regime as they have embraced Moscow's turn towards illiberal sources of legitimacy as a means of consolidating and preserving Putin's regime.

The Potemkin state

As mentioned in the Introduction, the corrupt organisation of the Russian state started to form – or perhaps reinvented itself in the new 'democratic' setting on the basis of the bribery practices of the Soviet Union – already in the 1990s. And already during Putin's first presidential term (2000–2004), it became obvious that his regime – although still corrupt[11] – differed from that of President Yeltsin.

If Yeltsin's rule had introduced powerful political technologists who were fighting against each other, during Putin's rule, 'the Kremlin established a monopoly of manipulation. . . . Instead of politics being a competition of rival puppet-masters', the Kremlin, or more specifically the Presidential Administration, became *the* political technologist.[12] Putin's Presidential Administration started building a Potemkin state: a pyramid-like kleptocratic system based on informal networks with Putin at the top – a system that would still present itself as a state but where state organs degenerated into imitations of real institutions.[13] The formal executive would be supplanted by a personified system of power; the parliament would become a rubber-stamp assembly; the power of the judiciary would only be directed against the opponents of the regime or presumptuous loyalists.

Reinstating state control over major mass media in Russia was the cornerstone of Putin's rise to authoritarian power. The freedom of press was far from ideal under Yeltsin, but these were media tycoons, or oligarchs, rather than the state, who set the political agenda for the media resources they owned and/or controlled. Putin understood well the power of the mass media, especially the major TV channels. Hence, Putin spent his first term crushing disloyal oligarchs Vladimir Gusinsky and Boris Berezovsky who controlled the most popular NTV and ORT TV channels respectively. Gradually, Putin re-established state control over all major mass media in Russia. Putin's regime used repressions, including 'lawsuits, bureaucratic obstruction, crude intimidation, and hostile corporate takeovers', to coerce independent voices into silence.[14] As Ben Judah puts it, 'TV editors would get calls from "up top" setting the agenda; the secret services would call reporters to tell them they had gone too far, and journalists were frequently murdered'.[15]

Other oligarchs, not necessarily connected to the media, were subdued: 'Putin wanted the oligarchs to understand that they would have rents from [their] companies only as a reward for loyal state service. But for an oligarch loyal to Putin there would be no restrictions on the profits that could be realized'.[16] Subdued oligarchs became Putin's 'own pockets' – he would turn to them to finance various projects.

Behind the suppression of the oligarchs lay Putin's belief that he would not have been able to preserve the regime had he not put under control those who could have funded rival political forces. The last prominent oligarch to be crushed during Putin's first term was the richest person in Russia and head of the YUKOS corporation Mikhail Khodorkovsky who dared to support political forces that were opposed to Putin. The arrest and subsequent imprisonment of Khodorkovsky was the last warning to the oligarchs who were presented with a choice:

> either to support the regime in all its undertakings, or retire to the sidelines.
> No longer can Russia's business elite establish their own parties and engage
> in open criticism of the government. . . . In this new social order there is
> no place for opposition, unpredictable elections, or insubordinate nouveaux
> riches . . . .[17]

Apart from the increasing centralisation of state power, suppression of the oligarchs and major mass media, an important difference from Yeltsin's era was the gradual rise of the so-called *siloviki*[18] – former or current representatives of the 'force institutions' such as the KGB, Federal Security Department (FSB, post-Soviet successor of the KGB),[19] Ministry of Internal Affairs, Ministry of Defence, Foreign Intelligence Service, Main Intelligence Directorate (or GRU), Federal Guard Service, Federal Drug Control Service and so on. In 1999, before Putin became President, he raised a toast at an FSB banquet: 'Dear Comrades, I would like to announce to you that the group of FSB agents that you sent to work undercover in the government has accomplished the first part of its mission'.[20] Whether Putin was joking or not, the reality was that, by the end of Yeltsin's rule, 17.4 per cent of the ruling elite were represented by the *siloviki*, yet every fourth member of Putin's ruling elite was a *silovik* by 2002.[21] By 2008, the share of the *siloviki* in the ruling elite would rise to 31.5 per cent.[22]

Already in autumn 2003, Gleb Pavlovsky, one of the main political technologists of Putin's regime who was opposed to the *siloviki*, voiced concern over their rise. He warned that they were forming 'a parallel centre of authority' that would subsequently replace the official one, and called it 'a creeping coup'. In his view, one of the major threats of the rise of the *siloviki* was the redistribution of property in their favour on the pretext of defending the state interests: 'the destroyed oligarchic system is being replaced by the new "force" oligarchy' that 'focuses on using the levers of the state and administrative resources for achieving its goals'.[23]

Pavlovsky belonged to the second group within the ruling elite that is sometimes called 'liberals' or 'system liberals' but there has never been anything deeply liberal about them, at least not in the political sense: they fully participated in the formation of Putin's kleptocratic authoritarian regime and did not oppose the curtailing of democratic freedoms. Prominent researchers of Russian political elites Olga Kryshtanovskaya and Stephen White argue that, rather than 'liberals', this group is best called 'non-siloviki' as they are 'officials with an economic or legal background who are not known to have an association with the force ministries'.[24] In 2003, members of the non-*siloviki* group had all the reasons to be concerned, especially if they initially failed to realise that Putin's own background in the KGB and FSB implied a particular mode of operation and thinking, or failed to see that security and military officials 'began to move into economic and political life in unprecedented numbers' *immediately* after Putin's election in 2000.[25] The *siloviki* did not form 'a parallel centre of authority'; rather, they were, to large degree, *the* authority.

It was already during Putin's first presidential term when the core of the *siloviki* group was formed: Igor Sechin, Viktor Ivanov, Sergey Ivanov, Nikolay Patrushev, Sergey Lavrov, Sergey Shoygu, Sergey Naryshkin, Vladimir Yakunin, Sergey Chemezov, Rashid Nurgaliyev, Mikhail Fradkov, Viktor Cherkesov and some others. The overwhelming majority of them have remained important members of the ruling elite to date, and have occupied prominent positions in the economic sphere. As Russian economic expert Vladislav Inozemtsev argues, huge revenues from oil and other Russian major Russian exports

> allowed Putin's power elite [i.e. *siloviki*] to commit practically any admin-
> istrative error, tolerate unprofessional decision making, and engage in all kinds
> of acts of favoritism, as oil revenues pushed the country forward despite ever-
> growing corruption. Starting in the critical period of 2003–04, public office
> became regarded as a special kind of 'business' that would bring the biggest
> amount of cash with a minimum of risk and responsibility. And Russia's
> president, whose close friends had already turned into oligarchs, made it
> repeatedly clear – using increasing bellicose terms – that he would not tolerate
> any attempt to change the country's course.[26]

Shevtsova, too, notes that 'Putin's regime that relies on the power structures and their control over property is genetically repressive and incapable of modernisation', while the 'praetorian [i.e. *silovik*] character of the authorities makes a struggle for its survival more violent and fierce'.[27] Possibly, already during his first presidential term, Putin and the *siloviki* arrived at a decision to never give up power, and were ready to do everything to preserve the existing regime. However, it would be inaccurate to perceive the *siloviki* as a monolithic group; rather, as specialist in Russian security issues Mark Galeotti argues, military, security and intelligence services 'are often divided, competitive, and poorly tasked'.[28] Moreover, Putin 'is presumably well aware of the danger in giving any one agency too much power', and 'he plays agencies off against each other, encouraging rivalries'.[29]

The *siloviki* – due to their education in the military and security institutions permeated with the spirit of the Cold War – were raised on the Soviet, anti-Western narratives, so it might have been expected that their rise would immediately bring anti-Westernism to the heart of Putin's foreign policy. This did not happen in 2000–2004, because the increasing economic integration of post-Soviet Russia into the globalised world and the opportunities that the West offered to the Russian elites – ranging from money laundering to education for their children in the world's best universities – dampened their intrinsic anti-Westernism. However, the 'wartime mindset' has been an intrinsic feature of the *siloviki*: 'even before the worsening of relations with the West, they appear genuinely to have felt that Russia was under serious, even existential threat, which demanded extreme responses'.[30]

The period 2000–2004 was Putin's personal political honeymoon with the West in general and the United States in particular. A first significant degradation of democracy in Russia was evident already in 2000–2001, but US President George Bush would still say in 2001 that he 'was able to get a sense of [Putin's] soul' and found him a 'very straight forward and trustworthy' man who was 'deeply committed to his country and the best interests of his country'.[31] In 2002, at the G8 summit in Kananaskis, Western leaders even noted 'the remarkable economic and democratic transformation that ha[d] occurred in Russia in recent years and in particular under the leadership of President Putin'.[32]

Just as in the 1990s, the West provided external legitimacy for Putin's regime:

> No longer was anyone thinking of the Kremlin's attack on the media, or of the destruction of the independent TV in Russia, or of the attempts to build an authoritarian 'vertical'. Western leaders who visited Moscow preferred not to meet with representatives of the opposition or the civil society – they could have hindered the process of building the 'horizontal' relations with the Kremlin. It was a policy of coaxing Putin's team with the aim of implementing Western interests.[33]

By turning the blind eye to all the non-democratic, corrupt practices in Russia, as well as assisting Russian ruling elites in laundering money in Europe, Western leaders not only emboldened those who were involved in these practices, but also created a very specific image of the West among the ruling Russian elites. The latter understood their own nature well, but the evident acceptance of their dubious practices by the West informed them that Western political and business leaders were as corrupt and double-faced as they were. 'Western values' are nothing more than a cover for the same dealings that characterised Russia under Yeltsin or Putin, 'camouflage for Westerners who are motivated solely by money'.[34] As Pavlovsky puts it, 'manipulating with left and right, strength and weakness', the ruling elites in Russia are 'confident that everybody else in the world is acting the same way. The world play is a series of fixed matches, where everybody manipulates everyone. The principles of humanity are only a procedure of bargaining'.[35]

The revival of anti-Westernism

Putin and his clique became convinced that the West accepted Moscow's rules of the game, but the paranoid nature of the *siloviki* manifested itself in 2004, during the Orange Revolution in Ukraine. The Orange Revolution was not a revolution, but a series of mass protests against the fraudulent victory of Ukraine's corrupt, pro-Russian Prime Minister Viktor Yanukovych in the presidential election.[36] For several weeks in November and December 2004, hundreds of thousands of Ukrainians protested on the streets of the Ukrainian cities, especially in the capital, Kyiv. These protests led to the second run-off of the presidential election in which Yanukovych's contender, pro-Western Viktor Yushchenko, won. The Kremlin was both furious and frightened. It was furious because Putin and the *siloviki* interpreted the Orange Revolution in Ukraine, which Moscow had always considered part of its sphere of influence, as a breach of an informal agreement between the West and Putin's Russia, as an act undermining the external (Western) legitimation of Putin's kleptocracy.

The Russian ruling elites know well about Zbigniew Brzezinski's book *The Grand Chessboard* and his argument that 'Ukraine, a new and important space on the Eurasian chessboard, is a geopolitical pivot because its very existence as an independent country helps to transform Russia. Without Ukraine, Russia ceases to be a Eurasian empire'.[37] The frequent quoting from Brzezinski provides further insights into the sentiments of Putin and the *siloviki* about Ukraine. With their Cold War mentality and bitterness over the demise of the Soviet Union, they perceived the 'loss' of Ukraine after the Orange Revolution as a continuation of the breakdown of the Soviet empire, as they never came to terms with the independence of Ukraine. Yet this was not the only reason why the Russian ruling elites were frightened. Not only did they intrinsically refuse to accept Ukraine's independence, they also truly believed that Russians and Ukrainians were one, wrongfully divided nation.[38] Apart from its emotional and imperialistic connotation, this argument had a very pragmatic implication closely related to the idea of the preservation of the existing regime in Russia. If Russians and Ukrainians were the same people, then Russians were – as the Ukrainian example had demonstrated – also capable of staging successful mass protests against the corrupt regime. Even more importantly, if Ukrainians were to transform, modernise and democratise their country along the Western lines, it would imply that the same was possible in Russia too – a development that would necessarily lead to the collapse of Putin's regime. It is with the aim of preventing countries such as Ukraine from modernising and democratising that Russia rejected their sovereign right to seek membership in the EU and NATO. As an instrument of political stabilisation, NATO – with its system of collective defence – provides a secure environment for implementing democratic reforms and makes it difficult for Russia to corrupt aspiring Westernising societies.

The year 2005 became a turning point for Putin's authoritarian kleptocracy, as it turned to the anti-Western measures to ward off the 'Orange threat' to the regime.[39]

The significant contribution of young, active Ukrainians to the success of the Orange Revolution prompted the Russian establishment to launch a pre-emptive defence force by reviving, mobilising and consolidating a pro-regime youth movement. In order to counter the largely imaginary 'Orange threat' in Russia, the authorities sanctioned the creation of several 'patriotic' youth movements. In February 2005, the declined youth organisation 'Idushchie vmeste' (Walking together) was revitalised as 'Nashi' (Ours) under the leadership of Vasiliy Yakemenko. Because of its straightforward pro-Putin position and aggressive attitudes towards the democratic opposition, 'Nashi' – like the 'Idushchie vmeste' before it – was dubbed 'Putinjugend' (Putin's youth, after Hitlerjugend).[40] The same month, Aleksandr Dugin's movement declared the formation of its National Bolshevik youth wing, Evraziyskiy soyuz molodezhi (Eurasian Youth Union, ESM), headed by Pavel Zarifullin and Valeriy Korovin. In April, a member of the State Duma Maksim Mischenko founded the 'Rossiya molodaya' (Young Russia) movement. In November, the declined youth organisation of the ruling party 'Yedinaya Rossiya' (United Russia) was reformed as the 'Molodaya gvardiya' (Young Guard) under the leadership of Tatyana Voronova.

Two major ideas behind the agenda of these youth movements were anti-Westernism (especially anti-Americanism) and the protection of Putin's regime. 'Nashi' claimed that the West was 'engaged in a great geopolitical game on the territory of the former USSR under the slogans of democracy and freedom – a game aimed at "squeezing" Russia out of the world politics and introducing external control over Russia itself.[41] The ESM declared that the United States, 'a civilisation of the wild West', 'smashed our Fatherland to pieces, cast the cobweb of dark presence over the continent, the whole world'.[42] The 'Rossiya molodaya' insisted that 'the sober-minded youth had to unite in order to prevent revolutions and coups leading to the colonisation of Russia', and that only the unity could 'defend our Motherland from the Western expansion, terrorism and corruption'.[43] The 'Molodaya gvardiya' claimed that they wanted to live in a country 'in which "great upheavals" or revolutions would never happen again', and they would 'never become a generation witnessing the end of the Russian state'.[44]

In February 2005, Putin created a new subdivision of the Presidential Administration, namely the Presidential Directorate for Interregional Relations and Cultural Contacts with Foreign Countries. Officially, it aimed at 'providing assistance to the President in implementing foreign policy'.[45] Russian journalists, however, interpreted the creation of this directorate as Putin's yet another instrument of thwarting 'colour revolutions'. Public relations expert Modest Kolerov was appointed to head the directorate on 22 March 2005, and a few days before his appointment, he published, on his website *Regnum*, a manifesto titled 'A Front against Russia' that argued that Western-inspired 'colour revolutions' in the post-Soviet space targeted Russia's sovereignty and territorial integrity: 'Today, the undisguised aim of Western "bad cops" is dismemberment of Russia; that of the "good cops" – "external control", restriction of its sovereignty, international supervision of its nuclear self-defence'.[46]

Gazprom's *Tribuna-RT*, too, alleged that Russia was the main aim of the 'colour revolutions' staged by 'Western political technologists'.[47] The most popular Russian tabloid *Komsomol'skaya Pravda* (Komsomol Truth) asserted that 'colour revolutions' were 'orchestrated not only to force pro-Russian elites from the former republic of the USSR, but also to destabilise Russia itself'.[48] *Rossiyskaya Gazeta*, the official daily of the Russian government, claimed that 'the US-led West and Russia fought a political battle over the control of the post-Soviet space'.[49]

The Russian Orthodox Church did not stand on the sidelines either, and launched, in July 2005, the SPAS TV channel aimed at 'forming a worldview and a system of moral coordinates required for the efficient development of the state on the basis of the indigenously Orthodox values'.[50] The SPAS TV would feature special programmes hosted, among others, by Aleksandr Dugin, Natalya Narochnitskaya of the 'Rodina' party, and Ilya Goryachev, the leader of the neo-Nazi organisations Boevaya organizatsiya russkikh natsionalistov (Combat Organisation of Russian Nationalists, also known as BORN) and 'Russkiy obraz' (Russian Image), as well as offering interviews with far-right ideologues such as Alain de Benoist, Lyndon LaRouche and some others.

Not that anti-Westernism was absent from the Russian political culture before; on the contrary, it had a very long history and manifested itself, in particular, in the concept of Russia's 'special path',[51] as well as being an integral ideological part of the 'red-brown' opposition to Yeltsin's regime. What Putin's regime started doing after 2004 was bringing to the forefront the anti-Western narratives that were previously either constrained or contained on the fringes of the society. This resulted in the de-marginalisation of the carriers of these narratives – they were moved into the mainstream to help the regime protect and legitimise itself by pushing the idea of a 'besieged fortress'.

Russian elites needed to deliberately mainstream anti-Americanism, as the most explicit manifestation of anti-Westernism, through previously marginalised figures because, as Vladimir Shlapentokh argues, 'the visceral hatred of America' has not been present in Russia: 'Anti-Americanism in Russia . . . does not come from below, from the general Russian population, but rather from above, from the elite. It is the elite, through its ability to control and manipulate the media, education and literature, which has the power to either foster or stifle xenophobia'.[52]

In his study on conspiracy theories in post-Soviet Russia, Ilya Yablokov explained that the process of mainstreamisation of the anti-Western conspiracy theories was helped by the arguments presented by First Deputy Chief of Russia's Presidential Administration Vladislav Surkov who offered a new narrative on Russia-West relations: the West was not 'the ultimate enemy' of Russia, but its 'shrewd competitor'. However, this particular reconceptualisation, rather than discarding anti-Western conspiracy theories, relocated them 'from the margins of Russian political discourse to its centre' and made 'criticism of the West – when framed within the conspiratorial narrative – a legitimate part of official political and media discourse'.[53]

Importantly, Putin's regime had sufficient financial resources to indulge anti-Westernism. In comparison to 1999, the windfall gains from oil revenues totalled \$133.7 billion in 2000–2003, but they were already \$153.6 billion in 2005 alone, and they amounted to \$894.4 billion in the period 2005–2008.[54] The increase in oil revenues was 'Dutch courage' for the ruling elites in their attitudes towards the perceived Westernising developments in Russia's neighbourhood, but the resulting accumulation of wealth, at the same time, made them even more scared of losing it.

Putin's speech at the 43rd Munich Conference on Security Policy in 2007 was an ultimatum to the West: 'the Kremlin was ready for the deterioration of the relations with the West', if the United States refused to review the rules of the game established after 1991.[55] In his speech, Putin, in particular, claimed:

> One state and, of course, first and foremost the United States, has overstepped its national borders in every way. This is visible in the economic, political, cultural and educational policies it imposes on other nations. [. . .]
>
> And of course this is extremely dangerous. It results in the fact that no one feels safe. I want to emphasise this – no one feels safe! Because no one can feel that international law is like a stone wall that will protect them.[56]

Putin's authoritarian kleptocracy felt threatened by the West, and urged the formation of 'the architecture of global security', based on 'a reasonable balance

between the interests of all participants in the international dialogue'.[57] Outside
the diplomatic doublespeak, this implied that Putin refused to acknowledge the
sovereignty of 'smaller nations' in Russia's neighbourhood with regard to their
political orders and foreign policy orientations, and called on the West to accept
the existence of Russia's sphere of influence in Eastern Europe that would serve
as a buffer against 'colour revolutions' allegedly posing a threat to Putin's regime.
Furthermore, Russia's East European sphere of influence would serve as a platform
for further integration of the Russian financial structures into the body of Western
economies with the aim of creating or deepening dependence on the workings of
Putin's regime. As James Sherr argues, Russia's 'overarching aim' is 'the creation
of an international environment conducive to the maintenance of its system of
governance at home'.[58] And, of course, possessing a sphere of influence recognised
as such by the West and, most importantly, by the United States, would produce
a feeling that Russia was a great power again – a feeling for which the *siloviki*
including Putin himself yearned since the demise of the Soviet Union.

The *siloviki* naturally benefited from Moscow's embrace of anti-Westernism.
As a report on the developments within the Russian elites in 2013 argued, 'the
use of the rhetoric of the external threat, [and the use of] power structures and
anti-corruption campaign to solve domestic issues resulted . . . in the *siloviki*
consolidating their position' in the ruling elites.[59]

Putin's rhetoric tactics worked, and major powers of the West recognised the
existence of Russia's sphere of influence with regard to Georgia and Ukraine.
At the 20th NATO Summit held in Bucharest in April 2008, Germany's Chancellor
Angela Merkel, France's President Nicolas Sarkozy and UK's Prime Minister
Gordon Brown refused to offer NATO Membership Action Plan to Georgia and
Ukraine, which had applied for NATO membership, as it 'would be an unnecessary
provocation to Russia'.[60] Taking advantage of this decision, Russia purposefully
provoked a war with Georgia in August 2008 – President Dmitry Medvedev called
this war a 'peace enforcement operation'[61] – and occupied the Georgian regions
of Abkhazia and South Ossetia. The West failed to meet the Russian aggression
against Georgia with sufficient fortitude, just as it failed to respond to Russia's massive
cyber-attack on Estonia, a member of NATO, in 2007.[62] In 2009, the PACE
approved a resolution that condemned 'the recognition by Russia of the
independence of South Ossetia and Abkhazia' in violation of the international law,
as well as 'the Russian non-mandated military presence and the building of new
military bases within the separatist regions of South Ossetia and Abkhazia'.[63]
Moscow ignored the resolution, and went unpunished.

Although the West turned out to be largely unable to meet the challenge of
Putin's regime, it would be unfair to say that all Western institutions remained
uncritical of the developments in Russia. Many Western NGOs and think-tanks
consistently reported on the curtailing of rights and freedoms, human rights violations and the solid increase of other authoritarian practices in Russia. Organisations
such as Freedom House, Economist Intelligence Unit, Amnesty International,
Transparency International and some others continuously registered the worrying

decline of democracy in Putin's Russia, but their research never translated into relevant policies.

The twist

Shevtsova writes that one of the main reasons that pushed Moscow to embrace 'anti-Western revisionism' was the fact that Putin's regime lacked – in contrast to the Soviet Union – an ideology that would consolidate the society; anti-Westernism was the only idea that could fill in the vacuum.[64] This is not entirely correct: while anti-Westernism has indeed been the main cross-cutting idea behind the Kremlin's attempts to present Russia as a 'besieged fortress', Moscow has experimented with various ideologies and ideological constructs to legitimise its anti-Western posture and to consolidate the Russian society to protect the kleptocratic regime. In a later work, Shevtsova reassessed her earlier argument stating that Putin was 'restlessly seeking new ideas to justify his claim to unrestrained rule. . . . For the Kremlin, ideas are instrumental. If an action is deemed necessary, ideas will be found to justify it'.[65]

In contrast to the totalitarian regimes that seek totality of an anthropological revolution of a deliberately politicised society, authoritarian regimes do not need ideology to the same extent. Putin's regime – already authoritarian in 2000–2004 – did not require an elaborate and all-encompassing ideology to legitimise his Potemkin state, and Putin himself claimed, in 2003, that 'a single state ideology [was] a sign of a totalitarian state'.[66] For once, Putin was right. Prominent Spanish political scientist Juan Linz, who contrasted authoritarian regimes to totalitarian ones, defined the former as 'political systems with limited, not responsible, political pluralism, without elaborate and guiding ideology, but with distinctive mentalities, without extensive nor intensive political mobilization, except at some points in their development'.[67]

As Sherr argues, 'unlike the Soviet Union, Russia [under Putin] does not seek a "social reordering of the world"'.[68] It only syringes very specific ideas into the body of the Russian society in order to achieve particular purposes. This is a typical mode of operation for authoritarian, not totalitarian, states that occasionally, rather than permanently, engage in political mobilisation of the society.

Every social development seen as potentially problematic for the Kremlin is resolved with an ideological tool honed for a specific situation. An example here is the tripartite series of Moscow's non-violent measures that fragmented and virtually destroyed the Russian opposition movement formed at the end of 2011. This movement emerged as a result of the protests against apparently fraudulent elections to the State Duma in December 2011. The protests, described by Miriam Lanskoy and Elspeth Suthers as 'the first real challenge to President Vladimir Putin and the political system that he ha[d] established in Russia',[69] continued for several months and intensified after the presidential elections in March 2012 in which Putin won in the first round. The Kremlin was scared of the opposition movement as it was scared of the repetition of the 'Orange scenario' in Russia in 2005: 'the street protests of late 2011 and early 2012 came as a shock to Putin and his group. The dangers of "colour revolutions" became a stock Kremlin warning'.[70] The police suppressed the protests, but the authorities predominantly took non-violent measures to fend off the threat of an imaginary 'colour revolution'. First, the Kremlin sensationalised the minor, allegedly sacrilegious performance of the Russian punk band Pussy Riot in Moscow's Cathedral of Christ the Saviour to bring division into the opposition movement on religious grounds.[71] Second, Russia adopted the so-called Dima Yakovlev Law that banned US citizens from adopting Russian orphan children in order to divide the opposition on the grounds of Russian nationalism intrinsically characterised by anti-Americanism. Third, it adopted the anti-LGBT[72] propaganda law officially to protect children from 'information advocating for a denial of traditional family values', but essentially to splinter the opposition movement exploiting the divisive LGBT issue. In addition to these measures and to further minimise perceived Western influence, Russian authorities changed the law on non-profit organisations (NPOs) declaring that those NPOs, which were engaged in vaguely defined political activities and received foreign funding, were obliged to register as 'foreign agents' – a term, which in Russian language is almost an equivalent to 'foreign spy'.[73] The revised law on the NPOs targeted Russia-based human rights organisations, educational and scientific centres, etc. that received funding from largely Western sources and were considered as a threat to Putin's regime.

The fact that Moscow has exploited so many different ideological tools produces an impression of Putinism as 'an eclectic and goal-oriented assemblage of precepts and philosophies that blends communist and Tsarist, nationalist and internationalist symbols together with disparate events and personalities from Russian history'.[74] Yet here is the twist: locked in a spiral of self-fulfilling prophecies, in which Moscow responded to each perceived anti-Russian move of the West with an increase in anti-Western rhetoric and further repression against the political opposition seen as the agents of the West, the Kremlin drove itself to a point where it *needed* to present a real ideology or at least a consistent ideological vision that would continue justifying Moscow's existential concern over the preservation of the authoritarian kleptocracy. Mimicking the practices of the Soviet Union, Putin's regime globalised its self-preservation drive in the form of assuming the role of a leader of the international movement struggling for a multipolar world, but intrinsically – against the United States. Anti-Westernism and 'ideological syringes' would still be used, but they alone were no longer considered sufficient for Russia's self-appointed global role.

Ten years after he claimed that 'a single state ideology [was] a sign of a totalitarian state', Putin voiced a different political opinion: 'It is evident that it is impossible to move forward without spiritual, cultural and national self-determination. Without this, we will not be able to withstand internal and external challenges, nor will we succeed in global competitions.'[75] Putin said these words in 2013 at a meeting of the Valdai International Discussion Club (or simply Valdai), a soft power tool of Russian foreign policy established in 2011. Despite the fact that Putin called for the creation of a Russian ideology, his speech also crowned several years of developing such an ideology by various pro-Kremlin actors: by declaring that it did not exist, he admitted that his regime ultimately failed to invent any consistent ideological system.

Several reasons determined this failure. First, no member of the ruling elite of the authoritarian kleptocracy actually believed in any ideology. Even when the regime wanted to exploit a certain ideological construct to mobilise the society for a particular cause, it 'outsourced' the task to the 'ideologues for hire' – true believers in religious fundamentalism, fascism, Russian ultranationalism, conservatism, etc. The regime cynically instrumentalised them, but never took them as anything more than political technologists or even looneys. Second, there was always an oversupply of ideologies – each of them could potentially serve as the main pro-Putin doctrine. But this oversupply reflected the diversity of often contrasting political opinions in the Russian society, so picking one doctrine would necessarily alienate the adherents of all others and, thus, fail as a consolidating worldview. Third, it seems that Putin was still wary about declaring a particular ideology as a state doctrine. Not so much because he could be accused of totalitarian practices, but mainly because having a single ideology would make the regime predictable and easily challenged in intellectual terms – a development that the Kremlin was always trying to avoid.

What is important in the context of this study is less Moscow's eventual failure to invent a state doctrine ideology than the complex of ideological constructs developed by pro-Putin forces and presented as a means of seeking international and domestic legitimation of the preservation of the kleptocratic regime. It would take nothing less than several separate volumes to explore these ideological constructs.[76] Here it suffices to briefly summarise the ideas on which Putin focused in his speech at Valdai in 2013, as they largely reflect the above-mentioned corpus of the elaborated ideological constructs.

In his speech, Putin rejected three ideologies: Soviet communism, Western liberalism, and Russian nationalism. While he also expressed criticism towards 'fundamental conservatism' that idealised 'pre-1917 Russia',[77] he seemed to be inclined to support conservatives in general. Embracing conservatism as a potentially consolidating ideology became the most popular idea among the top functionaries of the ruling 'Yedinaya Rossiya' since 2005. Over the years, the party organised several round-tables and workshops, often featuring Western politicians and experts, to discuss conservative trends in Europe. In the beginning of 2005, it also launched the Centre of Social-Conservative Politics founded on the 'principles of consistency of social and economic tasks, implementing reforms based on the Russian society's values, inadmissibility of any forms of extremism'.[78] In August 2008, the contemporary leader of 'Yedinaya Rossiya' and former Minister of Internal Affairs Boris Gryzlov officially declared that conservatism was the ideology of his party.[79] At the party congress at the end of 2008, Gryzlov specified that the ideology of the party was 'Russian conservatism'.[80]

For several years, Putin had seemed to remain uninterested in the idea of having 'Russian conservatism' as the underlying ideology of the regime, as he was satisfied with occasional instances of mobilising the society on the basis of various, rather than one, doctrines. The change in approach was largely a result of the perceived challenge of the Russian opposition movement that developed in 2011–2012. Just as in the period immediately after the Orange Revolution in Ukraine, the Kremlin radicalised its anti-Western stances, as the establishment believed that the West or, more specifically, the Americans were behind the protests of the Russian opposition. While the Kremlin used the above-mentioned tripartite series of the non-violent measures to partially disintegrate the opposition, it started probing for an outlook more efficient than anti-Westernism and more consistent than the eclectic mix of situational 'ideological syringes'.

As late as 2012, Putin attempted to simultaneously flirt with, and address the issue of, Russian nationalism – a move most likely informed by the fact that the protests in 2011 started with an unofficial protest rally organised by the ultranationalist organisation 'Russkie' (The Russians) that called for Putin's resignation. In his article published in the beginning of 2012, Putin called Russia 'a unique civilisation' whose 'fabric' was held together by ethnic Russians, that is 'russkiy narod', rather than 'rossiyskiy narod' which means the civic character of the Russian people. At the same time, Putin rejected the idea of a 'Russian "national", monoethnic state' that, in his view, was at odds with Russia's 'millenary' history. 'The self-determination of the [ethnic] Russian people is a poliethnic civilisation fastened together with the Russian cultural core. And this choice was confirmed by the [ethnic] Russian people again and again – and not by plebiscites or referendums, but by blood'.[81] This argument implied that not only ethnic Russians were deprived of a possibility to build a Russian nation-state because of the alleged sacredness of Russia's 'millenary' history, but all the other peoples of Russia were refused their own self-determination too, because ethnic Russians chose to have a 'poliethnic civilisation'. In his annual address to the Federal Assembly, Putin also stressed that Russia developed as 'a civilisation-state bonded by the Russian people, Russian language and Russian culture'. He insisted that, in order for Russia to be a 'sovereign and influential country', it had to 'secure a firm spiritual and moral foundation for our society', and 'support the institutions that [were] the carriers of traditional values'.[82] The focus on 'morality', 'spirituality', and 'traditional values' was already merely a step away from officially embracing conservatism.

Since 2013, Putin started talking about conservatism in a rather consistent manner. During an interview on the eve of the G20 (Group of Twenty) Summit in 2013, Putin said that he could call himself 'a pragmatist with a conservative perspective' who always took 'lessons from the distant and recent past into consideration'.[83] At the end of the same year, Putin argued that

> the point of conservatism is not that it obstructs movement forward and upward, but that it prevents the movement backward and downward. That, in my opinion, is a very good formula, and it is the formula that I propose.

There's nothing unusual for us here. Russia is a country with a very profound ancient culture, and if we want to feel strong and grow with confidence, we must draw on this culture and these traditions, and not just focus on the future.[84]

Putin's official embrace of conservatism was determined by domestic and international factors.[85] In the domestic context – despite Putin's arguments that conservatism was not 'about some kind of self-isolation and reluctance to develop'[86] – his support for this ideology in 2013 was largely a response to the failure of the modernising drive declared by Dmitry Medvedev who was Russia's President (2008–2012) in-between Putin's second and third presidential terms. By 2013, Russia had made little progress since the publication of Medvedev's wishfully optimistic article 'Go Russia!' in 2009, and, thus, could still be described, in Medvedev's own terms, as a backward, 'primitive economy based on raw materials and endemic corruption', with a weak civil society overwhelmed by paternalistic attitudes and low levels of self-organisation.[87] Instead of progress and reform, Russia continued a peculiar form of covert de-modernisation – a trend partially explained by the extractive, oil-dependent nature of its economy, and partially – by the lack of genuine willingness on the part of the ruling class (primarily the *siloviki*) to reform the country against the background of continuous windfall gains from oil revenues.

At least for some functionaries of the 'Yedinaya Rossiya', conservatism was simply an antithesis of liberalism. According to one head of a regional executive committee of the party, 'Russian conservatism has little in common with classic conservatism. . . . We had little choice: subscribing to liberal views or trying to build a political life without cataclysms and upheavals'.[88] 'Russian conservatism', or its pro-Kremlin, instrumental interpretation, is *okhranitel'stvo* – a Russian term that does not properly translate into English and is derived from the Russian word *okhranyat'* (to protect). *Okhranitel'stvo* implies protection of the authority that, in its turn, protects what is considered traditional values. Discussing the presumed values of the BRICS,[89] the head of the State Duma foreign affairs committee Aleksey Pushkov intrinsically interpreted them in terms of *okhranitel'stvo*: 'The BRICS countries have their own values system that differs from the Euro-Atlantic one. This, for example, is prevention of "orange revolutions", which are change of governments and power in other countries through external influence. Is this not a value?'.[90] Inozemtsev refers to 'Russian conservatism' as *okhranitel'stvo*, and writes that 'conservatism' of 'the Russian establishment and the politological crowd that services it' derives largely 'from the repudiation of the necessity of progress as such. "Conservatism" in Russia is a synonym of reactionary or, more precisely, retrograde politics'.[91]

In the international context, 'Russian conservatism' became a starting point for seeking legitimation of Putin's regime from a variety of Western political sources ranging from genuine conservatives to right-wing extremists. Moreover, Putin positioned Russia as a leader of international conservatism. In his annual address to the Federal Assembly at the end of 2013, he declared:

We will strive to be leaders, defending international law, striving for respect and national sovereignty and peoples' independence and identity. . . .

We know that there are more and more people in the world who support our position on defending traditional values that have made up the spiritual and moral foundation of civilisation in every nation for thousands of years: the values of traditional families, real human life, including religious life, not just material existence but also spirituality, the values of humanism and global diversity.[92]

Putin addressed these words to the domestic audience, trying to reassure the Russians that their country was not isolated in the world and that his regime found support – and, therefore, external legitimacy – from the like-minded Western forces. The same argument addressed to the Western audience was more specific and seemed to aim at garnering support from ultraconservatives, far right and Christian fundamentalists:

We can see how many of the Euro-Atlantic countries are actually rejecting their roots, including the Christian values that constitute the basis of Western civilisation. They are denying moral principles and all traditional identities: national, cultural, religious and even sexual. They are implementing policies that equate large families with same-sex partnerships, belief in God with the belief in Satan. . . .

I am convinced that this opens a direct path to degradation and primitivism, resulting in a profound demographic and moral crisis. . . .

Without the values embedded in Christianity and other world religions, without the standards of morality that have taken shape over millennia, people will inevitably lose their human dignity. We consider it natural and right to defend these values. One must respect every minority's right to be different, but the rights of the majority must not be put into question. . . .

In Europe and some other countries so-called multiculturalism is in many respects a transplanted, artificial model that is now being questioned, for understandable reasons. This is because it is based on paying for the colonial past. It is no accident that today European politicians and public figures are increasingly talking about the failures of multiculturalism, and that they are not able to integrate foreign languages or foreign cultural elements into their societies.[93]

In other words, for Putin, Europe and the West in general were decadent, plagued by same-sex marriages, moral crisis, failing multiculturalism and disrespect for the rights of the majority, that is the main narratives of the Western far right. Putin claimed that 'the institutions of international law and national sovereignty' were almost eroded, because the 'unipolar, standardised world [did] not require sovereign states; it require[d] vassals'.[94] The mastermind behind the 'unipolar world' was never named, but the United States was tacitly implied as such.

Already in 2012, Putin demonstrated somewhat a sympathy with the Western far right – a sympathy that would later develop into coded overtunes to the far right. For example, the specific language of Putin's article published in 2012 seemed to demonstrate his *understanding* of the agenda of the 'radical forces' in Europe as he explained that 'the rise of xenophobia among the native indigenous population' was a result of 'people being shocked by the aggressive pressure on their traditions [and a] familiar way of life, and [of people] being seriously scared of losing a nation-state identity'.[95]

As he increasingly started using arguments popular among the Western far right, Putin presented Russia as an alternative to the allegedly degenerate West: 'the desire for independence and sovereignty in spiritual, ideological and foreign policy spheres is an integral part of our national character'.[96] Moreover, to resist the alleged unipolarity and Western decadence, Russia would develop a geopolitical alternative to the EU – the Eurasian Economic Union (EEU, sometimes called the Eurasian Union), 'a project for maintaining the identity of nations in the historical Eurasian space in a new century and in a new world'.[97]

Despite the fact that the EEU would be presented as a mere successor to the Customs Union founded in 2010 by Russia, Belarus and Kazakhstan, that is post-Soviet states,[98] and despite the assurances that Moscow would not intend to set the process of Eurasian integration 'against other integration projects including the more mature European one',[99] one suspects that Putin imagined the Eurasian project to eventually extend to the entire European continent leading to the end of the 'decadent' EU. The conceptual rationale of the Russia-led Eurasian integration was underpinned not only by concerns about 'maintaining the identity of nations' but also by references to allegedly peaceful and mutually beneficial co-existence in Eurasia: 'the processes of the Eurasian integration contribute to the formation of a new architecture of economic cooperation on the territory from Lisbon to Vladivostok for the purposes of providing sustainable socio-economic development of the whole region'.[100] The idea of extending the Eurasian project to the European continent is generally accepted by the Russian 'intellectual elites' loyal to the Kremlin. For example, one of the leading Russian academics Sergey Karaganov, the dean of the Faculty of World Economy and International Affairs at the Higher School of Economics, also envisages the incorporation of Europe into Eurasia upon the pretext of 'preventing further destabilisation of the international community in the future': 'And we want a great power status. Unfortunately, we cannot give it up: over the last 300 years, this status has become part of our genome. We want to become a centre of a greater Eurasia, a zone of peace and cooperation. The European subcontinent will be included in this Eurasia.'[101]

Talking about Eurasian integration, Putin often referred to 'the territory from Lisbon to Vladivostok' reminiscent of the above-mentioned West European far-right plans. It is doubtful though that he played with the Thiriartian notion of the greater Europe 'from Vladivostok to Dublin', as the concept of 'a greater Europe from Lisbon to Vladivostok' has other sources in the Russian context independent from the Russian translations of Thiriart's articles.[102] However, certain elements of the Russian ruling elites were indeed aware of Thiriart's works. For instance, in 2010, contemporary Russian Railways CEO and *silovik* Vladimir Yakunin[103] favourably commented on the idea of Thiriart – Yakunin called him 'a Belgian geopolitician' and 'Belgian scholar' – of Europe joining forces with the USSR 'to break free of the American Thalassocracy' and build a Europe from Dublin to Vladivostok.[104] Curiously, commenting on Thiriart's ideas, Yakunin referred to the Russian translation of one of Thiriart's articles published in Dugin's *Elementy*.

Whether Putin did or did not refer to Thiriart's idea of Europe, his use of right-wing populist language has become more pronounced in recent years. Hence, it was hardly a coincidence that, during his annual 'direct line' in April 2014, Putin declared that talking directly to the peoples of the West was more important than talking to their leaders.[105] 'Talking directly to people' is a trope used by European populist parties that contrast 'ordinary people' to the 'political elites'. Likewise, there was a reason why Putin noted, during the same communication, that the electoral successes of Viktor Orbán, the Hungarian far-right party Jobbik, and the FN's leader Marine Le Pen evidently testified to the rise of 'conservative values' in the European countries.[106] By the end of 2013/beginning of 2014, it became clear that Putin's regime no longer appealed exclusively to Western *mainstream* political forces for the legitimation of his authoritarian kleptocracy as a normal state. Rather, the regime increasingly appealed to Western *illiberal* forces in its desperate quest for recognition as a global leader of 'conservative forces' and a truly sovereign state that challenged Western mainstream politics.

The 'beacon of hope'

The first two chapters of this book demonstrated that particular elements of the Western far right had, already for a long time, expressed Russophile attitudes, whatever the rationale of these sentiments was – tactical, ideological, or both. Since the demise of the Soviet Union, some far-right parties and leaders cooperated with their Russian counterparts, but, during Putin's first presidential term, there was little mutual interest between the Western far right and the Kremlin. For example, during his visit to Austria in 2001, Putin apparently met with the now late Governor of Carinthia Jörg Haider, who by that time had stepped down from the leadership of the far-right FPÖ, but remained the party's 'gray cardinal'. In the period 2000–2002, the FPÖ was a minor coalition partner in the government formed with the conservative ÖVP, so Putin met with Haider as one of the top Austrian politicians. Describing the meeting in an interview to a Russian newspaper 2003, Haider said: 'During Putin's visit to Austria, we had a very interesting conversation, and he invited me to visit Russia. I hope to use this invitation in the coming years'.[107] Haider never visited Russia and died more than 5 years after the interview.

Contemporary leader of the Front National Jean-Marie Le Pen, who visited Russia several times during Putin's first two presidential terms, was cautiously optimistic about Putin's regime. In 2003, Le Pen argued that 'the actions of monsieur

Putin' were reasonable, 'he made a great step forward'.[108] In 2004, Le Pen said that he 'found the politics of the Kremlin and Putin very sensible and wise'; it was 'on the right track'.[109] Still, these arguments were different from the lavish praise of Putin's regime on the part of the French far right after 2010–2011. The Russian authorities themselves were uninterested, up until 2012–2013, in establishing direct contacts with Western far-right politicians.

The positive narratives on Russia produced by the far right since Putin's third presidential term can be divided into the narratives on Russia in general and those on Putin's Russia. The former were not different from the far-right rhetoric on Russia during the Soviet times or in the 1990s: the European far right welcomed Russia as a geopolitical counterweight to the United States and NATO, as a state that could help Europe liberate itself from American influence, and as a country that was rich in mineral resources. The narratives on *Putin's* Russia followed a similar pattern that had, however, its peculiarities.

One of the very first far-right narratives on Russia under Putin's rule was that the country 'got up off its knees'. Andreas Mölzer of the FPÖ wrote that Putin 'had managed to steer the post-communist, crisis-ridden Russia into calmer waters'.[110] His fellow party member Johann Gudenus argued that, in the 1990s, Russian people 'were desperate, the country was characterised by high mortality rates, economic collapse. . . . And when Putin emerged – it was a salvation for Russia. He did a lot, if compared to the 1990s, and the results are evident'.[111] In a later interview, Gudenus alleged that Yeltsin was not only 'controlled by oligarchs', he was 'a puppet of the West'. Putin, at the same time, put 'the country back on its feet and consolidated Russia. He disciplined a large part of the oligarchs'.[112]

The 'anti-oligarchic' theme was indeed popular among the far right in their interpretation of Putin's Russia. Already during Putin's first presidential term, French New Right conspiracy theorist Jean Parvulesco, who wrote that Putin's 'dialectically envisaged rise to supreme power' signified 'the renewal and simultaneously over-coming of the entire pre-Soviet and Soviet path of Russia',[113] appealed to Putin for

> the liquidation of oligarchic structures and their socio-economic and political leadership, schemers and blackmailers inherited from the chaotic, rotten and stinking rule of Boris Yeltsin's 'family', and from regional heavy-handed feudal lords: all of this should be destroyed at any cost and as soon as possible.[114]

Márton Gyöngyösi, who is responsible for the foreign policy of the Hungarian Jobbik, largely echoes Gudenus' and Parvulesco's argument saying that 'throughout Boris Yeltsin's 10-year reign, the oligarchs and the West nearly drove Russia to dire straits, and the people of Russia were suffering'.[115] The FN's leader Marine Le Pen admitted that Putin 'inspired respect for his attempts to counter a group of oligarchs who had appropriated Russian national resources'.[116]

Some far-right activists and ideologues imbued the 'anti-oligarchic' narrative with their own specific messages. For example, the fascist BNP combined this narrative with the anti-Semitic message inherent in the party ideology, and claimed that Putin 'moved to stop the oligarchs who had grabbed control of the vast wealth of Russia looting any more. And nearly all those oligarchs happened to be Jewish and with close ties to international Zionist organisations'.[117] A far-right conspiracy theorist and former long-time associate of the LaRouche movement F. William Engdahl welcomed the arrest of Khodorkovsky who allegedly 'negotiated with George Herbert Walker Bush and powerful investors in Washington connected to the Pentagon and the CIA the transfer of 40 per cent of Yukos to the American interests'.[118] The LaRouchites themselves channelled their anti-British and anti-Semitic prejudice through the 'anti-oligarchic' narrative, as they insisted that Khodorkovsky was connected to the Rothschilds who allegedly ran British intelligence operation into Russia.[119]

Closely related to the argument that Putin 'got Russia up off its knees' is the idea that, under Putin, the Russians started to be proud of their nation again. In one interview, Marine Le Pen said she admired Putin because he 'managed to restore pride and contentment to a great nation that had been humiliated and persecuted for 70 years'.[120] Le Pen's then fellow party member Aymeric Chauprade, who was her advisor on international relations until spring 2015, argued that Putin 'restored Russia's positions in the economy and geopolitics, and Russia enjoyed deep respect in the world'.[121]

The European far right deplore the alleged loss of national sovereignty to Brussels, and consequently praise Putin for preserving Russia's sovereignty – an argument that Putin himself liked to stress during his later speeches. The LN's leader Matteo Salvini calls Putin 'a statesman who does not serve the interests of the globalists',[122] and argues that he 'defends the interests of his own people regardless of the world technocrats and Brussels' biddings'.[123] Engdahl maintains that Russia, 'especially after Vladimir Putin's return to the Kremlin, . . . made it very clear that it was going to defend its sovereignty, national interests and borders'.[124] Marine Le Pen considers Putin a patriot who 'cares about the sovereignty of his people'.[125]

Another important far-right narrative on Putin's Russia is the acceptance of the conservative posture of Putin's kleptocratic regime, and even its self-appointed global leadership in defending the so-called traditional values. This argument has been especially popular with American far-right and ultraconservative groups. Commenting on Putin's address to the Federal Assembly at the end of 2013, 'paleoconservative' political commentator Patrick Buchanan reflected on whether Putin was a paleoconservative too, and argued that Putin was 'not wrong in saying that he [could] speak for much of mankind' and that he might 'be seeing the future with more clarity than Americans still caught up in a Cold War paradigm'.[126]

Especially after the adoption of the anti-LGBT propaganda law in Russia, which was both an attempt to split the opposition to Putin and present Russia as standing up 'against Europe and America, offering an alternative modern project and a moral leadership for those dissatisfied with the West',[127] Putin achieved prominence among the American homophobic activists. American anti-gay activist Bob Vander Plaats, who compared homosexuality to secondhand smoke and slavery,[128] praised Putin for 'decisive leadership' in the attack on 'homosexual propaganda'.[129] Scott Lively, an American author who argued that gays were behind the rise of the Nazi regime and who, at the time of the writing, was facing charges of hate crimes,[130] wrote an open letter to Putin in which he expressed his 'heartfelt gratitude' that the Russian nation took 'a firm and unequivocal stand against this scourge by banning homosexualist propaganda in Russia'. According to Lively, Putin 'set an example of moral leadership that [had] shamed the governments of Western Europe and North America and inspired the peoples of the world'.[131]

Praise for Putin as a leader of conservative forces has not been limited to the United States. For example, Chauprade trusts that 'thanks to Putin, other people acquire hope and opportunity to defend family values. For the West, Russia is a beacon of hope'.[132] Fabrice Sorlin, the leader of the French Catholic ultranationalist organisation Dies Iræ (Day of Wrath) and former candidate for the FN, compared 'Russia's anti-gay stand to its protection of Europe against the Mongol hordes and against fascism in the twentieth century'.[133] The Italian far-right Fronte Nazionale (National Front) expressed its support for Putin's 'courageous position against the powerful gay lobby', as well as his political backing of Bashar al-Assad's regime in Syria, through dozens of posters in Rome announcing 'I am with Putin!'.[134] Jobbik's Gyöngyösi claims that the party's main enemy is liberalism, and 'the main ally in the fight against liberalism is Russia that has recognised traditional values. We will need the full cultural and economic weight of Russia to win in this struggle'.[135]

Putin's talk about Christian values did not go unnoticed by the far right either. Marine Le Pen's partner and the FN's Vice President Louis Aliot claims that Putin's Russia is 'one of the last European defenders of the Judeo-Christian values that form the basis of our civilisation'.[136] Roberto Fiore, the leader of the Italian fascist Forza Nuova (New Force) goes even further and alleges that 'Russian people have a particular role in history, which is to represent the rebirth of Europe and the rebirth of Christian Europe'.[137]

The 'salvation' narrative with regard to Putin's Russia and its potential role in defending or liberating Europe has also been popular among particular far-right activists. According to Gianluca Savoini, a spokesman for the LN's leader Matteo Salvini and President of the Associazione Culturale Lombardia Russia (Lombardy-Russia Cultural Association, ACLR), Putin 'has clearly stated his intention to protect the identity of peoples from the chaotic migration, international financial lobbies, and pressure from the influential external forces'.[138] Jobbik's Béla Kovács maintains that 'mother Russia will have to save Europe',[139] while Gudenus argues that 'a strong Russia gives [Europe] more independence, more freedom'.[140] According to the Austrian magazine *Info-Direkt* associated with the far-right Österreichische Landsmannschaft (Community of Austrian Compatriots), 'Putin is the beacon of hope for those who want to counterpose something to the challenges of global economic competition, namely something based on identity, homeland, and cultural rootedness'.[141] The authors of the Austrian far-right 'Freies Österreich' (Free Austria) blog believe that the 'Russia of Vladimir Putin . . . will give the people of Europe an incentive, a necessary external impulse, to rise against their anti-popular governments, with the mandate of their peoples and to reflect a policy of the identitarian return to eternal traditional, spiritual, ethnic values'.[142] However, the more sophisticated New Right intellectual Alain de Benoist – although claiming that Russia 'is now obviously the principal alternative to American hegemony' – believes that Putin is perhaps 'not the savior of humanity', but still 'there are many good reasons to be pro-Russian'.[143]

Some far-right party leaders in Russia's European neighbourhood spoke in favour of the EEU as the alternative to the EU. In his lecture at the Moscow State University in 2013, Jobbik's leader Gábor Vona said that Hungary would have to decide whether to stay in the EU, join the EEU, or try to remain independent. One way or another, Jobbik would have Hungary leave the EU, 'give way to transcendent values and quit the matrix of global capitalism'.[144] In a later interview, Vona referred to the works of the Russian theorist of Eurasianism Nikolay Trubetskoy and Russian neo-Eurasianist Aleksandr Dugin, and argued that 'the advantage of Eurasianism is that it allows for the preservation of the independence of the regions, and is based on the continental cooperation in contrast to the exploitation by the European Union'.[145] While Putin's project of the EEU had little to do with the Russian classic Eurasianism or Dugin's fascist neo-Eurasianism, Vona clearly identified it as such. Likewise, the Greek neo-Nazi XA welcomed the creation of the EEU and referred to it as 'Dugin's dream and the nightmare of the American-Zionists', as well as the 'rival to the EU'.[146] The political programme of the Bulgarian far-right party Ataka (Attack) at the 2014 European elections stated that the future belonged to 'Eurasia, to the combination of resources of Russia and technologies of other European countries'.[147] Addressing the nation at the end of 2014, Ataka's leader Volen Siderov claimed it was time for Bulgaria to choose: 'whether we continue breathing the Euro-Atlantic dust until we suffocate, or whether we will start searching for our roots of an old Eurasian people of state-builders'.[148] Siderov himself evidently preferred the second option and called for a referendum on Bulgaria's withdrawal from NATO and the EU. While campaigning for the holding of the referendum, Siderov declared that Bulgaria needed to align itself with the EEU.[149]

The brief discussion of the perceptions of Putin's Russia by particular Western far-right activists and ideologues demonstrate the uncritical and largely uninformed nature of these attitudes. Essentially, they are based either on the body of opinions elaborated by philo-Soviet or Russophile fascist and far-right ideologues since the 1920s, or the self-descriptions of Putin's regime. It is not incidental that some of the far-right perceptions of the Russian authoritarian kleptocracy largely coincide with the arguments put forward by Putin at the meetings of the Valdai International Discussion Club. Evidence suggests that individual far-right activists either participated in these meetings or, at least, closely followed them. For example, Aymeric Chauprade participated in the Valdai meeting in 2013, while Pat Buchanan, Nick Griffin and Marine Le Pen's niece and FN member Marion Maréchal-Le Pen were recommended by the Russians for participation in 2014.[150] A French far-right author Guillaume Faye compared Putin to former French

President Charles de Gaulle specifically on the basis of his analysis of one of Putin's speeches at Valdai.[151] The LN-dominated ACLR openly claims that its views 'fully concur with the worldview of the President of the Russian Federation enunciated at the meeting of the Valdai club in 2013, and can be presented in three words: Identity, Sovereignty, Tradition'.[152] In his turn, Jobbik's Márton Gyöngyösi seems to directly quote one of Putin's Valdai arguments. During the questions and answers session after his speech at the Valdai meeting in 2013, Putin argued that the Europeans were 'dying out' and, while Europe 'want[ed] to survive on account of immigrants', the European society could not 'take in such a large number of immigrants'.[153] Writing for the neo-Eurasianist pseudo-scientific *Journal of Eurasian Affairs*,[154] Gyöngyösi asserted that 'Western European and North American societies [were] unsustainable without immigrants, but the valuelessness of these societies prevent[ed] them from being able to integrate foreigners'.[155] Putin's tactical appeal to far-right and ultraconservative activists and ideologues in the search for unconditional Western legitimation of his regime state proved to be largely successful.

Conclusion

Russia in the Yeltsin era was a virtual state in which political manipulation played a greater role than the workings of its weak political institutions, while corruption largely substituted normal economic exchange. At the same time, Yeltsin's Russia was characterised by strong regional leaders and multiple centres of social and economic power – some of them belonged to the oligarchs and especially to those who controlled major Russian TV channels. This division of authority created an image of a weak, but still a democratic state.

When Putin became Russia's president, he took immediate steps towards liquidating or neutralising alternative centres of power in the country – a development that emerged as a vertical centralisation of the state structure. It turned out to signify the building of an authoritarian patrimonial system, in which ruling elites were recruited on the basis of loyalty to the president. Putin's regime monopolised political manipulation and corruption, and, while purging disloyal oligarchs, it kept the loyal ones, but also created a new class of oligarchs that consisted of the *siloviki*.

Similar to Yeltsin, Putin enjoyed external legitimation of his regime on the part of Western mainstream politicians, but started to feel threatened after a number of democratic, pro-Western developments in Russia's neighbourhood, first and foremost associated with 'colour revolutions' – successful protests against electoral fraud in favour of pro-Russian politicians. To fend off an imaginary threat of a 'colour revolution' in Russia, Putin's regime increasingly turned to anti-Western and especially anti-American rhetoric. This turn resulted in the de-marginalisation of fascist, imperialistic and ultraconservative ideologues (and their ideas) who, until 2004–2005, had remained on the fringes of the socio-political discussions in Russia. Moreover, the anti-Western, conspiratorial worldview of the *siloviki* increasingly became the new normal among the Russian ruling elites.

The anti-Western, anti-American turn of Putin's regime became even sharper after the anti-Putin protests in 2011–2013 allegedly inspired by the United States. In addition to the repressions against the opposition, the Kremlin used various right-wing 'ideological syringes' to divide the opposition, but gradually came to understand that it needed a proper ideology that would consolidate Putin's rule and mobilise the society to the defence of his regime. In foreign relations, this anti-Western turn implied presenting Russia as a leader of the international struggle for multipolarity, a global defender of 'traditional values' and a guardian of 'spiritual and moral foundations of civilisation'. Institutionally, this posture would be implemented on the international level as part of the agenda of the EEU as a rival alternative to the alliances of the 'decadent' West, in particular the EU.

Russia's anti-American turn, the perceived challenge it posed to the EU, the Kremlin's appeal to 'traditional values', national identity and rights of the majority, as well as Putin's populist language of the divide between the elites advocating for 'failing multiculturalism' and people shocked 'by the aggressive pressure on their traditions' allowed Putin's right-wing authoritarian kleptocracy to claim external legitimacy from illiberal political forces in the West, especially far-right ideologues, movements and parties, who started to consider Russia as a 'beacon of hope', a leader of the international crusade against the decadent West with its liberalism, multiculturalism and minority protection. For them, Putin's Russia has important symbolical value too. Since the end of the Second World War, far-right parties and movements have been on the fringes of socio-political life in their countries, while far-right worldviews were marginalised. Now, however, far-right politicians may claim that their ideology is congenial to that of Putin's Russia, and this claim – together with a reference to Russia's geopolitical importance – appears to them as legitimising their politics as no longer marginal within their own societies.

The next chapter examines how the Kremlin's concerns about 'colour revolutions' in post-Soviet space and the anti-Western turn of Putin's regime encouraged the emergence of the first institutionalised form of cooperation between Russian actors and the European far right, namely the network of political or politicised organisations and far-right activists involved in the politically biased electoral observation aimed at promoting Moscow's foreign policy interests.

Notes

1   "Cheka" is a short term for "Chrezvychaynaya komissya" (Emergency Committee), the first Soviet state security agency founded in 1917.
2   Zbigniew Brzezinski, "Moscow's Mussolini", *The Wall Street Journal*, 20 September (2004), www.wsj.com/articles/SB109563224382121790
3   Nicholas D. Kristof, "The Poison Puzzle", *The New York Times*, 15 December (2004), www.nytimes.com/2004/12/15/opinion/15kristof.html
4   "World: James Woolsey, Former CIA Director, Speaks to RFE/RL at Forum 2000", *RFE/RL*, 10 October (2005), www.rferl.org/content/article/1062001.html
5   Alexander J. Motyl, "Is Putin's Russia Fascist?", *The National Interest*, 3 December (2007), http://nationalinterest.org/commentary/inside-track-is-putins-russia-fascist-1888

6   Marcel H. van Herpen, *Putinism: The Slow Rise of a Radical Right Regime in Russia* (Basingstoke: Palgrave Macmillan, 2013), p. 202.

7   Ibid., pp. 202–203.

8   Roger Griffin's comment provided to the author in a private e-mail on 4 June 2016.

9   Andreas Umland, "Challenges and Promises of Comparative Research into Post-Soviet Fascism: Methodological and Conceptual Issues in the Study of the Contemporary East European Extreme Right", *Communist and Post-Communist Studies*, Vol. 48, Nos 2–3 (2015), pp. 169–181 (174).

10   James Sherr, *Hard Diplomacy and Soft Coercion: Russia's Influence Abroad* (London: Chatham House, 2013).

11   On corruption in Putin's Russia see Cheloukhine, Haberfeld, *Russian Organized Corruption Networks*; Boris Nemtsov, Vladimir Milov, *Putin. Itogi. 10 let* (Moscow: Solidarnost', 2010); Georgiy Satarov (ed.), *Rossiyskaya korruptsiya: uroven', struktura, dinamika: opyt sotsiologicheskogo analiza* (Moscow: Fond "Liberal'naya Missiya", 2013).

12   Wilson, *Ukraine Crisis*, p. 19. See also Peter Pomerantsev, *Nothing Is True and Everything Is Possible: The Surreal Heart of the New Russia* (New York: PublicAffairs, 2014).

13   On Putin's *sistema* see Alena V. Ledeneva, *Can Russia Modernise? Sistema, Power Networks and Informal Governance* (Cambridge: Cambridge University Press, 2013).

14   Alex Lupis, "Increasing Press Repression in Russia", *Nieman Reports*, Vol. 59, No. 2 (2005), pp. 118–120 (119).

15   Ben Judah, *Fragile Empire: How Russia Fell in and out of Love with Vladimir Putin* (New Haven: Yale University Press, 2013), p. 41.

16   Karen Dawisha, *Putin's Kleptocracy: Who Owns Russia?* (New York: Simon & Schuster, 2014), p. 277.

17   Olga Kryshtanovskaya, Stephen White, "The Rise of the Russian Business Elite", *Communist and Post-Communist Studies*, Vol. 38, No. 3 (2005), pp. 293–307 (306).

18   The word "siloviki" derives from the Russian word "*sila*" (force).

19   On the increase of political significance of the FSB in Putin's Russia see Andrei Soldatov, Irina Borogan, *The New Nobility: The Restoration of Russia's Security State and the Enduring Legacy of the KGB* (New York: PublicAffairs, 2010).

20   Quoted in Judah, *Fragile Empire*, p. 33. On the "FSB-isation" of Putin's Russia see the chapter "Putin's Rise: How the KGB Seized Power in Russia", in Edward Lucas, *The New Cold War: Putin's Threat to Russia and the West* (London: Bloomsbury, 2014), pp. 25–46.

21   Olga Kryshtanovskaya, Stephen White, "Putin's Militocracy", *Post-Soviet Affairs*, Vol. 19, No. 4 (2003), 289–306 (294).

22   Olga Kryshtanovskaya, "Novaya russkaya elita", *New Times*, No. 16, 21 April (2008), www.newtimes.ru/articles/detail/4324

23   Gleb Pavlovsky, "O negativnykh posledstviyakh 'letnego nastupleniya' oppozitsion-nogo kursu Prezidenta RF men'shinstva", *Russkiy zhurnal*, 2 September (2003), http://old.russ.ru/politics/20030902_gp-pr.html

24   Ol'ga Kryshtanovskaya, Stephen White, "The Sovietization of Russian Politics", *Post-Soviet Affairs*, Vol. 25, No. 4 (2009), pp. 283–309 (297).

25   Kryshtanovskaya, White, "Putin's Militocracy", p. 292.

26   Vladislav L. Inozemtsev, "Russia of 2010s: How to Live with It and How to Outlive It", *DGAPkompakt*, No. 7 (2015), p. 2.

27   Lilia Shevtsova, *My: zhizn' v epokhu bezvremen'ya* (Moscow: Politicheskaya entsiklo-pediya, 2014), pp. 117, 158.

28   Mark Galeotti, "Putin's Hydra: Inside Russia's Intelligence Services", *European Council on Foreign Relations Policy Brief*, No. 169 (2016), p. 2.

29   Ibid., p. 6.

30   Ibid., p. 5.

31   Caroline Wyatt, "Bush and Putin: Best of Friends", *BBC*, 16 June (2001), http://news.bbc.co.uk/2/hi/europe/1392791.stm

32 "Russia's Role in the G8", *2002 Kananskis Summit*, 26 June (2002), http://g8. utoronto.ca/summit/2002kananaskis/russiasrole.html

33 Shevtsova, *Odinokaya derzhava*, p. 53.

34 Edward Lucas, "Rethinking Russia: The Paradox of Paranoia", *Center for European Policy Analysis*, No. 34, 28 January (2013), p. 1, www.cepa.org/sites/default/files/documents/ CEPA%20Report%20No.%2034,%20Rethinking%20Russia.pdf

35 Gleb Pavlovsky, *Sistema RF v voyne 2014 goda. De Principatu Debili* (Moscow: Evropa, 2014), p. 45.

36 On the Orange Revolution see Andrew Wilson, *Ukraine's Orange Revolution* (New Haven: Yale University Press, 2005).

37 Zbigniew Brzezinski, *The Grand Chessboard: American Primacy and Its Geostrategic Imperatives* (New York: BasicBooks, 1997), p. 46. The book was published in Russian already in 1998 by the influential publishing house "International Relations" associated with the prestigious Moscow State Institute of International Relations (also known by the Russian acronym MGIMO) that belongs to Russia's MFA.

38 In 2015, Putin would declare: "We in Russia always saw the Russians and Ukrainians as a single people", see "Concert Celebrating Crimea and Sevastopol's Reunification with Russia", *President of Russia*, 18 March (2015), http://en.kremlin.ru/events/ president/news/47878

39 On the anti-Western shift in the Russian political system see also Andreas Umland, "Russia's New 'Special Path' after the Orange Revolution: Radical Anti-Westernism and Paratotalitarian Neo-Authoritarianism in 2005–8", *Russian Politics & Law*, Vol. 50, No. 6 (2012), pp. 19–40.

40 On the "Nashi" movement see Ivo Mijnssen, *The Quest for an Ideal Youth in Putin's Russia. Vol. 1. Back to Our Future! History, Modernity and Patriotism According to Nashi, 2005–2012* (Stuttgart: *ibidem*-Verlag, 2012); Jussi Lassila, *The Quest for an Ideal Youth in Putin's Russia. Vol. 2. The Search for Distinctive Conformism in the Political Communication of Nashi, 2005–2009* (Stuttgart: *ibidem*-Verlag, 2012).

41 Igor Yakovlev, Yuliya Ryshkina, Elena Loskutova *et al.* (eds), *Molodezhnye politicheskie organizatsii. Programmy i lyudi* (Moscow: ROO Tsentr "Panorama", 2007), p. 56.

42 "Katekhizis chlena Evraziyskogo Soyuza Molodezhi", *Evraziyskiy soyuz molodezhi*, 21 February (2005), www.rossia3.ru/katehizis.html

43 *Molodezhnye politicheskie organizatsii*, pp. 78–79.

44 *Ibid.*, p. 38.

45 "Presidential Executive Office Subdivisions", *President of Russia*, http://en.kremlin.ru/ structure/administration/departments

46 Modest Kolerov, "Front protiv Rossii", *Regnum*, 18 March (2005). See also Sinikukka Saari, "Russia's Post-Orange Revolution Strategies to Increase its Influence in Former Soviet Republics: Public Diplomacy *po russkii*", *Europe-Asia Studies*, Vol. 66, No. 1 (2014), pp. 50–66.

47 Konstantin Orekhov, "Kogda milee chuzhoy interes", *Tribuna-RT*, No. 3, 13 January (2005), p. 7.

48 Aleksandr Tsipko, "Rossiya zapolykhaet, esli vlast' ne stuknet kulakom", *Komsomol'skaya Pravda*, No. 51, 29 March (2005), p. 3.

49 Vitaliy Tret'yakov, "Mozhno li peredemokratit' Zapad?", *Rossiyskaya Gazeta*, No. 42, 3 March (2005), p. 3.

50 "Pervy obshchestvenny pravoslavny telekanal 'SPAS'", *Telekanal "SPAS"*, 28 July (2005), http://spas-tv.ru/history.html

51 Peter J.S. Duncan, *Russian Messianism: Third Rome, Holy Revolution, Communism and After* (London: Routledge, 2000); see also two Special Issues on the idea of Russia's "special path": *Russian Politics & Law*, Vol. 50, No. 5 (2012), and *Russian Politics & Law*, Vol. 50, No. 6 (2012).

52 Vladimir Shlapentokh, "The Puzzle of Russian Anti-Americanism: From 'Below' or from 'Above'", *Europe-Asia Studies*, Vol. 63, No. 5 (2011), pp. 875–889 (878).

53   Ilya Yablokov, *Conspiracy Discourse in Post-Soviet Russia: Political Strategies of Capture of the Public Sphere (1991–2014)*. A thesis submitted to the University of Manchester for the degree of Doctor of Philosophy in the Faculty of Humanities (Manchester: University of Manchester, 2014), pp. 91, 116.

54   Inozemtsev, "Russia of 2010s", p. 1.

55   Shevtsova, *Odinokaya derzhava*, p. 56.

56   Vladimir Putin, "Speech and the Following Discussion at the Munich Conference on Security Policy", *President of Russia*, 10 February (2007), http://en.kremlin.ru/events/president/transcripts/24034

57   Ibid.

58   Sherr, *Hard Diplomacy and Soft Coercion*, p. 96. The original italics omitted.

59   Yevgeniy Minchenko, " 'Politbyuro 2.0' nakanune perezagruzki elitnykh grupp", *Minchenko Consulting*, 19 February (2013), www.minchenko.ru/netcat_files/File/The%20Politburo%202_0%20%20on%20the%20eve%20of%20elite%20groups%20reload.pdf

60   "NATO's Eastward Expansion Rift to Dominate Summit", *Deutsche Welle*, 2 April (2008), www.dw.com/en/natos-eastward-expansion-rift-to-dominate-summit/a-3232477

61   "Press Statement Following Negotiations with French President Nicolas Sarkozy", *President of Russia*, 12 August (2008), http://en.kremlin.ru/events/president/transcripts/1072

62   Arthur Bright, "Estonia Accuses Russia of 'Cyberattack' ", *The Christian Science Monitor*, 17 May (2007), www.csmonitor.com/2007/0517/p99s01-duts.html

63   "Resolution 1647 (2009). The Implementation of Resolution 1633 (2008) on the Consequences of the War between Georgia and Russia", *Parliamentary Assembly*, 28 January (2009), http://assembly.coe.int/nw/xml/XRef/Xref-XML2HTML-en.asp?fileid=17708

64   Shevtsova, *Odinokaya derzhava*, p. 135.

65   Lilia Shevtsova, "Forward to the Past", *Journal of Democracy*, Vol. 26, No. 2 (2015), pp. 22–36 (25).

66   Vladimir Putin, "Excerpts from a Transcript of the Meeting with the Students of Kaliningrad State University", *President of Russia*, 27 June (2003), http://en.kremlin.ru/events/president/transcripts/22042

67   Juan J. Linz, "An Authoritarian Regime: Spain", in Erik Allardt, Yrjö Littunen (eds), *Cleavages, Ideologies, and Party Systems: Contributions to Comparative Political Sociology* (Helsinki: The Academic Bookstore, 1964), pp. 291–342 (297).

68   Sherr, *Hard Diplomacy and Soft Coercion*, p. 92.

69   Miriam Lanskoy, Elspeth Suthers, "Outlawing the Opposition", *Journal of Democracy*, Vol. 24, No. 3 (2013), pp. 75–87 (75).

70   Giles, Hanson, Lyne, Nixey, Sherr, Wood, *The Russian Challenge*, p. 51.

71   See Gulnaz Sharafutdinova, "The Pussy Riot Affair and Putin's Démarche from Sovereign Democracy to Sovereign Morality", *Nationalities Papers*, Vol. 42, No. 4 (2014), pp. 615–621.

72   LGBT stands for lesbian, gay, bisexual and transgender people.

73   See Françoise Daucé, "The Duality of Coercion in Russia: Cracking Down on 'Foreign Agents' ", *Demokratizatsiya: The Journal of Post-Soviet Democratization*, Vol. 23, No. 1 (2015), pp. 57–75.

74   Janusz Bugajski, "Russia's Pragmatic Reimperialization", *Caucasian Review of International Affairs*, Vol. 4, No. 1 (2010), pp. 3–19 (9).

75   Vladimir Putin, "Meeting of the Valdai International Discussion Club [2013]", *President of Russia*, 19 September (2013), http://en.kremlin.ru/events/president/news/19243

76   See, for example, some of the existing scholarship on the issue: Vera Tolz, *Russia* (London: Arnold, 2001); Laruelle, *In the Name of the Nation*; Kozhevnikova,

Shekhovtsov *et al. Radikal'ny russkiy natsionalizm*; Marlène Laruelle (ed.), *Russian Nationalism, Foreign Policy and Identity Debates in Putin's Russia: New Ideological Patterns after the Orange Revolution* (Stuttgart: *ibidem*-Verlag, 2012); Konstantin Sheiko, Stephen Brown, *History as Therapy: Alternative History and Nationalist Imaginings in Russia, 1991–2014* (Stuttgart: *ibidem*-Verlag, 2014); Mark Bassin, *The Gumilev Mystique: Biopolitics, Eurasianism, and the Construction of Community in Modern Russia* (Ithaca: Cornell University Press, 2016); Pål Kolstø, Helge Blakkisrud, *The New Russian Nationalism: Imperialism, Ethnicity and Authoritarianism 2000–15* (Edinburgh: Edinburgh University Press, 2016); Jardar Østbø, *The New Third Rome: Readings of a Russian Nationalist Myth* (Stuttgart: *ibidem*-Verlag, 2016); Clover, *Black Wind*.

77   Putin, "Meeting of the Valdai International Discussion Club [2013]".

78   "O TsSKP", *TsSKP*, www.cscp.ru/about/

79   Gennadiy Ryavkin, "Konservatizm vsemu golova", *Novgorodskie vedomosti*, No. 25, 9 August (2008), http://novved.ru/politika/24040-konservatizm-vsemu-golova.html.

80   "Ideologiya Partii osnovana na konservatizme", *Dagestanskaya Pravda*, No. 392, 17 December (2008).

81   Vladimir Putin, "Rossiya: natsional'ny vopros", *Nezavisimaya gazeta*, No. 7, 23 January (2012), www.ng.ru/politics/2012-01-23/1_national.html

82   Vladimir Putin, "Address to the Federal Assembly", *President of Russia*, 12 December (2012), http://en.kremlin.ru/events/president/news/17118

83   "Interview to Channel One and Associated Press News Agency", *President of Russia*, 4 September (2013), http://en.kremlin.ru/events/president/news/19143

84   "News Conference of Vladimir Putin", *President of Russia*, 19 December (2013), http://en.kremlin.ru/events/president/news/19859

85   On the official "conservative" turn of the Kremlin see also Marlène Laruelle, "Conservatism as the Kremlin's New Toolkit: An Ideology at the Lowest Cost", *Russian Analytical Digest*, No. 138 (2013), pp. 2–4; Andrey Makarychev, Alexandra Yatsyk, "A New Russian Conservatism: Domestic Roots and Repercussions for Europe", *CIDOB Notes Internacionals*, No. 93 (2014), pp. 1–6; Maria Engström, "Contemporary Russian Messianism and New Russian Foreign Policy", *Contemporary Security Policy*, Vol. 35, No. 3 (2014), pp. 356–379.

86   Vladimir Putin, "Meeting of the Valdai International Discussion Club [2014]", *President of Russia*, 24 October (2014), http://en.kremlin.ru/events/president/transcripts/46860

87   Dmitry Medvedev, "Go Russia!", *President of Russia*, 10 September (2009), http://en.kremlin.ru/events/president/news/5413

88   "Na X s'yezde 'Edinoy Rossii' predsedatel' vysshego soveta partii Boris Gryzlov nazval novoy partiynoy ideologiey rossiyskiy konservatizm", *Zvezda*, No. 169, 25 November (2008).

89   BRICS is the acronym for the association of emerging economies such as Brazil, Russia, India, China and South Africa.

90   " 'Est' kak minimum tri stsenariya "oranzhevoy revolyutsii" v Rossii' ", *Izvestiya*, No. 37, 4 March (2015), p. 3.

91   Vladislav Inozemtsev, "Konservatsiya Rossiyskoy Federatsii", *Moskovskiy komsomolets*, No. 143, 8 July (2014), p. 3.

92   Vladimir Putin, "Presidential Address to the Federal Assembly", *President of Russia*, 12 December (2013), http://en.kremlin.ru/events/president/news/19825

93   Putin, "Meeting of the Valdai International Discussion Club [2013]".

94   Ibid.

95   Putin, "Rossiya: natsional'ny vopros".

96   Putin, "Meeting of the Valdai International Discussion Club [2013]".

97   Ibid.

98   The Customs Union would later be joined by Armenia and Kyrgyzstan.

99   Putin, "Presidential Address to the Federal Assembly".

100 "Sovmestnoe zayavlenie Prezidenta Rossiyskoy Federatsii i Prezidenta Respubliki Balarus", *Prezident Rossii*, 31 May (2012), http://kremlin.ru/supplement/1226

101 "Interview mit Sergej Karaganow: Putin-Berater droht mit Vernichtung von Nato-Waffen", *Der Spiegel*, 11 July (2016), www.spiegel.de/spiegel/russland-sergej-karaganow-droht-mit-vernichtung-von-nato-waffen-a-1102108.html

102 See, for example, Yevgeniy Il'in, "Kontseptsiya Bol'shoy Evropy ot Lissabona do Vladivostoka: problemy i perspektivy", *Vestnik MGIMO*, No. 2 (2015), pp. 84–92.

103 Yakunin held the post of Russian Railways CEO in 2005–2015.

104 Vladimir Yakunin, *Zheleznye dorogi Rossii i gosudarstvo* (Moscow: Nauchny ekspert, 2010), pp. 228–229.

105 "Direct Line with Vladimir Putin", *President of Russia*, 17 April (2014), http://en.kremlin.ru/events/president/news/20796

106 Ibid.

107 Aleksandr Kuranov, Eduard Shtayner, "Yorg Haider: khochu v Rossiyu. Glavnoy tsel'yu svoey politiki lider avstriyskikh ul'trapravykh schitaet zabotu o 'malen'kom cheloveke'", *Nezavisimaya gazeta*, No. 135, 7 July (2003), p. 6.

108 Igor Chernyak, "Kak my pogovorili s glavnym frantsuzskim 'natsi'", *Komsomol'skaya Pravda*, No. 40, 5 March (2003), p. 5.

109 Konstantin Kachalin, "Gost' 'RV'. 'Budushchee Evropy – za severnoy dugoy'", *Rossiyskie Vesti*, No. 44, 8 December (2004), p. 4.

110 Andreas Mölzer, "Russland und die Muster-Demokraten", *Andreas Mölzer, Mitglied des Europaparlaments*, 6 March (2012), https://andreasmoelzer.wordpress.com/2012/03/06/russland-und-die-muster-demokraten/

111 Natalya Barabash, "My s Kadyrovym nashli obshchiy yazyk", *Vzglyad*, 10 May (2012), www.vz.ru/politics/2012/5/10/578121.html

112 "A Strong Russia Is Good for Europe!", *Manuel Ochsenreiter*, 18 April (2014), http://manuelochsenreiter.com/blog/2014/4/18/a-strong-russia-is-good-for-europe

113 Zhan Parvulesko [Jean Parvulesco], *Putin i Evraziyskaya imperiya* (Saint-Petersburg: TID Amfora, 2006), p. 230. This book is the Russian translation edited by Aleksandr Dugin; for the original French version see Jean Parvulesco, *Vladimir Poutine et l'Eurasie* (Charmes: Amis de la Culture Européenne, 2005).

114 Parvulesko, Putin i Evraziyskaya imperiya, p. 244.

115 "Keleten senki nem bízik Orbánban", *444*, 30 March (2015), http://444.hu/2015/03/30/jobbik-kulpol-gyongyosi/

116 Darya Aslamova, "Marin Le Pen: 'Evrosoyuz – eto SSSR v evropeyskom masshtabe. I tak zhe poterpel krakh'", *Komsomol'skaya Pravda*, No. 35, 11 March (2012), p. 6.

117 "Watch out – Warmongers about!", *British National Party*, 24 April (2014), https://web.archive.org/web/20140425212744/http://www.bnp.org.uk/news/national/watch-out-%E2%80%93-warmongers-about

118 Uil'yam Engdal [F. William Engdahl], "Zakat Imperii i budushchee Evrazii", in Aleksandr Dugin (ed.), *Leviafan*, No. 3 (2011), pp. 7–17 (13).

119 "Rothschilds Run British Intelligence Operation into Russia through JNR and Diligence", *LaRouche PAC*, 14 March (2010), http://archive.larouchepac.com/node/13871

120 "Le Pen: I Admire 'Cool Head' Putin's Resistance to West's New Cold War, *Euronews*, 1 December (2014), www.euronews.com/2014/12/01/le-pen-i-admire-cool-head-putin-s-resistance-to-west-s-new-cold-war/

121 Galina Dudina, "V Evrope pribavilos' kraynikh", *Kommersant. Daily*, No. 84, 20 May (2014), p. 7. Chauprade left the FN in November 2015 over the ideological conflict with Marine Le Pen and his role in helping two French pilots accused of drug-running escape from the Dominican Republic, see Charles Platiau, "MEP Quits Front National Accusing Marine Le Pen of Treason", *RFI*, 10 November (2015), http://en.rfi.fr/americas/20151110-mep-quits-front-national-accusing-marine-le-pen-treason

122 Niva Mirakian, "Evronadezhda na Rossiyu", *Rossiyskaya Gazeta*, No. 184, 15 August (2014), p. 6.
123 Evgeniy Tarasyuk, "Est' i drugaya Evropa", *Zavtra*, No. 42, 15 October (2014), p. 2.
124 Uil'yam Engdal [F. William Engdahl], "Rossiya – v avangarde sozdaniya novogo mira", *Nevskoe vremya*, No. 126, 17 July (2015), www.nvspb.ru/tops/rossiya-v-avangarde-sozdaniya-novogo-mira-58230
125 "Putin verteidigt Europas Zivilisation", *Kurier*, 17 May (2014), http://kurier.at/politik/eu/marine-le-pen-putin-verteidigt-die-werte-der-europaeischen-zivilisation/65.991.041
126 Patrick J. Buchanan, "Is Putin One of Us?", *CNSNews*, 17 December (2013), www.cnsnews.com/commentary/patrick-j-buchanan/putin-one-us
127 Emil Persson, "Banning 'Homosexual Propaganda': Belonging and Visibility in Contemporary Russian Media", *Sexuality & Culture*, Vol. 19, No. 2 (2015), pp. 256–274 (271).
128 Matt Sinovic, "Bob Vander Plaats: America's Most Powerful Bigot?", *Salon*, 9 August (2013), www.salon.com/2013/08/09/iowas_most_powerful_bigot_meet_bob_vander_plaats/
129 Brian Tashman, "Bob Vander Plaats Praises Russia's Ban on Pro-Gay Rights Speech", *Right Wing Watch*, 10 September (2013), www.rightwingwatch.org/content/bob-vander-plaats-praises-russia-s-ban-pro-gay-rights-speech
130 J. Lester Feder, "Anti-LGBT Persecution Can Form Basis for 'Crimes against Humanity' Lawsuit, Federal Judge Rules", *Buzzfeed*, 16 August (2013), www.buzzfeed.com/lesterfeder/pastor-who-helped-spark-ugandan-anti-gay-backlash-9a7s
131 Scott Lively, "An Open Letter to President Vladimir Putin", *Scott Lively Ministries*, 30 August (2013), www.scottlively.net/2013/08/30/an-open-letter-to-president-vladimir-putin/
132 Elena Chinkova, "Vladimir Yakunin, glava RZhD: Propishite v Konstitutsii, chto takoe 'brak'!", *Komsomol'skaya Pravda*, No. 103, 11 September (2014), p. 11.
133 Miranda Blue, "Globalizing Homophobia, Part 2: 'Today the Whole World Is Looking at Russia'", *Right Wing Watch*, 3 October (2013), www.rightwingwatch.org/content/globalizing-homophobia-part-2-today-whole-world-looking-russia
134 Fronte Nazionale Uffic., "Io sto con Putin", *Facebook*, 5 September (2013), www.facebook.com/photo.php?fbid=615875215114378
135 Darya Aslamova, "Vengerskiy politik Marton D'endeshi: My stali vassalami SShA i administratsii Evrosoyuza", *Komsomol'skaya Pravda*, No. 137, 4 December (2014), p. 6.
136 Jędrzej Bielecki, "Putin bohaterem Frontu Le Pena", *Rzeczpospolita*, 20 March (2014), www.rp.pl/temat/84807.html
137 Alliance for Peace and Freedom (APF), "Fiore Speaks in Russia – Moscow Is the Third Rome", *YouTube*, 17 May (2015), www.youtube.com/watch?v=oAt1a2_EiOg
138 Mirakian, "Evronadezhda na Rossiyu", p. 6.
139 Galina Sapozhnikova, "Deputat v Evroparlamente ot Vengrii Bela Kovach: Spasat' Zapad opyat' pridetsya Rossii", *Komsomol'skaya Pravda*, No. 116, 13 October (2014), p. 8.
140 "A Strong Russia Is Good for Europe!".
141 "Wir wollen einen wie Putin", *Info-Direkt*, No. 1 (2015), pp. 6–9 (7).
142 "In eigener Sache, März 2014", *Freies-oesterreich.net*, 30 March (2014), http://freies-oesterreich.net/2014/03/30/in-eigener-sache-maerz-2014/
143 Quoted in Andrew Higgins, "Far-Right Fever for a Europe Tied to Russia", *The New York Times*, 20 May (2014), www.nytimes.com/2014/05/21/world/europe/europes-far-right-looks-to-russia-as-a-guiding-force.html
144 "Gábor Vona Had a Lecture at Lomonosov University in Russia", *Jobbik*, 24 May (2013), www.jobbik.com/g%C3%A1bor_vona_had_lecture_lomonosov_university_russia

145 "Lider partii 'Yobbik – Za luchshuyu Vengriyu' Gabor Vona o evroatlantizme, Rossii, Gruzii, Sirii, rusinakh, Transil'vanii i Serbii", *IA REX*, 22 January (2014), www.iarex.ru/interviews/44688.html

146 "Σφοδρό χτύπημα στην εξωτερική πολιτική των ΗΠΑ: Ιδρύεται σήμερα η Ευρωασιατική Οικονομική Ένωση στο Καζακστάν", Χρυσή Αυγή, 29 May (2014), www.xryshaygh. com/enimerosi/view/sfodro-chtuphma-sthn-ejwterikh-politikh-twn-hpa-idruetai-shmera-h-eurwasiat

147 "Ataka – Evrozibory 2014", *Ataka*, www.ataka.bg/ep2014/

148 "Siderov ot parlamentarnata tribuna: Da sprem da dishame evroatlanticheskiya prakh, zashtoto shche se zadushim", *Ataka*, 5 December (2014), www.ataka.bg/index.php? option=com_content&task=view&id=7108&Itemid=1

149 "Siderov: Da se orientirame kam Evraziyskiya sayuz", *Novini*, 13 June (2014), www.novini.bg/news/210146-сидеров-да-се-ориентираме-към-евразийския-съюз.html

150 "The Interpreter Obtains List of Prospective Attendees for Russian Valdai Club Annual Meeting", *The Interpreter*, 15 October (2014), www.interpretermag.com/the-interpreter-obtains-list-of-prospective-attendees-for-prestigious-russian-valdai-club-annual-meeting/. The document reads that Chauprade participated in the Valdai meeting in 2012 too, but a 2013 interview with him suggests that he participated in the Valdai meeting in 2013 for the first time in his life which may or may not be true; see "Aymeric Chauprade: 'Si la Russie court derrière le modèle occidental, elle sera toujours en retard' ", *Égalité et Réconciliation*, 16 October (2013), www.egaliteetrecon ciliation.fr/Aymeric-Chauprade-Si-la-Russie-court-derriere-le-modele-occidental-elle-sera-toujours-en-retard-20768.html

151 Guillaume Faye, "Poutine: le De Gaulle russe?", *Guillaume Faye*, 19 November (2014), www.gfaye.com/poutine-le-de-gaulle-russe/

152 "L'Associazione Lombardia Russia", *Associazione Culturale Lombardia Russia*, 5 February (2014), www.lombardiarussia.org/index.php/associazione/lo-scopo

153 Putin, "Meeting of the Valdai International Discussion Club [2013]".

154 The journal is edited by Leonid Savin, and its advisory board features Dugin and Piskorski, as well as several Russian and international academics.

155 Márton Gyöngyösi, "Europe's Future: At the Crossroads of Eastern Relations and Western Fall", *Journal of Eurasian Affairs*, Vol. 3, No. 1 (2015), pp. 84–87 (85–86).

4

FAR-RIGHT ELECTION OBSERVERS IN THE SERVICE OF THE KREMLIN'S DOMESTIC AND FOREIGN POLICIES

Introduction

In his comparison of political systems in Russia and China, Ivan Krastev argues that 'observed from afar, [the Russian regime] certainly looks like a democracy', as it, in particular, 'enjoys a democratic constitution, runs elections, has a multiparty political system, [and] has some free media'.[1] At the same time, all these democratic institutions are largely a façade that is used to legitimise the authoritarian regime both domestically and internationally; 'Russia clearly has elections, but no rotation of power. . . . In the Russian system elections are used as the way to legitimise the lack of rotation'.[2]

Electoral authoritarianism, according to Andreas Schedler, has today become 'the modal type of political regime in the developing world':

> A large number of political regimes in the contemporary world . . . have established the institutional façades of democracy . . . in order to conceal (and reproduce) harsh realities of authoritarian governance. [. . .]
>
> Electoral authoritarian regimes play the game of multiparty elections by holding regular elections for the chief executive and a national legislative assembly. Yet they violate the liberal-democratic principles of freedom and fairness so profoundly and systematically as to render elections instruments of authoritarian rule rather than 'instruments of democracy'.[3]

In the post-Soviet space, to be sure, a number of attempts were made to confront electoral authoritarian regimes that posed as electoral democracies. After the Cold War, due to the increased focus on commitment to democracy in the countries of Central and Eastern Europe, as well as some other parts of the world, it became a norm that 'governments committed to democratic elections invite international monitors'.[4] According to the 'Declaration of Principles for International Election Observation' adopted at the UN in 2005, international election observation 'assesses election processes in accordance with international principles for genuine democratic elections and domestic law', and 'has the potential to enhance the integrity of election processes, by deterring and exposing irregularities and fraud and by providing recommendations for improving electoral processes'.[5] The most influential and reputable organisations involved in international election observation in the post-Soviet space are the OSCE, its Office for Democratic Institutions and Human Rights (ODIHR), European Union, PACE and European Commission. Since the mid-1990s, these organisations have conducted numerous election observation missions, and their evaluation of the fairness, openness and credibility of elections has become an important factor in assessing the level of democratisation of political systems in the post-Soviet space.

While international monitoring is not a panacea from electoral authoritarianism, 'negative reports from observers can lead to reduced international benefits and international observers can reduce election day fraud directly', and therefore international election monitors are 'more costly to pseudo-democrats than to true democrats'.[6] The significance of the international electoral observation missions has increased even more following a series of 'colour revolutions' in Georgia (2003), Ukraine (2004) and Kyrgyzstan (2005). The 'Revolution of Roses' in Georgia in November 2003 was largely modelled on the Serbian 'Bulldozer Revolution' (which had led to the overthrow of Slobodan Milošević's regime in 2000) and prevented pro-Russian Eduard Shevardnadze from 'winning' the fraudulent presidential elections. Already after the 'Revolution of Roses', Vladimir Putin's regime realised the threat of 'colour revolutions' to the Russian domination in post-Soviet space and started taking countermeasures against international election observation missions whose conclusions about unfair electoral procedures played an important role in mobilising societies against electoral fraud. One countermeasure was a failure: Russian representatives at the OSCE 'advocated reduced funding for OSCE/ODIHR missions and otherwise attempted to undermine the organization's work as an independent but prodemocracy judge of election quality',[7] but were unsuccessful. Other countermeasures were more sophisticated, and, following Rick Fawn, they could be placed in three categories in terms of tactics:

1   'asserting that double standards exist in the process' and 'advancing an alternative language for democratization';
2   'establishing alternative mechanisms and practices for [international election observer missions] that aim to give legitimacy to that alternative conception of democracy';
3   'using those tactics to deceive their own populations and undercut domestic opposition'.[8]

The second tactic refers to 'a shadow market for election monitoring' implying 'a supply of lenient monitoring organizations'[9] whose objective is anything but providing independent observation of elections. In particular, their activities may conceal practices of electoral authoritarianism or aim at legitimising elections that are deemed illegitimate by the international community. While these organisations may even present some methodology of conducting proper monitoring, they never use it and effectively turn the idea of independent electoral observation into a postmodern joke. By mocking independent international observation, which is essential for determining the level of compliance of a particular election cycle to democratic norms, they mock democracy itself.

This chapter explores several organisations of this type, but specifically focuses on the far-right element of the 'alternative' electoral observation missions that consistently employ evidently pro-Russian and/or controlled monitors who would attempt to legitimise controversial and/or unfair elections and, by doing so, assert Russian foreign policy interests in the post-Soviet space. First of all, the chapter discusses the history and activities of the most important organisation in this context, namely Commonwealth of the Independent States – Election Monitoring Organisation (CIS-EMO), that has been monitoring controversial elections in the post-Soviet space since 2004 and has pioneered in engaging ideologically loaded, far-right observers in their observation missions. Then the chapter looks at two Western organisations, which have been associated with CIS-EMO, and considers their activities, as well as connections between them and other Russian organisations involved in politically biased electoral observation.

CIS-EMO

The history of CIS-EMO is closely linked to the figure of Aleksey Kochetkov who headed the organisation from 2004 until 2013.[10] Kochetkov first rose to relative prominence in 1992 when he became editor of the *Russkiy poryadok* (Russian order), a newspaper of Aleksandr Barkashov's notorious fascist organisation RNE.[11]

The RNE took an active part in the violent part of the 1993 Russian constitutional crisis – a conflict between President Boris Yeltsin and a group within the Russian parliament heavily influenced by Russian ultranationalists and led by Vice President Aleksandr Rutskoy and Chairman of the parliament Ruslan Khasbulatov. For a better understanding of the subsequent discussion, it should be noted that Rutskoy was one of the first top Russian politicians who recognised, already in 1992, the 'independence' of Transnistria, a breakaway state in Moldova that became 'a transit point for regional enterprises in human trafficking, arms smuggling, and other illicit activities'.[12] Rutskoy's support for Transnistria paid off, and around 150 fighters from Transnistria were involved in Rutskoy's coup attempt in October 1993 in Moscow.[13] The RNE, too, was in contact with Transnistrian fighters, via the so-called 'Minister of State Security' of Transnistria Vladimir Antyufeev (alias Vadim Shevtsov), who retained his links with the RNE's leader Barkashov after 1993.[14]

The conflict between Yeltsin and the parliament ended in the shelling and consequent storming of the parliamentary building, and hundreds of fighters of the RNE – 22 of them were armed by Khasbulatov with machine guns[15] – were involved in fighting with the police and army forces loyal to Yeltsin. Kochetkov, among other members of the RNE, was arrested, but then granted amnesty in the beginning of 1994. In September 1995, Barkashov expelled several top members of the RNE, including Kochetkov, for alleged attempts at subversive activities and collaboration with security services and political movements opposing the RNE.[16]

In the second half of the 1990s, Kochetkov, like many former and actual members of Russian far-right groups, started a career of a *piarshchik* – a Russian term for a person involved in political consultancy promoting various candidates at elections in Russia.[17] This work was hardly ideological; all that mattered was money, although Kochetkov did indeed favour customers such as Sergey Baburin or Viktor Alksnis[18] who not only participated in various far-right movements but were also actively involved in the defence of the Russian parliament against pro-Yeltsin forces in October 1993. At the same time, Kochetkov maintained active contacts with Russian ultranationalists. As a member of the Russian Society of Friends of Saddam Hussein, an organisation founded by neo-pagan right-wing extremist Aleksey Andreev, Kochetkov visited Iraq in 1997 and published his pro-Iraqi and anti-American report in *Zavtra*, a National Bolshevik newspaper edited by Aleksandr Prokhanov.[19] As Robert Horvath notes, Kochetkov's official biography mentions that he 'worked in Iraq in 1998', but it gives no further details on his work.[20]

Founding CIS-EMO was a joint idea of Kochetkov, his then wife Marina Kochetkova and yet another *piarshchik* Viktor Karmatskiy. Marina Kochetkova did not have any political background, but, instead, had business acumen. Karmatsky was engaged in Yeltsin's presidential campaign in 1996, managed relations between Yeltsin's Presidential Administration and political parties in 1996–1997, and worked at the public relations office of the Ministry of Fuel and Energy in 1997–1999; he later resumed his career of a *piarshchik*.

In September 2003, when CIS-EMO was founded in Nizhny Novgorod under the name 'Autonomous Non-commercial Organisation for Monitoring Elections in CIS States',[21] it was not yet obvious that the project would be a success. 'Alternative mechanisms and practices' became relevant only after the 'colour revolutions' had taken place in Georgia and Ukraine, and Russian authorities became concerned with the perceived threat to Russia's electoral authoritarianism posed by organisations such as the OSCE and ODIHR.

At that time, Russia did have a state-controlled organisation that was involved in monitoring elections: this was one of the functions of the Russia-dominated Interparliamentary Assembly of the CIS Member Nations (IPA CIS). Democratisation researchers see the IPA CIS as politically biased and only created to water down criticisms coming from the OSCE and ODIHR. For example, Susan Hyde argues that the IPA CIS 'has earned a reputation for praising blatantly fraudulent elections in former Soviet states and issuing reports that are in direct opposition to the conclusions of the OSCE/ODIHR missions'.[22] In a similar vein, Judith Kelley writes that the monitoring activity of the IPA CIS 'is widely discredited and regarded as having been created merely to counter the criticisms of the OSCE in the former Soviet region'.[23] The problematic nature of the IPA CIS and its dependence on Russian foreign policy were too obvious, and the organisation never had the credentials of independence and impartiality comparable to those of the OSCE/ODIHR. This evidently irritated Moscow, but another problem was that Russia itself was a participating state of OSCE, and, while it had its grievances against the workings of this organisation[24] and even wanted to reduce funding for OSCE/ODIHR observation missions, the Kremlin could not – at least at that time – straightforwardly challenge it, not least because it was still trying to use the OSCE to weaken NATO.[25]

CIS-EMO, which was formally an NGO, was neither formally nor substantively an alternative to OSCE/ODIHR, but the Russian authorities could capitalise on its status of an NGO to strengthen the 'impartial image' of the IPA CIS. The late Roman Kupchinsky made a similar argument:

> One possible explanation [for the creation of CIS-EMO] is that after so many discrepancies between CIS [i.e. IPA CIS] monitors' conclusions and those arrived at by OSCE election observers, a 'neutral' NGO was needed to lend legitimacy to the official CIS reports and to thereby reinforce Russian policy goals.
> A certain amount of confusion resulted from the fact that this NGO had a very similar name to the official CIS monitors, and that its reports were almost carbon copies of those filed by the official CIS monitors.[26]

Kochetkov apparently used his older contacts to prominent ultranationalist politicians like Baburin, Alksnis and others, with whom he worked as a *piarshchik* in the past[27] in order to make his organisation visible in the world of Russian political technology and assert its usefulness for the Russian foreign policy interests. At that time, Alksnis was an MP, while Baburin became the Deputy Chair of the Russian parliament in the beginning of 2004. Karmatskiy, who had several years of civil service experience, also seemed to have contributed to establishing the links between CIS-EMO and the authorities.

Despite the arguably good start of the organisation's work, its observation of the 2004 presidential election in Ukraine was almost a disaster for the organisation. The election was marked by a political struggle between pro-Russian Viktor Yanukovych and pro-Western Viktor Yushchenko, and Moscow sent to Ukraine its best political consultants – including the Kremlin's 'gray cardinal' Gleb Pavlovsky – to help Yanukovych with the electoral campaign. Kochetkov himself acted as a *piarshchik* of Yanukovych's election campaign team, openly supporting his Partiya rehioniv (Party of Regions), and warning against Serbian and Georgian revolutionary 'scenarios' in Ukraine after the presidential election,[28] thus violating the principles of international election observation that insist on the strict impartiality of observers and unacceptability of any bias or preference in relation to political contenders.

Yanukovych, who was Prime Minister of Ukraine at that time, had almost all the advantages of administrative leverage that allowed him and his high-ranking supporters to rig the election and 'win' the second round. Yet the fraudulent nature of both rounds of the election was so obvious that even Dmitry Rogozin, then the leader of the far-right 'Rodina' party's parliamentary faction in the State Duma had to admit:

> These elections in Ukraine – its first round, as well as the second round – demonstrated that administrative leverage can do more harm than good. The administrative leverage destroyed the opportunities that Yanukovych could have seized had he not been Prime Minister. . . . Ukraine is doubtlessly facing a crisis of political power. International observers will unlikely declare these elections valid given the numerous violations that they have observed.[29]

Rogozin was right, as the international observers neither from OSCE/ODIHR, nor from the EU, PACE or NATO Parliamentary Assembly declared the elections free and fair. However, the political stakes were so high for the Kremlin that the Russian authorities had to keep insisting on the legitimacy of Yanukovych's 'victory'. Vladimir Rushaylo, then Chair of the Executive Committee of the CIS and head of the CIS observation mission, stated that some flaws and downsides 'had not exerted a significant impact on the free expression of the voters' will' and 'Ukraine's presidential elections were legitimate, free and fair';[30] Kochetkov, as head of CIS-EMO claimed the same.[31] In his turn, Putin declared that the OSCE's negative conclusions were 'inappropriate' and – turning to usual 'whataboutism'[32] – criticised the OSCE election observation missions in Afghanistan and Kosovo.[33]

The Kremlin eventually failed to secure Yanukovych's presidency in 2004, as Yushchenko won in the second run-off of the presidential election in December 2004. Despite the poor performance of CIS-EMO in Ukraine, its subsequent success was one of many other consequences of the Orange Revolution, as the Kremlin had to adapt its domestic and foreign policies to the perceived threats to Russia's dominant position in what it considered to be its sphere of influence. CIS-EMO, which had a status of an NGO but was intrinsically loyal to the Kremlin, promoted Moscow's interests in the post-Soviet space and Europe. According to Nicu Popescu, 'Russian authorities have been boosting a CIS election monitoring organisation (CIS-EMO) whose verdicts for elections conducted in the CIS have always been diametrically opposed to OSCE opinions on the elections'.[34] After the Orange Revolution, Kochetkov started cooperating with Modest Kolerov,[35] who, in March 2005, became the head of the Russian Presidential Directorate for Interregional Relations and Cultural Contacts with Foreign Countries that was aimed at preventing the spread of 'colour revolutions' in the post-Soviet space.

As Horvath argues, Kolerov's *Regnum* website 'regularly used CIS-EMO as a source of information and commentary'.[36]

Since 2005, CIS-EMO took part in more than 40 observation missions at elections in countries such as Azerbaijan, Estonia, France, Germany, Kazakhstan, Kyrgyzstan, Poland, Russia, Turkey and Ukraine, as well as in generally unrecognised, breakaway states such as Abkhazia, South Ossetia and Transnistria.

CIS-EMO's activities in each case corresponded to the interests of the Russian authorities in a peculiarly implicit manner. When CIS-EMO observed 'elections' or 'referenda' in Abkhazia, South Ossetia and Transnistria, that is the 'states' that Russia helped to separate from Georgia and Moldova to undermine their pro-Western aspirations, the objective was to *legitimise* those plebiscites by mere presence of international observers that would make the imitation of the normal electoral process more credible.

In Estonia, on the other hand, which Russia had been trying to discredit as a democratic member state of the EU, the objective was to draw attention to the allegedly discriminated Russian-speaking population and to dispute the democratic nature of the electoral process in Estonia. As CIS-EMO's report on the 2011 parliamentary elections in Estonia concluded, its 'observers [were] not warranted in maintaining that the electoral system and democratic institutions in Estonia fully conformed to the standards and requirements imposed on modern democratic states'.[37]

In Turkey, where the Kremlin wanted to diminish cooperation with NATO and the United States, CIS-EMO concluded that 'in terms of economic recovery, the democratic Islamisation on the basis of its own resources [had] turned out to be more efficient than the military administration under the aegis of NATO or following the principles of "Washington consensus" of the International Monetary Fund'.[38]

While there is no evidence that the CIS-EMO's activities were directly sanctioned by the Kremlin, the agenda of its work always complied with Russia's foreign policy. As Jakob Hedenskog and Robert Larsson argue,

> Several of [CIS-EMO's] observation missions have been controversial, as their findings have often been in sharp contradiction with the findings of other international organisations such as the OSCE, the Council of Europe, or the European Union. The CIS elections observation missions, which are often in fact purely Russian and which are labelled CIS in order to improve their legitimacy, are naturally often accused of being subservient to Kremlin foreign policy.[39]

Russian authorities seemed to appreciate CIS-EMO's work, and it received official support, in particular, from Russia's Foreign Ministry. For example, when Kochetkov and his colleague were arrested in Moldova for a brawl in July 2005,[40] it was Foreign Minister Sergey Lavrov himself who called the arrest 'an unacceptable act' and harshly linked the incident to the Transnistrian problem: 'It looks like the

Moldovan authorities are committed to do everything possible and impossible not only to block the Transnistrian reconciliation . . ., but also damage Russian-Moldovan relations even further'.[41]

Apparently hacked communications of Kochetkov provide further insights in the internal workings of the CIS-EMO. In the context of the 2010 presidential election in Ukraine, Kochetkov wrote:

> We have built a long track record of working in the area of the electoral processes of all levels that allows us to work not only in the capacity of independent arbiter of specific elections, but also to exert influence on the coverage of the electoral process, as well as its development (and, consequently, results of the elections). The implementation of the project will allow us to create an efficient mechanism of influencing the voters (shaping public opinion, attitudes towards a specific candidate, increasing or lowering voter turnout). Furthermore, the project will provide the information support for countering the structures engaged in the anti-Russian activities during the electoral campaign (supposedly OSCE ODIHR, UCCA [Ukrainian Congress Committee of America], NDI [National Democratic Institute], IRI [International Republican Institute], organisations that are financed by the US State Department, etc.). As a result, the implementation of the project will allow for exerting influence on the elections in the interests of the Russian Federation.[42]

According to one investigative journalist, Kochetkov wrote this in a memorandum addressed to Sergey Vinokurov who headed Russia's Presidential Directorate for Interregional Relations and Cultural Contacts with Foreign Countries in 2008–2012.[43] Kochetkov also specified the cost of the 'project': RUB 19,818,164 (approximately €476,010 at that time), including the total daily allowance for the participants in the amount of RUB 1,498,000 (€35,980) and the salaries for them in the amount of RUB 2,797,000 (€67,180).[44] At that time, Vinokurov was also in charge of Moscow's relations with Transnistria and South Ossetia,[45] and his position might be the original link between him and CIS-EMO that observed the 'electoral processes' there. It is unknown whether Kochetkov's 'project' was approved by Vinokurov, but CIS-EMO did send an observation mission consisting of 416 people to monitor the 2010 presidential election in Ukraine.

Documents recovered after the 2014 Ukrainian revolution from one of the offices of the Ukrainian Partiya rehioniv headed by former President Yanukovych provide further proof that CIS-EMO's services were a paid job. CIS-EMO monitored the regional elections in Ukraine in autumn 2010, and the documents testify that the total daily allowance for 65 observers amounted to $10,500, while the remuneration for the entire mission amounted to $51,000.[46]

The details about potential or actual payments for the work of CIS-EMO suggest that, rather than following someone's orders, the organisation offered its services to the interested parties, the choice of which was determined by Kochetkov's understanding of Moscow's foreign policy interests.

One of the features of CIS-EMO is that they have been inviting election observers not only from the CIS states, but from the EU too. This became possible after CIS-EMO had been re-registered in Moscow in October 2005 under the awkwardly worded name 'Autonomous Non-commercial Organisation "International Organisation for Monitoring Elections" "CIS-EMO"'. Widening the scope of the organisation's activities allowed for observing elections outside the CIS and engaging international, that is non-CIS, monitors – these changes became one of the factors of success for CIS-EMO.

Considering the CIS-EMO's loyalty to the Kremlin's foreign policy, the choice of observers that CIS-EMO could involve in their observation missions has always been largely limited to two main categories: election monitors taking part in CIS-EMO missions would be either pro-Russian or willing to turn the blind eye to the organisation's pro-Russian orientation. The majority of monitors – in terms of their ideological dispositions – have been actual or former members of pro-Russian, far-right and/or (far)-left movements or parties.

The far-right element of CIS-EMO's observation missions has been particularly visible. This can be explained by two factors. The first reason is both pragmatic and ideological. Kochetkov's background in the fascist RNE and his own views determined specific ideological affiliations of the people he could trust and, thus, engage in observation missions. There might also be an element of Kochetkov's gratitude to and/or dependence on his original patrons such as Baburin and Alksnis. Among the around 100 CIS-EMO's election monitors who made an unsuccessful trip to Moldova in March 2005 to illegitimately observe the parliamentary elections, there were, in particular, members of the ultranationalist party 'Narodnaya Volya' party led by Baburin and Alksnis, Vladimir Zhirinovsky's LDPR and Eduard Limonov's NBP.[47]

The ideological factor was also important with regard to non-Russian observers. Despite the fact that, by the time of the foundation of CIS-EMO, Kochetkov was not a known member of any far-right organisation, he still maintained right-wing views. At the same time, in the course of his work at CIS-EMO and under the influence of the individuals he worked with, Kochetkov seems to have shifted towards New Right and Eurasianist positions. As a sign of this shift, the website of the Centre for Monitoring Democratic Processes 'Quorum', which he founded in 2008 and which was merged with CIS-EMO, featured four articles by the Italian New Right geopolitical theorist and Dugin's associate Tiberio Graziani, then editor of *Eurasia: Rivista di studi geopolitici* (Eurasia: Review of geopolitical studies).[48] In these articles, Graziani, fully conforming to Eurasianist principles, attacked 'the hegemony of Washington on the Mediterranean Region', condemned ' "liberalist" practices imposed by the United States' on Europe, and praised Russia as 'the backbone of Eurasia' and 'the keystone of the multipolar system'.[49]

Two EU-based organisations acted as major subcontractors for CIS-EMO for several years recruiting international monitors for joint election observation missions: the Belgium-based Eurasian Observatory for Democracy & Elections and the Poland-based European Centre of Geopolitical Analysis. The next two sections focus on these organisations.

Eurasian Observatory for Democracy & Elections

The Eurasian Observatory for Democracy & Elections (EODE) was founded by Belgian Luc Michel in 2007 as an 'electoral monitoring organisation'. Although it claimed to be 'a non-aligned NGO', its political affiliation and ideological dispositions suggest otherwise.

Michel started his political life in his late teens and was a member of various fascist movements and groupuscules such as the Front de la jeunesse (Belgian Youth Front), Fédération d'action nationale et européenne (French Federation of European and National Action, widely known as FANE), Front Nationaliste (Nationalist Front)[50] and some others. In 1984, he founded the Parti Communautaire National-Européen (Communitarian National-European Party, PCN). The ideology of the PCN can be termed as 'national communist' or National-Bolshevik, while the organisation is an heir to the Parti Communautaire National (Communitarian National Party) founded in 1965 by above-mentioned pan-European fascist Jean Thiriart. Michel was a personal secretary and close associate of Thiriart from 1982 until the latter's death in 1992.[51] He is currently a keeper of Thiriart's archive and editor of Editions Machiavel, a publishing house established by Thiriart in 1982.

Following Thiriart, Michel and his PCN promoted the idea of the 'Euro-Soviet Empire from Vladivostok to Dublin' and strove to create a pan-European movement that would unite and consolidate the far-right and far-left tendencies. Their main enemy was the United States and a 'false "European" project' that was said to be modelled on 'Atlantism and Americano-Zionist imperialism'. Their ideal Europe was a 'European State-Nation, republican, unitary and socialist'; a Europe 'liberated of Yankee colonialism'; a 'Great-Europe, from Reykjavik to Vladivostok and from Quebec to the Sahara'.[52]

After Thiriart's death in 1992, Michel kept occasional contact with the Russian far right. Dugin and Prokhanov published Michel's texts in their periodicals *Elementy* and *Zavtra* respectively, while the two of them had a chance to meet Michel in 1996 at the 'anti-mondialist' congress in Tripoli[53] organised on the initiative of Muammar Gaddafi of whom Michel had been a long-time supporter.[54] After Dugin created, in 2003, his Mezhdunarodnoe evraziyskoe dvizhenie (International Eurasianist Movement, MED), the PCN welcomed the creation of this organisation that was, in their point of view, fighting against 'Yankee new colonialism, its "New World Order" and its military force: NATO, Hollywood, MacDonald's, [and] Coca-Cola'.[55] The PCN's message to the MED, fully in accordance with Thiriart's ideas, put high hopes on Russia as a perceived major opponent of the United States:

Only Russia . . . still has the demographic, geographic and human resources to give Europe an alternative to the 'New World Order'. For Russia, just as before when it was called the Soviet Union, is the last free and independent country in Europe. We believe in the Russian mission in Europe in the twenty-first century. . . .

For the Europe we fight for, the great and free Europe, from Vladivostok to Reykjavik, will indeed be the fourth Rome! Facing new-Carthage like America, the European Empire can only be a new Rome. With Moscow as a capital. Why not![56]

It was not until 2006, however, when Michel and his PCN established closer and more significant contacts with Russia. On 17 September 2006, Michel, as well as PCN's General Secretary Fabrice Beaur and a member of the party's political bureau Jean-Pierre Vandersmissen, took part – on the invitation from CIS-EMO – in observing the 'Transnistrian independence referendum'.

In Tiraspol, they were joined by a cohort of other observers of whom many were far-right activists: Baburin and Alksnis from the 'Narodnaya Volya'; the ESM's leader Pavel Zarifullin and his associates;[57] Natalya Narochnitskaya, an MP nominated by Rogozin's 'Rodina'; Yves Bataille, the leader of the French extreme-right Organisation Lutte du Peuple (People's Struggle Organisation); Stefano Vernole and Alberto Ascari, leaders of the Italian Eurasianist group Coordinamento Progetto Eurasia (Eurasia Coordination Project), among others.

During their visit to Transnistria both Michel and Vernole did not fail to promote the ideas of Thiriart. At a press conference held before the 'referendum', Michel declared that his PCN was committed to the 'unification of a Large Europe from Dublin to Vladivostok',[58] while Vernole claimed that 'the consensus on the Transnistrian issue could contribute to the formation of the integrated space on the territory of the EU countries and the Russian Federation – from Reykjavik to Vladivostok'.[59] After the 'referendum', Michel praised Tiraspol's anti-Americanism as 'a healthy self-defence movement' and argued that 'European views of Tiraspol' were reminiscent of those of ' "European Communitarianism" – namely a Eurasian Greater Europe that is not limited to the small European Union and the ideological horizon of which stretches from the Atlantic to Vladivostok'.[60]

The referendum was not recognised either by the OSCE or the EU, but the CIS-EMO's international observers concluded that the 'referendum' 'complied with the national [i.e. Transnistrian] law, recognised principles and norms of organising and holding democratic elections, the majority of which are equally applicable to democratic referenda'.[61]

The apparent financial success of the PCN's observation mission in Transnistria and the deepening of the cooperation with CIS-EMO gave Michel an idea of establishing their own electoral monitoring organisation. At first, Michel and Vandersmissen registered, in March 2007, an organisation named 'ECGA – Espace Francophone (Belgique-France-Suisse-Quebec)' (ECGA – Francophone Space (Belgium-France-Switzerland-Quebec)), where 'ECGA' stood for European

Centre of Geopolitical Analysis. This was the name of the organisation that the Kochetkovs registered in July 2004 for 'research purposes'. Later that year, however, in August 2007, another organisation was registered, EODE, with the aim of 'promoting democracy (especially patterns of expression of direct democracy that fully exercises the power of the people)' and 'controlling, monitoring and assessing the workings of democracy, especially electoral process and political, legal and constitutional systems'.[62] The PCN's Michel, Beaur and Vandersmissen became leading figures in the EODE.

The launch of the EODE was heralded by the publication of Michel's extensive report on Transnistria that was written, according to the author, 'for the mission of expertise and analysis conducted by European lawyers' in Transnistria 'under the direction of Mr Patrick Brunot'.[63] Brunot, a lawyer who, in 1997, represented Iraqi dictator Saddam Hussein in a libel case against the French magazine *Le Nouvel Observateur*, is also known for his long-time sympathies towards, and contacts with, the Russian far right. In particular, he published a book of his conversations with Zhirinovsky,[64] while Rogozin wrote a preface to Brunot's book on 'the false friends of America'.[65]

The EODE claims to be 'committed to a multipolar world' and to 'the unity of Eurasia, designed as geopolitical entity' within the 'multipolar world'.[66] They trace its 'Eurasian vision' back to the ideas of Thiriart and Michel – 'the vision of EODE was born in early 1980, with the Euro-Soviet School of Geopolitics'[67] – and argue that this vision 'is now shared by many governmental and political spheres, including the current Russian leadership and V.V. Putin'.[68]

The members of the EODE took part in several election observation missions in the territories occupied by the Russian forces in order to destabilise the countries to which these territories formally belonged. In 2007, Michel and Beaur – then as part of the Transeuropean Dialogue's international observation mission[69] – monitored the 'parliamentary elections' in Abkhazia, a breakaway region of Georgia. Political parties loyal to the now late 'President' Sergey Bagapsh won the 'elections'. Commenting on the 'elections', Michel declared: 'Today, we have become convinced that you have, indeed, a democratic state, while the information conveyed by Georgia does not correspond to the actual state of affairs'.[70] As a sign of gratitude, Bagapsh invited Michel and Kochetkova to his private birthday party. According to Michel, Grigore Mărăcuţă, a top Transnistrian politician, who was also present at Bagapsh's birthday party, 'hailed the memory of Jean Thiriart, the father of the Eurasian Greater Europe'.[71]

For the EODE, participation in the election observation activities was followed by other Russia-related events. In July 2007, Michel and the PCN's General Secretary Fabrice Beaur visited the Seliger camp, an annual 'educational forum' that had been held at the Seliger Lake by the pro-Kremlin Nashi youth movement since 2005. The Seliger camp is a high-profile series of lectures, debates, and conversations, and Putin himself visited the camp several times and delivered speeches there. It is not clear what exactly the PCN delegation was doing at the Seliger forum. In Michel's words, they 'had the honour of participating as trainers', and Michel lectured 'on the geopolitics of the "Greater Europe"'. At this forum, Beaur also met 'a senior officer' of Nashi whom he later married and, for this reason, moved to Russia.[72]

Throughout its history, the EODE has cooperated, apart from CIS-EMO, with a few other election monitoring organisations, in particular with the Poland-based European Centre of Geopolitical Analysis, a long-time partner of CIS-EMO. Since 2012, the EODE has also cooperated with the International Expert Centre for Electoral Systems established in 2005 in Israel and headed by Alexander Tsinker. Through Tsinker's Centre, the EODE sent Beaur, as well as the VB's Frank Creyelman and Johan Deckmyn, to observe the 2012 parliamentary elections in Ukraine. In March 2014, when the EODE observed the illegitimate 'referendum' on the independence of the Ukrainian Autonomous Republic of Crimea that was followed by the annexation of the region by Russia, Michel coordinated the organisation's activities with the European Centre of Geopolitical Analysis and the Russia-based Civic Control Association (see below).

European Centre for Geopolitical Analysis

Mateusz Piskorski, who founded the Europejskie Centrum Analiz Geopolitycznych (European Centre of Geopolitical Analysis, ECAG) in 2007 in Poland, started his international election monitoring career in 2004 when he was sent to observe parliamentary elections in Belarus[73] by now late Andrzej Lepper, leader of the right-wing populist Samoobrona Rzeczpospolitej Polskiej (Self-Defence of the Republic of Poland).[74] According to the joint report of OSCE and ODIHR, the 2004 parliamentary elections in Belarus 'fell significantly short of OSCE commitments', while 'the Belarusian authorities failed to create the conditions to ensure that the will of the people serves as the basis of the authority of government'.[75] Piskorski's conclusion, however, was predictably affirmative: 'There was nothing suggesting any violations.'[76]

Piskorski's political career did not start with Samoobrona which he joined in 2002. In the late 1990s, he was an active member of the Association for Tradition and Culture 'Niklot', a neo-pagan, 'metapolitical fascist' group that was influenced by the ideology of the Polish interwar neo-pagan fascist Zadruga movement. Apart from the indigenous Polish interwar influences, Niklot was inspired by *völkisch* ideology, writings of Italian fascist Julius Evola and French New Right thinker Alain de Benoist.[77] The group was also characterised by its Slavic ultranationalism and opposed 'the intermixture of cultures, languages, peoples and races'.[78] Niklot published neo-Nazi zines *Odala* and *Wadera*, and actively recruited its members from skinhead and National Socialist Black Metal subcultures.[79] The following quote from one of *Odala*'s articles provides a telling glimpse into the ideology of Niklot: 'Considering the decay and multiraciality of the West, only a united Slavdom – the northern empire of the rising sun – is the hope for the White Race and anyone in the West who does not support the Slavs betrays the White Race and himself.'[80]

A neo-pagan, pro-Slavic worldview became an ideological link between Polish and Russian neo-Nazis. By invitation of Pavel Tulaev, head of the Russia-based far-right Cultural Exchange Association, former co-editor of the journal *Nasledie predkov* and co-editor of the neo-pagan racist journal *Ateney*, Piskorski and Niklot's Marcin Martynowski, as well as members of other Polish neo-Nazi groups, paid their first visit to Russia in August 2000. They held meetings with leaders of several Russian far-right organisations to discuss prospects of cooperation between the two countries. Stressing their Slavic ultranationalism, Polish visitors expressed their concerns about the German influence in Poland. As Piskorski summed up in his article for the Russian newspaper *Ya – russkiy* (I am Russian), 'what is now going on between Poland and Germany is not a fair and open war, but a covert German economic invasion, inherently a kike method of penetration'.[81]

In the beginning of the 2000s, Niklot was successful in infiltrating established political parties and often joined protests alongside Samoobrona. This was a point of entry for Piskorski and some other Niklot's top members, including Martynowski, into the party. Piskorski rapidly progressed up the career ladder and became an important ideologue of Samoobrona and the party's international relations officer. It was apparently through Piskorski that representatives of Samoobrona took part in a conference of 'European environmental, peace and alternative movements' co-organised by the PCN and held in the Villepinte suburb of Paris in 2003.[82]

Initial contacts between Piskorski and Dugin's MED/ESM were established already in 2004, when Piskorski and Zarifullin observed the 2004 parliamentary elections in Belarus. Piskorski and Martynowski visited Moscow in 2005; in particular, they discussed the creation of the Polish branch of the MED but this project was never fully implemented.

A more fruitful result of Piskorski's contacts with Russian nationalists was his visit to Transnistria as an observer of the 'parliamentary elections' in December 2005. At a press conference of international observers, Piskorski declared that he would do everything to convince the Polish authorities to recognise Transnistria as an independent state.[83] Piskorski's trip to Transnistria and his statement provoked a scandal in Poland. Consequently, Samoobrona's leader Andrzej Lepper, who aimed at securing the position of Deputy Prime Minister following the party's success at the 2005 parliamentary elections that made it the third biggest party in the Polish parliament, threatened Piskorski to expel him from Samoobrona for his visit to, and behaviour in, Transnistria.[84] In other respects, however, the Transnistrian trip was beneficial to Piskorski as it was his first experience of working with CIS-EMO.[85]

Through CIS-EMO, Piskorski, as well as the EODE, built a variety of contacts with Russian officials, and their 'election observation' in favour of the Kremlin's interests became an entrance ticket to participation in other Russia-related activities. On 24 November 2006, a few days before the 19th NATO Summit in Riga, Moscow hosted a conference titled 'NATO and Security in Eurasia' that featured more than a hundred representatives of the Presidential Administration, Russian government, MPs, public and political figures, and foreign guests. Given the rising anti-Western sentiments in Russia, the contents of the conference were anything but unpredictable. The general idea of the conference can be succinctly described by a quote from the speech of Andrey Kokoshin, Chairman of the State Duma CIS and Compatriots Abroad Affairs Committee. Referring to the sovereign right of Central and East European states to join the preferred collective security organisation as the 'expansion of NATO to the East', Kokoshin continued:

> Russia will definitely continue strengthening and restoring its positions and securing its national interests and the interests of its friends, partners and allies. In Russia, a national consensus has practically been formed on the issues of foreign policy implemented by President Putin, on securing our real sovereignty, [and] on ensuring our defence capabilities and security.[86]

The problem for the organisers of this predominantly anti-NATO conference was that not many Western politicians and public figures were ready to participate in it. Naturally, the conference featured several pro-Russian politicians from ex-Soviet countries, as well as pro-Russian European lobbyists and academics such as Alexander Rahr, but the organisers presumably thought that these participants did not sufficiently signify the allegedly wide scale of anti-NATO sentiments in the West.

This seems to be the reason why the conference also hosted far-right activists and politicians such as Aleksey Kochetkov, Mateusz Piskorski, Luc Michel, Yves Bataille, Stefano Vernole, and one of the leaders of the Polish far-right Liga Polskich Rodzin (League of Polish Families, LPR) Sylwester Chruszcz – all of them were known as supporters of Putin's regime, as they had been engaged in pro-Kremlin electoral monitoring.[87] Despite the different type of activity, the Russian organisers invited them to the conference with a similar purpose: to condone anti-NATO and anti-American sentiments of Putin's regime. The far-right participants naturally met the expectations. Thus, Bataille delivered a speech in which he maintained that NATO aimed 'at attacking the space of great Russia, [and] the former Soviet space', while Vernole argued that the United States aspired 'to hamper the trade of Russian gas and oil, and force Russia to direct its supply streams through the corridors controlled by the Pentagon'.[88]

In January 2007, Piskorski and his associates registered their own organisation that would, in particular, provide electoral monitoring services to the interested parties. They chose the name that the Kochetkovs used for their organisation registered in 2004, the European Centre of Geopolitical Analysis, but unlike the PCN's leaders who first adopted this 'brand name' but then switched to the EODE, Piskorski and his team kept the name.

Piskorski's ECAG featured several Samoobrona members, including Martynowski, Konrad Rękas and Marcin Domagała, as well as Polish right-wingers such as Przemysław Sieradzan and Kornel Sawiński who would later become representatives of Dugin's MED in Poland.[89]

In 2009, there was an attempt to expand the ECAG internationally, and, in addition to the pre-existing organisation in Russia, a branch of the European Centre of Geopolitical Analysis was established in Germany under the management of Piotr Luczak, a member of the left-wing populist Die Linke. In its promotional booklet, the ECAG, as an international structure, did not conceal its Russo-centric nature. It claimed that their 'monitoring services [had] been already twice highly estimated by the Central Electoral Commission of Russian Federation', while its intended activities as a 'Euro-Russian dialogue platform' included 'publishing articles and/or interviews in Russian journals and on Russian websites, publishing books in Russian translation, participating in conferences, seminars and round-tables in Russia, [and] giving interviews for the main Russian massmedia'.[90] However, this international expansion of the ECAG proved unsuccessful, as the German branch eventually became an independent organisation (Europäisches Zentrum für Geopolitische Analyse e.V.) in 2011, while the Russian organisation was essentially CIS-EMO under a different name.

The ECAG provided over 20 monitors for the CIS-EMO observation mission at the 2010 presidential election in Ukraine. Apart from the functionaries of the ECAG (Piskorski, Domagała, Sawiński, Rękas), more than half of the Polish component of the mission consisted of actual and former members of Samoobrona (including Lepper) and the LPR. Both far-right parties were minor coalition partners of Jarosław Kaczyński's national-conservative Prawo i Sprawiedliwość (Law and Justice); their coalition government ruled Poland in 2006–2007. Moreover, Marian Szołucha, who was then Vice President of the ECAG, was close to the Młodzież Wszechpolska (All-Polish Youth), a youth organisation that was for some time affiliated with the LPR, so he might have helped engage its members in observation missions.

The pro-Kremlin nature of the entire ECAG/CIS-EMO cooperation manifested not only in their activities, but also in publications indirectly linked to their electoral monitoring. In 2009, Kochetkov and Piskorski – together with Aleksey Martynov, director of the International Institute of the Newly Established States – co-authored a Russian language book *South Ossetia: Armed Aggression and Peace-Making War* in which they attempted to condone Russia's war against Georgia in August 2008.[91] While grounded in the Kremlin's official narrative of Russia's 'peace enforcement operation' in Georgia, the authors' argument condoning Russia's war went beyond this official line and represented a point of view of Russian imperialism:

> For Russia, the participation in the events of 8 August in South Ossetia and their consequences became a certain 'point of no return'. A huge country that was humiliated for 17 years has now been revived as an empire. . . . An empire has a right for intervention beyond its borders. It has a sphere of influence and a sphere of strategic interests. Before 8 August 2008, the entire world was considered a sphere of influence of the USA. After that day, it became evident that the second military and political pole exists – the Russian Federation.[92]

The ECAG and CIS-EMO, however, have dramatically reduced cooperation since 2010–2011. Originally, Piskorski and Kochetkov explained the break in a similar manner. Piskorski referred to Kochetkov's right-wing extremist 'past': 'several people in Russia warned us that Kochetkov does not serve our reputation well. [That is] concerning his past'. Kochetkov, in his turn, explained that Piskorski would bring to their electoral observation missions 'rather suspicious company – leftists, neo-fascists'.[93]

In a later interview, Kochetkov argued that although Piskorski's 'radical nationalist' past was not a matter of principle, 'Piskorski was involved in various scandals including his continued friendship with particular structures in Europe accused, to a lesser or greater degree, of the rejection of the basic democratic values'.[94] However, Kochetkov also said that Piskorski, after he had finished his parliamentary career in 2007, started earning money from electoral monitoring and became associated 'with various structures [in Russia] including the Kremlin'.[95] Piskorski denied these allegations saying that he 'had not earned even a single rouble or zloty on any kind of monitoring missions because it was not a business'.[96]

Nevertheless, a more likely explanation for the break between Kochetkov and Piskorski could be a conflict over personal issues (Marina Kochetkova would divorce Kochetkov and partner with Piskorski) and competition for Russian financial support. Polish investigative journalists Michał Kacewicz and Michał Krzymowski suggest that Piskorski and the ECAG decided to establish direct – that is bypassing Kochetkov and CIS-EMO – relations with Russian actors who allocated financial resources provided for monitoring missions.[97] It is not clear what organisations or individuals provided these resources. A multinational investigation into the so-called 'Russian Laundromat', which was a scheme to move $20–80 billion out of Russia in 2010–2014 through a network of banks and letterbox companies – the scheme was named 'the biggest money-laundering operation in Eastern Europe' by the Organized Crime and Corruption Reporting Project[98] – shows that, in May 2013, the ECAG received €21 thousand for 'consulting services' from Cyprus-based Crystalord Limited that participated in the process of laundering Russian money.[99]

Cooperation with Civic Control

In 2011, another Russian electoral monitoring organisation, namely the Civic Control Association, started playing a more significant role in coordinating international observers at controversial elections. Civic Control is what can be called a 'GONGO', that is a 'government organised non-governmental organisation', as the groups that compose this association are loyal to the Kremlin, while the key figures in the management of the association are members of – or, at least, closely associated with – the State Duma and the Civic Chamber of the Russian Federation.[100] Interestingly, one of the groups that comprise the association, 'For Democracy and Rights of Peoples', lists Piskorski and Béla Kovács of the Hungarian far-right Jobbik among its 'experts'.[101] The implicit objective of Civic Control is to legitimise controversial elections and declare them free and fair, to criticise results of international monitoring missions from democratic institutions such as the OSCE, and, occasionally, to disapprove of the electoral procedures in Western countries such as the United States. For example, the preliminary report of the Civic Control on the 2012 presidential election in the United States concluded: 'no single generally recognised principle of the democratic elections is fully observed in the United States, except for one – regularity of elections'.[102]

As a consequence of the break-up between the ECAG and CIS-EMO, they started sending separate missions to elections. Since 2011, the backbone of the ECAG's observation missions has been a combination of far-right and left-wing political forces. The far-right element consisted of members of the LPR, Jobbik, VB, BNP, Ataka, Partij voor de Vrijheid (Party for Freedom, PVV),[103] Movimento Sociale – Fiamma Tricolore (Social Movement Social Movement – Tricolour Flame), and individual right-wing activists. The left-wing element was represented largely by the members of Die Linke.

In October 2011, Civic Control convened a conference, in the building of the Civic Chamber of the Russian Federation, titled the 'International Civic Observation in the Electoral Process: Principles, Development, International Experience'.[104] The composition of the conference participants seemed to indicate that Civic Control took charge of coordinating election observation activities of the ECAG and EODE that previously worked with CIS-EMO. In particular, the speakers at the conference included the ECAG's Piskorski and the EODE's Michel and Beaur, as well as a number of politicians who used to work with CIS-EMO in the past but crossed over to Civic Control together with the ECAG and EODE: Béla Kovács and Ádám Mirkóczki from Jobbik, Tanguy Veys from the VB, Piotr Luczak from Die Linke, and some others.

Naturally, the change of the Russian coordinator did not have any impact on the work of the ECAG/EODE-affiliated European observers. After observing the 2011 parliamentary elections in Russia, which the OSCE characterised as such that did not meet 'the necessary conditions for fair electoral competition',[105] Béla Kovács presented a report produced by his team of monitors that concluded that the elections had been held 'in compliance with the international electoral standards'.[106]

Nick Griffin, then the leader of the BNP, who was a member of the ECAG's observation missions in Russia (2011)[107] and Ukraine (2012), praised these 'young democracies' and expectedly attacked electoral procedures in the United Kingdom:

> [In Russia], I was stunned to discover instead a robust, transparent and properly democratic system that made me even more aware than ever of the truly shocking failings of the archaic and corrupted shambles that masquerades as free and fair elections in Great Britain.[108]
>
> The systems and checks and balances in place in Ukraine are hugely superior to the undemocratic farce that would make Britain an international laughing stock if the reality was exposed.[109]

Griffin was not the only observer who praised Russia's 'robust, transparent and properly democratic system' in order criticise the democratic workings in their home countries. After observing the 2012 presidential election in Russia, Ewald Stadler of the right-wing populist Bündnis Zukunft Österreich (Alliance for the Future of Austria, BZÖ) stated: 'The elections in the Russian Federation were conducted fully in accordance with democratic standards. There was no single election poster of any candidate by the polling stations, while in Austria this is happening very often'.[110] During the debates in the European Parliament about a resolution on the outcome of the 2012 presidential elections in Russia that, in particular, strongly criticised 'the shortcomings and irregularities in the preparation and conduct of these elections and the fact that voters' choice was limited',[111] Stadler declared that Putin's victory had been determined by the Russian voters' unwillingness to 'return to those thieving times under Mr Yeltsin, when many of those who now live in the West shamelessly profiteered on Russia's assets', and that the Russians 'wanted stability from these elections'.[112] It was the same Stadler who, together with Jörg Haider, concluded a $5 million agreement with the Iraqi authorities in 2002 for lobbying the interests of Saddam Hussein in Europe.

Civic Control headed by Aleksandr Brod, who is, ironically, also a head of the Moscow Bureau for Human Rights, seemed to have entrusted the ECAG and EODE with drawing up the main list of international observers for the Crimean 'referendum' in March 2014;[113] then this list was passed to the Crimean parliament that officially issued invitations to prospective election monitors. The international observation mission – as Russian political scientist Dmitry Oreshkin put it – consisted of 'trusted people who would not question its results'.[114] These 'trusted people' included both Michel and Piskorski, who later confirmed that he coordinated 'the international observation mission in Crimea',[115] as well as other members of European far-right organisations such as Jobbik, VB, LN, FPÖ, Ataka, Fiamma Tricolore, and Plataforma per Catalunya (Platform for Catalonia) among others. A number of representatives of the left-wing parties such as Die Linke and the Kommounistikó Kómma Elládas (Communist Party of Greece), as well as pro-Kremlin 'trusted people', observed the 'referendum' too.

The selection of the observation missions for the Crimean 'referendum' was competitive. For example, Sergey Zavorotny, a Moscow-based *piarshchik*, former advisor to Prime Minister Mykola Azarov in Ukraine under Yanukovych[116] and a member of the Russian ultranationalist Izborsk Club, sent his own observation mission proposal to the Russian authorities. The proposal listed 16 people, 8 of whom were Italian citizens. Zavorotny presented most of the proposed observers with a reference to their apparent suitability for the Crimean 'referendum'. For example, Alessandro Politi, director of the NATO Defence College Foundation, was noted for 'condemning the ultra-radicals of Maidan'; Danilo Taino was introduced as a correspondent of *Corriere della Sera* who 'criticised the organisers of the illegal power grab in Kyiv'; Frank Schumann was described as a contributor to *Neues Deutschland* and *Junge Welt* who 'exposed financial malpractice of [Ukraine's former Prime Minister Yuliya] Tymoshenko'. As Zavorotny wrote in the conclusion of his proposal, in case it were accepted, the observation mission would require 'an official invitation from the Crimean authorities', 'a [Russian] entry visa in the Sheremetyevo airport [in Moscow]', and 'the settlement of the relevant financial issues'.[117] Zavorotny's proposal, however, was not accepted by the Russian authorities, and this seemed to reflect the highly competitive nature of the struggle for the Russian funding between various electoral observation teams in general.

The text messages that were leaked by the Anonymous International hacktivist group revealed that the Russian Presidential Administration itself had been involved in inviting international observers to the Crimean 'referendum'.[118] On 10 March 2014, Timur Prokopenko, deputy chief of the Domestic Politics Department of the Presidential Administration of the Russian Federation, asked Konstantin Rykov, a Russian politician and influential media producer, to bring the FN's leader Marine Le Pen to Crimea. Rykov, who apparently owns a €2 million villa in Côte d'Azur and is a tax resident of France,[119] was in contact with Le Pen. He replied to Prokopenko saying that Le Pen was on tour campaigning for her party's municipal elections and was unlikely to go to Crimea, but one of her deputies could go in her stead. It was Aymeric Chauprade, then advisor on international relations to Le Pen, who went to observe the 'referendum'. *Libération* reported, with a reference to Chauprade's entourage, that he had been invited to Crimea by the EODE,[120] but the FN denied that the EODE had invited Chauprade, as the party presumably feared that the connection to the Belgian far-right activists could damage the FN's reputation on the eve of the municipal elections.[121]

The ECAG, EODE and Civic Control were also involved in organising the monitoring mission at the 'parliamentary elections' that were held on 2 November 2014 in the 'Donetsk People's Republic' (DNR) and 'Luhansk People's Republic' (LNR) – the territories in Eastern Ukraine controlled by pro-Russian separatists and Russian troops. On the eve of these 'elections', UN Secretary-General Ban Ki-moon deplored 'the planned holding by armed rebel groups in eastern Ukraine of their own "elections" on 2 November, in breach of the Constitution and national law'.[122] Nevertheless, the pro-Russian separatists held the 'elections' and arranged the arrival of more than 40 observers including members of the VB, Jobbik, Ataka, right-wing Forza Italia (Forward, Italy), ultranationalist Pokret za Srbiju (Movement for Serbia), and the Rassemblement bleu Marine (Marine Blue Gathering, RBM), a right-wing populist coalition created by the FN's Marine Le Pen in 2012.

One of the observers, Austrian politician Ewald Stadler, then the leader of the Die Reformkonservativen (Reform Conservatives, REKOS), chose not to take notice of the massive presence of the armed men at the 'polling stations', arguing in an interview to British self-described 'NewGonzo journalist' Graham Phillips, that 'there [was] no pressure to the people. Soldiers and people with guns [were] outside, not inside. Everybody [could] vote here free'.[123] Nevertheless, the number of irregularities at the 'parliamentary elections' in the DNR/LNR was apparently too high even for many an observer loyal to the Kremlin's foreign policy, and Jobbik's Márton Gyöngyösi acknowledged 'the fact that due to a close to six-month military conflict conditions for election [had been] far from ideal and the fighting represent[ed] a serious challenge for the region'. However, this did not prevent Gyöngyösi from declaring that Jobbik recognised 'the election as transparent, reflecting the will of the electorate'.[124]

The OSCE obsession

There is hardly any doubt that Russian and European organisations involved in electoral observation in favour of Moscow's interests understand that neither their reputation nor credibility can match those of the organisations and structures such as the European Parliament or OSCE. The analysis of the monitoring missions of the CIS-EMO, ECAG, EODE and Civic Control demonstrates a particular demand for Members of the European Parliament (MEPs) among them: this demand is driven by a permanent desire to lend credibility to the ideologically and politically motivated electoral observation or, at least, neutralise unfavourable reactions. For example, a report on the Transnistrian 'referendum' in 2006 published in a Russian newspaper *Izvestiya* (News) noted that the EU structures considered the 'referendum' illegitimate, but then continued: 'However, the Europeans did send observers to the referendum, including Members of the European Parliament'.[125] Naturally, this statement is manipulative in its nature. It creates a false impression that the EU, by denying the legitimacy of the Transnistrian 'referendum', is simply *pretending* to uphold the international law; the EU allegedly strikes an attitude, but eventually does send observers to the 'referendum' thus indirectly acknowledging its legitimacy. The fact, however, is that the EU did not send any observers. 'The Europeans' indicated in the *Izvestiya* report were the ECAG and EODE, which had nothing to do with any official EU structure, while the 'Members of the European Parliament' who observed the Transnistrian 'referendum' were MEPs who cooperated with the ECAG and EODE, but could not claim any connection between their work as observers and the European Parliament.

There seemed to be attempts to raise the status of the MEPs cooperating with the ECAG, EODE and Civic Control to those of the official representatives of the European Parliament. During a debate in the European Parliament in July 2011, Jobbik's Kovács declared that he had been invited by Civic Control to observe the 2011 parliamentary elections in Russia and expressed his hope that 'representatives of the European Parliament' would 'also be able to participate officially in Russian elections'.[126]

However, among other international institutions, the OSCE has become the primary victim of manipulations on the part of the Russian pro-Kremlin media and the organisations discussed in this chapter. Despite the fact that Russian authorities often accused the OSCE of having double standards and 'losing credibility',[127] this organisation remains an important reference point for the Russian officials, Russian media, and the election observation organisations loyal to official Moscow.

In pursuit of their legitimation and respectability, CIS-EMO has taken part in several events organised by the OSCE that are open to any NGO. In particular,

Aleksey and Marina Kochetkovs took part in the OSCE Human Dimension Seminar on the role of political parties in the political process in 2011. The next year, Kochetkova participated in the OSCE Supplementary Human Dimension Meeting on freedom of assembly and association. In 2013, Stanislav Byshok, an analyst at CIS-EMO and former member of the Russian neo-Nazi group 'Russkiy obraz', addressed the OSCE Human Dimension Implementation Meeting with a paper criticising Ukraine.

Since 2013, Ukraine has become the key topic for the activities of CIS-EMO at the OSCE events. Another employee of CIS-EMO, Aleksey Semenov, who co-authored with Byshok a book smearing a Russian opposition activist Aleksey Navalny,[128] criticised the early parliamentary elections in Ukraine at the 2014 OSCE Supplementary Human Dimension Meeting in Vienna. To strengthen the illusion of allegedly respectable status of CIS-EMO, members of this organisation actively use a feature on the OSCE website that allows to freely upload speeches and other materials of the participants of the OSCE events – they would then provide links to their materials uploaded on the OSCE website to lend weight to their works by disguising them as *OSCE-related* materials.

In 2014, Kochetkov and Byshok co-authored a book *Neonazis & Euromaidan: From Democracy to Dictatorship* exaggerating and sensationalising the role that Ukrainian far-right groups played during the Ukrainian revolution.[129] Byshok presented the book at numerous events – every presentation was widely publicised by the Russian state-controlled media – including the OSCE Human Dimension Implementation Meeting held in Vienna.

The EODE, on the other hand, renounces the OSCE by contrasting 'the Western NGOs sponsored by the OSCE, the EU and the United States' with 'non-aligned NGOs, claiming a scientific and neutralist monitoring'.[130] Considering Michel's attitude towards the OSCE, it is particularly absurd that Russian state-controlled Russia-24 news TV channel, when reporting on the Crimean 'referendum' in March 2014, deceitfully presented Michel as 'the organiser of the OSCE observation mission in Crimea'. Moreover, the same TV channel declared that 'around 100 OSCE observers would be working in Crimea'.[131] Russia-24 deliberately misinformed its audience – a few days before they aired their 'news', the OSCE Chairperson-in-Office Didier Burkhalter stated that the OSCE considered the 'referendum' illegal and 'ruled out the possibility of an OSCE observation of the planned referendum'.[132] The refutation of the OSCE's Chair did not prevent the Italian branch of the Russian state-funded Voice of Russia radio station from maintaining that Claudio D'Amico, a member of the Lega Nord, 'was present in Crimea during the referendum as an observer of the OSCE'.[133]

A similar manipulation took place on the eve of the 'parliamentary elections' in the temporarily occupied territories of Eastern Ukraine in autumn 2014. The OSCE's Didier Burkhalter denied the legitimacy of the 'elections' adding that they were 'not in line with Minsk Protocol', an agreement signed by the Ukrainian authorities and the aggressors to halt the warfare in Eastern Ukraine.[134] Nevertheless, the Russian state-controlled *RIA Novosti* ran a story claiming that 'OSCE officials had inspected polling stations in Donetsk',[135] one of the major cities occupied by the Russian troops and Russia-backed separatists. As in the case with '100 OSCE observers in Crimea', the story about the 'OSCE officials' inspecting 'polling stations' was run exclusively in Russian and, thus, was aimed at the domestic audience to strengthen the Kremlin's argument about the alleged legitimacy of its actions in Ukraine. The OSCE used its official Twitter handle to refute the manipulations of the Russian media by communicating the words of OSCE Secretary General Lamberto Zannier: 'No OSCE #observation of so-called "elections" in east #Ukraine Sunday 2 November and no OSCE monitors at polling stations'.[136] At a press conference of the observers Ewald Stadler and Forza Italia's Alessandro Musolino, the Chair presented them and other observers – in yet another attempt to associate their illegitimate observation mission with the prestigious OSCE – as members of the organisation called 'ASCE', 'Association for Security and Co-operation in Europe'.[137] Later Stadler had to admit that no 'ASCE' officially existed.[138] The 'ASCE' myth was only used to attribute importance to the illegitimate event.

Ironically, various manipulations involving references to the OSCE reveal the high-status value of this organisation even in the generally anti-Western context and among those far-right activists who attack the activities of the OSCE.

Conclusion

As Moscow perceived the 'colour revolutions' in Georgia, Ukraine and Kyrgyzstan as a Western, US-led conspiracy against Putin's regime and Russia's perceived domination in the post-Soviet space, the Kremlin became genuinely concerned with independent international election observation missions whose findings played an important role in mobilising societies against fraudulent elections. The Kremlin therefore supported 'alternative mechanisms and practices' that aimed at legitimising elections in the post-Soviet space which organisations such as the OSCE and ODIHR would unlikely consider free, fair or, in some cases, even legitimate.

Formally an NGO, CIS-EMO became one of the most important 'alternative' organisations that tried to legitimise practices of electoral authoritarianism and always remained loyal to the objectives of Russia's foreign policy in the post-Soviet space. Hardly surprisingly, results of CIS-EMO's observation missions generally contradicted those of the OSCE and ODIHR.

A salient characteristic of CIS-EMO and the organisations, through which it invited election observers outside the post-Soviet space, namely the Belgium-based EODE and Poland-based ECAG, is that they were all established by former and actual members of far-right organisations. The heads of these organisations have a positive view of Putin's regime and Russia's foreign policy, and are influenced by ideologies – first and foremost, neo-Eurasianism, National Bolshevism and Slavic ultranationalism – that praise Russia as a major anti-American and generally anti-Western power that is challenging the post-war liberal-democratic status quo. Thus, these election monitoring organisations are ideologically predisposed to take pro-Russian viewpoints and approve of practices of electoral authoritarianism.

Moreover, the backbone of the EODE's and ECAG's election observation missions comprise members of European radical right-wing movements and parties. Other members of these missions are often representatives of pro-Russian left-wing political forces that support the allegedly anti-globalist (in effect, anti-American) agenda of the Kremlin.

Russian media rarely, if ever, mention the ideological stances or political affiliations of far-right international observers engaged in monitoring elections. When referring to the monitors' favourable evaluations of controversial elections, they are usually presented as simply 'international observers' or 'experts' from particular countries. Some of them (for example, Michel and Ascari) are misleadingly presented as 'members of the European Parliament'[139] – a false description aimed at giving a greater degree of credibility to their words.

The assessments of CIS-EMO, ECAG, EODE and Civic Control – like those of other (politically or ideologically) biased electoral monitoring organisations – are usually disregarded by OSCE/ODIHR monitors, representatives of genuinely independent monitoring organisations and the international democratic community. However, Judith Kelley assumes that the activities of pseudo-observers 'may nonetheless be useful with some domestic audiences or with other autocratic governments, and . . . they may be useful in limiting the influence of more critical monitoring organizations'.[140] Perhaps more importantly the results of their work contribute to political consolidation of the international illiberal scene providing it with an 'alternative' institution of electoral monitoring.

Finally, it should be noted that Michel and Piskorski have gone beyond their activities as heads of international election monitoring organisations and have performed other services to the Russian authorities. In particular, they are often invited to conferences, discussion tables and other events in Russia to reinforce pro-Kremlin and anti-Western narratives.

Piskorski has also become a regular commentator for Russian state-controlled media such as RT (former 'Russia Today'), the Voice of Russia and Sputnik, and the next chapter explores yet another institutionalised form of cooperation between Russian actors and the Western far right, namely the cooperation between Russian pro-Kremlin media and far-right politicians and activists.

Notes

1   Ivan Krastev, "Is China More Democratic than Russia?", *Open Democracy*, 12 March (2013), https://opendemocracy.net/od-russia/ivan-krastev/is-china-more-democratic-than-russia.

2   Ibid.

3   Andreas Schedler, "The Logic of Electoral Authoritarianism", in Andreas Schedler (ed.), *Electoral Authoritarianism: The Dynamics of Unfree Competition* (London: Lynne Rienner, 2006), pp. 1, 3 (1–23).

4   Susan D. Hyde, *The Pseudo-Democrat's Dilemma: Why Election Monitoring Became an International Norm* (Ithaca: Cornell University Press, 2011), p. 158.

5   "Declaration of Principles for International Election Observation and Code of Conduct for International Election Observers", *OSCE*, 27 October (2005), http://osce.org/odihr/16935

6 Hyde, *The Pseudo-Democrat's Dilemma*, pp. 158, 156.

7 Ibid., p. 160.

8 Rick Fawn, "Battle over the Box: International Election Observation Missions, Political Competition and Retrenchment in the post-Soviet Space", *International Affairs*, Vol. 82, No. 6 (2006), p. 1133 (1133–1153).

9 Judith G. Kelley, *Monitoring Democracy: When International Election Observation Works, and Why It Often Fails* (Princeton: Princeton University Press, 2012), p. 45.

10 On CIS-EMO and Kochetkov's background see also Robert Horvath, "Fabricating Legitimacy: Russian Ultranationalism and Election Monitoring in the Former Soviet Space", *forthcoming*.

11 Vyacheslav Likhachev, Vladimir Pribylovsky, *Russkoe Natsional'noe Edinstvo. Vol. 1. Istoriya i ideologiya, 1990–2000* (Stuttgart: *ibidem*-Verlag, 2005), p. 27. On the RNE also see: Sven Gunnar Simonsen, "Aleksandr Barkashov and Russian National Unity: Blackshirt Friends of the Nation", *Nationalities Papers*, Vol. 24, No. 4 (1996), pp. 625–639; Shenfield, *Russian Fascism*, especially the chapter "Barkashov and the Russian National Unity", pp. 113–189; Mikhail Sokolov, "Russian National Unity: An Analysis of the Political Style of a Radical-Nationalist Organization", *Russian Politics and Law*, Vol. 46, No. 4 (2008), pp. 66–79.

12 Janusz Bugajski, *Cold Peace: Russia's New Imperialism* (Westport: Praeger, 2004), p. 107. Although Russia played a significant role in Transnistria's separation from Moldova, it has never recognised its independence. At the time of writing, Transnistria has only been recognised by three other "states" with limited recognition: Abkhazia, South Ossetia and Nagorno-Karabakh.

13 Stuart J. Kaufman, Stephen R. Bowers, "Transnational Dimensions of the Transnistrian Conflict", *Nationalities Papers*, Vol. 26, No. 1 (1998), pp. 131, 136 (129–146).

14 Ibid., p. 137. In summer 2014, Antyufeev appeared in the Russia-oganised separatist movement in Eastern Ukraine.

15 Likhachev, Pribylovsky, *Russkoe Natsional'noe Edinstvo*, p. 35.

16 Ibid., p. 64; Vasiliy Avchenko, "Nablyudateli spetsial'nogo naznacheniya", *Vladivostok*, No. 147, 4 October (2006).

17 The term "piarshchik" derives from the English abbreviation PR standing for "public relations".

18 Interview with Oleh Vernik, former employee of CIS-EMO (2004–2013), conducted in Kyiv on 12 September 2014.

19 Aleksey Kochetkov, "Nash brat Irak", *Zavtra*, No. 23, 9 June (1997), p. 5.

20 Horvath, "Fabricating Legitimacy".

21 For formal reasons, it was originally registered in the name of Aleksey Kamrakov. Since he resided in Nizhny Novgorod, it was convenient for the directors to submit tax reports through him. Kamrakov remained a formal director of the organisation until 2005 when it was re-registered in Moscow in the names of Kochetkov and Karmatskiy, see below. Karmatskiy remained an official co-director of the organisation until 2006 when it was taken over by the Kochetkovs.

22 Hyde, *The Pseudo-Democrat's Dilemma*, p. 159.

23 Kelley, *Monitoring Democracy*, p. 52. Note that both Hyde and Kelly refer to IPA CIS as simply "CIS", but this is not entirely correct.

24 In January 2003, Russia even decided not to extend the mandate of the OSCE Assistance Group to Chechnya, see Anna Politkovskaya, "Profanatsiya Evropy", *Novaya gazeta*, No. 1, 9 January (2003), p. 2. Furthermore, after the start of the Orange Revolution, Russia's Foreign Minister Sergey Lavrov published an article arguing that the OSCE had "stopped being a forum uniting states and peoples" and was "starting to contribute to their division". Consequently, Lavrov stated that Russia was "offering a clear-cut programme for OSCE reform". See Sergei Lavrov, "Reform Will Enhance the OSCE's Relevance", *Financial Times*, 28 November (2004), http://ft.com/intl/cms/s/1/d1af5d44-416b-11d9-9dd8-00000e2511c8.html

25 See Janusz Bugajski, *Dismantling the West: Russia's Atlantic Agenda* (Washington: Potomac Books, 2009), p. 65.

26 Roman Kupchinsky, "Monitoring the Election Monitors", in Ingmar Bredies, Andreas Umland and Valentin Yakushik (eds.), *Aspects of the Orange Revolution V: Institutional Observation Reports on the 2004 Ukrainian Presidential Elections* (Stuttgart: *ibidem*-Verlag, 2007), pp. 223–227 (227).

27 Interview with Oleh Vernik.

28 Tatyana Ivzhenko, "Prezumptsiya vinovnosti. Zapad mozhet ne priznat' itogi predstoyashchikh vyborov prezidenta na Ukraine", *Nezavisimaya gazeta*, No. 178, 23 August (2004), p. 6.

29 "Ukraina raskololas' po Dnepru", *Vremya novostey*, No. 214, 23 November (2004), p. 2.

30 Olga Klyueva, "Nablyudateli ot SNG nazyvayut vybory v Ukraine chestnymi i otkrytymi", *Podrobnosti*, 1 November (2004), http://podrobnosti.ua/podrobnosti/2004/11/01/156053.html

31 Viktor Tolokin, "Oranzhevaya oppozitsiya rastoptala zakon", *Pravda*, No. 133, 25 November (2004), p. 1.

32 On "whataboutism", i.e. the rhetorical tactic of shifting the focus of the discussion from one's own national context to that of the critics, see "Whataboutism", *The Economist*, 31 January (2008), http://economist.com/node/10598774

33 Andrey Kolesnikov, "Vladimir Putin nauchil Evropu ukrainskoy demokratii", *Kommersant. Daily*, No. 220, 24 November (2004), p. 2.

34 Nicu Popescu, "Russia's Soft Power Ambitions", *CEPS Policy Brief*, No. 115 (2006), p. 2.

35 Horvath, "Fabricating Legitimacy".

36 Ibid.

37 "Otchet o monitoringe vyborov v Riigikogu (parlament) Estonii 6 marta 2011 goda Mezhdunarodnoy organizatsii po nablyudeniyu za vyborami CIS-EMO", *Centre for Monitoring Democratic Processes "Quorum"*, 7 March (2011), http://cmdp-kvorum.org/news/materials/904

38 "Ekspertnaya otsenka monitoringovoy gruppy CIS-EMO po itogam parlamentskikh vyborov v Turtsii 12 iyunya 2011 goda", *Centre for Monitoring Democratic Processes "Quorum"*, 17 June (2011), http://cmdp-kvorum.org/news/center/924

39 Jakob Hedenskog, Robert L. Larsson, *Russian Leverage on the CIS and the Baltic States* (Stockholm: Totalförsvarets Forskningsinstitut, 2007), p. 26.

40 The Moldovan authorities never accredited CIS-EMO to observe any elections in their country. In March 2005, CIS-EMO monitors were deported from Moldova where they went to illegitimately observe the parliamentary elections. In July that year, Kochetkov and his colleague went to Moldova apparently to monitor – again, without any accreditation – the Chişinău mayoral election. See Vladimir Solov'yov, "Moldaviya vytyanula rossiyskuyu notu", *Kommersant. Daily*, No. 127, 13 July (2005), p. 10.

41 "Sergey Lavrov zhestko prokommentiroval zaderzhanie moldavskimi vlastyami rossiyskikh grazhdan", *Pervy kanal*, 13 July (2005), http://1tv.ru/news/world/53563

42 Sergey Il'ko, "Na vybory v Ukraine opredelen smotryashchiy ot Kremlya?", *UNIAN*, 23 February (2012), http://unian.net/politics/612744-na-vyiboryi-v-ukraine-opredelen-smotryaschiy-ot-kremlya.html

43 Kolerov was dismissed from the post in 2007 and replaced by Nikolay Tsvetkov who headed the Directorate in 2007–2008.

44 Il'ko, "Na vybory v Ukraine opredelen smotryashchiy ot Kremlya?".

45 In 2012, Vinokurov was "fired because of the failures in the presidential elections in South Ossetia and Transnistria that he supervised. There Moscow supported patently no-go candidates who eventually lost". See Vladimir Solov'yev, Ivan Safronov, Elena Chernenko, "SVR nashli pomoshchnika", *Kommersant. Daily*, No. 165, 5 September (2012), p. 6. Vinokurov was afterwards appointed deputy head of the Foreign Intelligence Service.

46 "Yak Yanukovych namahavsya kupyty loyal'nist' svitu (dokumenty)", *Espreso TV*, 21 May (2014), http://espreso.tv/article/2014/05/21/yak_yanukovych_namahavsya_kupyty_loyalnist_svitu_dokumenty

47 Denis Usov, "Moldavskiy gambit", *Novy Peterburg*, No. 12, 17 March (2005). Usov is a member of the Narodnaya Volya.

48 *Eurasia* has been edited by Jean Thiriart's Nazi Maoist disciple Claudio Mutti since 2011. See more details in Chapter 6.

49 See Tiberio Graziani, "Russia Keystone of the Multipolar System", *Centre for Monitoring Democratic Processes "Quorum"*, 10 June (2010), http://cmdp-kvorum.org/en/news/center/732; Tiberio Graziani, "Geopolitics in Republican Italy – A Limited Sovereignty Country", *Centre for Monitoring Democratic Processes "Quorum"*, 2 August (2010), http://cmdp-kvorum.org/en/news/center/796; Tiberio Graziani, "The Mediterranean and Central Asia: The Hinges of Eurasia", *Centre for Monitoring Democratic Processes "Quorum"*, 30 May (2011), http://cmdp-kvorum.org/en/news/center/921; Tiberio Graziani, "The Economic Crisis of the Western System. A Geopolitical Approach", *Centre for Monitoring Democratic Processes "Quorum"*, 28 May (2009), http://cmdp-kvorum.org/en/news/center/186

50 The full name of this organisation is simultaneously French and Flemish: Front Nationaliste/Nationalistisch Front.

51 "Who Is Luc Michel?", *Parti Communautaire National-européen*, http://pcn-ncp.com/editos/en/bio.htm; Lee, *The Beast Reawakens*, p. 479.

52 "Their 'Europe' Is Not Ours: PCN-NCP, the Party of the Unitary and Communitarian Europe, Says 'No' to the American False Europe of NATO and Capitalism!", *Nation-Europe*, No. 43 (May 2005), p. 39 (39–41).

53 Aleksandr Dugin, "Liviyskie impressii: po sledam poezdki v Dzhamakhiriyu", *Evraziya*, 1 March (2011), http://evrazia.org/article/1590. Also present at the congress in Tripoli was Ruslan Khasbulatov.

54 Pierre-André Taguieff, *La judéophobie des Modernes: Des Lumières au Jihad mondial* (Paris: Jacob, 2008), p. 638; Jean-Yves Camus, "Les amis de la Libye: rendez-vous estival à Paris", *Actualité juive*, No. 807 (July 2003).

55 "The Eurasian Vision of Another Europe!", *Nation-Europe*, No. 43 (May 2005), p. 46.

56 Ibid.

57 They were Leonid Savin, Aleksandr Bovdunov and Aleksandr Proselkov. The latter was killed in summer 2014 in Eastern Ukraine where he – like many other Russian far-right activists – went to fight against the Ukrainian forces.

58 "Deputat Evroparlamenta: 'Rossiya – neot'yevlemaya chast' Evropy'", *Regnum*, 16 September (2006), http://regnum.ru/news/706227.html

59 "Evropeyskie nablyudateli: 'Esli strany ES ne priznayut referendum v Pridnestrov'ye, znachit oni ne priznayut demokratiyu'", *Regnum*, 16 September (2006), http://regnum.ru/news/706222.html

60 "Etudes de Luc Michel", *Parti Communautaire National-européen*, http://pcn-ncp.com/editos/fr/ed-061218-1.htm

61 "Mezhdunarodnye nablyudateli prinyali zaklyuchenie po itogam referenduma v Pridnestrovye. Polny tekst", *Regnum*, 17 September (2006), http://regnum.ru/news/polit/706323.html

62 See the website of *La Direction de l'information légale et administrative*: http://journal-officiel.gouv.fr

63 Luc Michel, *La "Pridnestrovskaia Moldavskaia Respublika" (PMR): Construction d'un nouvel etat europeen et experience de democratie directe* (Brussels: EODE, 2007).

64 Vladimir Jirinovski [Zhirinovsky], Patrick Brunot, *Jirinovski m'a dit . . .* (Paris: [self-published], 1995).

65 Patrick Brunot, *Les Faux Amis de l'Amérique* (Coulommiers: Dualpha éd., 2006).

66 "Contact", *Eurasian Observatory for Democracy & Elections*, http://eode.org/contact/

67   "EODE: A Non-Aligned NGO!", *Eurasian Observatory for Democracy & Elections*,
       http://eode.org/eode-a-non-aligned-ngo/
68   "Contact", http://eode.org/contact/
69   The Transeuropean Dialogue was a short-lived organisation founded in 2007 and headed
       by Marina Kochetkova. The initial aim of founding another election monitoring
       organisation was to move away from the CIS-EMO's disrepute. To present the
       Transeuropean Dialogue as an organisation separate from CIS-EMO, Kochetkova even
       used her maiden name, Klebanovich, in public documents.
70   Ekaterina Pol'gueva, "Garantii prav obespecheny", *Sovetskaya Rossiya*, No. 30, 6 March
       (2007), p. 3.
71   Luc Michel, "Private Reception for the Birthday of the Abkhazian President",
       Facebook, 30 May (2011), https://facebook.com/media/set/?set=a.227941727216728.
       68471.137004106310491
72   "PCN TV Moscow: Interview of Luc Michel by Fabrice Beaur", *The Jamahiriyan
       Resistance Network*, 22 November (2011), http://elac-committees.org/2011/11/22/
       pcn-tv-moscow-interview-of-luc-michel-by-fabrice-beaur/
73   Rafał Pankowski, "Poseł ze swastyką w podpisie", *Gazeta Wyborcza*, No. 19, 23 January
       (2006), p. 17.
74   For a discussion of Samoobrona's ideology and the terms used to describe it see Rafał
       Pankowski, *The Populist Radical Right in Poland: The Patriots* (London: Routledge, 2010),
       pp. 135–146.
75   OSCE/ODIHR, *Republic of Belarus. Parliamentary elections. 17 October 2004. OSCE/
       ODIHR Election Observation Mission. Final Report* (Warsaw: OSCE/ODIHR, 2004),
       p. 1.
76   Pankowski, "Poseł ze swastyką w podpisie", p. 17.
77   "Mittendrin: Rechtspopulistische Parteien in Mittelosteuropa [Interview with Bartek
       Pytlas]", *Religionswissenschaftlicher Medien- und Informationsdienst*, 30 June (2014),
       http://remid.de/blog/2014/06/mittendrin-rechtspopulistische-parteien-in-mittelost
       europa/; Marta Zimniak-Hałajko, "Kultura słowiańska jako alternatywna", *Przegląd
       Humanistyczny*, No. 4 (2009), p. 116 (113–122).
78   "Jesienny zaciąg Leppera", *Newsweek*, 6 October (2002), http://polska.newsweek.pl/
       jesienny-zaciag-leppera,25460,1,3.html
79   Rafał Pankowski, Marcin Kornak, "Poland", in Cas Mudde (ed.), *Racist Extremism in
       Central and Eastern Europe* (London: Routledge, 2005) p. 154 (145–170).
80   Rafał Pankowski, "Polish Antisemite Takes Charge of Education", *Searchlight*, July
       (2006), p. 33.
81   Mateusz Piskorski, "Bratskaya Pol'sha", *Ya – russkiy*, No. 51 (September 2000).
82   Mateusz Piskorski, *Samoobrona RP w polskim systemie partyjnym. Rozprawa doktorska*
       (Poznań: Uniwersytet im. Adama Mickiewicza, 2010), p. 386. Villepinte was a place
       of Beaur's residence before he moved to the Russian city of Krasnodar after marrying
       a Russian.
83   Alena Get'manchuk, "Pridnestrov'ye 'obnovilos. OBSE protiv", *Zerkalo Nedeli*,
       No. 49 (2005).
84   Pankowski, *The Populist Radical Right in Poland*, p. 150.
85   Michał Kacewicz, Michał Krzymowski, "Euroazjaci w Warszawie", *Newsweek*, 15
       January (2013), http://swiat.newsweek.pl/euroazjaci-w-warszawie,100369,1,1.html
86   "NATO is bezopasnost' v Evrazii", *Moskovskie novosti*, No. 47, 8 December (2006),
       p. 22.
87   "Conferenza Internazionale. La Nato e la sicurezza eurasiatica", *Eurasia: Rivista di studi
       Geopolitici*, 22 November (2006), http://eurasia-rivista.org/cogit_content/articoli/
       EEyuElVFukysALSNUV.shtml
88   "NATO is bezopasnost' v Evrazii", p. 22.
89   "Polyaki podderzhali Rossiyu", *Evraziyskiy Soyuz Molodyozhi*, http://rossia3.ru/
       politics/foreign/polyakizaosetiu

90 *European Center of Geopolitical Analysis* (Moscow: [n.a.], 2009), p. 2.
91 Aleksey Kochetkov, Aleksey Martynov, Mateusz Piskorski, *Yuzhnaya Ossetiya: Vooruzhennaya agressiya i mirotvorcheskaya voyna* (Moscow: Knizhny mir, 2009).
92 Ibid., p. 85.
93 Kacewicz, Krzymowski, "Euroazjaci w Warszawie".
94 Interview with Aleksey Kochetkov conducted by Sanita Jemberga (*Re:Baltica*) in Warsaw on 30 September 2014. I am grateful to Jemberga for providing me with the transcript of this interview.
95 Interview with Aleksey Kochetkov.
96 Interview with Mateusz Piskorski conducted by Sanita Jemberga (*Re:Baltica*) in Warsaw on 31 March 2015. I am grateful to Jemberga for providing me with the transcript of this interview.
97 Kacewicz, Krzymowski, "Euroazjaci w Warszawie"; Michał Kacewicz, Michał Krzymowski, "Robił to jawnie", *Newsweek*, No. 23 (2016), http://newsweek.pl/plus/polska/mateusz-piskorski-kulisy-zatrzymania-rosyjskiego-szpiega,artykuly,386415,1,z.html
98 "The Russian Laundromat", *OCCRP*, 22 August (2014), https://reportingproject.net/therussianlaundromat/russian-laundromat.php
99 Wojciech Cieśla, Endy Gęsina, "Operacja Laundromat", *Newsweek*, No. 13 (2017), http://newsweek.pl/plus/spoleczenstwo/sledztwo-pralnia-brudnych-pieniedzy-z-rosji-w-polsce,artykuly,407167,1,z.html
100 The Civic Chamber of the Russian Federation was established in 2005, supposedly to provide intercommunication between the state and society. According to Krastev, however, the creation of the Civic Chamber aimed at controlling Russia's NGOs, and it was "political technologist" Gleb Pavlovsky who had "urged the Kremlin to adopt new legislation that would create" this new body. Ivan Krastev, "Democracy's 'Doubles'", *Journal of Democracy*, Vol. 17, No. 2 (2006), pp. 52–62 (57). Thus, the creation of the Civic Chamber seems to be one of the Kremlin's responses to the "colour revolutions" in Georgia and Ukraine, where independent NGOs played an important role in mobilising the protests against the electoral fraud.
101 "Nashi eksperty", *Za demokratiyu i prava narodov*, https://web.archive.org/web/20161030020218/http://pravanarodov.ru/экспертиза/наши-эксперты/
102 *Promezhutochny otchet o rezul'tatakh distantsionnogo monitoringa vyborov Prezidenta SShA 6 noyabrya 2012 goda* (Moscow: Grazhdanskiy kontrol', 2012), p. 53.
103 On the PVV see Koen Vossen, *The Power of Populism: Geert Wilders and the Party for Freedom in the Netherlands* (New York: Routledge, 2017).
104 "Konferentsiya 'Mezhdunarodnoe obshchestvennoe nablyudenie v izbiratel'nom protsesse: printsipy, razvitie, mirovoy opyt'", *Mezhdunarodny Institut Noveyshikh Gosudarstv*, 7 October (2011), http://iines.org/node/594
105 OSCE/ODIHR, *Russian Federation, State Duma Elections, 4 December 2011: Final Report* (Warsaw: OSCE/ODIHR, 2012), p. 1.
106 Maksim Dronov, "Mezhdunarodnye nablyudateli nazvali vybory 'chestnymi i demokraticheskimi'", *Moskovskiy komsomolets*, No. 278, 7 December (2011), p. 2.
107 Officially, Griffin was invited to Russia by Civic Control.
108 "Russian Elections 'Much Fairer than Britain's' – Initial Verdict from Nick Griffin", *British National Party*, 9 December (2011), https://web.archive.org/web/20120107204013/http://www.bnp.org.uk/news/national/russian-elections-%E2%80%9Cmuch-fairer-britain%E2%80%99s%E2%80%9D-%E2%80%93-initial-verdict-nick-griffin
109 "Ukraine Elections Put Britain's to Shame", *British National Party*, 20 November (2012), https://web.archive.org/web/20121123045633/ http://www.bnp.org.uk/news/national/ukraine-elections-put-britains-shame
110 Maksim Makarychev, "Ne nado pouchat' Rossiiu", *Rossiyskaya gazeta*, No. 51, 8 March (2012), p. 3.

111 "Outcome of the Presidential Elections in Russia", *European Parliament*, 15 March (2012), http://europarl.europa.eu/sides/getDoc.do?type=TA&reference=P7-TA-2012-0088&language=EN

112 "Thursday, 15 March 2012. Debates of the European Parliament", *European Parliament*, 15 March (2012), http://europarl.europa.eu/sides/getDoc.do?pubRef=-//EP//NONSGML+CRE+20120315+SIT+DOC+PDF+V0//EN&language=EN

113 "Predstaviteli 'Grazhdanskogo kontrolya' budut osushchestvlyat' nablyudenie na referendume v Krymu", *TASS*, 11 March (2014), http://tass.ru/politika/1036824

114 Anastasiya Kornya, Polina Khimshiashvili, "Osoboe priglashenie", *Vedomosti*, No. 44 (3548), 14 March (2014).

115 Sergey Naryshkin (ed.), *Novye izmereniya parlamentskogo dialoga v sovremenny period. Materialy tret'yego Mezhdunarodnogo parlamentskogo foruma* (Moscow: Izdanie Gosudarstvennoy Dumy, 2014), p. 57.

116 The leaked records of the off-the-book payments of Partiya rehioniv covering several months in 2012 bear evidence that the Partiya rehioniv illegally paid more than half a million US Dollars for various unspecified projects related to Sergey Zavorotny, see Sergey Leshchenko, Anton Marchuk, Sevgil Musaeva-Borovik, "Rukopisi ne goryat. Chernaya bukhgalteriya Partii regionov: familii, daty, summt", *Ukrayins'ka Pravda*, 31 May (2016), http://pravda.com.ua/cdn/graphics/2016/05/black-pr/index.html

117 This document was provided to the author by a trusted source.

118 "SMS perepiska iz Upravleniya vnutrenney politiki AP RF. 2011–2014 gg.", *Anonimny internatsional*, 31 March (2015), https://b0ltai.org/2015/03/31/смс-переписка-из-управления-внутренн/

119 "Bonjour les Patriotes! Russkaya Vesna na ville Triniti", *Navalny*, 26 August (2014), https://navalny.com/p/3763/

120 "Le FN dément envoyer des observateurs en Crimée", *Libération*, 13 March (2014), http://liberation.fr/politiques/2014/03/13/le-fn-dement-envoyer-des-observateurs-en-crimee_986838

121 Florence Morice, "French Far-Right Politician Endorses Crimea Vote", *EUObserver*, 21 March (2014), https://euobserver.com/eu-elections/123556

122 "Secretary-General Deplores Unconstitutional Elections Called by Armed Rebel Groups in Ukraine", *United Nations*, 29 October (2014), http://un.org/press/en/2014/sgsm16291.doc.htm

123 "Ewald Stadler – International Observer – on Donetsk Elections", *YouTube*, 2 November (2014), https://youtube.com/watch?v=ssxP9KZ4dgw

124 Cited in Juhász *et al.*, *"I Am Eurasian"*, p. 47.

125 Elena Shesternina, "Pridnestrov'e golosuet za nezavisimost' – v shestoy raz", *Izvestiya*, No. 171, 18 September (2006), p. 1.

126 Béla Kovács, "15. Preparations for the Russian State Duma Elections in December (Debate)", *European Parliament*, 6 July (2011), http://europarl.europa.eu/sides/getDoc.do?pubRef=-//EP//TEXT+CRE+20110706+ITEM-015+DOC+XML+V0//EN&language=en&query=INTERV&detail=3-548-000

127 Lavrov, "Reform Will Enhance the OSCE's Relevance".

128 Stanislav Byshok, Aleksey Semenov, *Navalny. Chelovek, kotory ukral les. Istoriya blogera i politika* (Moscow: Knizhny mir, 2014). The introduction to this book was written by a Russian ultranationalist Konstantin Krylov.

129 The above-mentioned book is an English translation of Stanislav Byshok, Aleksey Kochetkov, *Evromaidan imeni Stepana Bandery. Ot demokratii k diktature* (Moscow: Knizhny mir, 2014). On the participation of the Ukrainian far right in the Ukrainian revolution see Anton Shekhovtsov, "The Ukrainian Far Right and the Ukrainian Revolution", *New Europe College Black Sea Link Program Yearbook 2014–2015* (2016), pp. 215–237; Anton Shekhovtsov, Andreas Umland, "Ukraine's Radical Right", *Journal of Democracy*, Vol. 25, No. 3 (2014), pp. 58–63.

130 Luc Michel, "From the So-called 'Arab Spring' to the 'Russian Spring': Pro-Western Coup in Russia!", *The Jamahiriyan Resistance Network*, 8 December (2011), http://elac-committees.org/2011/12/08/luc-michel-from-the-so-called-arab-spring-to-the-russian-spring%E2%80%9D-pro-western-coup-in-russia/

131 See "V Krymu budut rabotat' okolo 100 nablyudateley OBSE", *Vesti*, 15 March (2014), http://vesti.ru/videos/show/vid/584634/

132 "OSCE Chair Says Crimean Referendum in Its Current Form Is Illegal and Calls for Alternative Ways to Address the Crimean Issue", *OSCE*, 11 March (2014), http://osce.org/cio/116313

133 Eliseo Bertolasi, "La sfida eurasiatica della Russia", *La Voce della Russia*, 7 July (2014), http://it.sputniknews.com/italian.ruvr.ru/2014_07_07/La-sfida-eurasiatica-della-Russia-6102/

134 "So-called Elections Not in Line with Minsk Protocol, Says OSCE Chair, Calling for Enhanced Efforts and Dialogue to Implement All Commitments", *OSCE*, 31 October (2014), http://osce.org/cio/126242

135 "Sotrudniki OBSE osmotreli izbiratel'nye uchastki v Donetske", *Ria Novosti*, 1 November (2014), http://ria.ru/world/20141101/1031302476.html

136 "No OSCE #observation of so-called 'elections' in east #Ukraine . . .", *Twitter*, 1 November (1014), https://twitter.com/osce/status/528645333195423744

137 "01 11 2014 V Donetske sostoyalas' press-konferentsiya mezhdunarodnykh nablyudateley ABSE", *YouTube*, 2 November (2014), https://www.youtube.com/watch?v=DLDxyMT2eHs

138 Roland Oliphant, "Ukraine Rebels Lure Voters to Polls – with Root Vegetables", *The Telegraph*, 2 November (2014), http://telegraph.co.uk/news/worldnews/europe/ukraine/11204433/Ukraine-rebels-lure-voters-to-polls-with-root-vegetables.html

139 See "V Pridnestrov'ye nakanune referenduma spokoyno, otmechayut nablyudateli", *RIA Novosti*, 16 September (2006), http://ria.ru/politics/20060916/53957224.html; "Pridnestrov'ye sdelalo shag v storonu Rossii", *Sankt-Peterburgskie vedomosti*, No. 174, 19 September (2006), p. 3.

140 Kelley, *Monitoring Democracy*, p. 46.

5

UNDERMINING THE WEST THROUGH MASS MEDIA

Introduction

As argued in Chapter 3, the state control over the major Russian mass media in Russia was a cornerstone of the authoritarian kleptocracy that Vladimir Putin has built during his presidency. Silencing (sometimes even through murders of journalists) and/or marginalising independent voices and alternative sources of information have eventually resulted in cultural hegemony of the ruling elites over the majority of population.

In 2004–2012, that is during Putin's second term and Dmitry Medvedev's presidential term, the repressions against, and murders of, journalists still took place. At the same time, the media increasingly developed self-censorship skills.[1] By Putin's third term (2012–today), the number of murdered journalists decreased, but the relative decrease of the repressions against the mass media in general testified to a new trend that was long in the making. It manifested itself as media conformism that implied 'both opportunism and routinized willingness to accept unquestioningly the usual practices or standards, which were originally imposed through coercion'.[2] Rather than being subjected to narratives produced by the Kremlin and then 'imposed coercively onto media personalities and reporters',[3] the major media produced their own – and genuinely creative – narratives that they perceived as being expected by the authorities.

The Russian mass media have thereby made a crucial contribution to the consolidation of Putin's regime by propagating conformist, pro-Kremlin ideas and marginalising rival views on Russian politics. Apart from this, Russian media succeeded, domestically, in creating a distorted image of Russia itself and international relations between Russia and other parts of the world. As Andreas Umland argues,

The primary reason for Putin's popularity in Russia is his far-reaching control over the media and the incredible propaganda campaign that is going on there every day on several channels in parallel. This is a huge brainwashing operation that has created, for tens of millions of Russians, an alternative reality.[4]

In addition, Putin's regime invested heavily in launching or reviving the Russian media operating outside the country, including TV, radio, Internet and printed resources. Especially in post-Soviet states, Russian or Russia-controlled media proved 'a useful instrument for influencing public opinion and political elites'.[5] Furthermore, as Janusz Bugajski writes,

An additional measure for influencing public and political opinion is the purchase of major media outlets in targeted states, especially television stations and popular newspapers with a wide audience. Russian businessmen with ties to the Moscow authorities have endeavored to acquire majority shares or outright ownership of media outlets in a number of countries. This provides a valuable means for airing opinions, commentaries, and discussions that enhance Moscow's foreign policy offensives.[6]

Today, Russian media operate in several foreign languages promoting, to various international target groups, Russian foreign policy, misinforming and/or confusing these audiences about the developments in Russia and the world, as well as subverting and undermining Western mainstream views on Russia.[7]

The use of international media as an important mechanism of soft power, public policy or propaganda is, naturally, not an exclusive invention of the Russian authorities: the major nations involved in the Cold War extensively used their international media in order to undermine their adversaries.[8] However, there are crucial differences between the Russian mass media and, for example, their Western mainstream counterparts. One difference is that, especially in recent years, the Russian media, which also include state-controlled media, started to engage with politicians, activists, publicists and commentators coming from the fringes of their countries' socio-political life, namely the far right, far left, conspiracy theorists, isolationists, etc. who approve of, or sympathise with, Russia's domestic and foreign policies.

This chapter looks at two particular aspects of the cooperation between the Russian media and the far right, but before doing this, the chapter discusses why this cooperation became needed in the first place. Then it examines how mainstream Russian media engage with far-right politicians, activists and publicists, and looks at the ideas and beliefs they articulate to justify the logic and direction of Russian foreign policy and to subvert the liberal-democratic consensus in the West. Finally, it explores the structural relations between Russian media and certain media initiatives of the European far right.

Failing soft power

Evidence suggests that engaging with far-right commentators is a relatively recent trend within Russian media the origins of which can be traced to 2008. Several important developments marked that year.

In August 2008, Russia invaded Georgia. Although Russia easily won this short war and the Russian society believed in the legitimacy of Moscow's actions in Georgia, the Russian establishment felt that it had lost the information warfare on the international level. One pro-Kremlin Russian journalist provided an insight into the establishment's thinking:

> The Russian military campaign in the Northern Caucasus can be considered a victorious one, but Russia has definitely lost the information war that the US waged on us. In the eyes of almost all the countries of the world, Russia is seen as an aggressor that has attacked a weak Georgian state.[9]

Discussing the international response to the Russian war on Georgia at a meeting of the Valdai International Discussion Club, Putin himself noted the 'power of the West's propaganda machine'.[10] At the same time, the Russian establishment realised that not only had the existing Russian international media failed to convince Western audiences in the alleged legitimacy of Russia's actions in Georgia; rather, the entire approach based on the traditional soft power concept of presenting an 'attractive image' of Russia had failed. In other words, the simple message that 'Russia is good' did not work.

The Russian media found a different approach to their Western audiences, and Peter Pomeranzev and Michael Weiss have argued that 'no organization better traces the transformation of Kremlin thinking from soft power to weaponization than the Kremlin's international rolling news channel, RT'.[11] RT was established in 2005 under the name 'Russia Today' and aimed – in Putin's own words – at breaking 'the Anglo-Saxon monopoly on the global information streams'.[12] Since then, Russia Today 'has gained a reputation for serving as the Kremlin's "propaganda machine" ',[13] but in 2009, in order to prevent the Western audiences from immediately associating the TV channel with official Moscow, all Western versions of Russia Today were rebranded as RT.[14] The content of its programmes changed too: less coverage of Russia, more deliberate provocations and conspiracy theories that were first advertised under the slogan 'Any story can be other story altogether' which later transformed into 'Question more' – an appeal to Western audiences to question the credibility of their national mainstream political leaders.[15]

RT's Editor-in-Chief Margarita Simonyan explained the transformation of Russia Today into RT in purely business terms: 'When we were a quiet, little-noticed channel telling stories from Russia, our audience was negligible. When we started being really provocative . . . our audience started to grow'.[16] However, in comparison to political goals, business considerations seemed to be of less importance to RT as a propaganda source and a tool of Russian public diplomacy.

Critics of RT maintained that 'far from improving Russia's image abroad, the channel [had] instead morphed into a platform for conspiracy theorists and other like-minded figures on the margins of debate – especially for those who espouse[d] anti-American views'.[17] Thus, a departure from the approach based on soft power, was – as software developers sometimes say – 'not a bug, but a feature': since 'Russia is good' did not work, then a combination of the 'Russian is good' narrative and that of 'the West is bad'[18] might do. A similar change of approach characterised other Russian international media too.

However, the new approach encountered a problem. The workings of the international media imply that these are international commentators, rather than domestic ones, who play a leading part. The anti-liberal policies implemented in Russia in recent years and the country's aggressive foreign policy alienated many Western liberal-democratic politicians from commenting positively on Russian domestic developments and international behaviour. Besides, they would hardly be ready to elaborate on the 'bad West' narrative anyway.

The increasingly racialist nature of post-Soviet Russian society[19] excludes the feasibility of engaging primarily with Black, Asian or Latin American politicians or activists from particular Third-World regimes who could potentially push anti-Western arguments. Only *white* Europeans and/or Americans can be seen as those whose views will be deemed as fully legitimate by Russian society. Therefore, the Russian media had to continue to rely on an ever-decreasing pool of Western mainstream politicians who would hold pro-Kremlin views or be interested in providing the required commentary. At the same time, they had to turn to white Europeans or Americans who would expose illiberal and/or anti-Western views, and, thus, corroborate the 'West is bad' argument.

As indicated earlier, as a result of the gradual radicalisation of the anti-Western sentiments in Russia since 2005, one could witness the growing ideological affinity between, on the one hand, mainstream discourse in Russia, which represented an amalgamation of various – sometimes conflicting, sometimes 'Russian conservative' – political concepts and myths, and, on the other hand, the scope of narratives produced collectively by the far right, far left, Christian fundamentalists and conspiracy theorists. In other words, Russia's mainstream socio-political discourse has created an alternative reality that, in the West, overlapped with the outlooks of the fringes of its socio-political life. Thus, fringe activists became uniquely suited to offer favourable political views of Putin's regime. On the part of the Russian media, this was 'nudge propaganda' that 'works by finding parties, politicians, and points-of-view that are already sure of their world-view . . ., and giving them a nudge – so long as these views are usefully anti-systemic'.[20]

To engage with the far right, anti-establishment figures and conspiracy theorists on the part of the Russian pro-Kremlin media such as RT seemed to be a deliberate decision. One former employee of the French edition of RT recollects: 'Initially, the idea [of the management] was to give voice to people we saw rarely in the media, including the left [. . .]. But [from October 2015] we were pressured to interview people of the extreme right'.[21] Liz Wahl, an American journalist who worked for RT for two-and-a-half years and publicly resigned on air over RT's coverage of the Russian invasion of Ukraine, says that journalists working for RT in the United States generally fall into two groups: those who see this job as 'a start, a chance to work in Washington DC and cover stories of real international significance' and those 'who come from anti-establishment movements with anti-Western views. . . . The more willing you are to twist the truth and spread conspiracy theories, the more likely you are to get a show on RT'.[22] Wahl also acknowledges that, while covering domestic US politics, she always had to get stories approved by 'the Russian news director. And you learned it would only get approved if it fit a general mould of making the US or the West look bad'.[23]

Russian state-controlled media engage with fringe anti-establishment commentators not only on the international level, but also domestically with a view to consolidating the Russian society. Working with the domestic audience, the Kremlin's media aim to show that Russia and its citizens are not isolated, that their country is not a 'lonely and castaway state'[24] and that, despite all the flirtations with the concepts of particularist 'Russian conservatism', Eurasianism or Russia's 'special path', the country is still considered part of the European civilisation by white Europeans or Americans themselves. By conveying pro-Kremlin views of Western illiberal activists, Russian state media strive to prove that Russia does appeal to particular Western politicians, and, furthermore, these particular politicians embrace Russia as the real Europe, in contrast to the degenerate Europe of liberal-democratic values, the 'Gayropa'.[25]

The Russian media operating domestically and internationally tend to omit the peculiar ideological credentials of the fringe politicians and activists they turn to, as well as relying heavily, especially in the international context, on *narrative laundering*. This process implies the movement of narratives in the media sphere, where the original source that produces these narratives is either forgotten or impossible to determine. Social networks with their frequent negligence towards the origins of shared information,[26] insufficient public expertise on particular socio-political phenomena and unpreparedness of other media actors for aggressive disinformation campaigns facilitate such narrative laundering. The Russian media that implant propagandistic narratives in the international media sphere are interested in a loss of their origin, so they cannot be traced back to Russia or to fringe commentators. When narrative laundering is successful, propagandistic narratives can become part of the mainstream media sphere. This process is also similar to a particular type of the Soviet active measures that Andrew Wilson refers to as 'an echo chamber effect': even the most 'blatant lies [that the Soviets disseminated] took on a life of their own through the sheer insistence of their repetition'.[27]

Bringing the rebels

In historical terms, the international Russian media granted space for propagating Western right-wing extremist views as early as 1996. That year, a Toronto-based

German neo-Nazi and Holocaust denier Ernst Zündel made an agreement with the Voice of Russia (VoR), the Russian government's by now discontinued international radio broadcasting service,[28] to broadcast his weekly 1-hour medium-wave radio shows called 'Voice of Freedom' from Kaliningrad.[29] In his broadcasts, which reached Germany, Zündel presented 'long monologues and quotations from the works of various Holocaust deniers' that were banned in Germany.[30] Zündel's radio shows produced an international scandal, and the VoR terminated his programme pleading that the management had been unaware of the contents of his broadcasts. It was not Zündel's first attempt to reach out to wider audiences, and while there is no direct connection between his earlier endeavours and the use of far-right activists by the Russian media today, an introduction to Zündel's 'Voice of Freedom' programme that he had launched in Canada before his cooperation with the VoR provides insight as to why activists like Zündel have become valuable for the Russian media in recent years:

> the 'Voice of Freedom' . . . is an attempt by us to bring you a . . . TV programme that differs from the mainstream media, because we . . . hope to bring you uncensored news, uncensored commentary. . . . We hope to be politically incorrect, uncorrect. . . . We want to bring you the rebels.[31]

More than a decade later, 'bringing the rebels' turned into major *modus operandi* for the Russian TV channels as they have started to engage with European and American far-right activists, racists and conspiracy theorists to promote directly or indirectly the pro-Kremlin agenda of undermining or eroding the mainstream political and social narratives in the West. Already in 2010, Sonia Scherr had called attention to the fact that RT 'reported with boosterish zeal on conspiracy theories popular in the resurgent "Patriot" movement, whose adherents typically advocate[d] extreme antigovernment doctrines'.[32] She observed that RT had been regularly giving exposure to fringe figures who promoted conspiracy ideas about 11 September attacks being 'an inside job'; Barack Obama having been born outside the United States and, thus, being ineligible for the presidency; or the United States being a 'tool of the New World Order'. Analysing conspiracy theories as an inherent feature of RT's contents, Ilya Yablokov identifies two types of conspiratorial ideas on RT: 'the first includes genuinely American conspiracy theories; and the second includes ideas of conspiracy in relations between the US and Russia'.[33] Yablokov argues that RT employs these ideas 'to undermine US domestic and foreign policies', as well as supporting 'the Russian government's actions, helping Russia's leadership to become a "spokesperson" on the side of the global community of "the people" against the global "Other" – the US'.[34]

The 11 September conspiracy theories promulgated by RT were not limited to those voiced by United States commentators. For example, the FN's then member Aymeric Chauprade appeared in RT's show '9/11: Challenging the official version'.[35] The TV channel introduced Chauprade as 'a dissident voice in the French academic world' and 'a critic of Western policies towards Russia', and asked him to discuss his dismissal from a chair at the Collège interarmées de défense following an accusation of supporting conspiracy theories around the 11 September attacks in his book *Chronique du choc des civilisations* (Chronicle of the clash of civilisations).[36]

American far-right activist Lyndon LaRouche obsessed with the idea of the Britons being instigators of almost every turbulent event in contemporary history is a darling of RT and some other Russian media too. In the wake of the Russian-Georgian War, when the pro-Kremlin media aspired to justify the Russian aggression in Georgia in August 2008, RT conducted an interview with LaRouche and highlighted his belief that 'the Georgian assault on South Ossetia was probably a British-led operation with US support'.[37]

In their attempts to justify the Russian invasion of Georgia not only internationally but also domestically, the Russian media turned to FPÖ leader Heinz-Christian Strache. In October 2008, that is after the Russian-Georgian War, he took part in the conference 'Europe-Russia-Georgia: Peace Building I' that was held in Vienna by the Austrian Technologies GmbH managed by FPÖ member Barbara Kappel.[38] At this conference, he made statements critical of Georgian President Mikheil Saakashvili known for his pro-Western views. The Russian media picked up these statements and quoted Strache as saying that Saakashvili 'had installed a dictatorial regime', that Russia 'had not acted as an aggressor' in its war on Georgia and that 'the EU member states should not take their cue from the US' in response to Russia's actions in Georgia.[39]

By turning to far-right politicians and activists for comments, the Russian media also tried to capitalise on particular soft spots of the EU, like the cohesion of the Eurozone or immigration, to prove the alleged failure of the democratic policies and integration agenda of the EU. When discussing, in one of its reports, an upcoming meeting of Eurozone finance ministers who would consider boosting the EU bailout fund in 2011, RT quoted three MEPs, none of whom could have possibly provided any optimistic or even neutral view on the future of the Eurozone: Nigel Farage and Godfrey Bloom of the Eurosceptic UK Independence Party (UKIP), and Morten Messerschmidt of the far-right Dansk Folkeparti (Danish People's Party, DF).[40]

The Russian media coverage of the riots in Stockholm suburbs in May 2013, which broke out after police had shot to death a machete-armed elderly man of non-Swedish origin, was also indicative of the strategy to insinuate that the integration project of the EU was failing. For example, out of seven people cited in RT's TV report 'They don't want to integrate',[41] four belonged to the far-right and racist circles: Kent Ekeroth, MP of the far-right SD; Ingrid Carlqvist and Lars Hedegaard, editors of the racist newspaper *Dispatch International*; and Gerolf Annemans, then chairman of the far-right VB. In a similar manner, the Italian service of the VoR interviewed Roberto Fiore of the fascist Forza Nuova asking him about his opinion on the immigration issue and whether Italy had a future in the EU.[42] (Ironically, in 2009, RT had called Fiore a 'convicted fascist terrorist',[43] but, 4 years later, the VoR considered him a legitimate commentator.) Such out-of-balance reports – prioritising far-right and generally fringe commentators over the mainstream or established ones – aimed at presenting views sceptical of, or even antagonistic towards, the EU project as of equal value with sober analyses of these problematic issues.

The Russian media also involved the far right to comment on topical international issues such as the challenges to the democratic transition in Libya or the civil war in Syria. For example, for comments on the Libyan and Syrian questions, RT turned, among other far-right activists, to Richard Spencer, president of the US-based think-tank National Policy Institute, whom the Anti-Defamation League called 'a leader in white supremacist circles that envision[ed] a "new" right that [would] openly embrace "white racial consciousness" '.[44] Despite these credentials, RT did not hesitate to transmit Spencer's ideas either to demonstrate the alleged failures of the West and, especially, the United States in their 'Libyan affair', or to 'prove' the involvement of the United States in the civil war in Syria: 'Russia is on the side of [Syria's] established sovereign authorities. . . . And Washington is playing a kind of dangerous game of both desiring hegemony in the region and trying to achieve that by creating chaos and riding the wave of Muslim discontent'.[45]

While one could observe a trend in the Russian media of engaging far-right politicians and activists already since 2008, this method became particularly evident in 2013–2014. That was the period of massive media-backed political mobilisation of the Russian establishment in connection with the imminent signing of the Association Agreement between the EU and Ukraine, the Ukrainian revolution (which was seen by 75.7 per cent of Russian elites as an American creation[46]), Russia's annexation of the Autonomous Republic of Crimea and invasion of Eastern Ukraine, and the consequent Western sanctions against Russia. Russian media extensively relayed – on a scale unseen before – narratives justifying Russia's foreign policy both to the domestic and international audiences.

In one of its shows, the VoR, discussing the prospective signing of the Association Agreement, noted 'some experts inside the EU' who said that Ukraine would 'lose its economic sovereignty as a whole number of its economic branches [would] be governed directly from Brussels'. However, only one such 'expert' was named in the programme: the 'prominent Polish geopolitical analyst Mateusz Piskorski'.[47]

Piskorski, indeed, became an important communicator of pro-Moscow narratives in Russian mass media – a status hardly commensurable to his limited political significance or the negligibility of his European Centre of Geopolitical Analysis in his home country, Poland. With a few exceptions, up until the second half of 2013, the Russian media mentioned Piskorski only in relation to his 'election observation' activities. Later, however, they started asking him to comment on other issues, and he readily talked on how 'a particular element of the "Ukrainian" protest had been developed and prepared in a local US embassy';[48] how the Ukrainian opposition parties during the revolution were 'calling for major violations of human rights';[49] or how the Americans would 'continue to use the situation in Ukraine as a means of destabilizing European Union countries and Russian Federation'.[50]

As mentioned earlier, Piskorski is usually described in the Russian media as 'a prominent geopolitical analyst' or 'geopolitical expert', but he is also pictured as a representative of a particular, 'nonconformist' trend in the EU. In a similar vein, presenting a narrative favourable to Russia's foreign policy as part of this trend, the VoR aired an interview with the FN's Marine Le Pen and introduced her as category witness that 'not everyone in Europe believes that Ukraine made a mistake by refusing to sign an association agreement' at the Eastern Partnership Vilnius Summit of 2013.[51]

Le Pen has become a regular commentator for pro-Kremlin media since the end of 2013. It is worth noting that, before this time, the media in Russia mentioned Le Pen largely as a *newsmaker*. However, with the beginning of pro-European protests in Ukraine, she started to appear in the Russian mainstream media sphere as an *opinion maker* offering her views on the 'legitimacy' of the Crimean 'referendum', the 'need' for the federalisation of Ukraine (an idea promoted by Russia), the EU 'waging Cold War on Russia', Russia bringing multipolarity back to the world, or the 'stupidity' of Western sanctions against Russia. These messages were, in particular, communicated by the most popular, state-controlled TV station Pervy kanal (First Channel),[52] the central state news agency ITAR-TASS,[53] and the most popular Russian tabloid *Komsomol'skaya Pravda*.[54] These media also readily conveyed her arguments about the allegedly counterproductive nature of the EU's sanctions, the anti-Russian Cold War, and a US-led conspiracy to extend its sphere of influence in Europe and the world.

The Russian media also utilised other leaders of the FN. For example, Chauprade started to appear in the Russian media regularly since the second half of 2013 – and Pervy kanal started using his comments from the start of the pro-European protests in Ukraine. Shortly before illegally going to the Russia-occupied Autonomous Republic of Crimea to observe the 'referendum' on the status of this region, Chauprade denied the fact that Russia invaded Ukraine, yet admitted that Russia could 'reserve its right to support ethnic Russians in Crimea with force', as well as pointing at the United States that, in his view, tried 'to solve any conflict in any part of the world by interfering into it with force'.[55]

In 2014, Russian media again invoked the 'expertise' of Strache who was largely forgotten after 2008, setting aside occasional references to electoral gains of the FPÖ. In an interview for *Parlamentskaya Gazeta* (Parliamentary Newspaper), the official newspaper of the State Duma, Strache repeated the unfounded, yet persistent, rumours about the involvement of Western security services in the Ukrainian revolution and a ban on the Russian language in Ukraine, as well as calling for lifting Western sanctions against Russia and proceeding with building South Stream, a pipeline project intended to transport Russian gas to the EU via the Black Sea bypassing Ukraine.[56] In a long article in *Tribuna*, an official newspaper of the Civic Chamber of the State Duma, that discussed the impact, in Austria, of the Russian counter-sanctions that banned agricultural imports from the EU, Strache was *the only* Austrian politician who was cited by the newspaper: 'Already in a couple of days after coming into effect, the [Russian] sanctions have damaged our agriculture'.[57]

Strache was not the sole representative of the European far right who was concerned about the problems of agricultural exports to Russia as communicated by the pro-Kremlin media. Discussing these problems in one of its reports, RT referred – of all the Italian politicians – to the LN's leader Matteo Salvini who wrote in one of his Facebook posts: 'Only fools, Brussels and Rome, could decide to impose economic sanctions against Russia, which now sends us back tons of Italian agricultural products worth more than €1 billion. Who will pay our farmers? [Matteo] Renzi? [Angela] Merkel?'.[58]

Since 2014, Salvini appeared often on RT, in both its English and Spanish versions, and some other established Russian media. It hardly seemed mere coincidence that this process ran concurrently with a marked deepening of the cooperation between Russian structures and the LN that resulted in the LN effectively turning into the Russian front organisation in Italy.[59] In October 2014, the LN even launched a group called 'Friends of Putin' in the Italian parliament.[60] As for the 'enemies of Putin', Salvini's views were unambiguous and duly reported by RT: 'Whoever plays against Putin is an imbecile. Those who want NATO tanks on the border with Russia are leading to a cold war that nobody wants'.[61]

Nor was the FPÖ's Strache the only one to mention South Stream in his comments. Discussing the suspension of South Stream in 2014, *Rossiyskaya Gazeta* asked for his opinion Alexander Simov, head of the Russophiles group within the Bulgarska sotsialisticheska partiya (Bulgarian Socialist Party), as well as Tiberio Graziani and Guillaume Faye, without mentioning the far-right credentials of the latter two.[62] The three commentators predictably argued that the suspension of South Stream delivered damage to the economy of their countries, and Faye and Simov blamed Washington and Brussels for the failure of the project. Faye had already appeared on the front page of *Rossiyskaya Gazeta* earlier that year, when he had talked about how Washington 'put obstacles to building a just world order'. A journalist of the newspaper presented Faye to the Russian readership as 'an ideologue of the "New Right", an adherent of an imperial and federal great Europe that should be united with Russia in "an inseparable union"'.[63]

The introductions of far-right commentators in the Russian media were sometimes overtly impudent. This was the case, for example, of Jobbik's Márton Gyöngyösi who, in 2012, urged the Hungarian government to draw up lists of Jews who posed a 'national security risk'.[64] In an introduction to the interview with him in *Komsomol'skaya Pravda*, the female journalist described Gyöngyösi as an 'elegant, handsome 37-year old man', a 'way-up and sophisticated . . . ardent patriot of Hungary' who 'could not care less' that 'he had been called an anti-Semite and a neo-Nazi'.[65] The journalist of *Komsomol'skaya Pravda*, which earlier reported on anti-Semitic activities of Jobbik, apparently needed this whitewashing and distracting introduction to play down Gyöngyösi's anti-Semitism and lend credibility to his words that the EU was a colony of the United States and that the CIA, the US State Department, George Soros and European politicians had allegedly orchestrated the Ukrainian protests.[66]

Arguably, the most regular far-right commentator and opinion maker on RT has been Manuel Ochsenreiter, the editor of the German magazine *Zuerst!* (At first!), which, in the words of its editorial staff, is 'committed only to the life and survival interests of the German people and the precious heritage of our European culture'.[67] As described by Adam Holland, 'in a format familiar to readers of mainstream news magazines, *Zuerst!* promotes Neue Rechte [New Right] and Völkisch ideas such as the preservation of "German ethnical (sic) identity", burnishing the image of the Third Reich in popular culture and opposing what it regards as the humiliating legacy of denazification'.[68]

RT first involved Ochsenreiter, alternately introduced as a 'political analyst', 'German journalist' and 'Syria expert', in 2013 to provide his opinion on 'the German government [selling] the privacy of German citizens to the US government'[69] and the US government's and, in particular, CIA's alleged involvement in the 'Syria conflict' which he called a 'proxy war'.[70] In March 2014, like Piskorski and Chauprade, Ochsenreiter illegally travelled to Russia-occupied Crimea to observe the 'referendum'. On 21 April, in an interview for the VoR Ochsenreiter denied the Russian occupation of Crimea,[71] although on 17 April Putin had himself admitted the deployment of Russian special ops units and troops in this Ukrainian republic.[72]

The year 2014 saw a surge of Ochsenreiter's comments for RT. In numerous interviews, he expounded his views on the situation in Ukraine from a pro-Kremlin perspective and even went so far as to declare that Ukraine was governed by people imposed by NATO and the EU, and effectively ceased to exist as a sovereign state.[73]

Far-right activists also appeared, as commentators and opinion makers, in national non-Anglophone versions of the VoR that broadcast and ran a website in 16 European languages. For example, by the end of December 2014, the French version of the VoR had aired around 20 interviews with Chauprade and Jean-Yves Le Gallou, a leading member of the far-right Mouvement National Républicain (National Republican Movement). Moreover, the same service aired 37 interviews with, and longer comments from, Luc Michel, the Head of the PCN and Director of the EODE. The Polish version of the VoR had broadcast 38 interviews with Piskorski in the period from 2010 to 2014, and more than half of these interviews had been aired in 2014 alone. In the same period, the Polish VoR aired more than 20 interviews with Konrad Rękas and Marcin Domagała who, like Piskorski, were presented as experts of the ECAG. To its Italian-speaking audience, the VoR aired six interviews with Salvini in the period from December 2013, when he became the chairman of the LN and started developing relations with Russia, to the end of 2014. The same service offered around 50 articles, longer comments and interviews with Graziani from 2009 to 2014. The Hungarian version broadcast six interviews with Jobbik's leaders Gábor Vona and Márton Gyöngyösi from 2013 to 2014. The Hungarian VoR also demonstrated particular cynicism when it reported, in 2012, on the anti-Semitic scandal that resulted from Gyöngyösi's suggestion to draw up lists of Jews who posed a 'national security risk',[74] but a year later interviewed Gyöngyösi – in a neutral way – on the anti-Semitic sentiments in Hungary only to allow him to dispel 'illusions' about threats to Hungarian Jews![75]

Not all far-right activists, however, have been equally solicited by the national services of the VoR. For example, the only long comment of RT's star Ochsenreiter appeared on the German VoR in October 2013. It appears that national perceptions of particular far-right activists play a certain role in the national editorial policies of the VoR. The Anglophone audience of RT may not be very well familiar with Ochsenreiter's background; hence, it is 'safe' to invite him for comments and interviews to English-language RT, but in Germany his *Zuerst!* is generally considered a 'right-wing extremist' magazine,[76] so the VoR's German service would not risk discrediting their pro-Kremlin and anti-Western narratives by engaging with a person with such a reputation.

Some of the names of the above-mentioned far-right commentators appear in a document titled 'Countries and persons, where [sic] there are grounds to create an elite club and/or a group of informational influence through the line of "Russia Today"' that was leaked by the Anonymous International hacktivist group.[77] The document was prepared by Aleksandr Dugin in December 2013 and sent to Georgiy Gavrish, a close associate of Dugin and of Russian ultranationalist oligarch Konstantin Malofeev.[78] In a footnote to the document, Dugin wrote that he or his representatives had met with all those people personally, and had talked directly or indirectly about a possibility of their participation 'in the organisational and/or informational initiative of the pro-Russian nature'. Among around 60 individuals based in the EU member states such as France, Germany, Greece, Hungary, Italy, Poland, Romania and Slovakia, Dugin listed, in particular, Ochsenreiter, Piskorski, Chauprade and Graziani. Other notable activists and politicians included Jobbik's Gábor Vona and Béla Kovács; the leading French New Right publicist Alain de Benoist; Italian 'Nazi-Maoist' Claudio Mutti; and Przemysław Sieradzan, a representative of Dugin's MED in Poland. The list also featured Roman Giertych described as the leader of the far-right Liga Polskich Rodzin, which implies that Dugin's knowledge of the European far-right scene, although impressive, was still limited: not only had Giertych left the LPR already in 2007, but he had also renounced far-right ideology by 2013.

There is no evidence that Dugin's list has influenced the interviewing policies of state-controlled media in Russia. Apart from Ochsenreiter, Piskorski and Chauprade, who established themselves in the Russian media space without any help from Dugin, the Russian media rarely, if at all, turned for comments to other far-right activists listed in the memo. The only exception might have been Gábor Vona, but it is not clear whether Dugin indeed played any role in promoting Vona as a commentator for the Russian media.

The memo might have served another purpose other than finding useful commentators for the state-controlled media. At the end of 2014, Malofeev's associates launched a think-tank called 'Katehon' aiming at defending 'the principle of a multipolar world' and challenging 'any kind of unipolar world order and global hegemony'.[79] Presided by Malofeev himself, the supervisory board of Katehon featured a number of notable figures, in particular, Dugin,[80] presidential advisor Sergey Glazyev, Leonid Reshetnikov, a retired Lieutenant General of Russia's Foreign Intelligence Service and then Director of the Russian Institute of Strategic Studies,[81] and Andrey Klimov, a senior member of the ruling 'Yedinaya Rossiya' party and deputy head of the Foreign Affairs Committee of Russia's Federation Council of the Federal Assembly. Dugin was an editor of Katehon's website that offered materials and commentary in eight European languages and Arabic. The website featured many authors mentioned in Dugin's memo, hence it might have been Katehon that Dugin referred to as 'the informational initiative of the pro-Russian nature'.

Pro-Kremlin 're-information' efforts and structural media relations

The frequent participation of Francophone far-right politicians in the broadcasts of the French service of the VoR does not only corroborate a tendency of the Russian media to engage with the European far right, but also reveals a seminal development, namely the establishment of structural relations between Russian state media and certain EU-based pro-Russian media outlets managed by far-right activists.

On 5–7 July 2012, Russia's central state news agency ITAR-TASS held a summit titled 'Global Media: Challenges of the Twenty First Century'. As the agency stated, 'over 300 top managers presenting 213 media outlets from 102 countries', including 'the leaders of such major news agencies, TV and radio channels as Associated Press, BBC, Reuters, NBC, Al Jazeera, Kyodo, Xinhua and MENA' arrived in Moscow 'to discuss pressing problems facing the media society'.[82] President Vladimir Putin and Russian Prime Minister Dmitry Medvedev, as well as UN Secretary General Ban ki-Moon via a video-link, greeted the participants of the summit.

The summit was also visited by Gilles Arnaud, Guillaume Tastet and Joseph-Marie Joly who represented Agence2Presse, a branch of the French association Groupe EDH Communication working in the media sphere. The association is headed by Arnaud and, apart from Agence2Presse, incorporates TVNorman-Channel, Agence2Presse and Editions d'Héligoland – all headed by the same Arnaud. He is a former regional advisor of the FN in Upper Normandy and contemporary member of the far-right Parti de la France (Party of France, PDF) that was founded in 2009 by Carl Lang and united many former members of the FN.

At the summit in Moscow, Arnaud and his colleagues had an opportunity to present their own TV project, namely the regional TVNormanChannel, founded by Agence2Presse and the identitarian regionalist Mouvement normand (Normandy Movement),[83] as well as establishing contacts with ITAR-TASS and, especially, the VoR. Upon Arnaud's return to France, he gave an interview that suggested that the Groupe EDH Communication had received funding from Russia for the development of a new TV channel in France. Arnaud said that his team always wanted to create a national TV that would become 'a re-information source' providing a platform to people with worldviews similar to those of Arnaud's team, but they constantly lacked funding. He believed that it was easier to work in Russia: 'When the decision is taken, once the project is studied and human contacts made, funds are made available. We can focus on the mission, without wasting time on excessive politeness or begging for the next instalment of funding'.[84]

Aleksandr Orlov, Ambassador of Russia to France, helped arrange signing of the contract between Arnaud and the Russian state media outlet. In September 2012, Arnaud launched the web-based TV channel under the ingenuous name 'ProRussia.TV', for which he received €115,000 for the first year of operation and €300,000 – for the next one.[85] With servers located in Russia and brandishing a logo closely resembling the logo of Russia's ruling party 'Yedinaya Rossiya', ProRussia.TV became yet another branch of the Groupe EDH Communication and was a product of the collaboration between Agence2Presse, which provided technological infrastructure, ITAR-TASS, the Russian news agency Interfax, VoR and the Iranian Mehr News Agency.[86]

Arnaud referred to ProRussia.TV and Agence2Presse as agencies of 're-information'. As explained by the author of this concept Jean-Yves Le Gallou, 're-information' implies propaganda of 'alternative views' which can be applied to all far-right media: 'Political correctness is imposed on the political, administrative and intellectual spheres through the traditional media. The principle of re-information is therefore to provide information and alternative points of views facing such a censorship'.[87]

Apart from Arnaud, the editorial staff of ProRussia.TV included, in particular, Alexandre Ayroulet, an employee of Editions d'Héligoland and a former head of the Front national de la jeunesse (National Front of Youth); Joseph-Marie Joly, a spokesperson of the identitarian Vague Normande (Normandy Wave) group; and Sylvie Collet, a former member of the FN, treasurer of the Editions d'Héligoland, and – like her husband Arnaud – contemporary member of the PDF.[88]

ProRussia.TV developed a strong partnership with the French service of the VoR. They shared materials, some members of their staff worked for both services, while Sylvie Collet presented a weekly news bulletin produced in collaboration with the VoR.

The content of ProRussia.TV's programmes was unequivocally pro-Kremlin, anti-American and very critical towards the workings of democracy in the EU. The TV channel broadcast interviews with EU-based far-right and Eurosceptic politicians, as well as representatives of the Russian establishment such as Yevgeniy Fyodorov, chairman of the Committee on Economic Policy and Entrepreneurship of the State Duma and the leader of the violent, extreme-right Natsional'no-osvoboditel'noe dvizhenie (National-Liberation Movement).[89] Despite the similarities between ProRussia.TV and the French VoR, the former was more radical in its editorial policy and sometimes engaged with far-right politicians, such as the FN's Marion Maréchal-Le Pen or Jobbik's Gábor Vona, whom the French VoR would not have.

A few weeks after he founded ProRussia.TV, Arnaud attempted to launch yet another TV project called 'Notre Antenne' (Our Antenna), in collaboration with Philippe Milliau, a co-founder of the Réseau identités (Identities Network), a 'community that defends the identity of the white peoples, [and] regional, national and European identities'.[90] Milliau was also a former member of GRECE who was one of the first representatives of that movement who put forward an idea of joining the FN. He was consequently a regional advisor of the FN in Île-de-France,[91] then left this party for the Mouvement National Républicain, and, after 2008, became involved in the identitarian movement.

On 22 September 2012, Arnaud and Milliau registered the web-based Notre Antenne TV. Describing the agenda behind the new TV channel, Milliau said:

> It is time for the Patriots to go beyond the quarrels of individual chapels or bloated egos and identify the common enemy; it is also time to understand that what unites us is stronger than what divides us. We must unite all forces available against a globalist system that brings people to their knees. We must defend our children against debilitating curricula; against philosophical theories, such as gender, presented as scientific dogmas; against the excesses of globalisation and multicultural society [. . .].[92]

The Notre Antenne TV project involved several far-right politicians. Most prominent of them were Yvan Blot and Jean-Yves Le Gallou who, in 1974, co-founded the New Right Club de l'Horloge (The Clock Club) that is described by Jean-Yves Camus as 'symptomatic of that faction of the [French] extreme right which wishes to become part of a large conservative coalition, combining populism with a racialist approach to national identity'.[93] Some other far-right activists involved in the development of Notre Antenne included Michel Marmin, one of the founding members of GRECE; Roger Holeindre and now deceased Pierre Descaves – both former members of the right-wing terrorist OAS and the FN, as well as contemporary members of the PDF; Paul-Marie Coûteaux, founder of the Souveraineté, indépendance et libertés (Sovereignty, Independence and Freedom), a party close to the FN; and far-right writers Jean Raspail and Renaud Camus.[94]

The Notre Antenne TV project, however, proved to be short lived, and Milliau moved on to another far-right TV project, on which more below. Milliau explained that some of the members of Notre Antenne TV were not happy with taking Russian money and wanted to be independent of the Kremlin's political agenda.[95] Apparently, these were Blot and Le Gallou who did not want to be openly associated with the Russian money. The Club de l'Horloge, which they co-founded, was influenced by the economic theories of Friedrich Hayek and Ludwig von Mises, and its pro-capitalist and pro-American attitudes put the Club de l'Horloge at odds with GRECE and other French far-right organisations and parties that were critical of neo-liberal economic models.[96] Moreover, when Blot and Le Gallou joined the FN in the mid-1980s, they – along with another member of the Club de l'Horloge Bruno Mégret – managed to modernise 'the FN's economic outlook, confirming the party in its turn away from neo-corporatism towards the neo-liberal economics', while Jean-Marie Le Pen's 'claim to have been a Reaganite before Reagan owed much to the infiltration of the FN by the Club de l'Horloge's ideas'.[97]

The economically neo-liberal agenda of Blot and Le Gallou does not imply, however, that they are anti-Russian or critical of the Kremlin's foreign policies. The decision of Milliau, which was presumably backed by Blot and Le Gallou, to distance from the Russian funding most likely stemmed from the willingness to shift the balance in the symbolic power relations within the political agenda of the TV channel. The direct Russian funding would position the project as evidently pro-Kremlin, while the idea was to present the new project as pro-French rather than anything else without excluding, however, the pro-Russian aspect. That Blot is hardly sceptical about Putin's regime is also proven by the fact that he is a member of the board of the openly pro-Moscow Association Dialogue Franco-Russe (French-Russian Dialogue Association, ADFR) established in 2004 under the patronage of Putin and France's then President Jacques Chirac, and co-chaired, since 2012, by Yakunin and Thierry Mariani, a prominent member of Sarkozy's conservative Union pour un mouvement populaire (Union for a Popular Movement).[98]

The considerations about the funding of a new TV project resulted in the creation of the web-based TV Libertés that was launched in the beginning of 2014. Apart from Milliau, Blot and Le Gallou, the following far-right activists became involved in the project: Robert Ménard, a co-founder of the international NGO Reporters Sans Frontières and mayor of Béziers who revealed his far-right sympathies in 2013; Martial Bild, a former member of the FN and contemporary member of the PDF; and Philippe Conrad, a historian and member of GRECE.

Without being overtly subservient to Russian foreign policy – as ProRussia.TV seemed to be – TV Libertés, nevertheless promoted unequivocally pro-Russian views on the international relations. In the beginning of September 2014, TV Libertés was the only TV channel allowed to cover a meeting with the then Chairman of the State Duma Sergey Naryshkin[99] held at the Russian Embassy in Paris[100] and organised by the ADFR.[101] Furthermore, when the DNR and LNR held, on 2 November 2014, illegitimate 'parliamentary elections', TV Libertés accompanied a French 'election monitor' Jean-Luc Schaffhauser of the RBM.

At the end of 2013, Putin ordered establishing an international information agency Rossiya Segodnya (translated as 'Russia Today' but not to be confused with RT) 'to provide information on Russian state policy and Russian life and society for audiences abroad'.[102] The same order discontinued the VoR. In spring 2014, Margarita Simonyan, the appointed editor-in-chief of Rossiya Segodnya, said that they would 'stop using obsolete radio broadcasting models, when the signal [was] transmitted without any control and when it [was] impossible to calculate who listen[ed] to it and where'.[103] Discontinuing the VoR automatically implied suspension of funds for ProRussia.TV. The last programme of the TV channel was aired in spring 2014, and the website of ProRussia.TV was disabled in autumn 2014.

In Italy, the VoR was also involved in the cooperation with the far-right Lega Nord, albeit on a lesser scale than in the French case.

In February 2014, Max Ferrari, the LN's member and contributor to the Italian service of the VoR, initiated the creation of the openly pro-Putin Associazione Culturale Lombardia Russia (ACLR) directly associated with the LN.[104] By slamming the 'ongoing misinformation' about Russia in the mainstream media, Ferrari made it clear that the ACLR would try to 're-inform' the public through its website; in doing so, it would 'take advantage of the collaboration with important Russian media, in particular with an official organ such as the Voice of Russia'.[105]

The scope of Ferrari's previous contribution to the workings of the VoR is not entirely clear. For example, Ferrari published on his website, decorated with the Russian national emblem and flag, an article discussing Putin's speech at the 2013 Valdai meeting.[106] Two days later, this article – under a slightly different title – appeared on the VoR's website without any mention of Ferrari's authorship and, thus, presented to the audience as the VoR's own analysis.[107]

The ACLR lists the Italian service of the VoR as its 'official partner', while the website of the Italian VoR used to have a link to the ACLR's website on its front page.[108] Eliseo Bertolasi, an associate researcher of Tiberio Graziani's Institute of Advanced Studies in Geopolitics and Auxiliary Sciences[109] and correspondent of the Italian VoR (and later of Rossiya Segodnya), also contributed to the development of the ACLR.

In October 2014, on their way to Moscow, the joint delegation of the LN and the ACLR visited Russia-annexed Crimea and allegedly reached an 'agreement on mutual exchange of information' with the 'Ministry of Domestic Policy, Information and Communications of Crimea' and the Kryminform news agency.[110] However, by the time of writing, this alleged cooperation has produced no results.

Structural relations also seem to be developing between the Slovak magazine *Zem & Vek* (Land and Age) and different Russian actors. *Zem & Vek* is a typical conspiracy theory magazine with a focus, as Matúš Ritomský argues, on three particular themes: politics, a search for social alternatives, and a return to nature.[111] The magazine is openly anti-Western and pro-Russian, as well as being particularly obsessed with 'exposing' the 'power of Jews and Americans', the LGBT 'conspiracy', and Slovak mainstream media slammed as 'mouthpieces of Zionism, Americanism, globalism, defamation of national values, primacy of the minority rights over the majority rights, [and] multiculturalism'.[112]

In May 2014, two editors of the magazine, Tibor Eliot Rostás and Dušan Budzák (he also directs Rádio Viva), met with Russia's then Ambassador to Slovakia Pavel Kuznetsov, and later published an interview with him.[113] In this interview, Kuznetsov, in particular, argued that the foreign policy of the Soviet Union had been based on the promotion of communist and socialist ideas internationally, and that the Soviet Union had paid money to the communist and socialist parties in the Warsaw Pact countries, as well as to the developing countries that had attempted to carry out socialist revolutions. With the demise of the Soviet system,

Kuznetsov maintained, this practice was abandoned, but the Americans started employing the same methods which the United States accused the Soviet Union of employing: instigating revolutions ('colour revolutions'), financing various NGOs, and promoting its own vision of democracy internationally.[114]

In June 2015, an audio file was leaked that contained an unedited version of Kuznetsov's interview for *Zem & Vek*.[115] It turned out that the magazine had not published certain parts of the conversation. Two major discussions were left out in the published version: (1) Kuznetsov's extended discussion of Russian foreign policy, and (2) the editors' attempts to establish closer relations with Russian institutions.

First, while talking about Russia allegedly abandoning the practice of 'interfering in the internal affairs of other states', Kuznetsov expressed his regret and voiced his hope that Russia would return to this practice. When asked by the editors whether Russia would potentially support a political force yet outside the Slovak political establishment that would proclaim Russian-Slovak 'Slavonic brotherhood' as its official political platform, Kuznetsov said:

> I am convinced that in Slovakia there is a good basis, and support among people for this kind of ideas, organisations, movements, which would contribute to the building of stronger relations between Russia and Slovakia. Naturally, we support and will support these movements [and] organisations that favour strengthening of cooperation and relationships with Russia. . . . This might have been our mistake that, in Russian foreign policy, we have abandoned what we used to call 'interference' – interference in the internal affairs of other states; [we have abandoned] support – not political, but financial support – of parties in other countries. . . . But I think that, one way or another, we will eventually return to the necessity of, indeed, a more active support – not simply on the political level – of those political forces in certain countries which favour cooperation with Russia. . . . I think that, in the coming years, there will be an increasing support from the Russian side for the political forces in other countries, including Slovakia, which are loyal to Russia. And also support for the media.[116]

The editors of *Zem & Vek* also mentioned that they were thinking of expanding their media business and asked Kuznetsov whether they could receive any support for their endeavours from Russia. In reply, Kuznetsov said that he would be glad 'to write to Moscow', 'to people who deal with these questions', and recommend establishing contacts between *Zem & Vek* and 'the relevant Russian structures'.[117]

In September 2014, Kuznetsov was replaced by Aleksey Fedotov as Russia's Ambassador to Slovakia, and the editors of *Zem & Vek* established contacts with him too. There is no evidence, however, that these contacts have led to any visibility of *Zem & Vek* or its authors in the Russian international or domestic media. Even when Rostás announced, in the beginning of 2015, that he and his associates would start collecting signatures for a petition demanding a referendum on Slovakia's withdrawal from NATO[118] – an effort that the Russian authorities would naturally embrace – the Russian media hardly covered this initiative.

Nevertheless, the attempts of *Zem & Vek*, which changed its subtitle from 'Information without censorship' to 'Geopolitical and cultural monthly' in February 2015, to establish relations with the Russian structures continued. Russian Ambassador Fedotov introduced, in Bratislava, Rostás and Budzák to Armen Oganesyan, the editor of the journal *Mezhdunarodnaya zhizn'* (International Affairs) that is officially associated with Russia's Ministry of Foreign Affairs (MFA). Russian Foreign Minister Sergey Lavrov heads the board of the journal, and Oganesyan is an unsalaried advisor to the foreign minister. This meeting resulted in Rostás's and Budzák's visit to Moscow in June 2015 where, upon the initiative of the Russian Embassy in Slovakia, the editors of *Zem & Vek* presented their idea of creating a media holding at the roundtable held at the editorial office of *Mezhdunarodnaya zhizn'*. Other participants included 'representatives of non-governmental organisations and foundations, as well as representatives of the governmental structures', while the roundtable was held 'in partnership with the Union of Oil & Gas Producers of Russia'.[119]

During his presentation at the roundtable, Budzák said that they were trying to expand their media business and launch a media house that would include not only the magazine, that is *Zem & Vek*, but also TV and radio stations, a daily newspaper, and online media. This media holding, as Budzák argued, would 'work against the mainstream that was largely financed by the American side and in the interests of NATO'.[120] In response to this presentation, Vasiliy Likhachev, an MP from the KPRF, assumed that their project would be carried out and inquired them about the time period they would require to endow it with 'transregional and Europe-wide significance'. Likhachev expressed confidence that 'Russian specialists [were] ready to take the most active part in processing and creating this kind of production', because Russia needed allies in competing with Brussels 'for the public opinion and the state of minds in Europe'.[121]

A report on the roundtable published by the Russian International Affairs Council, affiliated with Russia's MFA and Ministry of Education and Science, noted that the participants also discussed prospects of 'constructing' 'a Russia-friendly area in Central and Eastern Europe'.[122]

However, by the time of the writing, the idea of *Zem & Vek* to build a media holding has not been implemented, but the meetings and talks that Rostás and Budzák held with Russian representatives of different levels testify to the presence of mutual interest in developing structural relations between *Zem & Vek* and particular Russian groups.

The authors of '*I Am Eurasian*',[123] an insightful investigation into the links between the Kremlin and the Hungarian far right, suggest that a different type of structural involvement of the Russian actors exists in the Hungarian media space. The authors analyse, in particular, the illegal far-right website *Hídfő* (Bridgehead) maintained by anonymous contributors and presumably coordinated by István

Győrkös, the founder of the extreme-right paramilitary movement Magyar Nemzeti Arcvonal (Hungarian National Front, MNA).[124]

The emphatically pro-Russian and anti-Western *Hídfő* provides 'professional and regular content, exclusive information published on the portal, analyses revealing deeper-than-average familiarity with geopolitical, energy policy, economic and foreign affairs issues'.[125] At the same time, the website that could be, until spring 2015, accessed via the URL hidfo.net.ru,[126] sometimes published articles that resembled 'cables forwarded by foreign missions with underlined and highlighted text'.[127] Moreover, as the authors of the investigation argue, 'a number of articles run on Hídfő.net read as if they had not been written for Hungarian audience', as they tended to explain particular Hungary-related phenomena that require no explanation.[128] This and other evidence led the authors to the assumption that *Hídfő* was not just another Hungarian ultranationalist website, but 'a public messaging board and propaganda site maintained by Russian intelligence officers residing or operating in Hungary'.[129]

The case of *Hídfő* using the Russian domain registration service also provides an example of a growing trend in the Western far-right milieu, namely the use of the Russian Internet services. Already in 2003, Slovak neo-Nazis hosted their web portal *NS Info Slovensko* on several Russian free-hosting websites.[130] At the time of writing, mail servers of media sources such as *Szent Korona Rádió* and *Deres.TV*, apparently affiliated with the Hungarian far-right Hatvannégy Vármegye Ifjúsági Mozgalom (Sixty-Four Counties Youth Movement), are located in Russia and operated by the Moscow-based company LLC 'TC TEL'.[131] American right-wing extremist Dylann Storm Roof, suspected to have killed nine African Americans on 17 June 2015 in South Carolina (Charleston church shooting), chose a Russian company, REG.RU, to register and host his website lastrhodesian.com, where he published his racist manifesto.[132] The Austrian far-right *Freies Österreich* blog and the *Volksherrschaft* (People's rule) website, associated with the extreme-right party Arbeitsgemeinschaft für demokratische Politik (Working Group for Democratic Politics) are hosted by Russian companies too, and even have subtitles written in Russian language. Both were launched in the first half of 2014 and reveal straightforwardly pro-Russian stances.

The fact that some Western far-right organisations, groups and individuals host their websites on Russian servers does not directly fall into the category of the structural relations between the European far right and the Russian state. The growing trend of hosting their websites on Russian servers reflects the far-right groups' increasing distrust of the US-based hosting providers that, however, still remain the preferred option for European and even Russian far-right activists. Almost unrestricted freedom of speech in the United States has made it difficult for the European authorities to investigate cases of neo-Nazi activism and Holocaust denial involving European far-right groups that hosted their websites in the United States. However, after the Austrian police arrested Gottfried Küssel who had been involved in the workings of *Alpen-Donau.info*, a major neo-Nazi forum in Austria hosted in the United States, the confidence in the US hosting services was shattered as the arrest only became possible because the Austrian authorities 'had received help from US investigators to gain access to the website's servers'.[133] The threat of similar cases, as well as the US PRISM surveillance scandal, suggested to some pro-Russian and anti-American far-right activists to opt for Russian hosting providers, as they seemed to be confident that the Russian authorities would not cooperate with European prosecution. Evidence suggests that Russian hosting providers do not necessarily come up to expectations. After the German officials arrested, in January 2016, two German nationals in connection with the investigation into *Altermedia Deutschland*, 'a prominent nationwide right-wing extremist Internet news portal',[134] they asked the Russian service provider Mir Telematiki Ltd, which hosted the website, to shut it down,[135] and the Russians immediately complied with the request. Ironically, *Altermedia Deutschland* was previously hosted in the United States and migrated to Russia because the Americans shut it down.

In some cases, the cooperation between the Western far-right media and Russia goes beyond the use of Russian web-hosting services. This is the case of the Austrian, openly pro-Putin far-right printed magazine *Info-Direkt*. It was launched in March 2015 by the Linz-based Association for Freedom of Expression and Independent Journalism headed by Karl Winkler, who is also President of the far-right Österreichische Landsmannschaft (Community of Austrian Compatriots).[136] The magazine's first website (www.info-direkt.at) was hosted in Austria, but it registered a new address (www.info-direkt.eu) in September 2015 that was hosted in Russia. In August-September 2015, almost all the major Russian media publicised a story originating in *Info-Direkt* that alleged – with a dubious reference to an anonymous employee of the Austrian Defense Office – that the United States was involved in the illegal smuggling of refugees from Asia and Africa to Europe.[137] Moreover, the presentation of *Info-Direkt* took place in October 2015 during the soiree 'In the service of peace' organised by the Russian-born Nathalie Holzmüller within the framework of her Vienna-based cultural project 'The Faces of Russia'.[138] Holzmüller is also known for organising annual 'Russian Balls' in Vienna that are sponsored, in particular, by the Russian Embassy in Austria, the Russian federal government agency Rosso-trudnichestvo,[139] the Trade Agency of the Russian Federation in Austria, and the FPÖ.[140]

Conclusion

Like in many other national and international media, stories about successes and failures of far-right parties in the national and European elections, as well as scandals involving far-right politicians, appeared in the Russian media on a regular basis as a conventional part of the coverage of the political developments in the world. However, since 2008–2010, Russian state-controlled or pro-Kremlin media have increasingly changed their approach to the coverage of fringe politics in general and the far right in particular.

Fringe Western politicians and activists – especially on the far right – who are inherently critical of the United States, NATO, EU, Eurozone, liberal democracy, multiculturalism, human rights, etc. stopped being simple newsmakers for the Russian media, but started to appear as valuable commentators and opinion makers. By 2008–2010 some of them, for example, Luc Michel, Tiberio Graziani, Mateusz Piskorski and some others had already proved themselves useful to the Russian foreign policy agenda as compliant 'election observers'. Furthermore, already in 2008, after Russia's facile victory over Georgia, the Russian media realised that they could place more confidence in commentators such as Lyndon Larouche or Heinz-Christian Strache than in any mainstream, albeit more reputable, politician. To undermine the liberal-democratic consensus in the West, Russian media have engaged with the forces that are trying to undermine the West on their own accord. The pro-Russian sentiments of some of them constitute an added value.

From 2008 to the second part of 2013, the Russian media turned to politicians from the FN, DF, VB, SD and some other far-right parties to let them speak out their grievances about the 'bureaucratic monster' of the EU, Eurozone, immigration, multiculturalism, gay marriages. The explicit message was clear: the West is in decline and failing; the implicit message was about the stability of allegedly conservative, traditionalist Russia in comparison to the disorderly liberal West.

Simultaneously, particular Russian media that received generous funding from the state due to their enhanced significance in promoting the Kremlin's foreign policy, experimented with financing web-based TV channels in France run by far-right activists, first and foremost ProRussia.TV. This experiment has largely failed as the French far right proved unable to create a quality product.

The Ukrainian revolution that started at the end of 2013, the annexation of Crimea by Russia and the Russian invasion of the Donetsk Basin in 2014 have dramatically driven up the demand for far-right commentators and their conspiracy theories, anti-establishment ideas and anti-American vitriol. As a result, the number of interviews with far-right activists, as well as their shorter and longer comments considerably increased in domestic and international Russian media.

For the Russian audience, Western far-right commentators successfully play an allotted role of white European 'experts' on the alleged normalcy of the Kremlin's policies at home and in international relations. They do help create a comfortable feeling that Russia is not 'a lonely state' and that it has allies in Europe and the West in general. That these allies are fringe politicians and publicists with unsavoury reputations and doubtful political prospects the major part of the Russian audience does not know. Russian media tend either to omit their far-right credentials or even exaggerate their significance to present them in a more reputable way.

On the international level, only RT can be considered a successful media project, and the presence of far-right 'opinion makers' contributes to its image of a provocative supplier of alternative news. In contrast, the VoR was a failed project, because even in those countries where radio still has a wide reach people prefer to listen to their national radio stations rather than the Russian one. The influence of the more recent Sputnik and RIA Novosti websites on Western societies is still to be evaluated.[141]

There is no evidence that the impact of the far-right commentators engaged by Russian international media with the aim of *forming* or *shaping* political opinions in the West has been in any way significant. On the other hand, convincing the international audience of the alleged legitimacy of Russian foreign policy may not be the main goal of the Russian international media. As argued earlier, the failure of Russian soft power in the West informed the Russian authorities of a new approach in their information warfare: Russian state-sponsored media now implicitly aim not so much at justifying the Kremlin's domestic and foreign policies, but rather at undermining the confidence of international audiences in the legitimacy of their own governments and, in more general terms, of the liberal-democratic consensus. Thus, the combination of Russian media resources and Western radical right-wing elements became yet another alternative institution challenging the social institution of mainstream international media.

If Chapters 4 and 5 explored the involvement of Western far-right activists and politicians in pro-Kremlin activities within institutionalised frameworks originally established by Russian actors, the next chapter explores a different phenomenon, namely the European far-right pro-Kremlin efforts that originally developed without any Russian framework but were supported by various Russian actors afterwards.

Notes

1   Masha Gessen, "Fear and Self-Censorship in Vladimir Putin's Russia", *Nieman Reports*, Vol. 59, No. 2 (2005), pp. 115–118.
2   Elisabeth Schimpfossl, Ilya Yablokov, "Coercion or Conformism? Censorship and Self-Censorship among Russian Media Personalities and Reporters in the 2010s", *Demokratizatsiya*, Vol. 22, No. 2 (2014), pp. 295–311 (297).
3   Ibid., p. 310.
4   Šarūnas Černiauskas, "Andreas Umland: Putin Created Alternative Reality for Russians", *Delfi*, 28 January (2015), http://en.delfi.lt/central-eastern-europe/andreas-umland-putin-created-alternative-reality-for-russians.d?id=67020074
5   Bugajski, *Cold Peace*, p. 33.
6   Ibid.
7   Andrew Wilson, "Four Types of Russian Propaganda", *Aspen Review*, No. 4 (2015), pp. 77–81; Peter Pomerantsev, Michael Weiss, *The Menace of Unreality: How the Kremlin Weaponizes Information, Culture and Money* (New York: Institute of Modern Russia, 2014).
8   See, for example, Frederick Charles Barghoorn, *Soviet Foreign Propaganda* (Princeton: Princeton University Press, 1964); John Jenks, *British Propaganda and News Media in the Cold War* (Edinburgh: Edinburgh University Press, 2006); Nicholas John Cull, *The Cold War and the United States Information Agency: American Propaganda and Public Diplomacy, 1945–1989* (Cambridge: Cambridge University Press, 2008).
9   Anton Vuyma, "Pobediv Gruziyu, Rossiya proigrala informatsionnuyu voynu", *Rosbalt*, 31 August (2008), http://rosbalt.ru/main/2008/08/31/518977.html
10   Maksim Tovkaylo, "Vladimir Putin udivilsya moshchi zapadnoy propagandy", *Gazeta*, No. 173, 12 September (2008), p. 5.

11   Pomerantsev, Weiss, *The Menace of Unreality*, p. 14.

12   "Visit to Russia Today Television Channel", *President of Russia*, 11 June (2013), http://en.kremlin.ru/events/president/news/18319

13   Ilya Yablokov, "Conspiracy Theories as a Russian Public Diplomacy Tool: The Case of Russia Today (RT)", *Politics*, Vol. 35, Nos. 3–4 (2015), pp. 301–315 (301).

14   The TV channel's management, however, maintained the reference to Russia in its Arab version, Rusiya Al-Yaum (Russia Today).

15   Geir Hågen Karlsen, "Tools of Russian Influence: Information and Propaganda", in Janne Haaland Matlary, Tormod Heier (eds.), *Ukraine and Beyond: Russia's Strategic Security Challenge to Europe* (N.a.: Palgrave Macmillan, 2016), pp. 181–208.

16   Nikolaus von Twickel, "Russia Today Courts Viewers with Controversy", *The Moscow Times*, 17 March (2010), http://themoscowtimes.com/news/article/russia-today-courts-viewers-with-controversy/401888.html

17   Ibid.

18   As Pomerantsev and Weiss argued, RT was focusing on "making the West, and especially the US, look bad", see Pomerantsev, Weiss, *The Menace of Unreality*, p. 15.

19   See, in particular, Nikolay Zakharov, *Attaining Whiteness: A Sociological Study of Race and Racialization in Russia* (Uppsala: Uppsala University, 2013).

20   Wilson, "Four Types of Russian Propaganda", p. 78.

21   Dominique Albertini, Jérôme Lefilliâtre, "Russia Today: allo Paris, ici Moscou", *Libération*, 8 April (2016), http://liberation.fr/futurs/2016/04/08/russia-today-allo-paris-ici-moscou_1444970

22   Karolina Zbytniewska, "Former RT Presenter: Russian Disinformation Is a Weapon", *EurActiv*, 22 December (2016), http://euractiv.com/section/global-europe/interview/former-rt-presenter-russian-disinformation-is-a-weapon/

23   Ibid.

24   Shevtsova, *Odinokaya derzhava*, p. 218.

25   Oleg Riabov, Tatiana Riabova, "The Decline of Gayropa?", *Eurozine*, 5 February (2014), http://eurozine.com/articles/2014-02-05-riabova-en.html

26   Peter Pomerantsev, "Why We're Post-Fact", *Granta*, 20 July (2016), https://granta.com/why-were-post-fact/

27   Wilson, "Russian Active Measures".

28   In November 2014, the VoR and Russia's international news agency RIA Novosti were replaced by the international multimedia news service called "Sputnik".

29   Roger Boyes, "Neo-Nazis Fight to Take Over Extremist Publishing Empire", *The Times of London*, 14 November (1996).

30   "Zündel Silenced", *Searchlight*, No. 258 (1996), p. 20.

31   Ernst Zündel, "Introduction to 'Another Voice of Freedom'", *YouTube*, https://youtube.com/watch?v=is_DH4plBvo

32   Sonia Scherr, "Russian TV Channel Pushes 'Patriot' Conspiracy Theories", *Southern Poverty Law Center's Intelligence Report*, No. 139 (2010), http://splcenter.org/get-informed/intelligence-report/browse-all-issues/2010/fall/from-russia-with-love

33   Yablokov, "Conspiracy Theories as a Russian Public Diplomacy Tool", p. 307.

34   Ibid.

35   "9/11: Challenging the official version", *RT*, 11 March 2010.

36   Aymeric Chauprade, *Chronique du choc des civilisations* (Périgueux: Éditions Chronique-Dargaud, 2009).

37   "Interview with Lyndon Larouche", *RT*, 21 August (2008).

38   See more details on these conferences in Chapter 6.

39   Yuriy Politov, " 'Saakashvili – prestupnik' ", *Izvestiya*, No. 198, 22 October (2008), p. 2; Darya Yur'eva, "Diktator nedostoin diplomatii", *Rossiyskaya gazeta*, No. 220, 22 October (2008), p. 2; Vadim Novichikhin, "V Vene Saakashvili ne ponyali", *Parlamentskaya gazeta*, No. 73, 21 November (2008). None of these reports on the conference mentioned that the FPÖ was a far right or a nationalist party.

40   "Europe Cannot Afford Euro – MEP", *RT*, 18 January (2011), http://rt.com/news/cannot-afford-euro/

41   " 'They Don't Want to Integrate': Fifth Night of Youth Rioting Rocks Stockholm", *RT*, 23 May (2013), http://rt.com/news/stockholm-violence-outbreak-fires-671/

42   Ekaterina Sinitsyna Santoni, "Immigrazione e fallimento dell'Europa, intervista al leader di Forza Nuova", *La Voce della Russia*, 4 December (2013), http://it.sputniknews.com/italian.ruvr.ru/2013_12_04/Immigrazione-e-fallimento-dell-Europa-intervista-al-leader-di-Forza-Nuova/

43   "Ultra-nationalists Gaining Steel-toed Foothold in Europe", *RT*, 5 June (2009), https://rt.com/politics/ultra-nationalists-gaining-steel-toed-foothold-in-europe/

44   "Richard Spencer: A Symbol of the New White Supremacy", *Anti-Defamation League*, 14 May (2013), http://blog.adl.org/extremism/richard-spencer-a-symbol-of-the-new-white-supremacy

45   "Washington Ratcheting up Tension It Can't Afford", *RT*, 10 August (2013), http://rt.com/op-edge/usa-russia-tensions-snowden-333/. See also *RT*'s interview with Spencer: "Democratic Libya: 'Weak State Marred by Chaotic Infighting' ", *RT*, 9 July (2012), http://rt.com/news/libya-democratic-elections-results-685/

46   "Russian Elite 2016: Perspectives on Foreign and Domestic Policy", *Hamilton*, 11 May (2016), https://hamilton.edu/documents/russianelite2016final1.pdf

47   Andrey Fedyashin, Artyom Kobzev, "Kiev Makes Historic Choice: Free Trade with EU instead Customs Union?", *The Voice of Russia*, 21 September (2013), http://sputniknews.com/voiceofrussia/2013_09_21/Kiev-makes-historic-choice-Free-trade-with-EU-instead-Customs-Union-7461/

48   "Opiat' Maydan. Opiat' Takhrir?", *Nevskoe vremya*, No. 214, 3 December (2013).

49   "Human Rights Violated by Ukraine's Coup-appointed Govt – European NGO", *RT*, 12 March (2014), http://rt.com/news/ukraine-human-rights-violated-402/

50   "US to Use Situation in Ukraine for Destabilizing EU, Russia – Geopolitical Expert", *The Voice of Russia*, 23 April (2014), http://sputniknews.com/voiceofrussia/2014_04_23/US-to-use-situation-in-Ukraine-for-destabilizing-EU-Russia-geopolitical-expert-0743/

51   " 'European Union Has No Right to Demand Anything' – Marine Le Pen", *The Voice of Russia*, 14 December (2013), http://sputniknews.com/voiceofrussia/2013_12_14/European-Union-has-no-right-to-demand-anything-Marine-Le-Pen-1583/

52   "Lider frantsuzskogo Natsional'nogo fronta Marin Le Pen prokommentirovala sobytiya v Kieve", *Pervy kanal*, 14 December (2013), http://1tv.ru/news/polit/248339; "Lider Natsional'nogo fronta Marin Le Pen dala interv'yu Pervomu kanalu", *Pervy kanal*, 13 April (2014), http://1tv.ru/news/polit/256384

53   Anton Dolgunov, "Marin Le Pen: Evropa neset otvetstvennost' za proiskhodyashchee na Ukraine", *ITAR-TASS*, 1 June (2014), http://itar-tass.com/mezhdunarodnaya-panorama/1230269

54   Elena Chinkova, "Marin Le Pen: Sanktsii dadut obratny effect", *Komsomol'skaya Pravda*, 12 April (2014), http://kp.ru/daily/26219.7/3102470/

55   "French Journalist Accuses Ukraine's New Government of Infringing Human Rights", *The Voice of Russia*, 3 March (2014), http://sputniknews.com/voiceofrussia/2014_03_03/French-journalist-accuses-Ukraine-s-new-government-of-infringing-human-rights-8056/

56   Aleksandr Sobina, "Haints-Kristian Shtrakhe: S Rossii neobkhodimo snyat' vse sanktsii", *Parlamentskaya gazeta*, No. 38, 31 October (2014), p. 26.

57   Aleksandr Sobina, "Rossiya v izgoi ne goditsya", *Tribuna*, No. 44, 27 November (2014), p. 6. See also "Sanctions bite-back: Bickering, EU infighting over Russia retaliation", *RT*, 11 August (2014), http://rt.com/news/179348-russia-sanctions-europe-protests/

58   Matteo Salvini's post on Facebook, 14 August (2014), https://facebook.com/salvini official/posts/10152321781968155; "EU Sanctions Like 'Shooting Oneself in the Foot' – Hungary PM", *RT*, 15 August 15 (2014), http://rt.com/business/180564-eu-russia-sanctions-hungary/

59 See Chapter 6.
60 "Paolo Grimoldi sozdaet gruppu 'Druzya Putina' v parlamente Italii", *Arsenyevskie vesti*, No. 42, 21 October (2014).
61 "Político italiano: 'Quien juega contra Putin es imbécil' ", *RT*, 12 December (2014), http://actualidad.rt.com/actualidad/160119-juegos-contra-putin-estupidez-politico-italia-salvini
62 Leonid Pchel'nikov, Nikita Krasnikov, Niva Mirakyan, Vyacheslav Prokof'ev, "Bez ogliadki na Zapad", *Rossiyskaya gazeta*, No. 275, 3 December (2014), p. 2.
63 Viacheslav Prokof'ev, "Komu nuzhny novye steny?", *Rossiyskaya gazeta*, No. 258, 13 November (2014), p. 1.
64 Marton Dunai, "Anger as Hungary Far-right Leader Demands Lists of Jews", *Reuters*, 27 November (2012), http://reuters.com/article/2012/11/27/us-hungary-antisemi tism-idUSBRE8AQ0L920121127
65 Aslamova, "Vengerskiy politik Marton D'endeshi", p. 6.
66 Ibid.
67 "Über uns", *Zuerst!*, https://web.archive.org/web/20130326111023/http://www.zuerst.de/uber-uns/
68 Adam Holland, "RT's Manuel Ochsenreiter", *The Interpreter*, 21 March (2014), http://interpretermag.com/rts-manuel-ochsenreiter/
69 " 'German Government Sells the Privacy of German Citizens to the US' ", *RT*, 8 July (2013), http://rt.com/op-edge/german-government-sells-privacy-us-780/
70 "US Military Intervention in Syria Is not off the Table", *RT*, 14 September (2013), http://rt.com/op-edge/us-syria-crisis-intervention-867/
71 "Crimea: No Russian Invasion, Happy People – Manuel Ochsenreiter", *The Voice of Russia*, 21 April (2014), http://sputniknews.com/voiceofrussia/2014_04_21/Crimea-No-Russian-invasion-happy-people-Manuel-Ochsenreiter-9307/
72 "Putin Admits Russian Forces Were Deployed to Crimea", *Reuters*, 17 April (2014), http://uk.reuters.com/article/2014/04/17/russia-putin-crimea-idUKL6N0N921 H20140417
73 "Protesters in Eastern Ukraine See Kiev Govt as a 'Gang of Oligarchs' ", *RT*, 2 May (2014), http://rt.com/op-edge/156280-east-ukraine-civil-war/
74 Artyom Kobzev, "Magyarországon a Jobbik szeretné, ha listát készítenének a veszélyt jelentő zsidókról", *Oroszország Hangja*, 30 November (2012), http://hungarian.ruvr.ru/2012_11_30/Magyarorszagon-a-Jobbik-szeretne-ha-listat-kesz-tenenek-a-veszelyt-jelento-zsidokrol/
75 János Erős, "Gyöngyösi Márton: mocskos politikai játszmába sodorják Magyarországot", *Oroszország Hangja*, 21 October (2013), http://hungarian.ruvr.ru/2013_10_21/Gyongyosi-Marton-mocskos-politikai-jatszmaba-sodorjak-Magyarszagot/
76 Andreas Speit, "Plaudern mit Neonazis", *TAZ*, 7 March (2011), http://taz.de/!66991/; Tilman Tzschoppe, "Wider die 'herrschende Meinungsdiktatur der politischen Korrektheit': Magazin 'Zuerst!' ", *Netz-gegen-Nazis*, 16 April (2010), http://netz-gegen-nazis.de/artikel/wider-die-herrschende-meinungsdiktatur-der-politischen-korrektheit-zuerst-das-deutsche-nachrichtenmagazin-5554
77 "Cherny Internatsional: Malofeev i Dugin", *Anonimny internatsional*, 27 November (2014), https://b0ltai.org/2014/11/27/черный-интернационалмалофеев-и-дуги/
78 For more information on Malofeev see Chapter 6.
79 "About Us", *Katehon*, http://katehon.com/about-us
80 Dugin left Katehon in 2017.
81 Reshetnikov is also a member of the Supervisory Board of the Russian bank Tempbank, which, according to the US Department of the Treasury, provided millions of dollars to al-Assad's regime in Syria. For his position in Tempbank, Reshetnikov was sanctioned by the US in December 2016, see "Syria Designations; Counter Proliferation Designations", *US Department of the Treasury*, 23 December (2016), https://www.treasury.gov/resource-center/sanctions/OFAC-Enforcement/Pages/20161223.aspx

82   "Executives of leading media flock to Moscow for World Media Summit", *ITAR-TASS*, 4 July (2012), http://itar-tass.com/en/archive/678277

83   Founded in 1969, the Normandy Movement was originally close to GRECE headed by Alain de Benoist, see Jean-Yves Camus, "Strömungen der europäischen extremen Rechten – Populisten, Integristen, Nationalrevolutionäre, Neue Rechte", In Uwe Backes (ed.), *Rechtsextreme Ideologien in Geschichte und Gegenwart* (Köln: Böhlau, 2003), pp. 235–260 (257). In 2012, De Benoist himself wrote that he had been a member of the Normandy Movement for about 40 years, see Tamir Bar-On, *Rethinking the French New Right: Alternatives to Modernity* (London: Routledge, 2013), p.19.

84   "C'est toujours à l'Est que se lève le monde", *Le Magazine National des Seniors*, No. 16 (2012), pp. 4–6 (6).

85   Jauvert, "Poutine et le FN".

86   See http://livestream.com/prorussiatv

87   Jean-Yves Le Gallou quoted in Adrien Sénécat, "Wikistrike, Quenel+, TV Libertés: dans la nébuleuse des sites de 'vraie information'", *L'Express*, 3 December (2014), http://lexpress.fr/actualite/politique/wikistrike-quenelle-liberte-tv-dans-la-nebuleuse-des-sites-de-vraie-information_1628541.html

88   See also Stéphane Jourdan, Anya Stroganova, "Quand la Russie flirte avec le FN", *Slate*, 16 July (2013), http://slate.fr/story/75047/russie-fn

89   Founded in 2013, Fyodorov's National-Liberation Movement aims at "liberating the Russian Federation from colonial dependence on the US through the renewal of Sovereignty" where "Sovereignty" means the "restitution of Russia's territorial integrity lost in 1991", the year when the Soviet Union collapsed. See "Tseli i zadachi", Natsional'no-osvoboditel'noe dvizhenie, http://rusnod.ru/nod3.html

90   See https://web.archive.org/web/20160202053814/http://www.reseau-identites.org/

91   Madeleine Rebérioux, *L'Extrême droite en questions: actes du colloque* (Paris: Études et documentation internationales, 1991), p. 49.

92   "Philippe Milliau: Il nous faut une télévision internet alternative ouverte à tous les patriotes", *Riposte Laïque*, 22 October (2012), https://ripostelaique.com/philippe-milliau-il-nous-faut-une-television-internet-alternative-ouverte-a-tous-les-patriotes.html

93   Jean-Yves Camus, "Political Cultures within the Front National: The Emergence of a Counter-ideology on the French Far-right", *Patterns of Prejudice*, Vol. 26, No. 1–2 (1992), pp. 5–16 (10).

94   Olivier Faye, Abel Mestre, Caroline Monnot, "La télé identitaire, la drôle d'agence de presse et le 'soft power' russe", *Droite(s) extrême(s)*, 29 January (2013), http://droites-extremes.blog.lemonde.fr/2013/01/29/la-tele-identitaire-la-drole-dagence-de-presse-et-le-soft-power-russe/

95   "Une autre information: naissance de TV Libertés", *Observatoire des Journalistes et de l'Information Médiatique*, 17 February (2014), http://ojim.fr/une-autre-information-naissance-de-tv-libertes/

96   Michael Minkenberg, "The New Right in France and Germany: *Nouvelle Droite, Neue Rechte*, and the New Right Radical Parties", in Peter H. Merkl, Leonard Weinberg (eds.), *The Revival of Right-Wing Extremism in the Nineties* (London: Frank Cass, 1997), pp. 65–90 (72); Spektorowski, "The New Right", p. 116.

97   Shields, *The Extreme Right in France*, pp. 245–246.

98   In 2015, the party changed its name to Les Républicains (Republicans).

99   Naryshkin served as the Chairman of the State Duma until 5 October 2016 when Putin appointed him as the Director of Russia's Foreign Intelligence Service.

100 Although the Council of the European Union imposed, on 17 March 2014, a travel ban and asset freeze against Naryshkin as one of the Russian politicians responsible for actions which undermined or threatened the territorial integrity, sovereignty and

independence of Ukraine, he was able to travel to Paris on the invitation of the Parliamentary Assembly of the Council of Europe.

101 François Clemenceau, "Ce lobby qui défend Poutine", *Le Journal du Dimanche*, 7 September (2014), http://lejdd.fr/International/Europe/Ce-lobby-qui-defend-Poutine-685316

102 Vladimir Putin, "Ukaz o merakh po povysheniyu effektivnosti deyatel'nosti gosudarstvennykh SMI", *Prezident Rossii*, 9 December (2013), http://kremlin.ru/news/19805

103 "Russia Today's English newswire to be launched in April", *The Voice of Russia*, 23 March (2014), http://sputniknews.com/voiceofrussia/news/2014_03_23/Russia-Today-s-English-newswire-to-be-launched-in-April-1119/

104 See Chapter 6 for more details about this Association.

105 "Nasce 'Lombardia-Russia' ", *La Prealpina*, 20 February (2014).

106 Max Ferrari, "L'Europa di Putin: identità, tradizione, demografia. Il discorso di Valdai censurato dai giornali", *Max Ferrari*, 22 September (2013), https://web.archive.org/web/20131108234046/http://maxferrari.net/2013/09/22/leuropa-di-putin-identita-tradizione-demografia-il-discorso-di-valdai-censurato-dai-giornali. Although Ferrari does not speak Russia, he has a Russian language version of his website: http://maxferrarirussia.wordpress.com. The Russian translation of the article was published there too.

107 "L'Europa di Putin: il discorso di Valdai 'trasformato' dai giornali", *La Voce della Russia*, 24 September (2013), http://it.sputniknews.com/italian.ruvr.ru/radio_broadcast/6931403/121859556/

108 See *La Voce della Russia*, https://web.archive.org/web/20140626014219/http://italian.ruvr.ru/

109 See Chapter 6 for more details about the Institute of Advanced Studies in Geopolitics and Auxiliary Sciences.

110 "Soglashenie o sotrudnichestve s Ministerstvom vnutrenney politiki, informatsii i svyazi Respubliki Krym i agentstvom novostey Krym Inform", *Associazione Culturale Lombardia Russia*, 11 November (2014), http://ru.lombardiarussia.org/index.php/component/content/article/57-categoria-home-/257-2014-11-11-12-44-23

111 Matúš Ritomský, "Zem a Vek nebezpečných konšpirácií", *Priestori*, 25 September (2014), http://priestori.sk/zem-a-vek-nebezpecnych-konspiracii-priestori/

112 Anton Smataník, "Slovenskí vojnoví Štváči", *Zem & Vek*, July (2014), pp. 37–39 (37).

113 Tibor Eliot Rostás, "Slovanská vzájomnosť je aj ruským záujmom", *Zem & Vek*, June (2014), pp. 46–53.

114 Ibid., pp. 47–48.

115 "Rostas Budzak Kuznecov.mp3", *Ulož.to*, http://ulozto.sk/xoqiiKVd/rostas-budzak-kuznecov-mp3. The audio file was later uploaded on YouTube by a Slovak anti-corruption activist Juraj Smatana, see "Rostás (ZEM A VEK) žiada ruského veľvyslanca o podporu na médium a politiku", *YouTube*, 3 February (2016), https://youtube.com/watch?v=0t2yAax3_2s

116 "Rostas Budzak Kuznecov.mp3".

117 Ibid.

118 Grigorij Mesežnikov, "West Should Launch Counterattack in War with Russia", *Charter97*, 20 July (2015), https://charter97.org/en/news/2015/7/20/160609/

119 Sergey Filatov, " 'My nakhodimsya v epokhe informatsionnoy voyny', – govoryat gosti iz Slovakii", *Mezhdunarodnaya zhizn'*, 6 June (2015), https://interaffairs.ru/news/show/13270

120 "Zem a Vek: Naše ambície nemajú hranice", *Nie je to tak*, 23 June (2015), http://niejetotak.sk/zem-a-vek-nase-ambicie-nemaju-hranice/

121 "Zhurnalisty iz Slovakii Dushan Budzak i Tibor Rostas – gosti zhurnala 'Mezhdunarodnaya zhizn' ' ", *Mezhdunarodnaya zhizn'*, 16 June (2015), https://interaffairs.ru/news/show/13319

122 "Roundtable on Constructing a Russia-Friendly Territory in CEE", *Russian International Affairs Council*, 4 June (2015), http://russiancouncil.ru/en/inner/?id_4= 6072

123 Juhász et al., *"I Am Eurasian"*.

124 In October 2016, Győrkös fired at two police officers (killing one) when they arrived at his home to investigate whether he possessed illegal weapons in his house, see Justin Spike, "Suspected Neo-Nazi Shoots, Kills Police Officer near Győr", *Budapest Beacon*, 26 October (2016), http://budapestbeacon.com/news-in-brief/suspected-neo-nazi-shoots-kills-police-officer-near-gyor/41560

125 Juhász et al., *"I Am Eurasian"*, p. 37.

126 As the URL suggests, the website was registered with RU-CENTER, the largest domain name registrar in Russia. The website itself, however, was hosted on the US servers. In April 2015, *Hídfő.net* moved to hidfo.ru also registered with RU-CENTER but hosted on a US server.

127 Juhász et al., *"I Am Eurasian"*, p. 38.

128 Ibid.

129 Ibid., p. 37.

130 Martina Pisárová, "Website Urges Violence on", *The Slovak Spectator*, 18 August (2003), http://spectator.sme.sk/c/20020127/website-urges-violence-on.html

131 "Orosz szerveren üzemel a Deres.TV és a Szent Korona Rádió", *Atlatszo.hu*, 5 July (2013), http://atlatszo.hu/2013/07/05/orosz-szerveren-uzemel-a-deres-tv-es-a-szent-korona-radio/; "Nemzeti radikális hírportálok: Oroszország magyar hangjai", *Atlatszo.hu*, 26 August (2014), http://atlatszo.hu/2014/08/26/nemzeti-radikalis-hirportalok-oroszorszag-magyar-hangjai/

132 Lenny Bernstein, Sari Horwitz, Peter Holley, "Dylann Roof's Racist Manifesto: 'I Have No Choice'", *The Washington Post*, 20 June (2015), https://washingtonpost.com/national/health-science/authorities-investigate-whether-racist-manifesto-was-written-by-sc-gunman/2015/06/20/f0bd3052-1762-11e5-9ddc-e3353542100c_story.html

133 "Austria Arrests Former Neo-Nazi Leader Gottfried Kuessel over Website", *The Telegraph*, 13 April (2011), http://telegraph.co.uk/news/worldnews/europe/austria/8447175/Austria-arrests-former-neo-Nazi-leader-Gottfried-Kuessel-over-website.html

134 Innenministerium des Landes Mecklenburg-Vorpommern (Hrsg.), *Verfassungsschutz-bericht 2009* (Schwerin: Abteilung Verfassungsschutz, 2009), p. 13.

135 Kathleen Schuster, "Suspected Neo-Nazi Website Operators Arrested in Germany", *Deutsche Welle*, 27 January (2016), http://dw.com/en/suspected-neo-nazi-website-operators-arrested-in-germany/a-19006861

136 "Prorussischer Rechtsextremismus", *Dokumentationsarchiv des österreichischen Wider-standes*, August (2015), http://doew.at/erkennen/rechtsextremismus/neues-von-ganz-rechts/archiv/august-2015/prorussischer-rechtsextremismus

137 "Insider: Die USA bezahlen die Schlepper nach Europa!", *Info-Direkt*, 5 August (2015), http://info-direkt.eu/insider-die-usa-bezahlen-die-schlepper-nach-europa/. In the Russian media space, the story was publicised, in particular, by the country's largest TV channel, Pervy kanal, see "Stary Svet ishchet vykhod iz migratsionnogo krizisa, kotory narastaet den' oto dnya", *Pervy kanal*, 3 September (2015), http://1tv.ru/news/world/291480

138 See Chapter 6 for more information on Holzmüller, her projects and contacts with the FPÖ.

139 In an interview, Holzmüller mentioned the Russian Centre of Science and Culture instead of Rossotrudnichestvo, but all Russian Centres of Science and Culture across the world were restructured into different offices of Rossotrudnishestvo created in 2008.

---

140 Yuriy Kuzmin, "Nataliya Khol'tsmyuller: kogda ya vizhu schastlivye litsa gostey bala, vse trudnosti zabyvayutsya", *Boss*, No. 11 (2014), pp. 72–74. See Chapter 6 for more details.
141 On Sputnik see Ben Nimmo, "Sputnik: Propaganda in Orbit", *CEPA Information Warfare Initiative*, No. 2 (2016), http://infowar.cepa.org/Reports/Sputnik-propaganda-in-orbit

6

FAR-RIGHT STRUCTURES IN EUROPE AS PRO-MOSCOW FRONT ORGANISATIONS

Introduction

Chapter 2 briefly mentioned that joint conferences of Russian and Western ultranationalists continued into Putin's second presidential term and beyond. These meetings were not limited to Vladimir Zhirinovsky's World Congress of Patriotic Parties. Both old and new actors have been involved in hosting international far-right conferences since 2005.

As could be expected – given his extensive international cooperation in the 1990s – Aleksandr Dugin retained his position as the most active Russian advocate of the international far-right cooperation. In 2008, Dugin was appointed Professor at the Sociology Department of the Moscow State University, and, on the basis of this Department, Dugin established the Centre of Conservative Research, a think-tank promoting the New Right agenda. Among many other events, this think-tank co-organised the International Scientific Conference 'Against Post-Modern World' that was held in 2011 and attended, in particular, by Claudio Mutti and Christian Bouchet (then already a member of the FN since 2008). Presented as a 'scientific conference', the event had a clearly political agenda reflecting the New Right's approach to Integral Traditionalism that implies using Traditionalist vocabulary as a camouflage for far-right ideas.[1] The conference was sponsored by the Moscow-based Tempbank, whose CEO Mikhail Gagloev was then vice chair of Dugin's MED. It seems that Gagloev took such anti-liberal initiatives seriously. According to the US Department of the Treasury, his Tempbank 'provided millions of dollars in cash and facilitated financial services to the Syrian regime. . . . Gagloev [had] personally travelled to Damascus to make deals with the Syrian regime on behalf of Tempbank'.[2] Gagloev also provided funding for the MED and ESM.[3]

Apart from Dugin, several other Russian right-wing extremists have been involved in the international cooperation with like-minded Western actors. For instance, Richard Arnold and Ekaterina Romanova detail, in a separate paper, particulars of the conference 'The Future of the White World' held in Moscow in 2006 and organised by Pavel Tulaev's *Ateney* journal and the 'Russian branch' of Synergies européennes. Several far-right authors and intellectuals attended this rather ambitious conference, including Guillaume Faye; Pierre Vial, the leader of the French identitarian neo-pagan Terre et Peuple (Land and People) group; Pierre Krebs, a German-French author and the head of the extreme-right Thule-Seminar think-tank; David Duke, a former 'Grand Wizard' of the Ku Klux Klan; Enrique Ravello, a former member of CEDADE and contemporary member of the Spanish branch of the Terre et Peuple; and a number of others.[4] The conference 'proposed a new ideology and structure of cooperation for racists, Euro-Russia' defined as 'a union of the white peoples of the world and a sanctuary for the cultivation and protection of the white race'.[5] Later that year, a similar gathering took place in Belgium under the title 'Can Europe be without Russia?' It was organised by Kris Roman, a former member of the far-right Vlaams Blok and founder of the fringe Euro-Rus association (possibly consisting of only Roman himself) that promotes the idea of a 'white Europe' from Gibraltar to Vladivostok. The meeting was attended by Faye, Duke, Tulaev, Nick Griffin, and a few other, less known right-wing extremists.[6]

New Russian ultranationalist actors became involved in the international cooperation too. Czech researchers Miroslav Mareš and Martin Laryš write, in particular, that the Russian neo-Nazi group 'Russkiy obraz' established, in 2009–2011, contacts with the Greek neo-Nazi XA, Roberto Fiore, and Robin Tilbrook, leader of the far-right English Democrats.[7]

These meetings and conferences, while introducing some Western far-right activists to Russia or strengthening the Russian connections of others, were nevertheless marginal. However, concurrently to these fringe fora, a related and far more important phenomenon started to take shape since Putin's second presidential term, namely organised pro-Russian efforts undertaken by various Western far-right organisations. These new initiatives are different from the activities described in Chapters 4 and 5. Electoral observation to the benefit of Moscow's foreign policy and the cooperation with Russian media implied the existence of a Russian structure that initially determined the course of the corresponding activities even if they could later develop without that Russian structure. In contrast, the far-right pro-Kremlin efforts analysed in this chapter originally developed and assumed organisational forms without any initial Russian framework, but later were supported by various Russian actors directly or indirectly linked to the Kremlin, thus turning the far-right organisations involved in these activities into effectively pro-Moscow front organisations.

This chapter explores such activities drawing on the evidence from three particular cases. Namely, the chapter looks into the sources, nature and development of far-right pro-Russian efforts in Austria, Italy and France, as well as identifying their patterns and individuals and Russian structures that supported and furthered these efforts.

Austria

In certain cases, joint conferences of Western far-right activists and Russian mainstream actors preceded the entrance of the former into the Russian media, 'electoral observation' missions, and other Russia-related activities. A few meetings held in Austria under the auspices of the FPÖ and Austrian Technologies GmbH in 2008–2010 developed from a series of relatively marginal events into active cooperation between the FPÖ and the Russian authorities as well as other actors.

Austrian Technologies is the name of a company that was founded in 2001 and was originally named Bundesinstitut für internationalen Bildungs- und Technologietransfer (Federal Institute for International Education and Technology Transfer, BIB). Despite the name suggesting its structural association with Austrian state institutions, the BIB was a private company that, nevertheless, received annual funding from various state departments, including the Federal Ministry for Transport, Innovation and Technology.[8] In 2005, the BIB was renamed into Austrian Technologies and presented itself as Bundesagentur für Technologietransfer und Sicherheitsforschung (Federal Agency for Technology Transfer and Security Research) again suggesting the structural link to the state institutions. Moreover, its website (www.austriantechnologies.gv.at) used, as the URL implies, a domain reserved by the Austrian governmental bodies (i.e. gv.at), while the website of the Federal Ministry for Transport, Innovation and Technology officially provided a link to the Austrian Technologies website in its innovation and technology section.[9]

In the period between 2005 and 2009, the BIB/Austrian Technologies received €585,689 from the Ministry for Transport, Innovation and Technology.[10] As the company acquired federal funds, it was supposed to be free of political influence, but its links to the FPÖ were evident. The BIB's Vice President in 2003–2004 was Barbara Kappel, who was also President of the BIB/Austrian Technologies in 2004–2007. Kappel was considered a protégé of Thomas Prinzhorn, one of the richest Austrian industrialists and a prominent member of the FPÖ until 2006.[11] She was head of Prinzhorn's office when he was a member of the National Council in 1996–1999, as well as heading his office in the period 2000–2006 when Prinzhorn was Second and Third President of the National Council in 1999–2002 and 2002–2006 respectively.[12] In 2010, Kappel would become a member of the FPÖ's federal executive, coordinator of the party's economic and financial policy, as well as member of the Vienna Landtag (regional parliament).

In 2006, a new organisation appeared, namely Austrian Technologies GmbH, and Kappel became its Managing Director. It had no relation to either the Austrian state institutions such as the Ministry for Transport, Innovation and Technology, or even Austrian Technologies as a 'federal agency'.

The reasons for creating this organisation are not entirely clear, but the following developments may throw light on this question. In April 2005, Jörg Haider, the head of the FPÖ in 1986–2000 left the party and established the less radical, right-wing populist BZÖ. The FPÖ's member Hubert Gorbach who was Minister for Transport, Innovation and Technology (2003–2007) left the party together with Haider and joined the BZÖ too. Furthermore, Thomas Prinzhorn switched from the FPÖ to the BZÖ in 2006. The departure of these important figures from the FPÖ coincided with a marked decrease of funding for the 'federal agency' Austrian Technologies from the Ministry for Transport, Innovation and Technology: the inflow of funding decreased from €295,000 in 2005 to €161,500 in 2006 and to €99,015 in 2007.[13] This might be the reason why Kappel, who remained president of Austrian Technologies until 2007, decided to start a new company that would not be dependent on the Ministry for Transport, Innovation and Technology, but would be able to relate superficially to the 'federal agency' and perform similar activities. As the website of Austrian Technologies GmbH stated, its focus was 'on project design for international, high-performance projects, and on the worldwide transfer of know-how and Austrian technologies. We support our clients in their search for strategic partners and advantageous local conditions according to the motto, "We think global, act global and go global"'.[14]

Despite its declared business-oriented focus, the public activities of Austrian Technologies GmbH were heavily politicised, while its association with the FPÖ was even more evident. In October 2008, the company co-organised a conference 'Europe-Russia-Georgia: Peace Building I'.[15] Other co-organisers included the FPÖ-affiliated institution 'Freedom Academy', which sponsored the event,[16] and the Centre for Strategic Studies of Religion and Politics of the Modern World, a think-tank established by a Russian nationalist journalist and TV presenter Maksim Shevchenko. Kappel and the FPÖ's leader Heinz-Christian Strache represented the Austrian side, while the Russian side was represented by Shevchenko, who at that time was also a member of the Civic Chamber of the Russian Federation, and two other members of the Civic Chamber: Russian Orthodox Bishop Theophan (Ivan Ashurkov) and Olga Kostina, a Russian public figure and wife of Konstantin Kostin, then deputy chief of the Domestic Politics Department of the Presidential Administration of the Russian Federation.[17] Georgian businessman Levan Pirveli spoke on behalf of the political opposition to Georgia's President Mikheil Saakashvili. The participants of the conference criticised the United States, denounced Saakashvili blaming him for the conflict with Russia, and praised Moscow's foreign policy. Strache argued that Europe needed to pursue its own geopolitical interests, to deepen and develop cooperation with Russia, since Russia was 'a part of Europe'.[18] For Strache, these statements became a point of entry into the Russian media.

Strache's pro-Russian sentiment was apparent already in 2007. As a leader of a party represented in the Austrian parliament, Strache met with Putin on 23 May 2007 during the Russian president's visit to Austria. It seems that Putin made an impression on Strache, and, the next day after his meeting with Putin, the FPÖ published a press release quoting Strache as saying that Europe was 'unthinkable without Russia' and that it was essential 'to further expand and deepen our friendship and cooperation with Russia in order to secure peace in Europe and strengthen democracy, economic and social security together with Russia'.[19] In the same press release, Strache assumed Moscow's adverse position with regard to the construction of the US missile shield installations in Poland and the Czech Republic.

The involvement of the FPÖ in the political activities of Austrian Technologies GmbH seemed to have helped the party build closer links to Russian officials. In December 2008, the FPÖ delegation consisting of Strache, Kappel, Johann Gudenus, Johannes Hübner, Harald Vilimsky and Hilmar Kabas travelled to Moscow and met with then Moscow Mayor Yuriy Luzhkov to discuss with him 'the development of friendly relations between Moscow and Vienna'.[20] During their visit to Moscow, the members of the FPÖ also met with the representatives of the Russian Orthodox Church and several MPs from the ruling 'Yedinaya Rossiya' party.

In the beginning of 2009, Maksim Shevchenko invited Aleksandr Dugin to Vienna.[21] Shevchenko introduced Dugin to the leadership of the FPÖ, in particular to Strache and Kappel; moreover, Dugin became a guest at the Ball des Wiener Korporationsrings (Ball of the Viennese Union of the Incorporated), an annual ball organised by Viennese right-wing student fraternities, the so-called Burschenschaften.[22]

Shevchenko continued cooperating with Austrian Technologies GmbH, and, in May 2009, they held the second conference on the same topic as in the previous year, 'Europe-Russia-Georgia: Peace Building II'. The conference featured not only Strache, Kappel, Shevchenko and Pirveli, but also two Russian MPs from 'Yedinaya Rossiya', Grigoriy Ivliev and Viktor Zvagel'sky.[23] Later that year, in November, Shevchenko – possibly upon Dugin's recommendation – brought two of Dugin's associates, namely the economist Mikhail Khazin and Russian Islamist Geydar Dzhemal,[24] to yet another conference co-organised with Austrian Technologies GmbH, 'Conflict versus Dialogue: Are There Any Solutions to the Crises of the Modern World?'.[25] The conference, however, addressed only particular spheres of the 'Modern World'. Strache talked about 'problematic events in the post-Soviet republics' referring to 'colour revolutions' in Ukraine and Georgia. Khazin prophesised, as he had been doing for years, the inevitable economic downfall of the United States, while Shevchenko praised the FPÖ as 'one of the few European parties embodying freedom' and Strache – as 'a politician of a new type'.[26]

The year 2010 was the last year when Austrian Technologies GmbH co-organised its Russia-related conferences but they turned out to be of a higher profile than the previous ones. In January 2010, four organisations – Austrian Technologies GmbH, 'Freedom Academy', Maksim Shevchenko's above-mentioned Centre, and the Russian federal government agency Rossotrudnichestvo – organised a conference titled '55 Years of the Austrian State Treaty – Reflections from the Austrian-Russian Perspective'.[27] Apart from the usual participants (Kappel, Strache and Shevchenko), the conference was attended by two Austrian academics –

Wilhelm Brauneder and Lothar Höbelt[28] – one way or another connected to the FPÖ, as well as a Russian MP from 'Yedinaya Rossiya' Irina Rodnina and a Russian academic Igor Maksimychev, a senior fellow of the Institute of Europe of the Russian Academy of Sciences.

According to its official website, Rossotrudnichestvo 'carries out projects aimed at strengthening international ties, close cooperation in the humanitarian sphere and formation of a positive image of Russia abroad'.[29] It was created in 2008, and has become Russia's major instrument of soft power in foreign countries. In 2013, Putin issued an edict raising the budget of Rossotrudnichestvo from 2 billion to 9.5 billion Russian roubles (i.e. approximately from €48 to €228 million at that time) by 2020.[30] Orysia Lutsevych describes Rossotrudnichestvo as 'an umbrella organization for a network of Russian compatriots' that 'funds various "public diplomacy" projects' and 'operates an extensive network of 60 Russian Centres of Science and Culture and 25 representative offices in Russian embassies, and employs 600 people internationally'.[31] Jānis Kažociņš, former head of Latvia's state security service Constitution Protection Bureau, considers bodies such as Rossotrudnichestvo 'government-organised non-governmental organisations which work outside the Russian Federation furthering Russian foreign policy objectives in all sorts of ways including through culture, through political pressure, [and] through diplomatic pressure'.[32]

In its article on the conference '55 Years of the Austrian State Treaty', Rossotrudnichestvo reported:

> Presentations . . . noted the tremendous role of the Soviet Union in preventing the division of Austria following the German model; highlighted the great significance of [Austria's] politics of *neutrality* that . . . allowed the country to become a reliable link between the West and the East in the Cold War period.[33]

Neither this kind of rhetoric nor the pro-Russian activities of the FPÖ were radically new for Austria. As Chapter 1 showed, the emphasis on the country's neutralism from an ultranationalist perspective was the *raison d'être* of Adolf Slavik's far-right neutralist Nationale Liga that operated as a Soviet front organisation in 1950–1955 with the only aim: to promote Austria's nationalist neutralism and rapprochement with Soviet Russia.

The last Russia-related conference co-organised by Austrian Technologies GmbH was devoted to 'Coloured revolutions in the CIS countries and their current impact'.[34] On that occasion, the usual hosts such as Kappel, Strache and Shevchenko were joined by participants from the countries that experienced 'colour revolutions': Vladyslav Lukyanov, a Ukrainian MP from the Partiya rehioniv; Bermet Akayeva, a former Kyrgyz MP and daughter of Kyrgyzstan's former president of Askar Akayev who fled to Russia after the 'Tulip Revolution' in 2005; and two Georgian opposition politicians and businessmen – Levan Pirveli and Gogi Topadze. The Russian side at the conference was represented by Geydar Dzhemal and Sergey

Markov, an MP and member of both the Supreme Council of 'Yedinaya Rossiya' and the Council on Foreign and Defence Policy of Russia.

A brief report on the conference was published in *Sootechestvennik* (Compatriot), a discontinued monthly Russian language newspaper published for *sootechestvenniki*, that is Russian expats in Austria. In his introduction, according to the report in *Sootechestvennik*, Strache argued that the United States and organisations such as United States Agency for International Development (also known as USAID) and NDI prepared and financed 'colour revolutions', as well as accusing non-commercial organisations of 'advancing the US interests in different countries under the pretence of advancing democracy'. In his turn, Markov discussed 'the political technologies and mechanics of "colour revolutions"', suggesting that there were 'attempts at preparing such a coup in Russia'.[35] In other words, the last conference co-organised by Austrian Technologies GmbH impeccably followed the established pro-Kremlin ideological pattern that lay in the foundation of all the FPÖ's previous Russia-related conferences.

Since then, Austrian Technologies have not held any political conferences, but this did not mark the end of the FPÖ's pro-Russian activities. On the contrary, the party leadership became even more active in promoting Moscow's interests, keeping in mind its own far-right agenda.

One of many examples of such intersection is the trip of the FPÖ delegation to Russia's Chechen Republic for a meeting with its head, Ramzan Kadyrov, and other republican leaders in February 2012. The FPÖ was represented by Johann Gudenus and Johannes Hübner, and the latter explained that the aim of their trip was to

> make sure that peace and order were reigning [in Chechnya], and that the true state of affairs did not correspond to the picture of the Chechen Republic presented by our media. It is also important for us to make sure that those who will return to the Republic will find normal conditions for living.[36]

The Austrian media criticised the FPÖ's meeting with Kadyrov, pointing out numerous human rights violations in Kadyrov's Chechnya.[37] Kadyrov's name was particularly infamous in Austria. In Vienna, in 2009, four Chechens killed Kadyrov's former bodyguard Umar Israilov who had been granted asylum in Austria as he had accused his former patron of creating illegal prisons and practising torture and extrajudicial executions in Chechnya. Austrian prosecution incriminated Kadyrov with the killing of Israilov, but took no further action.[38]

Upon the FPÖ members' return from Chechnya, they declared that they were convinced that there was no persecution in Kadyrov's Chechnya and that Chechens seeking asylum in Austria could safely return to their homeland. Thus, the FPÖ's visit to Chechnya had a double agenda. Domestically, they played an anti-immigrant card claiming that most of the Chechens in Austria, rather than being genuine refugees, were 'asylum scammers and economic migrants', who should be sent back to allegedly peaceful Chechnya.[39] Internationally, they sought to whitewash Kadyrov's regime, which was beneficial to him personally and the Russian authorities in general. It is unclear who exactly came up with the idea of the FPÖ's trip to Chechnya in the first place, but Gudenus claimed that the trip had taken place 'through intermediary of Russian friends'.[40] Gudenus did not reveal the names of 'Russian friends', but also present at the FPÖ's meeting with Kadyrov was Levan Pirveli, while Maksim Shevchenko later confirmed that the idea of the Austrians' trip had come from the Chechen authorities and that he had helped organise their trip.[41] Shevchenko is known for having good relations with Kadyrov whom he would call 'the foundation stone of stability and security of the Russian Federation'.[42]

Among the FPÖ's leadership, Johann Gudenus is the most energetic advocate of the pro-Russian position of the party, and has long-standing relations with Russia. Following the political footsteps of his now late father, FPÖ member John Gudenus, Johann Gudenus started his political career early, was a member of the FPÖ's youth movement, and, in 1996, became the youngest member of a Viennese district council in the Austrian capital.[43] His career in the FPÖ steadily progressed, and he became the party's deputy chairman in 2011.

Gudenus learned Russian language at school, and travelled regularly to take part in summer schools at the Moscow State University from 1995 until 2003. By the end of this period, he spoke Russian fluently and acquired, in 2004, a Test of Russian as a Foreign Language certificate. In 2005, while studying at the Diplomatic Academy in Vienna for the degree of Master of Advanced International Studies, Gudenus lived in Russia for about a year studying at the Diplomatic Academy of Russia's MFA. His diploma thesis was devoted, in his own words, to 'the political and diplomatic path of Russia in contemporary history, from 1995 to Khodorkovsky'.[44]

In the beginning of the 2010s, Gudenus forged relations with Russian-born Nathalie Holzmüller who had lived in Austria since 1991 and launched, in 2007, the Viennese 'Russian Ball', a dinner dance social event held annually since then and aiming at promoting Russian culture and Russian political interests in Austria. Over the years, 'Russian Balls' have become a meeting point of Russian and pro-Russian politicians, businessmen, diplomats, and cultural figures. Holzmüller also launched another project, 'The Faces of Russia', with the aim of 'rallying people on the basis of interest in Russia, its history and culture'.[45] Gudenus became a regular guest of 'Russian Balls' and soirees held three times a year within the framework of 'The Faces of Russia' project. Furthermore, according to Holzmüller herself, the FPÖ became one of the sponsors of the 'Russian Balls'.[46] The main page of the website of the 'Russian Ball' features a report from the Russian ITAR-TASS news agency that singled out Gudenus as 'the main sponsor' of one of the soirees held in 2012; the same report also noted that he had been 'a regular guest and sponsor of the Russian balls and musical soirees'.[47]

The 'Russian Ball' has increasingly become political in its self-representation; in one letter, Holzmüller refers to it as a 'cultural and patriotic project', and continues:

The project is helped by the Freedom Party of Austria [i.e. FPÖ] that is officially supporting President V.V. Putin's politics. The Russian ball stirs wide interest in Austria whose government understands the absurdity of the sanctions [against Russia] that have caused extensive damage to the economy of the Austrian republic.[48]

Holzmüller also helped organise, in May 2014, a secret international meeting of European and Russian far-right activists and politicians in Vienna, which will be discussed later. The Austrian, openly pro-Putin far-right magazine *Info-Direkt* published an article about Holzmüller in its first edition where she was quoted as saying that 'the media in Austria had not always reported the truth and therefore created a false [i.e. negative] impression of Russia'.[49] The soiree held in October 2015 as part of the 'The Faces of Russia' and titled, in a typical, Soviet-style manner of 'peace-making' active measures, 'In the service of peace' included the presentation of *Info-Direkt*. At the same event, Holzmüller publicly read a letter from Sergey Aksyonov, EU-sanctioned 'Prime Minister' of Russia-annexed Crimea, in which he expressed his gratitude for Holzmüller's support.[50] Back in March 2014, when the Russian authorities held the 'referendum' in occupied Crimea, Johann Gudenus and Johannes Hübner travelled to Crimea to 'observe' this illegitimate process.

The FPÖ also established contacts with the straightforwardly pro-Kremlin Österreichisch-Russische Freundschaftsgesellschaft (Society of Austrian-Russian Friendship, ORFG). Three members of the party (Gudenus, Kappel and Peter Fichtenbauer) entered the extended board of the ORFG – in comparison, only one member of the SPÖ and one member of Die Grünen (Greens) are on the extended board of the ORFG.[51] No member of the ÖVP is on the extended board, but its contemporary President, Ludwig Scharinger, has been close to the ÖVP.

Speaking at a meeting held by the ORFG in March 2015, Strache enunciated a mixture of Kremlin's propaganda narratives and Austrian far-right neutralist arguments: intelligence agencies played a role in the Ukrainian revolution in 2014; foreign actors provided funding for NGOs in Ukraine; the change of the Ukrainian government was unconstitutional; sanctions against Russia are damaging to Austria which should remain a neutral country; hawks in the US government are thinking about the Third World War; NATO, rather than Russia, is the aggressor expanding to the Russian borders. The ORFG's President Ludwig Scharinger seemed to share Strache's views, and declared: 'we have to let the Americans know that they cannot divide us in Europe and that they should not constantly incite us against Russia'.[52]

Despite all the pro-Moscow efforts of the FPÖ and its affiliated structures, as well as the party members' participation in Nathalie Holzmüller's 'cultural' projects and their cooperation with the ORFG, there is no indication that the Kremlin has achieved any tangible results in terms of improving its image in Austria. Mainstream media in the country rarely cover the FPÖ's pro-Russian efforts, while the vigour of the ORFG and Holzmüller's projects is limited to preaching to the converted. Even within their own party, the leaders of the FPÖ find it difficult to spark the interest in their openly pro-Moscow positions. For example, at an FPÖ's semi-closed meeting in a Viennese café in August 2014, where Strache narrated to his fellow party members the Kremlin's version of the contemporary developments in Ukraine, as well as calling for building a new 'Holy Alliance' between continental Europe and Russia, few seemed to be thrilled. They were instead more interested in the anti-American thrust of Strache's speech.[53]

The pro-Russian activities of particular members and leaders of the FPÖ developed concurrently with their Russia-related business initiatives, some of which even preceded the FPÖ's pro-Moscow efforts.

As Austrian investigative journalist Herwig Höller wrote, Johann Gudenus was, between October 2006 and March 2010, managing director of Donowan Invest Trading GmbH, an Austrian company engaged in wholesale trade of raw cotton and yarn.[54] The company had a subsidiary in Moscow, Donovan Invest Trading Rus, while the Austrian company itself was owned, from 2007, by a Russian citizen. The balance sheet, which Donowan Invest Trading GmbH submitted to the Austrian relevant authorities to cover the period until the end of 2007, indicated that the company had a debt of approximately €300,000 – Gudenus never explained the nature of this debt. The company submitted no balance sheets afterwards. Gudenus left the position of managing director of Donowan Invest Trading GmbH in 2010, and it was liquidated a year later.

One of the objectives of the 'federal agency' Austrian Technologies was promotion of Austrian businesses abroad, and, during the time when Barbara Kappel was the company's President, Austrian Technologies tried to mediate between Austrian businesses and potential Russian customers. In Russia, the company was represented by Julia Vitoslavsky, a Russian citizen who had studied Economics in Vienna and later headed the 'Information and Business Centre of the city of St. Petersburg' in Austria. Vitoslavsky, in particular, promoted various Austrian construction technologies in Russia,[55] as well as cooperating with the Austrian state agencies in presenting 15 Austrian companies at a showcase event in St Petersburg in June 2007.[56]

In 2009–2011, Kappel was a co-founder, vice president and member of the board of directors of Aquabionica, a multi-level marketing business (or, simply, a pyramid scheme) that sold various 'bionic products' in Eastern Europe including Russia and Ukraine.[57] One of the products was 'bionic water' described as 'clear natural water, structured by minerals with the use of nanotechnologies' and released 'from all harmful informational effects',[58] and was ultimately drinking water sold for around €45 per two vials[59] to gullible East European customers. Kappel's Austrian Technologies GmbH owned 5 per cent of the Cyprus-registered company Win Worldwide International Network Ltd that owned the product, brand and distribution rights for the production of Aquabionica.[60] Yevgeniy Merkel, who worked as a consultant at Kappel's husband's Joachim Kappel Management Consultants GmbH, was a co-director of Win Worldwide International Network Ltd and executive vice president of Aquabionica.

The FPÖ's representatives frequently discussed economic issues at the meetings with their Russian contacts. As it was reported, already in 2008, during the FPÖ's meeting with Moscow's contemporary Mayor Yuriy Luzhkov, the latter had suggested meeting Strache again 'to deepen the amicable relationship and discuss economic potentials'.[61]

In 2010, the FPÖ started the initiative of inviting children from Russian orphan homes to visit Austria, as well as regularly passing Christmas presents to orphan Russian children via contemporary Russian Ambassador Sergey Nechaev meeting him either at the Russian Centre of Science and Culture affiliated with the Austrian office of Rossotrudnichestvo or at the Russian Embassy in Vienna.[62] Explaining these activities to the media, Strache said that it was his 'humanitarian duty to offer [their] help to the Russian friends'.[63] However, these activities seemed to go beyond the 'humanitarian duty'. During a meeting, in May 2011, of an FPÖ delegation with the then governor of the Moscow Region Boris Gromov, Strache said – in response to Gromov's words of gratitude for the FPÖ's humanitarian actions: 'Children are goodwill ambassadors, and it is through the children we hope to develop further cultural and *economic* cooperation with the Moscow Region'.[64] A Minister of Foreign Economic Relations of the Government of the Moscow Region was present at that meeting too. Apparently, the FPÖ used its humanitarian help to create a favourable impression on potential Russian business partners.

Furthermore, it was reported, that during the visit to Chechnya of Johann Gudenus and Johannes Hübner, the latter said that they 'intended to study the investment potential of the Chechen Republic, so Austrian businessmen could invest in the regional economy'.[65] When two members of the Legislative Assembly of the Chechen Republic, including a deputy chairman of the Chechen Committee for the budget, banks and taxes, visited Vienna shortly after the FPÖ's trip to Checnhya, they met with the representatives of the party and again discussed 'a possibility of investments in the economy of the Chechen Republic by Austrian businesses, as well as a possibility of sending the best pupils of the Chechen Republic to study in Vienna and other Austrian cities'.[66]

However, no details on the economic relations, if any, possibly deriving from the FPÖ's meetings with Luzhkov, Gromov, or Chechen politicians are available so far.

On 14–16 April 2016, two MPs from the FPÖ, namely Axel Kassegger and Barbara Rosenkranz, took part in a big conference titled 'Second Yalta International Economic Forum' that took place in annexed Crimea. The organising committee was headed by Sergey Aksyonov, while the conference itself aimed at promoting the alleged investment potential of Crimea. According to the organisers, 1100 people participated in the conference; of them 70, described as 'politicians, civic figures, and business leaders', came from outside Russia.[67] The conference was important for Russia for two major reasons. First, the sanctions introduced by the West against Russia effectively barred foreign companies from investing in Crimea to pressure Russia into returning the annexed republic to Ukraine. Second, by inviting foreign participants to the conference, Russia aimed to show that the sanctions were not working and Russia was not internationally isolated.

The issue of sanctions was of particular concern to the participants who feared that a violation of the sanctions regime could damage them politically or economically. Hristo Marinov, the head of administrative apparatus of the Bulgarian far-right Ataka party, which recognised the Russian annexation of Crimea as a legitimate act and tried – apparently unsuccessfully – to do business in Crimea,[68] explained the difficulties of investing in Crimea during his visit to the conference in Yalta:

> We have had several bad experiences when businessmen from the European Union came to Crimea; they liked everything here and they wanted to invest, but then in their main countries of residence they were subjected to 'arm twisting'. We had an experience of dealing with one Indian company that considered a possibility of investing in Crimea, and we would be operating as intermediaries. But then Europe and Canada started to shut the door on them, and they had to abandon the plans.[69]

Taking into account these difficulties, the conference featured a separate discussion on how both Russian and non-Russian businesses could circumvent the sanctions, but this discussion was not made public. The organisers claimed that, during the conference, 12 contracts had been signed worth 20 billion Russian roubles (approximately €267.311 million at that time),[70] but neither the details nor the names of the contractors were revealed. According to one of the press releases of the Second Yalta International Economic Forum, FPÖ's Kassagger 'requested details of the plans to develop tourism in Crimea'. He also expressed his hope that Austria and Russia would return to business as usual, 'especially in the field of tourism', as he thought that it had a 'huge potential for collaboration, particularly in the area of training tourism staff'.[71]

Apart from the FPÖ's MPs and Ataka's Hristo Marinov, the far-right segment of the foreign participants was represented, among others, by Stefano Valdegamberi who was elected to the Venetian regional council on the personal list of Lega Nord's Luca Zaia; Marcus Pretzell, an MEP from the far-right Alternative für Deutschland (Alternative for Germany, AfD), and Markus Frohnmaier, a co-founder of the AfD's youth wing Junge Alternative für Deutschland (Young Alternative for Germany, JAfD); Mitsuhiro Kimura, the leader of the Japanese Issuikai group; Ewald Stadler's employee Robert Stelzl; and Mateusz Piskorski accompanied by Marina Klebanovich (ex-wife of Aleksey Kochetkov).

Despite all their pro-Russian efforts, however, the FPÖ for a long time did not succeed in establishing relations with the highest quarters of political power in Russia. While enjoying the multifaceted support from the FPÖ, the Russian authorities seem to have kept the Austrian right-wing radicals at arm's length, because the FPÖ is the major opposition to the mainstream Austrian parties, and the Russian ruling circles have been unwilling to compromise political and economic relations with them by openly supporting or, at least, rendering honours to their opposition. More specifically, Russian economic and business leaders continued to enjoy mutually beneficial and high-profile relations with the Austrian bank Raiffeisen Bank International, the subsidiary of which, namely ZAO Raiffeisenbank, is one of Russia's major banks. At the same time, the Raiffeisen Banking Group, 'a powerful conglomerate of agricultural cooperatives, banks, and dairy producers', has close ties to the ÖVP.[72] On the other hand, the ÖVP's prominent member Christoph Leitl, who is the President of the Wirtschaftskammer Österreich (Austrian Federal Economic Chamber) that represents and coordinates the activities of all Austrian businesses on the domestic and international levels, has business interests in Russia,[73] while the Wirtschaftskammer Österreich itself is involved in the business relations with Russia, which maintains a considerable economic presence in Austria.[74] When Putin visited Vienna in June 2014, he was hosted by Austria's contemporary President Heinz Fischer and Leitl, while Raiffeisen Bank International's CEO Karl Sevelda was present at Putin's address to the Wirtschaftskammer Österreich and held talks with the Russian businessmen accompanying Putin on his trip to Vienna. However, no FPÖ member was seen amid Putin's Austrian hosts. With Leitl consistently opposing the EU's sanctions against Russia[75] and Sevelda's pledge not to wrap up Raiffeisen's business in Russia despite the sanctions[76] – Sevelda made this pledge at a meeting with the ORFG – the FPÖ remained a useful, but not Moscow's most important ally in Austria.

However, the situation changed in 2016. FPÖ member and Third President of the National Council Norbert Hofer won the first round of the presidential elections. For the first time in the Austrian post-war history, neither a representative of the SPÖ or ÖVP made it to the second round of the presidential election. After the annulled second round of the election, Hofer eventually lost the re-run to Alexander Van der Bellen supported by Die Grünen with 46.21 per cent of the vote on 4 December 2016. But the failure of the SPÖ and ÖVP – parties that formed grand coalition governments for many years – as well as results of public opinion polls suggesting that the FPÖ will likely win the parliamentary elections in 2018 with over 30 per cent of the vote,[77] might have signalled to Moscow that political power of their mainstream partners in Austria was in decline and that the far right could become the Kremlin's primary ally. The FPÖ would hardly be able to form a federal government without a coalition partner, but there were strong supporters of a coalition government both inside the SPÖ and ÖVP. Although there was also strong opposition to such a coalition among Austrian social-democrats and conservatives, the chances were still high that, after the 2018 parliamentary elections, Austria would be ruled by a pro-Moscow, FPÖ-led coalition government.

These considerations might have underpinned the decision of the Presidium of the General Council of 'Yedinaya Rossiya' to conclude an agreement on collaboration and cooperation (*Zusammenwirken und Kooperation*) with the FPÖ. 'Yedinaya Rossiya' took this decision on 28 November, that is less than a week before the second re-run of the presidential election, and was possibly hoping to congratulate Hofer on the victory in December. Although Hofer lost, the FPÖ delegation went to Moscow 2 weeks after the re-run.[78] Featuring top leaders of the party such as Strache, Hofer, Vilimsky, Hübner and Gudenus, the delegation met, on 19 December, with Deputy Chairman of the State Duma Pyotr Tolstoy and Deputy Secretary of the General Council of 'Yedinaya Rossiya' Sergey Zheleznyak. Strache and Zheleznyak officially signed the agreement on cooperation between the two parties. In particular, they agreed to exchange information on topics such as 'current issues on the situation in the Russian Federation and the Republic of Austria, bilateral and international relations', and to exchange 'experiences in the field of party building, organisational work, youth policy, economic development as well as other areas interesting for both sides'.[79] Moreover, 'Yedinaya Rossiya' and the FPÖ agreed to

> actively contribute to the development of mutually beneficial collaboration and cooperation [*Zusammenwirkens und der Kooperation*] between youth, women, education, aid and other social organizations in order to strengthen the friendship and education of young generations in the spirit of patriotism and the joy in work [*Arbeitsfreude*].[80]

The agreement also envisages that the two parties 'will support the development of economic, trade and investment cooperation between the two countries'[81] – an arrangement that FPÖ members frequently discussed during their previous trips to Russia too.

During the signing ceremony, Strache stated: 'We are very dissapointed that the EU and Russian government impose mutual sanctions. Our party is against the sanctions against Russia. I am sure that, eventually, the EU will adopt the same position and start developing cooperation with your country'.[82]

At the time of writing, it is not yet clear what forms cooperation between 'Yedinaya Rossiya' and the FPÖ will take, but the signing of the above-mentioned agreement is so far the most important stage of the relations between the FPÖ and Russian actors.

Italy

Aleksandr Dugin was crucial in establishing the initial contacts with Italian right-wing radicals – the contacts that eventually led to launching various pro-Moscow campaigns in Italy in recent years.[83] Three main factors determine the significance of Dugin's role in the Italian case. First, Dugin has been in contact with several authoritative figures in the Italian far-right scene, including Claudio Mutti and now late Carlo Terracciano, since the 1990s. Second, ideological roots of Dugin's neo-Eurasianism lie, in particular, in the works of Italian fascist thinker Julius Evola, which makes Dugin's doctrine congenial to the contemporary Italian far right still influenced by Evola.[84] Third, Dugin's contacts with Russian actors with a higher status in Russian political life made it possible to advance his relations with the Italian far right and raise them to a new level.

In 2004, Nazi–Maoist Claudio Mutti, Dugin's Italian associate and former disciple of Jean Thiriart, launched a journal *Eurasia: Rivista di studi geopolitici* published by his own publishing house Edizioni All'insegna del Veltro. Tiberio Graziani, a New Right geopolitical author and translator of extreme-right literature, was *Eurasia*'s editor until his split with Mutti in 2011 after which Mutti started to edit the journal himself. The first issue of the journal opened with articles by Dugin and Russian theorist of Eurasianism Nikolay Trubetskoy – as Giovanni Savino argues, this was 'a clear declaration of intention by [the journal's] editors'.[85] The same issue also featured articles, in particular, by Mutti, Graziani, Stefano Vernole, and Carlo Terracciano, who had known Dugin since 1992 when Terracciano visited Moscow in 1992 together with Thiriart and other contemporary representatives of the European Liberation Front.

Also in 2004, the circle around *Eurasia* established the group Coordinamento Progetto Eurasia (Eurasia Coordination Project, CPE) that would disseminate the neo-Eurasianist and New Right ideas of *Eurasia* on the socio-political level; Stefano Vernole became the leader of the CPE. In 2005, the CPE started publishing the information bulletin *Continente Eurasia* under the editorship of Daniele Scalea – the name of the bulletin referred to the title of Dugin's book, *Continente Russia*, published by Edizioni All'insegna del Veltro in 1991.

In one of the issues of *Continente Eurasia*, the CPE presented itself as the Italian branch of Dugin's MED, and declared that its objectives included, inter alia, 'the birth of a united Europe', 'establishing close political and military relations with the Commonwealth of Independent States', 'cooperation between Europe and the Arab world', and 'support for the anti-imperialist struggle of the peoples of Africa and Latin America'.[86] Furthermore, the CPE stated that North American 'imperialism' was a 'military arm' of globalisation and called for abolishing 'all instruments of military, economic and financial imperialism' such as NATO, World Trade Organization, International Monetary Fund, World Bank, International Atomic Energy Agency, UN Security Council and multinational companies.[87]

To this end, the CPE would organise workshops, seminars, publish periodicals, and establish relations with like-minded international groups. Initially, however, the CPE's activities were limited to the fringes of the Italian socio-political life, but still they seemed to be in demand for pro-Russian activities. As was discussed earlier, the CPE's Stefano Vernole and Alberto Ascari observed the 'Transnistrian independence referendum' in 2006, while Vernole took part in the conference 'NATO and Security in Eurasia' in Moscow the same year. In March 2008, around 20 activists of the CPE, including Mutti and Vernole, protested against the United States at the base of the Italian Air Force in Ghedi where the 704th Munitions Maintenance Squadron of the US Air Force is located. In addition to banners in Italian, the CPE activists held posters with slogans in Russian language: 'Putin makes us free' and 'Italy and Russia united against America'.[88]

The constant flow of articles glorifying Putin's Russia and its anti-Western foreign policy, as well as diverse pro-Russian efforts and general anti-American stances, won the CPE attention from Russia's official representatives in Italy. On 6

November 2010, *Eurasia* organised a conference 'Economic and Cultural Relations between Italy and Russia' that featured Graziani, Italian economist Giampaolo Caselli, Italian journalist Stefano Grazioli, and Aleksey Paramonov, contemporary Consul-General of the Russian Federation in Milan.[89] Graziani set the tone of the conference in his introductory address, stressing the importance of 'greater synergy in relations between the two countries in every field' as these relations 'would ensure greater autonomy and sovereignty of Rome from the United States'. Moreover, Graziani argued, the 'recovered economic and political significance of the Russian Federation, China and India, [was] an opportunity for Italy and the EU to withdraw from the Atlantic Pact and, more generally, from the area of the US influence in Europe'. Caselli seemed to embrace Putin and his *siloviki* for initiating 'the reforms needed to boost the economy and enhancing international prestige' of Russia by means of 'state intervention for establishing control over strategic companies and ouster of the oligarchs from institutions'. In his turn, Paramonov focused on the economic relations between Russia and Italy, and tried to convince the audience that the EU would benefit from increased economic cooperation with Russia.[90]

The CPE's contacts with Paramonov, however, did not result in any tangible cooperation with other Russian officials. This might be due to two major factors. First, the CPE seemed to suffer from a clash with Graziani over the orientation of *Eurasia*; Graziani withdrew from the journal in 2011 and founded a new one, *Geopolitica*.[91] Second, Russian officials did not seem to see much political significance or potential of the CPE; its members could be useful as election observers or participants in anti-American conferences, but hardly anything else. Even Russian media did not seem to be interested in engaging with either Mutti or Vernole. After all, the CPE remained a marginal group, not even a political party that could theoretically aspire to gain political power.

Graziani and Daniele Scalea founded *Geopolitica* as an official journal of the Istituto di Alti Studi in Geopolitica e Scienze Ausiliarie (Institute of Advanced Studies in Geopolitics and Auxiliary Sciences, IsAG) that was established in 2010 and co-directed by Graziani and Scalea. Graziani and his associates became more successful than the CPE in establishing relations with Russian actors and institutions, as well as becoming major far-right promoters of Russia's interests in Italy at that time.

In 2011, the IsAG became an official partner of the World Public Forum 'Dialogue of Civilisations' established by Vladimir Yakunin in 2002 when he was First Deputy of Minister of Railway Transport of the Russian Federation. Over the years, conferences organised by the 'Dialogue of Civilisations' on the Greek island of Rhodes (these conferences are also called 'Rhodes Forums') have become a significant international project aimed at advancing the ideas of a multipolar world – a Russian politically correct euphemism for anti-Americanism. In 2012, Graziani presented a paper at the 10th Rhodes Forum in which he voiced his hope that the features of 'unipolarism' such as 'neoliberalism, individualism and un-equal neocolonialist exchange' would not 'represent the global rule' in the imminent 'new multipolar order' succeeding 'unipolarism'.[92] Since then, representatives of the IsAG became regular contributors to the 'Dialogue of Civilisations' project.

In December 2011, Graziani took part in a large, 2-day conference titled 'Innovations Forum Italy-Russia' organised by the Fond 'Russkiy Mir' (Russian World Foundation, FRM) and the Centre of the Russian Studies at the Sapienza University of Rome. The FRM was established by Putin in 2007 'to popularise Russian language' and 'support programmes of studying Russian language abroad',[93] but its agenda has always been broader than this. Like Rossotrudnichestvo, the FRM is an instrument of Russia's soft power,[94] and aims 'to promote values that challenge Western traditions',[95] especially in the countries that were Soviet republics before 1991. For example, the Estonian Security Police 'has indicated that members of the "former Soviet intelligence cadre are active within the Estonian chapter" of the FRM, which suggests that the foundation also works to advance Russia's foreign policy interests in the Baltics'.[96]

The Centre of the Russian Studies at Sapienza was established by the FRM,[97] so it is possible to suggest that the conference 'Innovations Forum Italy-Russia' was an initiative of the Foundation, rather than Sapienza. In his paper presented at this conference,[98] Graziani discussed economic and diplomatic relations between Italy and Russia, and specifically focused on the energy supplies from Russia. In this part of his paper, Graziani essentially lobbied for the building of the South Stream pipeline that would transport Russian natural gas to the EU. Not surprisingly, Graziani was sceptical about the usefulness to Italy of the competing Nabucco pipeline that would transport non-Russian natural gas to the EU.[99] The conference 'Innovations Forum Italy-Russia' was attended by dozens of Italian and Russian officials and academics, as well as Russian business lobbyists and representatives of major Russian companies such as Lukoil and Transneft.[100]

The IsAG became an official partner of several Russian organisations in 2012 signalling the increased cooperation with the Russian officials and other actors. In particular, the IsAG established partnership with the Russian Fund of High Tech Development; Diplomatic Academy of Russia's MFA; Russian State University of Trade and Economics; Institute of Democracy and Cooperation (IDC), a Paris-based Russian soft power operation headed by Natalya Narochnitskaya and John Laughland (see the next section); and *Mezhdunarodnaya zhizn'* (International Affairs), the official journal of Russia's MFA that would later also build relations with Slovak far-right conspiracist *Zem & Vek* magazine.

Graziani might have first met the IDC's Narochnitskaya during the observation of one of the illegitimate electoral processes in Transnistria in 2006. In 2012, both Narochnitskaya and Laughland became members of the scientific committee of *Geopolitica*. Graziani started publishing his *Geopolitica* in 2012 under the imprint of the national-revolutionary publishing house Avatar Éditions owned by former extreme-right militant Gilbert Dawed.[101] The first issue of the journal was entirely devoted to Russia, and, symbolically, its presentation was held at the Rome-based Russian Centre of Science and Culture affiliated with the Italian office of

Rossotrudnichestvo, and, along with Graziani, the IDC's Narochnitskaya and Laughland were main participants of the presentation.

Although the IsAG cooperated with organisations from other countries, the Russian element of its international cooperation has been most prominent, while the scope of its pro-Kremlin activities in Italy has been much broader than that of the CPE. The IsAG is also more influential than the CPE, although, of course, its political influence remains largely limited to particular segments of the Italian academic and intellectual life, rather than political sphere. However, the IsAG is also involved, since 2013–2014, in coordinating the Master in Geopolitics and Global Security degree programme at Sapienza, and Graziani is a member of the scientific board of this programme.[102] It seems viable to suggest that, by taking part in educating Master students, the IsAG and its New Right, pro-Russian ideas may have deeper influence on the Italian political milieu in the mid- and long-term perspective.

The IsAG has also cooperated with yet another Italian far-right organisation, the cultural association Millennium, which was inspired by the works of Dugin and Italian fascist intellectuals such as Julius Evola and Claudio Mutti, as well as being involved in promotion of Russia's interests in Italy. Millennium was created in 2011, with Orazio Maria Gnerre as its leader and Andrea Virga – as the chief ideologue of the association. Millennium 'advocates a European revolution against modernity',[103] and is openly pro-Eurasianist and anti-American. In Putin's Russia, the leader of Millennium sees a model state that opposes Western multiculturalism and at the same time rejects the idea of the nation based on ethnicity – instead, Putin's Russia, according to Gnerre, offers an idea of communities 'organically oriented' towards the Russian cultural axis.[104]

Another Dugin-inspired Italian far-right organisation involved in the pro-Russian activities is Stato & Potenza (State and power) that is led by Stefano Bonilauri and can be described as National Bolshevik, as it combines extreme-right and extreme-left ideas, while its activists come from the Italian far-right and far-left political camps. If Millennium cooperated with the IsAG, Stato & Potenza preferred to maintain contacts with the CPE and Claudio Mutti, although the latter cooperated with Millennium too.

Since its creation at the end of 2010, pro-Russian efforts of Stato & Potenza, which was renamed into Socialismo Patriottico (Patriotic Socialism) in 2014, were largely confined to online propaganda activities on social networking websites such as Facebook. However, from 2014, this group also took part in a number of street protests. One of them was a small rally against the anti-Russian sanctions that was held in June 2015 in Bologna and co-organised with the Italy-Russia Committee led by Riccardo Rompietti who was close to Socialismo Patriottico. As activists explained, they saw the sanctions imposed by the EU on Russia for its war on Ukraine as an 'absolutely unjustified and groundless' measure and 'a serious violation of the sovereignty and the right for the free development of both Russia and Italy as well as of other countries'.[105] On 3 October 2015, the Italy-Russia Committee held another small rally, titled 'I am with Putin', with three official slogans: 'To defeat Islamic terrorism', 'To stop the migration crisis', and 'To regain sovereignty'.[106] Another major slogan was, naturally, 'No sanctions against Russia'.

The phrase 'I am with Putin' ('Io sto con Putin') was coined in 2013 by the fascist Italian political party Fronte Nazionale led by Adriano Tilgher. In the beginning of September 2013, activists of the Fronte Nazionale posted several dozens of posters with an image of Putin and the slogan 'I am with Putin'. By this act, Tilgher's party expressed its agreement with Putin on three points: 'no' to the military intervention in Syria, 'no' to the homosexual propaganda and adoption of children by gay couples, and 'no' to the European Union, which does not consider the South Stream pipeline a priority.[107]

So far, there has been no evidence that the pro-Moscow actions either of Millennium or Stato & Potenza/Socialismo Patriottico or the Fronte Nazionale have exerted any major impact on the Italian politics. However, these efforts demonstrate the degree of penetration of the pro-Kremlin narratives into the Italian far-right milieu and the readiness of this milieu to promote these narratives and operate, effectively, as Russian front organisations in Italy.

However, despite the plethora of Italian far-right movements and organisations that helped advance Moscow's interests in the country, Russian stakeholders kept looking for a more prominent political force that would be more efficient as a pro-Kremlin front organisation. The developments since 2013 suggest that they found such an organisation in the radical right-wing populist Lega Nord.

As briefly mentioned in Chapter 2, the LN cooperated with Zhirinovsky already in the 1990s and early 2000s. Already then, there was an ideological affinity between the LN and Russian ultranationalists, with anti-Americanism being the basis of this affinity. As Marco Tarchi argued, at that time, the LN's press 'nurtured' its criticism of the United States by strong attacks

> against the so-called 'Atlantic warriors', whose secret plotting aimed to weaken Russia, which the Europeans should look upon as a powerful and potential ally 'without the deforming lens of the old anti-Soviet propaganda' in view of a continental defence 'independent from Washington and separated from the NATO infrastructures'.[108]

However, those were only Russian ultranationalists, rather than (self-nominated) representatives of Putin's regime, who were interested in developing contacts with the LN. The situation started to change when Putin's regime decided to take a 'conservative' turn in 2011–2013, but in that period the LN was in decline, while Moscow lacked an operator who would establish contacts with the party.

Such an operator appeared in 2013. Aleksey Komov, the official representative of the World Congress of Families in Russia, travelled to Turin in December 2013 and took part, together with a Russian MP from the 'Yedinaya Rossiya' Viktor Zubarev, in the LN's congress that elected Matteo Salvini as a new leader of the party. Komov and Zubarev were clearly treated as VIPs at the congress and were seated in the first row together with Geert Wilders, the leader of the Dutch right-wing populist PVV, and Ludovic de Danne, a prominent member of the FN's political bureau. The LN's congress enthusiastically applauded Komov's speech in which he referred to the Russian organisations he represented as the LN's 'brothers in Russia' who supported 'our common Christian European values'.[109]

The participation of Komov in the LN's congress in Turin was hardly accidental: it was a deliberate attempt to establish contacts between the LN and Russian actors. Apart from being linked to the international 'pro-family', homophobic association World Congress of Families, Komov is the head of the international department of the Patriarch's Commission on the Family Issues created by the Holy Synod of the Russian Orthodox Church in 2011.

Most importantly, Komov is closely associated with several projects of a Russian 'Orthodox oligarch' Konstantin Malofeev. Given the latter's significance in establishing other contacts with European far-right and ultraconservative circles, it appears likely that, in comparison to Komov, Malofeev acts as an operator of the European/Russian contacts of a higher level. Therefore, his position in the Russian context requires a separate discussion to understand better the Italian and some other cases.

Malofeev has access to the ruling elites in Russia through several key figures. There are two main lines of these connection: (1) business relations around the Svyazinvest, which was Russia's largest state-controlled telecommunications company, and the telecommunications company Rostelecom to which Svyazinvest was joined in 2012–2013; (2) activities in the Russian Orthodox milieu.

The founder of the investment company Marshall Capital Partners, Malofeev was elected to the Board of Directors of Svyazinvest as the head of the strategic planning committee of the company in February 2009.[110] During his tenure as a member of the Board, Malofeev invited several employees of Marshall Capital Partners into the management of Svyazinvest,[111] while his investment company itself bought several Svyazneft's subsidiaries. As Svyazneft owned 51 per cent of the shares of Rostelecom, Malofeev obtained 7 per cent of the shares in Rostelecom.[112]

The CEO of Svyazinvest Yevgeniy Yurchenko seemed to be disaffected with what he saw as Malofeev's seizure of control over Svyazinvest,[113] but Malofeev's actions were backed by a powerful ally, namely Igor Shchegolev, then Minister of Telecom and Mass Communications, who had direct access to Putin[114] and had known Malofeev before his appointment to the Svyazinvest's Board. Shchegolev also chaired the Svyazinvest's Board of Directors in 2010–2011, and requested from Yurchenko to give a resignation notice.

Moreover, Russian economic investigative journalists suggested that Malofeev concluded the purchase of Rostelecom's shares in favour of a major *silovik*, namely then Deputy Prime Minister Sergey Ivanov who supervised telecommunications. Ivanov's son at that time was a deputy CEO of Gazprombank, and it was this bank that sold Rostelecom's shares to Marshall Capital Partners. Further evidence seems to corroborate this suggestion: as it emerged, at least some of Rostelecom's shares owned by Malofeev's Marshall Capital Partners were in fact operated by Gazprombank.[115] In June 2015, Sergey Ivanov became a chair of Rostelecom's Board of Directors.

Yet another influential person with whom Malofeev enhanced relations through his work for Svyazinvest and Rostelecom is Count Alexander Trubetskoy, a French descendant of one of the Russian noble families who immigrated to Europe after the Russian Revolution. On the invitation from Shchegolev and with the support of Sergey Ivanov, Trubetskoy became a chair of the Svyazinvest's Board of Directors in October 2011.[116] According to Trubetskoy, he formed relations with Malofeev and Shchegolev thanks to their conversations on the Christian Orthodox issues: 'They [i.e. Malofeev and Shchegolev] are very close to Father Tikhon, and this played a certain role. Moreover, Konstantin Malofeev, as a businessman, shared some ideas with me regarding Svyazinvest, and I hope he can give me some advice in the future. But importantly, I know him as a true Russian Orthodox patriot'.[117]

Trubetskoy, who is Executive President of the ADFR, is also part of Malofeev's Orthodox circle of friends. 'Father Tikhon' mentioned by Trubetskoy is Georgiy Shevkunov, a rabidly anti-Western ultranationalist and influential member of Russian Orthodox clergy, who is widely believed to be Putin's personal confessor.[118] Malofeev's long-time friendship with Shevkunov, whom some sources consider Malofeev's confessor too,[119] provided him with access to the highest circles of the Russian Orthodox Church. Moreover, the supervisory board of the Saint Basil the Great Charitable Foundation, which Malofeev founded in 2007, includes, in particular, Shchegolev, Shevkunov, Count Zurab Chavchavadze,[120] and ultranationalist filmmaker Sergey Mikhalkov.

In 2011, when Malofeev was still a member of the Boards of Directors of Svyazinvest and Rostelecom, and Shchegolev was still Minister of Telecom and Mass Communications, the Saint Basil the Great Charitable Foundation established – with support from Shchegolev's Ministry – the Safe Internet League. Shchegolev headed the supervisory board of the League that also included, in particular, high-ranking officials from various power ministries and representatives of Russian Internet companies. In particular, the League was supported by the large international software security company Kaspersky Lab[121] headed by Eugene Kaspersky, a graduate of the Fourth (Technical) Department of the Higher School of the KGB.[122] Officially, the League aimed at countering the distribution of illegal contents in the Internet, and later it emerged that the League became the major Russian lobbyist of censorship in the Internet. At the end of 2011, the League drafted what became known as the Internet Restriction Law that the State Duma adopted in 2012 and that since then has been used by the Russian authorities to censor the Internet.[123]

Komov, who participated in the LN's congress at the end of 2013, is associated with two projects of Malofeev: he is a foreign projects manager of the Saint Basil the Great Charitable Foundation and a member of the Board of the Safe Internet League. Apparently, Komov's visit to Italy was coordinated with Malofeev who seems to enjoy patronage of the influential figures such as Father Tikhon

(Shevkunov), Igor Shchegolev who became an aide to President Putin in 2012, and, possibly, Sergey Ivanov, a powerful *silovik* in Putin's inner circle,[124] who was Chief of the Presidential Administration of the Russian Federation from December 2011 until August 2016. However, there is no evidence that any of them was involved in establishing relations with the LN.

Shortly after Komov's visit to Italy, Max Ferrari, a member of the LN and contributor to the party's official newspaper *La Padania* and the Italian service of the Voice of Russia, came up with a proposal to establish the Associazione Culturale Lombardia Russia (ACLR). As Giovanni Savino argues, Ferrari's initiative was 'enthusiastically supported' by the LN,[125] and the ACLR was founded in February 2014 with Aleksey Komov as its honorary president, Salvini's spokesman and vice chairman of the Lombardy Regional Communications Committee Gianluca Savoini – as President, and Ferrari – as General Secretary.

According to Ferrari, the cultural objective of the ACLR 'fully concurred with the worldview that Putin enunciated during the Valdai meeting': 'Identity, Sovereignty, Tradition'[126] – it was a reference to Putin's Valdai speech, discussed in Chapter 3, in which he said that it was 'impossible to move forward without spiritual, cultural and national self-determination'.[127]

The website of the ACLR has published articles praising Putin as the great leader of Russia and presenting the Europeans with a choice between 'Eurabia'[128] as a project that would lead to 'the denial of Europe', and Eurasia from Brittany to Vladivostok that would successfully compete with the United States and China.[129] Thus, it was not surprising that, apart from the interviews with Komov, the website also published several interviews with another associate of Malofeev, Aleksandr Dugin, who described Matteo Salvini as 'the only politician who [could] represent the real interests of the Italians'.[130] One of the interviews was conducted by Savoini[131] during Dugin's visit to Italy upon the invitation of the ACLR: on 4 July 2014, Dugin spoke at a special event, titled 'The Eurasian Challenge of Russia', co-organised by the ACLR and LN in Milano.[132] Moreover, when the ACLR started establishing its branches across northern Italy, Dugin became an honorary president of the Associazione Culturale Piemonte-Russia (Piedmont-Russia Cultural Association).

The materials on the ACLR's website largely followed the changes in the relations between Russia and the West. At the end of the revolution in Ukraine, the ACLR called for the division of Ukraine into 'Ukrainian' and 'Russian' parts; it then attempted to legitimise the 'referendum' in Russia-occupied Crimea (the head of the LN's foreign relations department Claudio D'Amico was one of the international observers at the 'referendum') and, later, to justify its annexation by Russia. After the Western countries introduced sanctions against Russia, the ACLR published numerous articles condemning the sanctions and calling to lift them.

The ACLR did not confine their activities to the pro-Russian online publications; rather, they seemed to focus largely on actions outside the Internet that included demonstrations, public discussions, and various presentations – sometimes in collaboration with the Russian Embassy in Rome and the Russian Consulate General in Milan.[133] Moreover, possibly in its bid to cement their reputation of the devoted pro-Russian forces, the ACLR and LN cooperated with individual representatives of other Italian far-right and right-wing organisations. For example, in November 2014, the ACLR's secretary and treasurer Luca Bertoni took part in the conference 'Economic effects of the sanctions against Russia'[134] together with CPE's Stefano Vernole and Forza Italia's Fabrizio Bertot who was also an observer at the Crimean 'referendum'. In 2015, the ACLR and LN twice invited Eliseo Bertolasi, an expert from Graziani's IsAG and correspondent of Rossiya Segodnya, to the conferences they co-organised: 'The Russian challenge to mondialism'[135] and 'Russia, the West, and the Ukrainian crisis' (Bertot was invited to this conference too).[136]

Already in spring 2014, the Association built important relations with the organisation Rossiysko-Ital'yanskaya molodyozh (Russian Italian Youth, RIM), an organisation founded in 2011 to represent young Russians in Rome. It was founded by Irina Osipova, a Russian student and a daughter of Oleg Osipov, the head of the Rossotrudnichestvo office in Italy. Political views of Irina Osipova are not entirely clear, but her social networking profiles[137] feature photos that suggest friendly relations with a number of Italian far-right individuals and organisations such as convicted fascist bomb-thrower Maurizio Murelli and Italian fascist Andrea Palmeri who volunteered to fight against the Ukrainian government forces in Eastern Ukraine, as well as the leadership of the LN and the fascist movement CasaPound.

Owing to her family connection to Rossotrudnichestvo, Osipova has signifi-cantly contributed to the pro-Russian efforts of the ACLR and LN, as well as having helped them advance their relations with the representatives of the Russian state.[138] On 11 July 2014, Osipova's RIM co-organised and moderated the conference 'What is Russia in 2014?' that hosted, in particular, Vitaliy Fadeev, the counsellor of the Russian Embassy in Italy, Luca Bertoni from the ACLR, and Alfonso Piscitelli, a regular contributor to the ACLR's website. In an interview that followed this conference, Osipova told the VoR's Italian service that 'the Italian right-wing parties' favoured Russia and shared Putin's 'traditionally conservative positions', and that Russia was seen in the West as 'an example that inspire[d] those who [were] fed up with having to live in a regime of so-called democracy'.[139] In September 2014, Osipova arranged a trip to Moscow for several members of the ACLR and other far-right movements, including the Forza Nuova and CasaPound.[140] Osipova also invited Bertoni and Piscitelli to the conference 'Rome – The Third Rome' that she organised, in November 2014, at the Russian Centre of Science and Culture in Rome.[141] On 28 November 2015, following Turkey shooting down a Russian jet that had apparently violated Turkish airspace during Russia's Syrian campaign,[142] the ACLR and Osipova's RIM co-organised – together with the pro-Assad European Solidarity Front for Syria founded by Matteo Caponetti, the leader of the Evola-inspired, fascist Associazione Culturale Zenit (Zenith Cultural Association) – a manifestation in Rome 'in support of Russia and against Turkey's terrorism and aggression'.[143]

The activities of the LN and ACLR in October 2014 were especially important for the development of their Russian connections that led to an increase of their pro-Russian efforts. That month, a delegation of the LN/ACLR visited Russia-annexed Crimea – their trip was coordinated with the Russian Embassy in Rome[144] – and met with the EU-sanctioned 'Prime Minister' of Crimea Sergey Aksyonov. After Crimea, the LN/ACLR delegation went to Moscow where they met with a number of high-ranking Russian officials and politicians such as Chairman of the State Duma Sergey Naryshkin, his deputy and the head of the 'Yedinaya Rossiya' State Duma group Vladimir Vasilyev, the head of the Duma foreign affairs committee Aleksey Pushkov, and deputy Foreign Minister Aleksey Meshkov. The LN/ACLR delegation also visited a session of the State Duma; according to the official transcript of the session, Naryshkin personally welcomed the delegation:

> Dear colleagues, . . . I would like to turn your attention to the presence of the leadership and regular members of the Lega Nord party on the guest balcony. This is one of Italy's political parties that is unalterably opposed to the anti-Russian sanctions introduced by the United States and the European Union – let us greet them! (Heavy applause.)
>
> A sweatshirt, which the leader of the party Mr. Salvini is wearing, reads: 'No to the anti-Russian sanctions!'. (Heavy applause.) Let us wish our colleagues best of luck! (Applause.)[145]

While in the State Duma, Salvini stated: 'We take to heart all the developments in Crimea. Next week we will return to Brussels and we will be ready to start our fight for the recognition of the Crimean Republic and for the lifting of the anti-Russian sanctions'.[146]

Salvini was able to meet and talk to Putin for 20 minutes during a break at the Asia-Europe summit in Milan on 17 October 2014.[147] Salvini described the conversation with Putin in an interview to the IsAG's Eliseo Bertolasi:

> We talked about the absurd sanctions against Russia introduced by the cowardly EU that defends the interests not of its own citizens, but rather those of the economic oligarchs and lobbies of the representatives of the world power. We also discussed together important topics ranging from the protection of national autonomy to the fight against illegal immigration and defence of traditional values.[148]

The same day Salvini met with Putin in Milan, an Italian MP from the LN Paolo Grimoldi, who visited Moscow as part of the LN/ACLR delegation, declared the launch of the cross-party group 'Friends of Putin' in the Italian parliament. As Grimoldi explained, this initiative was aimed at maintaining dialogue with Russia, which he called an 'essential trade and economic partner' of Italy. The LN hoped that the 'Friends of Putin' group would attract 'several hundreds of supporters among the MPs and senators'.[149] When asked why the group had to be called 'Friends of Putin' rather than 'Friends of Russia', Salvini replied that, unlike Yeltsin, Putin represented Russia and defended the prosperity of the Russians, and that his party admired Putin and hoped that he would 'become an example for all the European nations'.[150] On 3 December 2014, Grimoldi sent an official letter to the Chamber of Deputies, the lower house of the Italian parliament, inviting MPs to join the 'Friends of Putin' group.[151] The letter said that the aim of this group was to 'contribute to pacifying diplomatic, political and economic relations' between Italy and Russia, because 'the sanctions and the recent termination of the South Stream gas pipeline produced untold damage to our economy'.[152]

The LN/ACLR trip to Moscow in October 2014 marked the beginning of a series of frequent visits of the LN leadership to Russia and their meetings with high-ranking officials and politicians from the 'Yedinaya Rossiya' party. On 22 October 2014, Claudio D'Amico met with Andrey Klimov, a member of the supervisory board of Malofeev's Katehon think-tank and a senior member of the 'Yedinaya Rossiya' who was responsible for the party's foreign relations in 2012–2016. During this meeting, D'Amico reiterated the LN's opposition to the sanctions against Russia, and suggested that the LN and 'Yedinaya Rossiya' signed an agreement on cross-party cooperation.[153] Klimov and Salvini discussed this idea further during the latter's visit to Moscow in February 2015.[154] The two of them continued discussing tentative official cooperation between the parties on 17 December 2015 when Salvini, Savoini and D'Amico arrived in Moscow for a 2-day visit.[155] It was not, however, until 6 March 2017, that Salvini and Zheleznyak signed a coordination agreement between the LN and the 'Yedinaya Rossiya'. The parties agreed to exchange information on current affairs, international relations, to exchange experiences in the sphere of youth policies and economic development; to regularly exchange delegations at different levels, hold bilateral and multilateral seminars, conferences and roundtables on the most topical issues of Russian-Italian reactions; and to contribute to the unification of all forces in the fight against Islamic terrorism, combat illegal immigration, and defend traditional values.[156]

Although the coordination agreement with the 'Yedinaya Rossiya' was signed only in 2017, the LN and ACLR continued its pro-Russian efforts in Italy, sometimes combining pro-Russian actions with its far-right and socially conservative agenda. On 18 October 2014, the LN, CasaPound and several other far-right organisations held an anti-immigration protest in Milan, and 'the crowd displayed posters hailing Putin' as well as waving flags of the DNR.[157] On 7 November the same year, the ACLR organised an event 'Family Tradition Identity: Russia's Challenge to Mondialism' in Varese that featured, in particular, Savoini and Komov.[158] The ACLR continued discussing the 'Ukrainian question' at the meeting titled 'Beyond the Ukrainian crisis: For a New Dialogue between Europe and Russia' in April 2015 in Milan,[159] and the same month co-organised a cultural event titled 'Music of the World: Russia Special' in Varese.[160] In June 2015, the ACLR held a public discussion 'The Rebirth of Empire: Vladimir Putin's Russia' in Milan.[161]

Like their Austrian counterparts, concurrently with their pro-Moscow efforts the LN attempted to develop business relations with various Russian actors. On one particular occasion, the leaders of the LN were the only Italian politicians at the conference 'Russia-Italy: maintaining trust and partnership' co-organised by the Italian-Russian Centre of the Russian Presidential Academy of National Economy and Public Administration and the State Duma Committee on Economic Policies, Innovative Development and Business. This conference was attended, apart from the LN's leaders, by more than 100 academics and official trade representatives from both countries, and aimed at 'consolidating academic and business communities of Russia and Italy interested in developing Russia-Italian relations'.[162]

However, it seemed that the most active business-related contacts between the LN and various Russian actors developed in the context of Russia-annexed Crimea.

As mentioned earlier, the joint delegation of the LN and ACLR – in coordination with the Russian Embassy in Rome – made a trip to Crimea in October 2014. Apart from the political side of the meetings that the LN/ACLR delegation held in Crimea – discussing the 'legitimacy' of the annexation of Crimea and criticising Western sanctions against Putin's Russia – there was also an evidently economic component to them.

During his meeting with the LN/ACLR delegation, Crimean 'Prime Minister' Sergey Aksyonov said that Crimean 'authorities' intended to consider 'cooperation projects in the areas of recreation, education, healthcare, agriculture and others'.[163] In his turn, Presidential Plenipotentiary Envoy to the 'Crimean Federal District' Oleg Belaventsev stated that Crimea 'was interested in building mutually beneficial Russian-Italian cooperation in economic, cultural and tourist spheres'.[164] Consequently, the LN/ACLR delegation met with 'first deputy Minister of Economic Cooperation' Konstantin Ipatov and 'Minister of resorts and tourism' Elena Yurchenko who articulated their own vision of possible cooperation. Yurchenko claimed, after the meeting with the LN/ACLR, that they had reached an agreement on cooperation in the sphere of tourism.[165]

Following up on the LN/ACLR meetings in Crimea, the ACLR and Russia's now defunct Ministry of Crimean Affairs co-organised a conference 'Russia and Crimea – two great opportunities for our companies' in Padua on 15 December 2014. Apart from the leadership of the LN and around 100 businessmen from various Italian regions, the conference featured several high-ranking figures including Deputy Minister of Crimean Affairs Elena Abramova; advisor on investment policies of the Ministry of Crimean Affairs Vadim Tretyakov; 'Minister of Economic Development of Crimea' Nikolay Koryazhkin; Consul-General of the Russian Federation in Milan Aleksandr Nurizade; the representative of Confindustria[166] in Russia and Italy's Honorary Consul in Lipetsk Vittorio Torrembini; Mayor of Padua Massimo Bitonci; and regional Minister of Tourism and International Trade Marino Finozzi – the latter two also represented the LN-affiliated far-right Liga Veneta (Venetian League).[167]

At this conference, Abramova declared that the Ministry of Crimean Affairs would 'lend full support to those businessmen who would decide to use their capabilities and potential for doing business on the Crimean territory'. In his turn, Koryazhkin was more specific saying that Crimea needed 'technologies for storage and processing of fruit and vegetables, [and] winegrowing and wine production'.[168]

The ACLR and the Ministry of Crimean Affairs held the second conference on the same topic in Milan on 20 March 2015. The second conference also hosted Abramova, Tretyakov and Koryazhkin, and aimed, as Savoini argued, at 'presenting to the Italian business circles the vast potential of Crimea that [was] a special economic zone'.[169] Moreover, Savoini stated: 'Business residents of Crimea, including foreign investors, will be exempt from taxes. I can assure you that, already at this initial stage, there are very many Italian companies intending to invest in Crimea'.[170] Among major economic sectors, in which Italian businesses were presumably prepared to invest, Savoini mentioned tourism and healthcare.

However, further developments showed that the LN and ACLR were interested in other potential spheres of economic cooperation. In May 2015, the ACLR announced that it teamed up with the Russia-based company ItalAgro that specialised in sales and delivery of Italian equipment for agriculture and food production purposes to Russian customers, and opened an office of ItalAgro in Moscow to lobby for Italian companies.[171] The same month, Irina Shcherbinina, one of the founding members of the ACLR, managed a joint ItalAgro/ACLR presentation of 15 Italian companies at the exposition 'Crimea – The South of Russia' held in Russia-annexed Sevastopol. At the end of May 2015, the ACLR's delegation also had a meeting with Crimea's then 'Minister of Agriculture' Vitaliy Polishchuk to discuss 'possibilities that Crimea offered to Italian companies in the agricultural sector'.[172]

The LN is not the only Italian far-right organisation that has tried to establish economic relations with Russian actors in Crimea. On 22 May 2015, representatives of several Crimean 'Ministries' had a meeting with a delegation of the Alexandrite Association that included several Italian producers of wine and metalwork, as well as representatives of the companies engaged in marble production and construction business.[173] The Alexandrite Association keeps a low profile in Italy, and its 'office' in Rome is located in the office of the private company Italiana Servizi Postali (Italian Mail Services). This postal services office is headed by Beniamino Iannace, a former member of Roberto Fiore's fascist Forza Nuova. In September 2012, Fiore and Iannace took part in the International Business Summit in the Russian city of Nizhniy Novgorod as representatives of the Alexandrite Association, while the programme of the event introduced Fiore as the head of this Association.[174] At the summit, Fiore declared that they wanted to develop business in Nizhniy Novgorod in the areas of food production, tourism and *haute couture*, and were ready to establish around 20 enterprises and invest around one million Euros in each.[175] However, there is no evidence that Fiore's Alexandrite Association has managed to develop economic relations successfully either in Nizhniy Novgorod or Crimea. Interestingly, until the end of the Ukrainian revolution in February 2014, Fiore and his Forza Nuova cooperated with the Ukrainian far-right party Vseukrayins'ke ob'yednannya 'Svoboda' (All-Ukrainian Union 'Freedom') and sympathised with the revolution,[176] but later severed all ties to the Ukrainian ultranationalists and assumed a firmly pro-Putin and anti-Ukrainian position.

France

Although the Front National and its leader Marine Le Pen are currently the most vocal supporters of Moscow's foreign and domestic policies in France, the first far-right pro-Kremlin efforts in this country were started, like in Italy, by smaller organisations and less significant far-right activists.

Arguably the first French far-right activist to have been involved in organised, openly pro-Kremlin efforts was André Chanclu, a former member of the Groupe Union Défense (Defence Union Group, GUD),[177] a violent extreme-right groupuscule that was, since its foundation in 1968, engaged 'in running battles with left-wing groups on university campuses'.[178] In late 2008, Chanclu founded a small organisation Collectif France-Russie (France-Russia Collective, CFR) as a response to 'the blatant disregard by the French media of the cynical Georgian aggression in South Ossetia'.[179] During his visit to Moscow and the headquarters of Dugin's MED in May 2009, Chanclu said that the people who founded the CFR were 'Russophiles' who believed they needed to promote three ideas: (1) support for Russia's foreign policy and the Russian government; (2) the 2008 economic crisis offered an opportunity to 'turn our back to the Americans and their dollar', and develop profitable trade relations with Russia instead; (3) the Americans impose their culture on the French and force them to forget cultures of 'their friends, including the great Russian culture'.[180]

The CFR claimed that they were not 'subservient to any political movement or ideology' and that their only creed was 'the defence of eternal Russia'.[181] The group lavishly praised Putin for 'strengthening the industrial complex, developing the economy while fighting the mafia oligarchs, reforming institutions, initiating major projects in the sectors of justice, defence and territorial administration'.[182]

In November 2009, the CFR, together with the activists of the Égalité et Réconciliation (Equality and Reconciliation) founded by Alain Soral, a former member of the Parti communiste français (French Communist Party) and FN, organised a demonstration to greet Putin on his visit to France in the capacity of prime minister. The CFR and Égalité et Réconciliation apparently coordinated this demonstration with the Russian Embassy in France.[183] In March 2010, around a dozen of people mobilised by the CFR took part in a demonstration welcoming the visit of Russia's President Dmitry Medvedev in Paris.

In Russia itself, Chanclu's initial contacts were the neo-Eurasianists, in particular the MED and Prava narodov (People's Rights), a small neo-Eurasianist group established by Pavel Zarifullin who had left the MED/ESM after a conflict with Dugin. In July 2009, together with representatives from the MED and 'Prava narodov', Chanclu organised a conference in Paris 'South Ossetia: A Year on' upholding and justifying the Kremlin's position on the Russian-Georgian war in August 2008.[184] A similar conference with the same ideological message was held in August 2009 in Warsaw and featured Zarifullin, as well as Mateusz Piskorski and Przemysław Sieradzan of the ECAG.[185]

Chanclu's cooperation with the Russian neo-Eurasianists appeared to have had a significant ideological impact on him. This was particularly evident in his declaration of the creation of yet another organisation, Novopole.[186] Dugin was the only ideologue mentioned in the declaration, and Chanclu seemed to have embraced the so-called 'fourth political theory' that Dugin put forward in 2009.[187] According to Dugin, the three ideologies (or 'political theories') that dominated the twentieth century – liberalism, communism and fascism – lost their relevance today. Fascism was defeated first, and then communism lost the struggle against liberalism. However, after its triumph, liberalism disappeared and turned into 'post-liberalism'. Accordingly, Dugin came up with the 'fourth political theory' that he considered to be an alternative to 'post-liberalism' and a 'crusade' against 'postmodernity', 'the post-industrial society', 'liberal thought realised in practice', and 'globalisation, as well as its logistical and technological bases'.[188] Chanclu adopted the vocabulary of Dugin's 'fourth political theory', and his Novopole was involved in the activities promoting the pro-Russian and anti-American ideas, and defending regimes such as that of Bashar al-Assad.

During the Russian-Ukrainian war in 2014–2015 and Moscow's Syrian campaign in 2015, Chanclu provided convenient commentary for the daily *Rossiyskaya Gazeta*,[189] but he generally failed to develop his CFR into an efficient organisation or establish relations with high-profile figures in Russia, and none of his pro-Moscow efforts gained any traction.

In 2009, Fabrice Sorlin, the leader of the Catholic ultranationalist organisation Dies Iræ and former candidate for the FN, formed yet another patently pro-Moscow organisation, the Alliance Europe-Russie (Europe-Russia Alliance) that was later renamed into the Association Alliance France-Europe Russie (Association France-Europe-Russia Alliance, AAFER). Discussing the rationale behind the AAFER, the executive officer of the organisation and a member of the FN Jean-Claude Philipot argued that a stronger connection between Europe and Russia would unite the Christian civilisation that would stand up to the rise of Islam, help Europe resist 'American hegemony', and strengthen the economies of European states and Russia through establishing an internal market.[190] The AAFER also insisted on the need for creating 'a greater Europe from Brest to Vladivostok', and aimed at bolstering three particular pro-Russian efforts: (1) developing partnership policies in the spheres of politics, culture, economy and science; (2) disseminating ideas of the need for deeper cooperation between Russia and France; and (3) 're-informing' the public about 'the reality of politics and Russian geopolitics'.[191] According to the AAFER, these pro-Russian activities would be carried out through conferences, debates, roundtables, writing articles, etc.

The AAFER organised several events, and managed to involve people such as the Russian Honorary Consul in the city of Biarritz Alexandre de Miller de La Cerda and Spanish Prince Sixtus Henry of Bourbon-Parma who was connected to the FN through his vice-presidency of the NGO 'SOS Enfants d'Irak' presided by Jany Le Pen, wife of Jean-Marie Le Pen.[192] Like Chanclu, Sorlin would also provide his commentary to the *Rossiyskaya Gazeta*.[193] Yet in the same manner as Chanclu's CFR, the AAFER failed to develop into an efficient organisation, but – compared to the failure of the CFR – the main reason for this was different. The AAFER's proximity to the FN implied that it would be the established political party FN, rather than a small group such as the AAFER, that would develop and expand the pro-Moscow activities of the politicians affiliated with the FN.

It would still be a mistake to argue that the minor pro-Russian efforts of the CFR and AAFER did not exert influence on attitudes within the French far right. When Marine Le Pen's FN made a definite pro-Kremlin turn in 2010–2011, some of the pro-Russian ideas she articulated seemed to draw on the body of the pro-Kremlin narratives produced by smaller organisations. For example, in Le Pen's statement that the '[financial] crisis could give an impetus to the changes in domestic and foreign policies of France that needed to stop obeying the United States and turn to Russia'[194] one could hear an echo of Chanclu's argument that the 'economic crisis offer[ed] us a rare opportunity to turn our back to the Americans and their dollar, which cost us dearly, and develop profitable trade relations with Russia'.[195] Jean-Yves Camus and Nicolas Lebourg suggest that it was the AAFER's Emmanuel Leroy, a former member of Alain de Benoist's GRECE and one of Dugin's French contacts, who contributed to the pro-Kremlin turn of the FN.[196] French journalist Gaïdz Minassian notes that Leroy, a member of the FN and advisor to Le Pen, 'tried – without success – to establish high-level contacts between Le Pen and the Russian leadership, through his Russian wife [who was] close to the IDC and the Russian Embassy in Paris'.[197]

The Institute of Democracy and Cooperation (IDC) was created in 2008 with two headquarters – in New York and Paris – to promote the Kremlin's perspective on a number of issues: 'the relationship between state sovereignty and human rights', 'East-West relations and the place of Russia in Europe', 'the role of non-governmental organisations in political life', 'the interpretation of human rights and the way they are applied in different counties', 'the way in which historical memory is used in contemporary politics'.[198] Russian academic Andrey Makarychev argued that the foundation of the IDC could be 'interpreted as a direct response to the activities of European and American foundations and think-tanks in Russia and, simultaneously, as an alternative to the Western interpretations of normativity in world politics'.[199] Indeed, the launch of the IDC project owes to Putin's comments that he made in Portugal in autumn 2007 when he spoke about the idea of establishing an institute that would 'address the issues of electoral monitoring, situation with national minorities and migrants, freedom of speech'. As Putin argued, 'the EU helps developing, through grants, Western institutions of this kind in Europe. I think it is time for Russia to do the same in the EU'.[200]

Natalya Narochnitskaya, former Russian MP nominated by the Russian far-right 'Rodina' party,[201] became a director of the Paris chapter of the IDC, and was joined, as director of studies, by John Laughland, a British Eurosceptic journalist who had been described as a 'right-wing anti-state libertarian and isolationist' and a 'PR man to Europe's nastiest regimes'.[202] While the IDC is also intended to promote Moscow's interests in the West, it is still different from Rossotrudnichestvo or the FRM. On the one hand, unlike these two, the IDC is not *officially* funded by the Russian state – in fact, the sources of the IDC's funding are unclear. On the other hand, the IDC has always been much more ideological than Rossotrudnichestvo or the FRM, and this resulted in a particular choice of Western organisations and individuals that the IDC cooperated with over the years, ranging from Eurosceptic national-conservatives through right-wing populists to the far right – all both anti-American and sympathetic towards Russia. As was mentioned above, the IDC cooperated with Tiberio Graziani's *Geopolitica* in Italy, and, in Germany, it cooperated with the right-wing populist *Compact* magazine edited by Jürgen Elsässer.[203]

There were also other figures close to the FN who, at the same time, have had relations with Russia: Frédéric Chatillon and Xavier Moreau. Chatillon, the former leader of the extreme-right GUD, supporter of Assad's regime in Syria and the Lebanon-based Islamist Hezbollah movement,[204] often travelled to Russia on business and was one of the unofficial advisors to Marine Le Pen.[205] Former paratrooper officer Moreau, who holds dual French-Russian citizenship, owns the Moscow-based Sokol Holding that employs, as its website claims, former members of French Army elite troops and Russian security services,[206] as well as providing consultancy and security to French companies.[207] Moreau, for some time, regularly contributed to the Internet-based Realpolitik.TV channel founded by Aymeric Chauprade,[208] while a prominent member of the FN Bruno Gollnisch described the relations between Moreau and the FN as 'friendly'. Moreover, Gollnisch seemed to acknowledge, without going into a detail, that Moreau had contributed to establishing the relations between the FN and Russian actors: 'He's a businessman, an influential boy. He has friendships there [in Russia] and especially with Mr. Putin. I think he is still one of our contacts in Russia. He served as an intermediary in some circumstances'.[209]

Marlène Laruelle notes that Chauprade, a prominent contemporary member of the FN who officially advised Marine Le Pen on international relations from autumn 2013 until spring 2015, worked with Moreau, as well as Sorlin and Leroy of the AAFER.[210] Cécile Vaissié puts Chauprade into special focus arguing that it was him, rather than Chatillon, Sorlin or Leroy, who contributed most to the explicitly pro-Putin turn of the FN.[211] It needs to be stressed, however, that – as Chapter 2 demonstrated – the FN was characterised by pro-Moscow positions in its foreign policy orientations since the 1990s and Jean-Marie Le Pen even tried (unsuccessfully) to meet with Putin in 2002. Moreover, already during the Cold War and immediately after the demise of the Soviet Union, a significant element of the French or Francophone far right revealed pro-Soviet/pro-Russian inclinations. Those were particularly associated with Jean Thiriart and the French/Belgian New Right, while the Thiriartian myth of a Europe 'from Dublin to Vladivostok' – in its different variations – has become ingrained in many far-right discourses even outside the Francophone world.

Nevertheless, the pro-Moscow turn of the FN under Marine Le Pen in 2010–2011 gained prominence. Already in March 2010, when President Medvedev visited France, Le Pen 'saluted to the arrival of Dmitry Medvedev to Paris and to Russia as a great nation [and] a friend of France'.[212] This statement was hardly noticed then, and only after she became the FN's president in January 2011, her consistent pro-Moscow position became conspicuous. At a press conference in April 2011, she said that she would favour partnership with Russia for 'obvious civilisational [and] geostrategic reasons' and because of 'interests in [France's] energy independence'.[213] In an interview for *RT* the same month, she declared that she believed that France 'should turn to Russia for economic and energy partnerships' and that she thought 'very objectively' that 'this "Cold War" imposed by America on relations with Russia [was] a huge political error'.[214]

At the same time, Le Pen and her party started thinking of a trip to Russia with the objective of meeting 'people in power', as Ludovic de Danne, Le Pen's advisor on European affairs, formulated. One senior official of the FN said that there were 'proposals to meet, if not Putin, then his entourage or [representatives of] his party', that is the 'Yedinaya Rossiya', although a meeting with Putin would be 'much better'.[215]

However, Le Pen did not travel to Russia either in 2011 or in 2012. In his book about Marine Le Pen, an established Russian journalist and long-time foreign correspondent of *Pravda* Vladimir Bol'shakov argued that the FN was planning her trip to Moscow in the beginning of 2012, but Le Pen cancelled the trip, because – as he suggested – the level of protocol was lower than she expected.[216] This can be explained by a reference to the electoral processes in Russia and France. On the one hand, the Russian political elites were busy throughout 2011 preparing for the parliamentary elections in December 2011 and presidential elections in March 2012. On the other hand, France had presidential elections in late spring 2012, and the Russian political elites did not want to sour relations with the two most popular presidential candidates, that is François Hollande and Nicolas Sarkozy, by doing another presidential candidate, namely Le Pen, high honour on the eve of the French presidential elections.

The lack of progress in the talks about Le Pen's visit to Russia in 2011 did not discourage the FN from pushing its pro-Russian foreign policy agenda. In an interview for the Russian *Kommersant* newspaper, Le Pen declared that she, to a certain degree, admired Putin: 'I think that Putin has a character and a vision of the future required for bringing to Russia the prosperity it deserves. And active cooperation between Russia and European countries can speed up this process'.[217] In November 2011, Le Pen published her presidential programme and, out of 11 foreign policy positions, Russia was mentioned in five of them; the first two positions offering the ultimate expression of the pan-European far-right narrative on Russia:

1   The advent of a Europe of Nations, a withdrawal from NATO integrated command and offering Russia a strategic alliance based on a

close military and energy partnership, rejection of military interference, and support for international law.

2   A joint proposal to form a trilateral alliance Paris-Berlin-Moscow.[218]

After he easily won the presidential election in March 2012, Putin visited France and held talks with President Hollande. This meeting revealed deep disagreement between French and Russian presidents over the situation in Syria. The French investigative journalist Vincent Jauvert identifies Hollande's criticism of Russian support for Assad as a turning point in the attitudes of Russia's political elites towards those in France:

> After he just settled at the Élysée, François Hollande strongly criticised the Kremlin's position on Syria; ministerial visits have become seldom, the Franco-Russian dialogue has dried up. Therefore, the Kremlin needed a new footing in Paris. [Russia's] Ambassador Aleksandr Orlov and his adviser on French political parties, Leonid Kadyshev, proposed trying Marine Le Pen and her movement. The Kremlin gave its blessing![219]

It was the time when Orlov helped French far-right activist Gilles Arnaud to establish the Internet-based ProRussia.TV and secure Russian funding for the project. Simultaneously, Ambassador Orlov and minister-counsellor Kadyshev started, according to Jauvert, meeting regularly and discreetly with the leaders of the FN at the Russian Embassy in Paris and the Russian diplomatic residence.[220]

The first major breakthrough in the FN's attempts to approach 'people in power' in Russia took place in December 2012 when Marine Le Pen's niece Marion Maréchal-Le Pen went to Moscow and took part in the First International Parliamentary Forum 'Contemporary Parliamentarianism and the Future of Democracy' held at the initiative of the State Duma and presided by Sergey Naryshkin.[221] The latter is a representative of the *siloviki* group within the Russian political elite. A graduate of the Higher School of the KGB, he headed the Presidential Administration in 2008–2011 (under Medvedev's presidency) and, since December 2011 until October 2016, was Chairman of the State Duma. Opening the forum, Naryshkin personally greeted Maréchal-Le Pen, although she was not supposed to deliver an address at the forum:

> This forum hosts representatives of 23 countries of the world; they have very different political views and they are of different age, including the youngest member of the National Assembly of France Marion Maréchal-Le Pen who celebrates her birthday today. Allow me, on behalf of all the participants of the forum, to wish Madame Maréchal-Le Pen a happy birthday and every success and prosperity.[222]

Upon her return to France, Maréchal-Le Pen gave an interview to ProRussia.TV in which she said: 'Russia seeks a certain number of partners; they may have set their sights – as I hope anyway – on the Front National'.[223] She also suggested that meetings between the FN's representatives and Russian officials would continue.

Indeed, the FN's Bruno Gollnisch visited Moscow in May 2013 and took part in a number of meetings with Russian politicians. On 13 June the same year, a French delegation led by the AAFER's Sorlin and consisting of Chauprade, the president of the Mouvement Catholique des Familles (Catholic Movement of Families) François Legrier, the president of the association 'Catholiques en Campagne' (Catholics in Campaign) Hugues Revel, and an activist of the 'pro-life' Alliance Vita (Life Alliance) Odile Téqui took part in the roundtable 'Traditional Values – the Future of European Nations' in Moscow.[224] The roundtable was organised by Malofeev's Saint Basil the Great Charitable Foundation under the auspices of the State Duma Committee on Women, Family and Youth Issues, and was essentially focused on the demonisation of gay marriages seen as an existential threat to the 'Christian civilisation'. The roundtable also featured managing director of the Saint Basil the Great Charitable Foundation Zurab Chavchavadze, as well as a number of Russian politicians, in particular, deputy head of the Central Office of the State Duma Yuriy Shuvalov and chair of the State Duma Committee on Women, Family and Youth Issues Yelena Mizulina. The latter was one of the MPs who tabled the revised Internet Restriction Law initially drafted by Malofeev's Safe Internet League. One of the results of the roundtable was a resolution signed by Mizulina and Aleksey Pushkov recommending the State Duma to amend the laws on adoption of orphan children in such a way that would ban adoption of orphans by same-sex foreign couples from those countries that recognised their union as marriage, as well as by single people or unmarried couples from those countries. The French far-right/ultraconservative delegation was invited to this roundtable to present 'European support' for the amendments. During the roundtable, Chauprade even said:

> Patriots across the world who are devoted to the independence of peoples and foundations of our civilisation have now directed their eyes to Moscow. And, with a great hope, do they look at Russia that opposes . . . public legalisation of homosexuality, interference of non-governmental organisations which are nihilistic and are manipulated by the American services, and adoption of children by same-sex couples.[225]

Also in June 2013, Marine Le Pen – accompanied by her partner and the FN's vice president Louis Aliot and Ludovic de Danne – visited Sevastopol and a number of other Crimean cities on the invitation of French businessman and long-time resident of Sevastopol Thierry Jean Cipière, a founder of several Swiss-registered companies engaged in real estate and ship trade, as well as investments. After visiting Crimea, the FN's delegation went straight to Moscow. During their visit, the delegation met with Sergey Naryshkin, Aleksey Pushkov, Dmitry Rogozin and Aleksey Zhuravlyov, an MP from the 'Yedinaya Rossiya' parliamentary group and the leader of the 'Rodina', and some other politicians. During his meeting with Le Pen, Naryshkin stated:

> You are well known in Russia and you are a respected political figure. . . . We see France as one of the key strategic partners of Russia in Europe and worldwide. We follow the decisions taken by the new [French] government, which are often taken in different ways by the society. We follow the developments with interest and we draw conclusions.[226]

Naryshkin's statement could be interpreted as an acknowledgement of what Maréchal-Le Pen suggested after her own meeting with Naryshkin – that Moscow was looking for political partners in France and considered the FN as its potential ally. According to the reports, during the closed meeting of Le Pen and Naryshkin, they discussed same-sex marriages and the Syrian issue;[227] Le Pen insisted that the FN was the only political party in France that opposed foreign intervention in Syria. At that time, this position coincided with Moscow's position.[228] After the meeting with Naryshkin, Le Pen declared:

> I think we have common strategic interests, I think we also have common values, that we are European countries. . . . I have the feeling that the European Union is leading a Cold War against Russia. Russia is presented with a demonised face . . . a sort of dictatorship, a country totally closed. That is not, objectively, the reality. I feel more in tune with this model of economic patriotism than with the model of the European Union.[229]

The exchange of political niceties between Naryshkin and Le Pen, as well as Le Pen's Moscow meetings in June 2013 in general, laid the foundations of closer relations between the NF and Russian actors. In October 2013, Chauprade was invited to participate in the meeting of the Valdai International Discussion Club, and, from the second half of 2013, he became a regular commentator for the Russian media, which was also determined by the start of pro-European protests in Ukraine in late autumn 2013 and Russia's increased need for European support of its opposition to Ukraine's rapprochement with the EU.

From the beginning of 2014, two major processes connected to the financial relations between the FN and Russian officials – reported by French investigative journalists from *Mediapart* and, in particular, Marine Turchi – were running in the background of official meetings and pro-Moscow activities of the FN. First, Chauprade introduced Jean-Marie Le Pen to Malofeev in order to help the FN's founder get money for a political funding association Cotelec that was used to lend funds for electoral campaigns of FN members.[230] In April 2014, Cotelec received €2 million from Vernonsia Holdings Ltd, a Cyprus-registered offshoot of the Investment Company of Vnesheconombank (or VEB Capital) that, in its turn, is a 100 per cent subsidiary company of the Russian state corporation 'Bank of Development and Foreign Economic Affairs' (or Vnesheconombank). At that time,

General Director of VEB Capital was Yuriy Kudimov. A former UK-based staff correspondent for the daily *Komsomol'skaya Pravda* during the Soviet times, Kudimov was expelled from the United Kingdom in 1985 after he had been accused – together with 24 other Soviet diplomats, officials and journalists based in the United Kingdom – of taking part in espionage work.[231] Malofeev and Kudimov have known each other since at least 2010 when they both served on the Board of Directors of Rostelecom, so Malofeev's help in securing a loan from Vernonsia Holdings Ltd for Cotelec seems consistent. According to Jean-Marie Le Pen, Chauprade himself borrowed €400,000 from Cotelec to fund his electoral campaign for the 2014 elections to the European Parliament, and *Mediapart* suggested that he received this loan 'for the promise of Russian money to help fund Jean-Marie Le Pen's micro-party', that is Cotelec.[232]

Second, *Mediapart*'s Marine Turchi presumes that Marine Le Pen made a secret trip to Moscow in February 2014 and met with Putin and Aleksandr Babakov.[233] In 2006, the latter was briefly the leader of 'Rodina' following Rogozin's resignation from the leadership of the party, but eventually joined the 'Yedinaya Rossiya' and was elected to the State Duma in 2011. In June 2012, Putin appointed Babakov Special presidential representative for cooperation with organisations representing Russians living abroad. Babakov is also indirectly affiliated to Rossotrudnichestvo that, in particular, engages with the Russians living abroad. Moreover, both Babakov and Rogozin share a connection to Russia's defence industry: Rogozin is the top official responsible for the Russian military-industrial complex, while Babakov is the head of the State Duma commission in charge of the legal groundwork for the development of organisations of the military-industrial complex. According to Turchi, Babakov was essential in Le Pen's negotiations with the Russian officials about a €9 million loan to the FN that the party obtained from the First Czech-Russian Bank (FCRB) in September 2014.

More than 90 per cent of the charter capital of the FCRB belongs to Stroytransgaz, a Russian engineering construction company in the field of oil and gas,[234] while the majority of the shares of Stroytransgaz is owned by companies and holdings that belong to Gennadiy Timchenko,[235] a major Russian business-man from Putin's inner circle.[236] It seems – and *Mediapart*'s assumption that Le Pen met with Putin personally reinforces this suggestion – that Putin was directly involved in making the final decision to provide a loan to the FN.

Another person identified by Turchi as one who had contributed to the negotiations about the Russian loan is the RBM's Jean-Luc Schaffhauser. In 1991, Schaffhauser was involved in a project aiming at reconciliation between the Vatican and the Russian Orthodox Church, and built contacts related to the Russian military-industrial complex in the mid-1990s. According to his own words, Schaffhauser became acquainted with Babakov in the mid-2000s through the Orthodox Church connections.[237] Moreover, Schaffhauser is the president of the European Academy, a Paris-based organisation that aims at fostering relations between European states and Russia. According to *Mediapart*, in 2014–2015, the European Academy received €250 thousand from two companies managed by

Babakov's business partners.[238] In June 2014, the European Academy co-opted Aleksandr Vorobyov and Mikhail Plisyuk, directors of the Moscow-based Institute of the Collective Security Treaty Organisation, who started sending Schaffhauser recommendations for Russia- and Ukraine-related statements.[239] It was also Plisyuk who arranged Schaffhauser's trip to the DNR to observe illegitimate 'parliamentary elections'.

The FN's economic strategist Bernard Monot said that Schaffhauser was essential in securing the deal with the Russian actors, and Schaffhauser himself confirmed that he had been paid €140,000 for his mediation.[240] As the FN's treasurer Wallerand de Saint-Just explained, the party had turned to many French and European banks for a loan. Allegedly they all refused, so the FN asked for a loan from a Russian bank.[241]

Confronted with critique, Marine Le Pen denied that the first Russian loan implied Russian political influence on the FN. In certain Russian pro-Kremlin analytical circles, however, the loan to the FN was considered as purchase of political leverage. In one of his interviews, the director of the Russian Institute of Strategic Planning Aleksandr Gusev, discussing presumable Russian successes in buying political influence in Europe, said:

> We have provided financial assistance [to the FN] through the First Czech-Russian Bank controlled by a person I will not name. . . . It is a private bank, but the decision was unlikely taken without our political leaders.[242]

The Russian-Ukrainian war deepened cooperation between various Russian actors and the FN. In March 2014, Chauprade travelled to Russia-occupied Crimea to observe the illegal 'referendum'. Marine Le Pen paid another visit to Moscow in April that year. As the EU imposed sanctions on several prominent Russian officials for the annexation of Crimea, she declared, during a meeting with Naryshkin, that she was 'surprised a Cold War on Russia [had] been declared in the European Union'[243] and that the sanctions were counterproductive. She also backed Russia's idea to federalise Ukraine. Naryshkin thanked her for her 'balanced position on the developments in Ukraine'.[244]

The 'Ukrainian question' was the focus of the speech of Naryshkin's deputy Andrey Isayev at the FN's 15th Congress that took place on 29–30 November 2014. Accompanied to the congress by Andrey Klimov, Isayev insisted that 'the developments in Ukraine were instrumentalised to put pressure on Russia' and that the United States forced the EU to introduce anti-Russian sanctions.[245] The FN's congress also hosted the FPÖ's Heinz-Christian Strache, LN's Matteo Salvini, PVV's Geert Wilders, and Krasimir Karakachanov, a former collaborator of the State Security agency in socialist Bulgaria[246] and leader of the far-right Balgarsko Natsionalno Dvizhenie (Bulgarian National Movement).[247] Isayev's participation in the FN's congress seemed to have strengthened Le Pen's conviction that Russian ruling elites were willing to cooperate with the FN. After the congress, she sent a letter to Isayev, republished on the website of 'Yedinaya Rossia', that, in particular, read: 'Your participation as a political ally and friend in our struggle for the European of Nations and Freedoms has done us a high honour. . . . The strengthening of the voice of people in Europe portends a great future for our cooperation'.[248]

At the end of May 2014, as revealed by Austrian investigative journalist Bernhard Odehnal, Malofeev convened – with the logistical help from Nathalie Holzmüller – a secret meeting in Vienna.[249] Among the participants of the meeting, several people were identified by Odehnal's sources: the FN's Marion Maréchal-Le Pen and Aymeric Chauprade; Aleksandr Dugin and nationalist painter Ilya Glazunov; Heinz-Christian Strache, Johann Gudenus and Johann Herzog from the FPÖ; Bulgarian far-right Ataka's leader Volen Siderov; Prince Sixtus Henry of Bourbon-Parma; and Serge de Pahlen, president of the Swiss financial company Edifin Services. The official topic was the 'Congress of Vienna', referring to a series of meetings of representatives of European states and Russia that were held in 1814–1815 and eventually established the 'Holy Alliance' that aimed at containing the spread of secularism and republicanism in Europe, and 'confirmed that the big countries had certain *legitimate interests* and established *specific spheres* of influence' in Europe[250] – a development that Putin's regime would be willing to duplicate. Despite the official theme, the participants of the far-right meeting discussed how to 'save Europe from liberalism and the "satanic" gay lobby'.[251]

To a certain extent, this secret meeting was a prelude to a major conference called 'Large Family and Future of Humanity' that was held in Moscow on 10–11 September 2014. This conference was originally planned as an annual meeting of the anti-LGBT 'pro-family' organisation World Congress of Families (WCF) represented in Russia by Malofeev's associate Aleksey Komov. But the main office of the WCF located in the United States decided to refashion the event because the United States imposed sanctions on several Russian officials who would take part in the meeting and the WCF did not want to risk its reputation at home.[252] Officially, the conference in Moscow was organised by the Centre of National Glory of Russia and St Andrew the First-Called Foundation – both organisations controlled by Vladimir Yakunin who at that time was still Russian Railways CEO – with the support of Malofeev's Saint Basil the Great Charitable Foundation and the Patriarch's Commission on the Family Issues headed by Komov. This high-profile event hosted around 1500 people from 45 countries. Oleg Morozov, then chief of the Domestic Politics Department of the Presidential Administration, communicated Putin's address to the participants of the conference.[253] Chauprade had the privilege to take part in the plenary session of the conference sitting at one table with Patriarch of Moscow and All Rus Vladimir (Kirill) Gundyaev, Chief Rabbi of Russia Berel Lazar, Supreme Mufti of Russia Talgat Tajuddin,[254] Yakunin, Malofeev, Morozov, Mizulina and some other important figures.

In his speech, Chauprade talked about the fight against those who 'lobbied the interests of people and organisations promoting the interests of non-traditionally oriented citizens.' He claimed that there was 'an ideological struggle, a geopolitical struggle, . . . a struggle of the values of the so-called liberal philosophy, the philosophy of materialism, but in fact of the force of the dictatorship of the matter, dictatorship of materialism against the ideology of spirit'.[255]

Also present at the conference were Fabrice Sorlin and Johann Gudenus. The latter criticised the Western sanctions against Russia, lambasted US politics, and attacked 'trends towards gender equality' in Europe.[256] According to the communications leaked by the Anonymous International hacktivist group,[257] Yakunin's St Andrew the First-Called Foundation covered Chauprade's and Sorlin's travelling expenses, while Chauprade, Gudenus and Sorlin were invited by Malofeev's Saint Basil the Great Charitable Foundation to a gala dinner closing the conference. Other notable invitees to the gala dinner included the leaders of the WCF, Dugin, Komov, Zurab Chavchavadze, Igor Shchegolev, and Georgiy Shevkunov (Father Tikhon).

In July-August 2014, three members of the FN from Saint-Nazaire – namely Gauthier Bouchet (Christian Bouchet's son), Jean-Claude Blanchard and Stéphanie Sutter – started yet another pro-Russian effort launching a group called 'Mistral, gagnons!' (Mistral, win!) that supported delivery of two French Mistral helicopter carriers to Russia. The two Mistral carriers stationed in Saint-Nazaire, indeed, were to be delivered to Russia in 2014, but, due to the annexation of Crimea and Russia's aggression against Ukraine, President Hollande first put the deal on hold and then cancelled it altogether. 'Mistral, gagnons!' organised various protests against the suspension of the delivery and distributed appeals arguing that, by delivering the Mistral carriers to Russia, they would 'protect the Saint-Nazaire industry', express their freedom to trade with whoever they wanted, and show that 'the weight of international relations [could not] prevent us from fellowship by trade'.[258] The activities of 'Mistral, gagnons!' were not determined by economic considerations alone: the presence of flags of the DNR at the protests organised by the group put the activities of 'Mistral, gagnons!' in ideological perspective.[259]

'Mistral, gagnons!' were not the only French far-right activists who expressed their sympathies towards the DNR. Schaffhauser travelled to Eastern Ukraine to observe the illegitimate 'elections' held by the DNR on 2 November 2014. In May 2015, he also was one of the initiators of the conference 'Donbass: Yesterday, Today, Tomorrow' held in Donetsk, the 'capital' of the DNR. Officially, the conference discussed 'peace settlement in and development of Donbass'.[260] But it was essentially an attempt at demonising the liberal West supporting Ukraine, as well as legitimising the unrecognised 'state' of the DNR through participation in the conference of various foreign politicians, activists and journalists.[261] The conference hosted over 20 foreign participants representing different political forces ranging from the far left to the far right of the political spectrum.[262] Apart from Schaffhauser, the far right was represented by Manuel Ochsenreiter, editor of the German magazine *Zuerst!*, and Markus Frohnmaier of the JAfD. Schaffhauser participated in the plenary session sitting together with the leaders of the DNR and Aleksey Zhuravlyov of the 'Yedinaya Rossiya' and 'Rodina'. During his speech at the conference, Schaffhauser recited the Soviet-style narrative about the 'hawkish Other' and 'dovish Us':

If Paris, Berlin, Moscow and Beijing come together, the US will turn into a small island, but they are not fine with this. . . . Europe does not want the end of the war [in the Donetsk Basin]. As for us, we need peace, and we have to find partners for bringing peace.[263]

The conference was also attended by Alain Fragny, a former member of the French far-right Bloc Identitaire (Identitarian Bloc) in Cannes, and Emmanuel Leroy of the AAFER and FN.[264] Following the tradition of the Le Pen family who founded the implicitly pro-Hussein NGO 'SOS Enfants d'Irak' in 1995, Fragny and Leroy established, in September 2014, a 'humanitarian association' Urgence Enfants d'Ukraine (Children of Ukraine Emergency), with Fragny as president and Leroy as vice-president. The main objective of the association was 'to provide help and moral and material aid to Ukrainians affected by the conflicts, especially children in difficult circumstances'.[265] Introducing their association, Leroy revealed the ideological side of the initiative going beyond helping Ukrainian children, linking it to his understanding of geopolitics: 'We clearly understand the reasons why NATO wants to increase pressure on Russia through destabilisation or taking control of former states of the Soviet Union such as Georgia and Ukraine, and even through the war in Syria'.[266] During their visit to Donetsk in May, representatives of Urgence Enfants d'Ukraine supposedly brought €3,000 to buy clothing and toys to children in an accident hospital,[267] and then decided to change the name of their association into Urgence Enfants du Donbass (Donbass Children Emergency), because the word 'Ukraine' was allegedly associated in the DNR with 'death, tortures, [and] abominations'.[268] In December 2015, the representatives of Urgence Enfants du Donbass went to Donetsk again, and donated, according to their own report, €8,000 for the renovation of a children's home, purchase of toys and the treatment of four children injured in the Russian-Ukrainian war.[269] The second visit of Urgence Enfants du Donbass was reported in French and English by the Russian website Sputnik,[270] but the international media ignored these activities.

There is no publicly available evidence that FN's leadership or members attempted to develop potential business relations with the Russian representatives. However, the case of Philippe de Villiers seems to point in this direction. De Villiers is the French businessman and politician. He is the founder of the historical theme park 'Puy du Fou' in France and was a presidential nominee of the conservative and Eurosceptic Mouvement pour la France (Movement for France) for the 2007 presidential election. Chauprade was an international advisor to de Villiers before the former joined the FN.[271] In April 2014, de Villiers visited Russia-annexed Crimea and had talks with 'Prime Minister' Sergey Aksyonov. On 14 August the same year, de Villiers met with Putin in Yalta. The next day the media reported that de Villiers, Aksyonov and Malofeev signed an agreement stating that de Villiers would build an historical theme park in Crimea by the year 2019 for 4 billion Russian roubles (around €83 million at that time).[272] By the time of the writing, however, no further developments in this direction have been reported.

Due to the sanctions imposed on Russia and Crimea, de Villiers may have problems doing business in the annexed Ukrainian republic. It may also be the case that the publicised plan to build a theme park in Crimea were a stunt aimed at showing that some successful Western businessmen recognised Crimea as 'an entity of the Russian Federation'.

Despite the seemingly good relations between the FN and Putin's regime, their 'love affair' seemed to stumble in 2016. The first allusions to an emerging rift surfaced in February 2016 when the FN's treasurer Wallerand de Saint-Just claimed that the party experienced problems with applying for loans from French banks to run the 2017 parliamentary and presidential campaign, and that the party had applied for a €27 million loan from an unnamed Russian bank.[273] The latter statement suggested that the deal with the FCRB was somehow thrown into question. In March 2016, Russian media reported that the workings of the FCRB had been limited by banking regulators already in January that year,[274] and, later, the state-controlled Central Bank of Russia withdrew a banking licence from the FCRB and, eventually, declared it bankrupt.[275] Also in March that year, Jean-Luc Schaffhauser was trying – with the help of Babakov and Latvian consultant Vilis Dambiņš – to find another Russian bank from which the FN could borrow money, and Dambiņš suggested the Moscow-based bank 'Strategiya',[276] which was previously involved in the 'Russian Laundromat' scheme.[277] The FN's executive bureau officially decided to borrow €3 million from 'Strategiya' in June 2016 to finance electoral campaigns,[278] but a month later the Central Bank of Russia revoked a banking license from 'Strategiya',[279] and there is no evidence that the FN managed to obtain a loan from it. After the failure of the deal with 'Strategiya', the FN was trying to obtain the same €3 million loan from the Russian bank NKB, but its banking license was also revoked in December 2016.[280]

The financial problems of the FN seemed to have less to do with the FCRB as such as with the internal political dynamics in France and their interpretation by the Russian ruling elites. The year 2016 was the year when the French centre-right party Les Républicains held its primaries to select a candidate for the 2017 French presidential election. In these primaries, which took place in November 2016, François Fillon defeated Alain Juppé. Among many differences between these two candidates, Fillon was known for his Moscow-friendly positions, while Juppé was, on the contrary, quite sceptical about Russia's domectic and international activities.[281]

Various public opinion polls conducted in November-December 2016 showed that Fillon would have a slight advantage over Le Pen in the first round of the 2017 presidential election but would win by a landslide in the second round against Le Pen.[282] Moscow seems to consider Fillon and Le Pen as 'pro-Russian' candidates, but since Fillon would likely win, the Kremlin's continuous support for Le Pen in the run-up to the presidential elections could compromise apparently good relations with the elected president. Another possible indication that there was a certain rift between Moscow and the FN was that it was Marion Maréchal-Le Pen, rather than Marine Le Pen, who travelled to Moscow in November 2016, which might imply that, at that time, there had been no agreement between the FN and Russian officials on the visit of the presidential candidate Marine Le Pen to Russia.

The situation started to change in January-February 2017 with the dramatic decline of popularity of Fillon and the rise of the pro-EU and Russia-sceptic candidate Emmanuel Macron. Public opinion polls suggested that Macron and Le Pen would win the first round of the presidential election, hence Le Pen would be the only 'Russia's candidate' in the second round. In the beginning of February, Russian state-controlled media outlets such as RT and Sputnik started publishing materials aimed at undermining the growing popularity of Macron. RT focused on Macron's highly paid position at Rothschild & Cie Banque controlled by the Rothschild family,[283] thus playing the anti-globalist and anti-Semitic card.[284] Referring to Nicolas Dhuicq, a French MP representing Les Républicains and a member of the board of the ADFR, Sputnik alleged that Macron was 'an agent of the big American banking system' and backed by a 'very wealthy gay lobby', as well as spreading rumours that Macron was secretly gay himself.[285]

Moscow's aim might still be the reversion of Fillon's decline, but since public opinion polls showed no hint at the recovery of Fillon's popularity, the Kremlin seemed to have been compelled to provide political support for Le Pen. At the invitation of the State Duma foreign affairs committee, Le Pen travelled to Moscow and met, on 24 March 2017, with Chairman of the State Duma Vyacheslav Volodin and, later, with President Putin. During the meeting, Putin claimed that Russia did not 'want to influence the events [i.e. the French electoral campaign] as they unfold[ed]', but admitted that he saw the FN as a representative of a European political force that was 'growing quickly'.[286] In her turn, Le Pen asserted that she urged 'the restoration of cultural, economic and strategic ties between Russia and France' and called for 'a truly global strategy' in the fight against terrorism[287] – a narrative promoted by official Moscow itself. FN's officials, including Ludovic de Danne, denied that Le Pen discussed possibilities of obtaining Russian financial support during her visit to Moscow.[288]

Conclusion

Nine patterns have characterised the development of pro-Russian efforts of the far-right groups and political parties in Austria, Italy and France, which have increasingly started operating as pro-Kremlin front organisations in these countries.

First, the pro-Russian efforts in Italy and France drew upon the pre-existing pro-Russian sentiments within the far-right milieus of these countries. The Austrian case is different, because the FPÖ, which has largely monopolised the far-right political scene in Austria, was never characterised by these sentiments until its pro-Moscow turn in 2007–2008.

Second, pro-Russian activities in Italy and France were initially undertaken by marginal far-right groups that had limited or no political influence in their respective societies. This also applies to the Austrian case with one caveat: Austrian Technologies GmbH, which launched the initial pro-Russian actions, was a politically insignificant organisation too, but had strong links to the FPÖ. Barbara Kappel's Austrian Technologies GmbH can be partially compared to the French Association Alliance France-Europe Russie run by Fabrice Sorlin and Emmanuel Leroy: Kappel, Sorlin and Leroy headed marginal organisations, but were connected to established political parties that picked up their pro-Moscow initiatives and brought them to a new, more significant level.

Third, the Russian-Georgian war in August 2008 became a trigger for the launch of the first far-right pro-Russian activities in Austria and France. This war, interpreted from a Russian perspective as Georgia's aggression against South Ossetia, was in the focus of Austrian Technologies GmbH and André Chanclu's Collectif France-Russie. In contrast, the Russian-Georgian war garnered little attention in the Italian far-right circles.

Fourth, there are six types of structures and individuals – referred to here as 'operators' – who furthered, at various stages, cooperation between the far right in the above-mentioned countries, on the one side, and Russian actors linked to the Kremlin, on the other:

1   *'Russophile' activist operators.* Individuals such as Johann Gudenus, Max Ferrari, Fabrice Sorlin and Aymeric Chauprade played an important role in either initiating or consolidating the pro-Russian turns of their respective parties.
2   *Russian activist operators.* Individuals such as Aleksandr Dugin and Maksim Shevchenko contributed to the consolidation of the European far right's pro-Russian efforts. Their involvement seemed to be driven by their own political or ideological interests and resembled earlier attempts of Russian ultranationalists to build and develop relations with Western far-right activists and politicians – attempts that had earlier failed to produce any meaningful results.
3   *Russian soft power operators.* Rossotrudnichestvo, an institution aiming to influence public opinion outside Russia and cooperating with Russian-speaking diasporas, was an important actor that helped forge closer relations between Austrian and Italian far-right organisations, on the one hand, and Russian elites, on the other. The FRM seems to have played a certain role in forging such relations in the Italian case, but failed to advance them because Tiberio Graziani's Istituto di Alti Studi in Geopolitica e Scienze Ausiliarie, with which it cooperated, was too marginal to be of interest to the Russian elites. Natalya Narochnitskaya's Paris-based Institute of Democracy and Cooperation provided a useful Russian connection in the Italian and French cases, but only at the initial stages of the development of far-right pro-Russian efforts.
4   *Ultraconservative operators.* Aleksey Komov and, especially, Konstantin Malofeev were important in introducing Italian, French, and – to a lesser extent – Austrian far-right politicians into the Russian ultraconservative, religious and homophobic milieu that had access to Russian policy-makers through high-level contacts of Malofeev and Vladimir Yakunin.

5   *Diplomatic operators.* Russian embassies and consulates in the three countries helped formalise the relations between the far-right organisations and Russian officials.
6   *Russian power operators.* 'Yedinaya Rossiya' members encouraged pro-Russian efforts of the far-right organisations in the three countries. Especially important, in the Italian and French cases, were Chairman of the State Duma Sergey Naryshkin and the head of the Duma foreign affairs committee Aleksey Pushkov, who became key points of contact for the Lega Nord and Front National in their relations with the Russian ruling elites.

Fifth, pro-Russian efforts of the far-right organisations involved a repetition of narratives propagated by the Russian authorities: the Russian-Georgian war in August 2008 is a fault of Georgia's then President Mikheil Saakashvili; the South Stream pipeline is beneficial to the EU countries involved in the project; the Russian annexation of Crimea is legitimate; the territories in Eastern Ukraine controlled by pro-Russian separatists and Russian troops are legitimate 'People's Republics'; Western sanctions against Russia in response to the annexation of Crimea and invasion of Eastern Ukraine damage European economies; the United States forced the EU to introduce anti-Russian sanctions; France should deliver Mistral helicopter carriers to Russia; homophobic laws adopted in Russia are justified.

Sixth, far-right politicians in Austria and France used the issue of helping children in Russia and occupied East Ukrainian territories as a means of creating a favourable impression on the Russian officials with whom they wanted to cooperate. This tradition in the far-right milieu goes back to the 1990s when the Le Pen family founded 'SOS Enfants d'Irak' to strengthen relations with Saddam Hussein.

Seventh, the FPÖ and LN have been interested in developing business relations with various Russian actors in addition to their political pro-Russian efforts. This may also be indirectly true in the French case: Philippe de Villiers, who wanted to build theme parks in Moscow and Russia-occupied Crimea, has cooperated with Aymeric Chauprade, but de Villiers is not officially affiliated with the FN.

Eighth, the pro-Russian efforts of the far right in the three cases ran concurrently with, or were complemented by, the participation of politicians such as Johannes Hübner, Johann Gudenus, Claudio D'Amico, Aymeric Chauprade, and Jean-Luc Schaffhauser in international observation of illegitimate 'electoral procedures' in Crimea and Eastern Ukraine.

Ninth, only the French and Italian far-right leaders had the honour to talk to the most influential figure in Russia, although there is no conclusive evidence that Matteo Salvini's 20-minute talk with Vladimir Putin in 2014 has resulted in any significant Russian support for the LN. At the same time, only the FPÖ and LN have been so far successful in concluding agreements on collaboration with the ruling 'Yedinaya Rossiya' party – a move that offers, at least in the FPÖ's case, vast opportunities for further cooperation with official Moscow.

The final chapter looks at pro-Kremlin activities of European far-right politicians at conferences organised by Sergey Naryshkin, and during particular sessions of the European Parliament debating Russia-related resolutions.

Notes

1   See also Anton Shekhovtsov, Andreas Umland, "Is Aleksandr Dugin a Traditionalist? 'Neo-Eurasianism' and Perennial Philosophy", *The Russian Review*, Vol. 68, No. 4 (2009), pp. 662–678.

2   In 2014, Tempbank and Gagloev were sanctioned by the US "for providing material support and services to the Government of Syria", see "Treasury Sanctions Syrian Regime Officials and Supporters", *US Department of the Treasury*, 8 May (2014), https://treasury.gov/press-center/press-releases/Pages/jl2391.aspx

3   Clover, *Black Wind*, pp. 275–276, 279.

4   "Historic Moscow Conference", *DavidDuke.com*, 20 June (2006), http://davidduke.com/historic-moscow-conference-press-release/

5   Arnold, Romanova, "The 'White World's Future?'", p. 97.

6   " 'Euro-Rus', une association d'Indo-européens blancs pour la 'Grande Europe' ", *RésistanceS*, 22 December (2006), http://resistances.be/eurorus.html

7   Miroslav Mareš, Martin Laryš, "The Transnational Relations of the Contemporary Russian Extreme Right", *Europe-Asia Studies*, Vol. 67, No. 7 (2015), pp. 1056–1078 (1065).

8   "4655/AB XXII. GP", *Österreichisches Parlament*, 10 November (2006), https://parlament.gv.at/PAKT/VHG/XXII/AB/AB_04655/imfname_070540.pdf.

9   See https://web.archive.org/web/20080530013741/http://www.bmvit.gv.at/service/links/innovation/index.html

10   "943/AB XXIV. GP", *Österreichisches Parlament*, 10 April (2009), https://parlament.gv.at/PAKT/VHG/XXIV/AB/AB_00943/fname_155513.pdf

11   Katrin Burgstaller, Benedikt Narodoslawsky, " 'Unsere Politik ist nicht populistisch, sondern pragmatisch' ", *Der Standard*, 11 May (2011), http://derstandard.at/130455 1367527/derStandardat-Interview-Unsere-Politik-ist-nicht-populistisch-sondern-pragmatisch

12   "Barbara Kappel", *European Parliament – MEPs*, http://europarl.europa.eu/meps/en/125024/BARBARA_KAPPEL_cv.html

13   "943/AB XXIV. GP".

14   "We Think Global, Act Global and Go Global", *Austrian Technologies*, https://web.archive.org/web/20160405183335/http://www.austriantechnologies.at

15   "Konferenz 'Europe-Russia-Georgia: Peace Building I' ", *Austrian Technologies*, 20 October (2008), https://web.archive.org/web/20090607034041/http://www.austriantechnologies.at:80/unser-fokus/konferenzen-und-workshops/europe-russia-georgia-peace-building-i/

16   *Bericht des Rechnungshofes. Förderung der staatsbürgerlichen Bildungsarbeit in den Bildungseinrichtungen der politischen Parteien* (Vienna: Rechnungshof, 2014), p. 328.

17   The strong connection to the Civic Chamber led the Russian media to claim that the Civic Chamber was the Russian co-organiser of the conference; they do not mention Shevchenko's Centre. In its turn, Austrian Technologies GmbH did not mention the Civic Chamber.

18   Yur'eva, "Diktator nedostoin diplomatii", p. 2.

19   "Strache: Europa ist ohne Russland nicht denkbar", *APA-OTS*, 24 May (2007), http://ots.at/presseaussendung/OTS_20070524_OTS0059/strache-europa-ist-ohne-russland-nicht-denkbar

20   "Überaus herzlicher Gedankenaustausch von HC Strache und Moskauer Oberbürgermeister Luschkow", *APA-OTS*, 16 December (2008), http://ots.at/presseaussendung/

OTS_20081216_OTS0054/ueberaus-herzlicher-gedankenaustausch-von-hc-strache-und-moskauer-oberbuergermeister-luschkow

21 Aleksandr Dugin, "V Evrope mnogo druzey Rossii", *Russia.ru*, 19 February (2009), www.russia.ru/video/duginbal/

22 "Eurasischer Rechtsextremismus in Wien", *Dokumentationsarchiv des österreichischen Widerstandes*, June (2014), http://doew.at/erkennen/rechtsextremismus/neues-von-ganz-rechts/archiv/juni-2014/eurasischer-rechtsextremismus-in-wien

23 "Konferenz 'Europe-Russia-Georgia: Peace Building II'", *Austrian Technologies*, 25 May (2009), https://web.archive.org/web/20100124144014/http://www.austriantechnologies.at/unser-fokus/konferenzen/europe-russia-georgia-peace-building-ii/

24 In 2011, Dugin, Shevchenko, Khazin and Pirveli would join the Florian Geyer Conceptual Club established by now late Dzhemal and named after Florian Geyer who lead the peasants during the German Peasants' War (1524 to 1525). The NSDAP praised Geyer as a hero and, in 1944, the 8th SS Cavalry Division was named after him.

25 Manfred Andexinger, "Woche der Diplomatie", *Neue Freie Zeitung*, No. 47, 26 November (2009), pp. 14–15 (15).

26 Ivan Shataev, "Dialog protiv konflikta", *Socialist*, 26 November (2009), http://socialistinfo.ru/comments/387.html

27 "Konferenz: '55 Jahre Staatsvertrag – eine Betrachtung aus österreichisch-russischer Sicht'", *Austrian Technologies*, 29 January (2010), http://austriantechnologies.at/vap/1262/Db/p16/i5/konferenz_55_jahre_staatsvertrag_eine_betrachtung_aus_oesterreichisch-russischer.html. The page is no longer available.

28 Curiously, Lothar Höbelt is also the author of former FPÖ leader Jörg Haider's biography, see Lothar Höbelt, *Defiant Populist: Jörg Haider and the Politics of Austria* (West Lafayette: Purdue University Press, 2003).

29 "About Rossotrudnichestvo", *Rossotrudnichestvo*, http://rs.gov.ru/en/about

30 Elena Chernenko, "'Myagkuyu silu' snabzhayut sredstvami", *Kommersant. Daily*, No. 95, 5 June (2013), p. 1.

31 Lutsevych, *Agents of the Russian World*, p. 10.

32 Quoted in Juris Pakalniņš (dir.), *The Master Plan* (Riga: Mistrus Media, 2016).

33 "Mezhdunarodnaya konferentsiya '55 let Gosudarstvennogo dogovora – razmyshleniya s rossiyskoy i avstriyskoy storony'", *Rossotrudnichestvo*, 29 January (2010), http://old.rs.gov.ru/node/8378. My emphasis. The page is no longer available.

34 "Konferenz mit Russland-Schwerpunkt: 'Farbige Revolution in den GUS-Ländern und ihre aktuellen Auswirkungen'", *Austrian Technologies*, 4 June (2010), http://austriantechnologies.at/vap/1262/Db/p16/i6/konferenz_mit_russland-schwerpunkt_farbige_revolution_in_den_gus-laendern_und_ih.html. The page is no longer available.

35 "Ob itogakh 'tsvetnykh revolyutsiy'", *Sootechestvennik*, No. 56 (2010), http://sootechestvennik.com/index.php/news/1-info/407-colorrev

36 "V Groznom obsudili obshchestvenno-politicheskuyu situatsiyu v respublike", *Grozny-inform*, 6 February (2012), http://www.grozny-inform.ru/news/society/31804/

37 Eduard Steiner, "Gudenus: Geheime FPÖ-Mission nach Tschetschenien", *Die Presse*, 7 February (2012), http://diepresse.com/home/politik/innenpolitik/730447/Gudenus_Geheime-FPOMission-nach-Tschetschenien; "FPÖ-Delegation besucht tschetschenischen Präsidenten Kadyrow", *Der Standard*, 7 February (2012), http://derstandard.at/1328507166001/Geheime-Mission-am-Kaukasus-FPOe-Delegation-besucht-tschetschenischen-Praesidenten-Kadyrow; "'Frieden und Ruhe' in Grosny", *ORF*, 9 February (2012), http://news.orf.at/stories/2103993/2103995/

38 Nikolay Sergeev, Sergey Mashkin, Seda Yegikyan, "Na Ramzana Kadyrova vozlagayut Venu", *Kommersant. Daily*, No. 76, 29 April (2010), p. 1.

39 "FP-Gudenus/Hübner: FPÖ-Erfolg für Österreich – Präsident Kadyrow will Wirtschaftsflüchtlinge zurückholen!", *APA-OTS*, 8 February (2012), http://ots.at/presseaussendung/OTS_20120208_OTS0180/fp-gudenushuebner-fpoe-erfolg-fuer-oesterreich-praesident-kadyrow-will-wirtschaftsfluechtlinge-zurueckholen

40 Steiner, "Gudenus: Geheime FPÖ-Mission".

41 Herwig G. Höller, "Moskaus blaue Freunde", *Die Zeit*, 29 September (2014), http://zeit.de/2014/40/russland-oesterreich-kreml-fpoe/komplettansicht.

42 "Osoboe mnenie", *Ekho Moskvy*, 25 February (2016), http://echo.msk.ru/programs/personalno/1718570-echo/

43 Saskia Jungnikl, Benedikt Narodoslawsky, "Blitzblaues Blut", *Datum*, 1 March (2011), www.datum.at/artikel/blitzblaues-blut/seite/alle/

44 "Über mich", *Johann Gudenus*, http://jgudenus.at/zur-person/; Natalya Barabash, " 'My s Kadyrovym nashli obshchiy yazyk' ", *Vzglyad*, 10 May (2012), http://vz.ru/politics/2012/5/10/578121.html

45 Kuzmin, "Nataliya Khol'tsmyuller", p. 74.

46 Ibid.

47 Yuriy Kozlov, "Muzykal'noe suare 'Iz Rossii – s lyubov'yu' stalo prekrasnym rozhdestvenskim podarkom dlya avstriyskikh lyubiteley muzyki", *ITAR-TASS*, 7 December (2012), republished on the website of the "Russian Ball", see http://russianball.info/rus/about.php

48 Holzmüller's letter republished in Sergey Golovinov, "Vitse-gubernatora Kolkova obvinyayut vo lzhi?", *Zebra-TV*, 27 January (2015), http://zebra-tv.ru/novosti/chetvertaya-rubrika/vitse-gubernatora-kolkova-obvinyayut-vo-lzhi/

49 "Kultur im Dienste Russlands", *Info-Direkt*, No. 1 (2015), pp. 42–43 (43).

50 I am grateful to Herwig Höller for sharing this information with me.

51 "Erweiterter Vorstand der ORFG", *Österreichisch-Russische Freundschaftsgesellschaft*, http://orfg.net/?page=7-erweiterter-vorstand-der-orfg

52 "Strache: 'Nicht Russland ist Aggressor der letzten Jahrzehnte' ", *Die Presse*, 24 March (2015), http://diepresse.com/home/politik/innenpolitik/4692491/Strache_Nicht-Russland-ist-Aggressor-der-letzten-Jahrzehnte; "Zhurfiks s Khaynts-Kristianom Shtrakhe", *Österreichisch-Russische Freundschaftsgesellschaft*, 24 March (2015), http://orfg.net/?news=show&id=48

53 I am grateful to Bernhard Odehnal for sharing these observations with me.

54 Höller, "Moskaus blaue Freunde". See also Sofia Khomenko, "FPÖ: Aus Liebe zu Russland", *Mokant*, 30 June (2015), http://mokant.at/1506-fpoe-russland-ukraine-geld/

55 Ilya Vinogradov, "Avstriya stala blizhe", *Kapital*, No. 6, 22 February (2006); Anastasiya Tyuleneva, "Chto v Rossii avstriyskogo", *Stroitel*, No. 282, 12 March (2008), p. 3.

56 "Austria Showcase Russian Federation. St. Petersburg 'Exportinitiative Umwelttechnologien', 17.06. – 19.06.2007", *Advantage Austria*, http://advantageaustria.org/ru/oesterreich-in-russia/news/local/BusinessGuide08062007.pdf

57 Herwig G. Höller, "Die Mutter des Wunderwassers", *Die Zeit*, 27 October (2011), http://zeit.de/2011/44/A-Kappel

58 "Bionic Water", *Aquabionica*, https://web.archive.org/web/20131010224732/http://en.aquabionica.com/products/product/water/

59 *The Official Catalog of the Company "Aquabionica Life"* (Vienna: Aquabionica Life, 2013), pp. 6–7.

60 Höller, "Die Mutter des Wunderwassers".

61 "Überaus herzlicher Gedankenaustausch".

62 "Vstrecha s rukovodstvom Avstriyskoy partii svobody v RTsNK v Vene", *Rossotrudnichestvo*, 21 December (2011), http://old.rs.gov.ru/node/29083; "Avstriyskie pravye peredali rozhdestvenskie podarki rossiyskim sirotam, *RIA Novosti*, 13 December (2014), http://ria.ru/world/20141213/1038013138.html

63 "Moskauer Kinder von FPÖ empfangen", *APA-OTS*, 22 September (2010), http://ots.at/presseaussendung/OTS_20100922_OTS0051/moskauer-kinder-von-fpoe-empfangen-bild

64 "Soobshchenie press-sluzhby gubernatora Moscovskoy oblasti", *Moskovskaya oblast*, 11 May (2011), http://old.mosreg.ru/oficial_chronicle/60539.html. My emphasis.

65 "V Groznom obsudili obshchestvenno-politicheskuyu situatsiyu v respublike".
66 "Chechenskie parlamentarii pobyvali v Avstrii", *Parlament Chechenskoy Respubliki*, 18 May (2012), http://old.parlamentchr.ru/content/view/1474/
67 "Summing-up YIEF-2016 – Two Records, 70 Billion Roubles of Investment . . . and a Resounding NO to Sanctions", *Yalta International Economic Forum*, 16 April (2016), http://forumyalta.com/news/81/
68 "Bolgariya namerena sozdat' bioenergeticheskiy klaster v Krymu", *Business Place*, 15 February (2015), http://businessplace.info/175-investicii-bolgarii-v-krym.html
69 "II YaMEF glazami uchastnikov: zarubezhnye delegaty", *Yalta International Economic Forum*, 14 April (2016), http://forumyalta.com/news/54/?langswitch=ru
70 "Summing-up YIEF-2016".
71 "Time to Invest in Russia. On the Sidelines of the 2nd YIEF, a Meeting Was Held between Foreign Delegations and Leaders of Crimea", a press release of the Yalta International Economic Forum Foundation, p. 2.
72 Oliver Treib, "Party Patronage in Austria: From Reward to Control", in Petr Kopecký, Petr Mair, Maria Spirova (eds), *Party Patronage and Party Government in European Democracies* (Oxford: Oxford University Press, 2012), pp. 31–53 (35).
73 Ashwien Sankholkar, "Das Comeback des Herbert Stepic", *Trend*, 3 April (2014), http://trend.at/home/comeback-herbert-stepic-5586808; Andrea Hodoschek, "Übergabe bei Leitls", *Kurier*, 19 July (2015), http://kurier.at/wirtschaft/uebergabe-bei-leitls/142.177.153
74 See more on Russia's economic ties to Austria in Roman Kupchinsky, *Gazprom's European Web* (Washington: Jamestown Foundation, 2009).
75 "Leitl kritisiert Sanktionen: 'Wirtschaft nicht missbrauchen'", *Der Standard*, 30 July (2014), http://derstandard.at/2000003713801/Leitl-kritisiert-Sanktionen-Wirtschaft-nicht-missbrauchen; "Leitl: 'Sanktionen gegen Russland sind Unsinn und bewegen nichts'", *Der Standard*, 29 December (2015), http://derstandard.at/2000028245568/Leitl-Sanktionen-gegen-Russland-sind-Unsinn-und-bewegen-nichts
76 "Raiffeisen Remains Committed to 'Attractive' Russian Market", *The Moscow Times*, 5 September (2014), http://themoscowtimes.com/news//business/article/raiffeisen-remains-committed-to-attractive-russian-market/506541.html
77 "Hofer besser als Strache", *OE24*, 9 December (2016), http://oe24.at/oesterreich/politik/Hofer-besser-als-Strache/261658295
78 According to Claus Pandi, editor of *Kronenzeitung*, also part of the FPÖ delegation was Stefan Magnet, who is presumably directly connected to the Austrian, openly pro-Putin far right printed magazine *Info-Direkt* discussed briefly in Chapter 5, see "Öllinger zu FPÖ-Moskau-Reise: Offenlegung aller Details des blauen Moskau-Deals gefordert", *APA-OTS*, 19 December (2016), http://ots.at/presseaussendung/OTS_20161219_OTS0112/oellinger-zu-fpoe-moskau-reise-offenlegung-aller-details-des-blauen-moskau-deals-gefordert
79 "FPÖ schließt Fünf-Jahres-Vertrag mit Kreml-Partei", *Die Presse*, 19 December (2016), http://diepresse.com/home/politik/innenpolitik/5136136/FPOe-schliesst-FuenfJahresVertrag-mit-KremlPartei
80 Ibid. *Arbeitsfreude* is a controversial term in German language today. Originally, it was "the guiding spirit of the German Werkbund, a 1907 alliance of artisans, craftsmen, and industrialists who aimed at revitalizing German culture by combining industry with artistry" and wanted "to reject Victorian excess and revive the craftsmanship that had existed in medieval times", see Richard Donkin, *The History of Work* (Basingstoke: Palgrave Macmillan, 2010), pp. 192–193. However, the NSDAP hijacked the term *Arbeitsfreude* and used it for its own propaganda purposes.
81 "FPÖ schließt Fünf-Jahres-Vertrag mit Kreml-Partei".
82 "'Yedinaya Rossiya' podpisala soglashenie o sotrudnichestve s Avstriyskoy partiey svobody", *Yedinaya Rossiya*, 19 December (2016), https://er.ru/news/149954/

83 See Giovanni Savino, "From Evola to Dugin: The Neo-Eurasianist Connection in Italy", in Laruelle (ed.), *Eurasianism and the European Far Right*, pp. 97–124 (114).

84 See also a discussion on Dugin and Evola between Andreas Umland and A. James Gregor in Roger Griffin, Werner Loh, Andreas Umland (eds), *Fascism Past and Present, West and East: An International Debate on Concepts and Cases in the Comparative Study of the Extreme Right* (Stuttgart: *ibidem*-Verlag, 2006).

85 Savino, "From Evola to Dugin", p. 108.

86 "Documento politico del Coordinamento Progetto Eurasia", *Contitente Eurasia*, No. 5 (2006), p. 13.

87 Ibid., p. 13.

88 "Presidio C.P.E. davanti alla base di Ghedi", *Facebook*, 30 March (2008), https://facebook.com/roberto.quadrelli.7/media_set?set=a.1355848147045.48614.1556721197

89 Luca Rossi, "I rapporti economici tra Italia e Russia: cronaca del seminario", *Coordinamento Progetto Eurasia*, 23 November (2010), http://cpeurasia.eu/1248/i-rapporti-economici-tra-italia-e-russia-cronaca-del-seminario

90 Ibid.

91 Savino, "From Evola to Dugin", p. 110.

92 Tiberio Graziani, "From the Universal Imposition of Western Standards to a Peer-to-Peer Dialogue of Civilizations", *World Public Forum "Dialogue of Civilizations"*, 18 October (2012), http://wpfdc.org/blog/society/18662-from-the-universal-imposition-of-western-standards-to-a-peer-to-peer-dialogue-of-civilizations

93 "Ukaz Prezidenta Rossiyskoy Federatsii ot 21.06.2007 No. 796 'O sozdanii fonda "Russkiy mir"'", *Prezident Rossii*, 21 June (2007), http://kremlin.ru/acts/bank/25689

94 Sherr, *Hard Diplomacy and Soft Coercion*, pp. 87–88.

95 Andrew Foxall, "The Kremlin's Sleight of Hand: Russia's Soft Power Offensive in the UK", Russia Studies Centre Policy Paper No. 3 (London: The Henry Jackson Society, 2015), p. 3, http://henryjacksonsociety.org/wp-content/uploads/2015/02/The-Kremlins-Sleight-of-Hand.pdf

96 Heather A. Conley, Theodore P. Gerber, Lucy Moore, Mihaela David, *Russian Soft Power in the 21st Century: An Examination of Russian Compatriot Policy in Estonia* (Washington: Center for Strategic & International Studies, 2011), p. 15.

97 "V Rimskom Universitete La Sap'yentsa otkrylsya Tsentr rossiyskikh issledovaniy Fonda 'Russkiy mir'", *Rossotrudnichestvo*, 12 December 2010, http://old.rs.gov.ru/node/21725

98 "Tiberio Graziani al Forum Innovazioni Italia-Russia", *Istituto di Alti Studi in Geopolitica e Scienze Ausiliarie*, 14 December (2011), http://istituto-geopolitica.eu/143/tiberio-graziani-al-forum-innovazioni-italia-russia

99 Both projects are currently suspended. The South Stream project has suspended because it does not comply with the competition and energy legislation of the EU (Third Energy Package).

100 "Italia-Russia Forum Innovazioni 12–13 dicembre 2011", *Istituto di Studi Politici Economici e Sociali*, 9 December (2011), http://eurispes.eu/content/italia-russia-forum-innovazioni-12-13-dicembre-2011

101 François Stéphane, Schmitt Olivier, "L'extrême-droite française contemporaine et le monde: une vision 'alternative' des relations internationales", *¿Interrogations?*, No. 21 (2015), http://revue-interrogations.org/L-extreme-droite-francaise

102 See the website of the Master in Geopolitics and Global Security degree programme: http://mastergeopoliticaesicurezza.it

103 Savino, "From Evola to Dugin", p. 111.

104 Orazio Maria Gnerre, "La Comunità Economica Eurasiatica, modello di sviluppo multipolare", *Nomos*, No. 2 (2012), pp. 7–9 (8–9).

105 "Rally Against Anti-Russia Sanctions Takes Place in Italy's Bologna", *Sputnik*, 13 June (2015), http://sputniknews.com/europe/20150613/1023333742.html

106 Carlo Correr, "Putin Italian Fan Club", *Avanti!*, 6 October (2015), http://avantionline.it/2015/10/putin-italian-fan-club/

107 Fronte Nazionale Uffic., "Io sto con Putin"; Robert Mackey, "Italy's Far Right Salutes Putin for Anti-Gay Law and Support for Assad", *The Lede: The New York Times News Blog*, 12 September (2013), http://thelede.blogs.nytimes.com/2013/09/12/italys-far-right-salutes-putin-for-anti-gay-law-and-support-for-assad/

108 Marco Tarchi, "Recalcitrant Allies: The Conflicting Foreign Policy Agenda of the *Alleanza Nazionale* and the *Lega Nord*", in Christina Schori Liang (ed.), *Europe for the Europeans: The Foreign and Security Policy of the Populist Radical Right* (Aldershot: Ashgate, 2007), pp. 187–207 (194).

109 "Congresso Federale Lega Nord 2013 – Ambasciatore Russo Nazioni Unite Alexey Komov", *YouTube*, 18 December (2013), https://youtube.com/watch?v=DsgJtcNZZwQ

110 "Sovet direktorov (s 10 fevralya 2009 goda)", *Svyazinvest*, 10 February (2009), https://web.archive.org/web/20090221183128/http://svyazinvest.ru/manage

111 Rinat Sagdiev, Timofey Dzyadko, Irina Reznik, "Ne zamministra, a drug ministra", *Vedomosti*, No. 191, 11 October (2010), p. 16.

112 Igor Tsukanov, "Marshall pokupaet", *Vedomosti*, No. 171, 13 September (2010), p. 11.

113 Inna Erokhina, "Evgeniy Yurchenko nazval prichinu svoego uvol'neniya", *Kommersant. Daily*, No. 170, 15 September (2010), p. 13.

114 Andrei Soldatov, Irina Borogan, *The Red Web: The Struggle Between Russia's Digital Dictators and the New Online Revolutionaries* (New York: PublicAffairs, 2015), p. 196.

115 Oleg Sal'manov, "Kto spryatalsya v 'Rostelekome' ", *Vedomosti*, No. 239, 17 December (2012), http://vedomosti.ru/newspaper/articles/2012/12/17/kto_spryatalsya_v_rostelekome; Roman Shleynov, "Vysokie otnosheniya", *Vedomosti*, 18 March (2013), http://vedomosti.ru/politics/articles/2013/03/18/vysokie_otnosheniya

116 Roman Shleynov, "Knyaz'-svyaznoy", *Vedomosti*, No. 150, 15 August (2011), p. 1.

117 Ibid.

118 Timur Polliannikov, "The Logic of Authoritarianism", *Russian Politics and Law*, Vol. 44, No. 1 (2006), pp. 55–63 (61); John B. Dunlop, "Foreword", in Marlène Laruelle (ed.), *Russian Nationalism and the National Reassertion of Russia* (London: Routledge, 2009), pp. xvii–xix (xix).

119 Ivan Osipov, Roman Badanin, "Minoritariy ot Boga: put' Konstantina Malofeeva ot bogatstva do obyska", *Forbes*, 21 November (2012), http://forbes.ru/sobytiya/lyudi/215436-minoritarii-ot-boga-put-konstantina-malofeeva-ot-bogatstva-do-obyska

120 Chavchavadze is also a member of the supervisory board of Malofeev's Katehon think-tank.

121 " 'Laboratoriya Kasperskogo' prisoedinyaetsya k rabote 'Ligi bezopasnogo Interneta' ", *Kaspersky Lab*, 8 February (2011), http://kaspersky.ru/news?id=207733419

122 Paul J. Springer, *Cyber Warfare: A Reference Handbook* (Santa Barbara: ABC-CLIO, 2015), p. 164. In 1992, the Department was reorganised into the Institute of Cryptography, Telecommunications and Computer Science.

123 Rachel Nielsen, "Internet Restriction Law Comes On Line", *The Moscow Times*, No. 5006, 2 November (2012), p. 47.

124 Minchenko, " 'Politbyuro 2.0' nakanune perezagruzki elitnykh grupp".

125 Savino, "From Evola to Dugin", p. 114.

126 "Identity, Sovereignty, Tradition" is most likely a reference to a group in the European Parliament called "Identity, Tradition and Sovereignty" that consisted of 23 far-right MEPs and existed from January until November 2007.

127 Putin, "Meeting of the Valdai International Discussion Club [2013]".

128 "Eurabia" is a concept popularised by Bat Ye'or (pen name of Gisèle Littman) that means "a gradual overtaking of Europe by Muslim populations", see Paul Jackson,

"2083 – A European Declaration of Independence: A License to Kill", in Matthew Feldman, Paul Jackson (eds), *Doublespeak: The Rhetoric of the Far Right since 1945* (Stuttgart: *ibidem*-Verlag, 2014), pp. 81–100 (84).

129 Max Ferrari, "Eurasia o Eurabia: UE al bivio", *Associazione Culturale Lombardia Russia*, 4 June (2014), http://lombardiarussia.org/index.php/component/content/article/57-categoria-home-/300-eurasia-o-eurabiaue-al-bivio

130 Antonio Rapisarda, "L'ideologo di Putin lancia la Lega: 'Ultima speranza per l'Italia' ", *Il Tempo*, 23 June (2015), http://iltempo.it/politica/2015/06/23/l-ideologo-di-putin-lancia-la-lega-ultima-speranza-per-l-italia-1.1429396

131 Gianluca Savoini, "Intervista ad Aleksander Dugin", *Associazione Culturale Lombardia Russia*, 8 July (2014), http://lombardiarussia.org/index.php/component/content/article/57-categoria-home-/329-intervista-ad-aleksander-dugin

132 "La sfida Euroasiatica della Russia", *Associazione Culturale Lombardia Russia*, 23 June (2014), http://lombardiarussia.org/index.php/stampa-eventi-cultura/eventi/319-la-sfida-euroasiatica-della-russia

133 Gianluca Savoini, "5 Febbraio 2014 – 5 Febbraio 2016: auguri a tutti noi", *Associazione Culturale Lombardia Russia*, 4 February (2016), http://lombardiarussia.org/index.php/component/content/article/57-categoria-home-/585-5-febbraio-2014-5-febbraio-2016-auguri-a-tutti-noi

134 "Conferenza 'Gli effetti economici delle sanzioni alla Russia' ", *Associazione Emilia Russia*, 17 November (2014), http://emiliarussia.org/?p=26

135 "La sfida russa al mondialismo", *Associazione Culturale Lombardia Russia*, 6 January (2015), http://lombardiarussia.org/index.php/stampa-eventi-cultura/eventi/431-la-sfida-russa-al-mondialismo

136 "Russia, Occidente e crisi Ucraina. La verità che i media occidentali non vi dicono", *Associazione Culturale Lombardia Russia*, 8 March (2015), www.lombardiarussia.org/index.php/stampa-eventi-cultura/eventi/476-russia-occidente-e-crisi-ucraina-la-verita-che-i-media-occidentali-non-vi-dicono

137 See http://vk.com/id188344 and www.facebook.com/osipova

138 Giovanni Savino, "L'infatuazione putiniana della Lega, tra neofascisti italiani e Dugin", *MicroMega*, 22 October (2014), http://temi.repubblica.it/micromega-online/linfatuazione-putiniana-della-lega-tra-neofascisti-italiani-e-dugin/

139 Marina Tantushyan, "Che cos'è la Russia nel 2014?", *La Voce della Russia*, 14 July (2014), http://it.sputniknews.com/italian.ruvr.ru/2014_07_14/Che-cos-e-la-Russia-nel-2014-0439/

140 Savino, "From Evola to Dugin", p. 114.

141 "Konferentsiya Rim – Tretiy Rim v RTsNK", *La Rappresentanza di RosSotrudnichestvo in Italia*, http://ita.rs.gov.ru/it/node/3384

142 See "2015 Russian Sukhoi Su-24 Shootdown", *Wikipedia*, https://en.wikipedia.org/wiki/2015_Russian_Sukhoi_Su-24_shootdown

143 "Manifestazione a favore della Russia, contro il terrorismo e l'aggressione Turca", *Associazione Culturale Lombardia Russia*, 25 November (2015), http://lombardiarussia.org/index.php/component/content/article/57-categoria-home-/578-manifestazione-a-favore-della-russia-contro-il-terrorismo-e-laggressione-turca

144 "Lega: non solo Mosca, a ottobre Salvini anche in Crimea", *AGI*, 29 September (2014), http://archivio.agi.it/articolo/0bfa7ef9c5edcfe859c15a32acd39633_20140929_lega-non-solo-mosca-a-ottobre-salvini-anche-in-crimea/

145 "Zasedanie No. 190", *Gosudarstvennaya Duma*, 14 October (2014), http://api.duma.gov.ru/api/transcriptFull/2014-10-14

146 "Skazano!", *Komsomol'skaya Pravda*, No. 117, 15 October (2014), p. 3.

147 Savino, "From Evola to Dugin", pp. 113–114; Matteo Salvini, "20 minuti di incontro . . .", *Facebook*, 17 October (2014), https://facebook.com/salviniofficial/photos/a.10151670912208155.1073741827.252306033154/10152465922593155/

148 Eliseo Bertolasi, "Interv'yu s Matteo Salvini i Gianluca Savoini iz partii 'Lega Nord' (Italiya) po vozvrashchenii iz Moskvy", *Mezhdunarodnaya zhizn'*, 8 November (2014), https://interaffairs.ru/news/show/12061

149 "Paolo Grimoldi sozdaet gruppu 'Druz'ya Putina' v parlamente Italii".

150 Irina Shcherbinina, Polina Solov'yova, "'My voskhishchaemsya tem, chto delaet Putin'", *Vzglyad*, 17 October (2014), http://vz.ru/world/2014/10/17/711106.html. One of the authors of the interview, Irina Shcherbinina, is a co-founder of the ACLR.

151 Michela Scacchioli, "Lettera della Lega Nord ai parlamentari: 'Iscriviti anche tu agli Amici di Putin'", *Repubblica*, 5 December (2014), http://repubblica.it/politica/2014/12/05/news/lega_nord_promuove_in_parlamento_l_associazione_amici_di_putin_-102198610/

152 Ibid.

153 "Andrey Klimov vstretilsya s predstavitelem 'Ligi Severa'", *Yedinaya Rossiya*, 22 October (2014), http://er.ru/news/123924/

154 "Klimov vstretilsya s federal'nym sekretaryom partii 'Liga Severa'", *Yedinaya Rossiya*, 17 February (2015), https://er.ru/news/127882/

155 "'Yedinaya Rossiya' i ital'yanskaya partiya 'Liga Severa' proveli konsul'tatsii v Moskve", *Yedinaya Rossiya*, 21 December (2015), http://er.ru/news/138115/

156 Matteo Salvini, "Storico accordo questa mattina a Mosca fra Lega e Russia Unita di Putin . . .", Facebook, 6 March (2017), https://facebook.com/salviniofficial/photos/a.278194028154.141463.252306033154/10154567614898155/; "ER zaklyuchila dogovor o vzaimodeystvii s ital'yanskoy partiey 'Liga Severa'", RIA Novosti, 6 March (2017), https://ria.ru/politics/20170306/1489367218.html; "Accordo tra Lega e il partito di Putin", *ANSA*, 7 March (2017), http://ansa.it/sito/notizie/topnews/2017/03/06/accordo-tra-lega-e-il-partito-di-puntin_d19ae3ed-dd84-40c7-ad94-0ddcc3d7a61b.html

157 Savino, "From Evola to Dugin", p. 113.

158 "Famiglia Tradizione Identita'. La sfida della Russia al mondialismo", *Associazione Culturale Lombardia Russia*, 21 October (2014), http://lombardiarussia.org/index.php/stampa-eventi-cultura/eventi/383-famiglia-tradizione-identita-la-sfida-della-russia-al-mondialismo

159 "Oltre la crisi Ucraina. Per un nuovo dialogo tra Europa e Russia", *Associazione Culturale Lombardia Russia*, 12 April (2015), http://lombardiarussia.org/index.php/stampa-eventi-cultura/eventi/494-oltre-la-crisi-ucraina-per-un-nuovo-dialogo-tra-europa-e-russia

160 "Musiche dal Mondo – Speciale Russia", *Associazione Culturale Lombardia Russia*, 4 July (2015), http://lombardiarussia.org/index.php/stampa-eventi-cultura/eventi/553-musiche-dal-mondo-speciale-russia

161 "Rinascita di un Impero – La Russia di Vladimir Putin", *Associazione Culturale Lombardia Russia*, 3 July (2015), http://lombardiarussia.org/index.php/stampa-eventi-cultura/eventi/520-rinascita-di-un-impero-la-russia-di-vladimir-putin

162 "'Rossiya-Italiya: sokhranit' doverie i partnerstvo' – nauchno-prakticheskaya konferentsiya 8 dekabrya 2014 goda", *Komitet Gosudarstvennoy Dumy po ekonomicheskoy politike, innovatsionnomu razvitiyu i predprinimatel'stvu*, 5 December (2014), http://komitet2-7.km.duma.gov.ru/site.xp/052057124049050053050.html; "'Rossiya-Italiya: sokhranit' doverie i partnerstvo' – konferentsiya 8 dekabrya 2014 goda v Gosudarstvennoy Dume", *Komitet Gosudarstvennoy Dumy po ekonomicheskoy politike, innovatsionnomu razvitiyu i predprinimatel'stvu*, 11 December (2014), http://komitet2-7.km.duma.gov.ru/site.xp/052057124049050054056.html

163 "Sergey Aksyonov prinyal uchastie vo vstreche s ital'yanskoy delegatsiey", *Pravitel'stvo Respubliki Krym*, 13 October (2014), http://rk.gov.ru/rus/index.htm/news/287272.htm

164 "V Krym pribyla delegatsiya iz severnoy Italii", *Gosudarstvenny Sovet Respubliki Krym*, 13 October (2014), http://crimea.gov.ru/ru/news/13_10_14

165 "Krym budet razvivat' sotrudnichestvo s Severnoy Italiey", *Ministerstvo kurortov i turizma Respubliki Krym*, 13 October (2014), http://mtur.rk.gov.ru/rus/index.htm/news/287308.htm; "Sostoyalas' vstrecha s delegatsiey ital'yanskoy partii 'Liga Severa' i predstavitelyami Assotsiatsii 'Lombardiya-Rossiya'", *Ministerstvo ekonomicheskogo razvitiya Respubliki Krym*, 13 October (2014), http://minek.rk.gov.ru/rus/index.htm/news/287300.htm

166 Confindustria is the major association representing manufacturing and service companies in Italy, as well as a national chamber of commerce.

167 "Russia e Crimea – due grandi opportunita' per le nostre imprese", *Associazione Culturale Lombardia Russia*, 11 December (2014), http://lombardiarussia.org/index.php/stampa-eventi-cultura/eventi/414-russia-e-crimea-due-grandi-opportunita-per-le-nostre-imprese; Alexander Prokhorov, "Crimea – grandi opportunita' per le imprese italiane in Russia", *La Voce della Russia*, 31 December (2014), http://it.sputniknews.com/italian.ruvr.ru/2014_12_31/281828809/

168 "Nikolay Koryazhkin prinyal uchastie v biznes-missii v Italiyu", *Ministerstvo ekonomicheskogo razvitiya Respubliki Krym*, 17 December (2014), http://minek.rk.gov.ru/rus/index.htm/news/291423.htm

169 Niva Mirakyan, "V Milane otkrylas' konferentsiya, posvyashchennaya Krymu", *Rossiyskaya gazeta*, 20 March (2015), http://rg.ru/2015/03/20/konf-site-anons.html

170 Ibid.

171 "Fiera agroalimentare della Russia del Sud – Crimea 2015", *Associazione Culturale Lombardia Russia*, 21 May (2015), http://lombardiarussia.org/index.php/component/content/article/57-categoria-home-/506-fiera-agroalimentare-della-russia-del-sud-crimea-2015

172 "Oltre le sanzioni. Fiera agroalimentare della Russia del Sud – Crimea 2015", *Associazione Culturale Lombardia Russia*, 1 June (2015), http://lombardiarussia.org/index.php/stampa-eventi-cultura/eventi/518-oltre-le-sanzioni-fiera-agroalimentare-della-russia-del-sud-crimea-2015

173 "Predprinimateli iz Italii zainteresovany v uchastii v industrial'nykh parkakh Kryma", *Ministerstvo promyshlennoy politiki Respubliki Krym*, 22 May (2015), http://mprom.rk.gov.ru/rus/index.htm/news/304212.htm

174 The programme can be found here: http://ovvs.su/imglib/summitprogram.pdf

175 Olga Borisova, "Rezul'taty prevzoshli ozhidaniya", *Tribuna*, No. 40, 4 October (2012), p. 3.

176 Anton Shekhovtsov, "The Old and New European Friends of Ukraine's Far-right Svoboda Party", *Searchlight*, No. 455 (2013), pp. 5–7.

177 Olga Bronnikova, *Compatriotes et expatriotes: le renouveau de la politique dans l'émigration russe. L'émergence et la structuration de la communauté politique russe en France (2000–2013)*. Thèse soutenue le 27 janvier 2014 à l'Institut national des langues et civilisations orientales pour obtenir le grade de Docteur l'INALCO (Paris: INALCO, 2014), p. 122.

178 Shields, *The Extreme Right in France*, p. 159. On the GUD see also Roger Griffin, "Net Gains and GUD Reactions: Patterns of Prejudice in a Neo-fascist *Groupuscule*", *Patterns of Prejudice*, Vol. 33, No. 2 (1999), pp. 31–50.

179 "My podderzhivaem vneshnyuu politiku Rossii", *Geopolitika*, 18 May (2009), https://web.archive.org/web/20130129064601/http://geopolitica.ru/Articles/596/

180 Ibid.

181 Olivier Faye, Abel Mestre, Caroline Monnot, "L'extrême droite en mode Raspoutine; pas de liste GUD; des SMS racistes", *Droite(s) extrême(s)*, 12 March (2010), http://droites-extremes.blog.lemonde.fr/2010/03/12/pas-de-liste-gud-lextreme-droite-en-mode-raspoutine/

182 "Qui est Vladimir Poutine? 2ème partie", *Collectif France-Russie*, 17 August (2009), https://web.archive.org/web/20091128132353/http://collectiffrancerussie.com/2009/08/17/qui-est-vladimir-poutine-2eme-partie/

183 Olivier Faye, Abel Mestre, Caroline Monnot, "Alain Soral et son association font les yeux doux à Poutine", *Droite(s) extrême(s)*, 26 November (2009), http://droites-extremes.blog.lemonde.fr/2009/11/26/alain-soral-et-son-association-font-les-yeux-doux-a-poutine/

184 "Evropa boitsya pravdy o voyne v Yuzhnoy Osetii", *Prava narodov*, 11 September (2009), http://peoples-rights.ru/evropa-boitsya-pravdy-o-vojne-v-yuzhnoj-osetii/

185 "V Pol'she i Frantsii proshli konferentsii, posvyashchennye godovshchine tragedii v Yuzhnoy Osetii", *Alaniyainform*, 7 August (2009), http://osinform.org/15504-v-polshe-i-francii-prooshli-konferencii.html

186 André Chanclu, "Pourquoi Novopole?", *Novopole*, 20 January (2013), https://web.archive.org/web/20130222040744/http://novopole.org/?p=18

187 Aleksandr Dugin, *Chetvertaya politicheskaya teoriya: Rossiya i politicheskie idei XXI veka* (Saint Petersburg: Amfora, 2009). See also Alexander Dugin, *The Fourth Political Theory* (London: Arktos, 2012), which is a shorter version of the Russian language book on the same topic.

188 Ibid., p. 21. Despite the different name, a closer analysis of the ideological tenets of Dugin's "fourth political theory" reveals that it does not differ from neo-Eurasianism: it is significantly influenced by imperialist geopolitics, opposes liberal democracy, detests the West and the US, and calls for a revolution against the perceived enemies of Russia.

189 See, for example, Viacheslav Prokof'ev, "Moskva zhdet 'Mistraley' ili deneg", *Rossiyskaya gazeta*, No. 233, 13 October (2014), p. 3; Ekaterina Zabrodina, "Na flagi ne posmotreli", *Rossiyskaya gazeta*, No. 247, 2 November (2015), p. 8.

190 Jean-Claude Philipot, "Une alliance avec la Fédération de Russie comme alternative à l'impérialisme états-unien . . .", *Synthèse nationale*, 22 October (2009), http://synthesenationale.hautetfort.com/archive/2009/10/22/une-alliance-avec-la-federation-de-russie-comme-alternative.html

191 "A propos de l'Alliance France-Europe Russie", *Alliance France-Europe-Russie*, https://web.archive.org/web/20120206083254/http://alliance-france-europe-russie.org/s-a_propos_de_aafer.html

192 Huguette Pérol, *Secrets de princes: un capétien au coeur de la France: Sixte-Henri de Bourbon-Parme* (Paris: Nouvelles Éditions Latines, 2009), p. 162.

193 Vyacheslav Prokof'ev, "Frantsiya ushla nalevo", *Rossiyskaya gazeta*, No. 59, 23 March (2010), p. 8.

194 Elena Chernenko, "Frantsiya vyydet iz NATO", *Kommersant. Daily*, No. 192, 13 October (2011), p. 7.

195 "My podderzhivaem vneshnyuu politiku Rossii".

196 Jean-Yves Camus, Nicolas Lebourg, *Les Droites extrêmes en Europe* (Paris: Éditions de Seuil), p. 268. See more on Leroy in Pierre Vaux, "Marine Le Pen's Closest Advisor Comes out of the Shadows in Donetsk", *The Daily Beast*, 14 May (2015), http://thedailybeast.com/articles/2015/05/14/marine-le-pen-s-closest-advisor-comes-out-of-the-shadows-in-donetsk.html

197 Gaïdz Minassian, "Les réseaux français de Poutine: une intelligentsia hétéroclite", *Le Monde*, 18 November (2014), www.lemonde.fr/international/article/2014/11/18/les-reseaux-francais-de-poutine-une-intelligentsia-heteroclite_4525583_3210.html. See also Marine Turchi, "Les réseaux russes de Marine Le Pen", *Mediapart*, 19 February (2014), https://mediapart.fr/journal/france/190214/les-reseaux-russes-de-marine-le-pen

198 "The Institute of Democracy and Cooperation", *Institute of Democracy and Cooperation*, http://idc-europe.org/en/The-Institute-of-Democracy-and-Cooperation

199 Andrey S. Makarychev, "In Quest of Political Subjectivity: Russia's 'Normative Offensive' and the Triple Politicisation of Norms", in *What Prospects for Normative Foreign Policy in a Multipolar World?* European Security Forum Working Paper No. 29 (2008), pp. 12–17 (12).

200 Ekaterina Grigor'yeva, "Rossiya profinansiruet evropeyskuyu demokratiyu, *Izvestiya*, No. 198, 29 October (2007), p. 2; Aleksandr Koptev, " 'Vy eshche ne lyubite Rossiyu? Togda – idyom k vam . . .' ", *Argumenty i fakty*, No. 6, 6 February (2008), p. 4.

201 On Narochnitskaya and her ideology see Jardar Nuland Østbø, "Excluding the West: Nataliia Narochnitskaia's Romantic-Realistic Image of Europe", in Helge Vidar Holm, Sissel Tone Ågot Lægreid and Torgeir Skorgen (ed.), *The Borders of Europe: Hegemony, Aesthetics and Border Poetics* (Aarhus: Aarhus Universitetsforlag, 2012), pp. 92–105.

202 David Aaronovitch, "PR Man to Europe's Nastiest Regimes", *The Guardian*, 30 November (2004), http://theguardian.com/media/2004/nov/30/pressandpublish ing.marketingandpr

203 On the *Compact* magazine see Christian Fuchs, Fritz Zimmermann, "Hauspost für die Wütenden", *Die Zeit*, No. 25 (2016), p. 25.

204 Caroline Monnot, Abel Mestre, "Le 'nouveau FN' de Marine Le Pen", *Le Monde*, 6 September (2011), http://lemonde.fr/election-presidentielle-2012/article/2011/09/06/le-nouveau-fn-de-marine-le-pen_1568382_1471069.html

205 Turchi, "Les réseaux russes de Marine Le Pen".

206 "Organization", *Sokol Group*, http://sokol-corp.com/organization

207 See "Kamerton drugogo zvuchaniya", *Ekonomicheskie strategii*, No. 6 (2010), pp. 40–43.

208 Turchi, "Les réseaux russes de Marine Le Pen"; Minassian, "Les réseaux français de Poutine".

209 Turchi, "Les réseaux russes de Marine Le Pen".

210 Marlène Laruelle, "Russia's Radical Right and Its Western European Connections: Ideological Borrowings and Personal Interactions", in Mats Deland, Michael Minkenberg (eds), *In the Tracks of Breivik: Far Right Networks in Northern and Eastern Europe* (Berlin: Lit Verlag, 2014), pp. 87–104 (102).

211 Cécile Vaissié, *Les réseaux du Kremlin en France* (Paris: Les Petits Matins, 2016), pp. 186–187.

212 Quoted in Faye, Mestre, Monnot, "L'extrême droite en mode Raspoutine".

213 Quoted in "Marine Le Pen veut aller en Russie", *Le Figaro*, 2 May (2011), http://lefigaro.fr/flash-actu/2011/05/02/97001-20110502FILWWW00503-marine-le-pen-veut-aller-en-russie.php

214 "I Want to Free France from EU Straitjacket – Far-right Party Leader", *RT*, 27 April (2011), https://rt.com/news/france-eu-immigrants-pen/

215 Quoted in "Marine Le Pen veut aller en Russie".

216 Vladimir Bol'shakov, *Zachem Rossii Marin Le Pen* (Moscow: Algoritm, 2012), p. 144.

217 Chernenko, "Frantsiya vyydet iz NATO", p. 7.

218 "Discours de Marine Le Pen prononcé le samedi 19 novembre 2011 à Paris à l'occasion de la présentation de son Projet Présidentiel", *Front National*, 19 November (2011), http://frontnational.com/videos/presentation-du-projet-presidentiel-de-marine-le-pen/

219 Jauvert, "Poutine et le FN".

220 Jauvert, "Poutine et le FN".

221 See Chapter 7 for more details.

222 Sergey Naryshkin (ed.), *Sovremenny parlamentarizm i budushchee demokratii. Materialy pervogo Mezhdunarodnogo parlamentskogo foruma* (Moscow: Izdanie Gosudarstvennoy Dumy, 2013), p. 13.

223 Quoted in Marine Turchi, "Au Front national, le lobbying pro-russe s'accélère", *Mediapart*, 18 December (2014), https://www.mediapart.fr/journal/france/181214/au-front-national-le-lobbying-pro-russe-saccelere. Maréchal-Le Pen's interview for ProRussia.TV was also aired by the French service of the Voice of Russia as part of the structural cooperation between the two media companies, see "Journal hebdomadaire de La Voix de la Russie – 4 mars 2013", *La Voix de la Russie*, 4 March

(2013), https://fr.sputniknews.com/actualite/201303041022561808-journal-hebdom adaire-de-voix-de-la-russie-4-mars-2013/. The video, however, is no longer available online, as it was hosted by the now terminated ProRussia.TV.

224 "Evropa zhdyot ot Rossii konsolidatsii zdravykh sil i organizatsii soprotivleniya sodomizatsii mira", *Sem'ya, lyubov', otechestvo*, 13 June (2013), https://web.archive.org/web/20150515024402/http://semlot.ru/regions/regions-news/301-evropa-zhdjot-ot-rossii-konsolidatsii-zdravykh-sil-i-organizatsii-soprotivleniya-sodomizatsii-mira

225 "Vystuplenie Emrika Shoprada – grazhdanskogo aktivista, geopolitika", *Komitet Gosudarstvennoy Dumy po voprosam sem'i, zhenshchin i detey*, 13 June (2013), http://komitet2-6.km.duma.gov.ru/site.xp/052057124053057048.html

226 Quoted in Emmanuel Grynszpan, "Moscou déroule le tapis rouge devant Marine Le Pen", *Le Figaro*, 21 June (2013), http://lefigaro.fr/politique/2013/06/20/01002-20130620ARTFIG00642-moscou-deroule-le-tapis-rouge-devant-marine-le-pen.php

227 Ibid.; Isabelle Weber, "Gros succès pour la visite en Russie de Marine Le Pen", *Nations Presse*, 26 June (2013), http://nationspresse.info/geopolitique/gros-succes-pour-la-visite-en-russie-de-marine-le-pen

228 Russia started its military intervention in the Syrian Civil War only in September 2015.

229 Quoted in "A Moscou, Marine Le Pen rend hommage à une Russie 'diabolisée' ", *Libération*, 19 June (2013), http://liberation.fr/france/2013/06/19/a-moscou-marine-le-pen-rend-hommage-a-une-russie-diabolisee_912158; Marine Turchi, "Le Front national décroche les millions russes", *Mediapart*, 22 November (2014), www.mediapart.fr/journal/france/221114/le-front-national-decroche-les-millions-russes

230 Fabrice Arfi, Karl Laske, Marine Turchi, "La Russie au secours du FN: deux millions d'euros", *Mediapart*, 29 November (2014), https://mediapart.fr/journal/france/291114/la-russie-au-secours-du-fn-deux-millions-d-euros-aussi-pour-jean-marie-le-pen

231 Raymond Walter Apple, Jr., "K.G.B. Defector Is Called a British Double Agent", *The New York Times*, 14 September (1985), http://nytimes.com/1985/09/14/world/kgb-defector-is-called-a-british-double-agent.html

232 Arfi, Laske, Turchi, "La Russie au secours du FN".

233 Turchi, "Le Front national décroche les millions russes". See also Marine Turchi, Mathias Destal, "Le Pen-Putin Friendship Goes back a Long Way", *EUObserver*, 22 April (2017), https://euobserver.com/elections/137629

234 Svetlana Petrova, " 'Stroytransgaz' zanyalsya bankovskim biznesom", *Vedomosti*, 14 July (2003), http://vedomosti.ru/newspaper/articles/2003/07/14/strojtransgaz-zanyalsya-bankovskim-biznesom

235 Anastasiya Agamalova, "Holding Timchenko uvelichil dolyu v 'Stroytransgaze' do 94.55%", *Vedomosti*, 13 September (2013), http://vedomosti.ru/business/articles/2013/09/13/holding-timchenko-uvelichil-dolyu-v-strojtransgaze-do-9455

236 Christopher M. Matthews, Andrew Grossman, "U.S. Money-Laundering Probe Touches Putin's Inner Circle", *The Wall Street Journal*, 5 November (2014), www.wsj.com/articles/u-s-money-laundering-probe-touches-putins-inner-circle-1415234261. Stroytransgaz was expected to be involved in constructing the South Stream pipeline, but withdrew from the project before it was suspended because the US imposed sanctions on Timchenko and several of his companies, including Stroytransgaz, see "Announcement of Additional Treasury Sanctions on Russian Government Officials and Entities", *U.S. Department of the Treasury*, 28 April (2014), https://treasury.gov/press-center/press-releases/Pages/jl2369.aspx

237 Agathe Duparc, Karl Laske, Marine Turchi, "Argent du FN: les hommes de la filière russe", *Mediapart*, 8 December (2014), https://www.mediapart.fr/journal/france/081214/argent-du-fn-les-hommes-de-la-filiere-russe

238 Agathe Duparc, "Le Front national a traité avec des banques mafieuses russes", *Mediapart*, 2 May (2017), https://mediapart.fr/journal/international/020517/le-front-national-traite-avec-des-banques-mafieuses-russes

239 Duparc, Laske, Turchi, "Argent du FN".
240 Ibid.
241 Turchi, "Le Front national décroche les millions russes".
242 "Aleksandr Gusev. My zaplatili Marin Le Pen", *YouTube*, 26 March (2015), https://youtube.com/watch?v=BnEchxquvjo. According to one article, the FN obtained the loan at a 6% interest rate, see Olivier Faye, Benoît Vitkine, "La justice russe saisie sur le prêt bancaire consenti au Front national", *Le Monde*, 4 January (2017), http://lemonde.fr/politique/article/2017/01/04/la-justice-russe-saisie-sur-le-pret-bancaire-consenti-au-front-national_5057637_823448.html
243 Alessandra Prentice, "France's Le Pen, in Moscow, Blames EU for New 'Cold War' ", *Reuters*, 12 April (2014), http://reuters.com/article/us-ukraine-crisis-le-pen-russia-idUSBREA3B09I20140412
244 Chinkova, "Marin Le Pen", p. 2.
245 "Evrope navyazany sanktsii protiv Rossii – Isayev", *Yedinaya Rossiya*, 30 November (2014), http://er.ru/news/125366/
246 Clive Leviev-Sawyer, "Four of Bulgaria's Presidential Candidates Were Communist-era State Security Collaborators", *The Sofia Echo*, 27 September (2011), http://sofiaecho.com/2011/09/27/1163815_four-of-bulgarias-presidential-candidates-were-communist-era-state-security-collaborators
247 Alexej Hock, "Russlands rechtes Netzwerk. Die Einflussnahme Russlands auf rechte Strukturen in der EU", *Politik in Gesellschaft*, July (2015), p. 34.
248 "Marin Le Pen: U sotrudnichestva 'Yedinoy Rossii' i 'Natsional'nogo fronta' velikoe budushchee", *Yedinaya Rossiya*, 5 December (2014), https://er.ru/news/125726/
249 Bernhard Odehnal, "Gipfeltreffen mit Putins fünfter Kolonne", *Tages-Anzeiger*, 3 June (2014), http://tagesanzeiger.ch/ausland/europa/Gipfeltreffen-mit-Putins-fuenfter-Kolonne/story/30542701
250 Carl Henrik Fredriksson, "In a Backyard that Doesn't Exist", *Eurozine*, 6 May (2016), http://eurozine.com/articles/2016-05-06-fredriksson-en.html
251 Odehnal, "Gipfeltreffen mit Putins fünfter Kolonne".
252 See also Anton Shekhovtsov, "The Kremlin Builds an Unholy Alliance With America's Christian Right", *War Is Boring*, 13 July (2014), https://medium.com/war-is-boring/the-kremlin-builds-an-unholy-alliance-with-americas-christian-right-5de35250066b; Miranda Blue, " 'Cancelled' World Congress of Families Kremlin Conference Begins Today, Possibly with Special Guest Star Brian Brown", *Right Wing Watch*, 10 September (2014), http://rightwingwatch.org/content/cancelled-world-congress-families-kremlin-conference-begins-today-possibly-special-guest-sta
253 *Mezhdunarodny forum "Mnogodetnaya sem'ya i budushchee chelovechestva"* (2015), p. 4.
254 Tajuddin is also a member of the High Council of the MED led by Dugin.
255 "Vystuplenie deputata Evropeyskogo Parlamenta Emerika Shoprada", in *Mezhdunarodny forum "Mnogodetnaya sem'ya i budushchee chelovechestva"*, p. 34.
256 "Vystuplenie chlena venskogo parlamenta, Avstriyskoy partii svobody Yohana Gudenusa", in *Mezhdunarodny forum "Mnogodetnaya sem'ya i budushchee chelovechestva"*, pp. 114–115.
257 "Cherny Internatsional: Malofeev i Dugin".
258 "Nazairiens! Téléchargez et diffusez notre premier tract", *Mistral, gagnons!*, 14 August (2014), http://mistralgagnons.fr/?p=214
259 See http://facebook.com/Mistralgagnons/photos
260 "International Forum 'Donetsk: Yesterday, Today, Tomorrow' to Be Held in DPR", *TASS*, 11 May (2015), http://tass.ru/en/world/794049
261 The argument that this and similar conferences aimed – at least to a certain extent – at providing legitimacy to the DNR is further supported by a description of the agenda of a roundtable, which the Moscow-based Agency for Strategic Communications proposed to hold in Donetsk in October 2015. As the Agency argued, by inviting European politicians from the right-wing parties such as VB, Forza Italia, REKOS,

Team Stronach and Srpska napredna stranka (Serbian Progressive Party) to Donetsk, they would "demonstrate [to the people of the DNR] the attention to Donetsk as an independent subject of political process on the part of some representatives of the European community". This description is found in an e-mail sent by the Agency for Strategic Communication to the office of Putin's aide Vladislav Surkov on 7 October 2015. This and other e-mails were leaked to the public by the Ukrainian Cyber Alliance, see Falcon Bjorn, "SurkovLeaks (Part 2): Hacktivists Publish New Email Dump", *InformNapalm*, 3 November (2016), https://informnapalm.org/en/surkovleaks-part2/. The roundtable proposed by the Agency for Strategic Communications never took place.

262 "V Donetske sostoyalsya mezhdunarodny forumPravdorub, 11 May (2015), http://pravdoryb.info/v-donetske-sostoyalsya-mezhdunarodnyy-forum.html
263 Ibid.
264 Vaux, "Marine Le Pen's Closest Advisor".
265 "Annonce No. 80", *Annexe au Journal officiel de la République française. Lois et décrets*, No. 41 (2014), http://journal-officiel.gouv.fr/publications/assoc/pdf/2014/0041/JOAFE_PDF_Unitaire_20140041_00080.pdf
266 Laurent Brayard, "Emmanuel Leroy – 'Nous savons que chacun des obus qui tombent peut enlever la vie des enfants du Donbass' ", *DONi International Press Center*, 23 December (2015), https://dnipress.com/fr/posts/emmanuel-leroy-nous-savons-que-chacun-des-obus-qui-tombent-peut-enlever-la-vie-des-enfants-du-donbass/
267 "Conférence de presse de l'association 'Urgence enfants du Dombass' à Paris", *Synthèse nationale*, 14 December (2015), http://synthesenationale.hautetfort.com/archive/2015/12/14/conference-de-presse-de-l-association-urgence-enfants-du-dom-5730714.html
268 Brayard, "Emmanuel Leroy".
269 "Conférence de presse de l'association 'Urgence enfants du Dombass' à Paris".
270 See "Une délégation française vire des fonds pour traiter les enfants du Donbass", *Sputnik*, 4 December (2015), https://fr.sputniknews.com/international/201512041020059327-france-fonds-traitement-enfants-donetsk/; "French Charity Visits Donbass, Transfers Money to Help Wounded Children", *Sputnik*, 4 December (2015), http://sputniknews.com/europe/20151204/1031272273/donbass-children.html
271 Karl Laske, Marine Turchi, "Le troisième prêt russe des Le Pen", *Mediapart*, 11 December (2014), https://mediapart.fr/journal/france/111214/le-troisieme-pret-russe-des-le-pen
272 "Frantsuzy postroyat v Krymu park razvlecheniy, posvyashchenny russkoy istorii, za 4 mlrd rubley", *Kryminform*, 15 August (2014), http://c-inform.info/news/id/10744; Blandine Le Cain, "Un Puy du Fou russe va ouvrir en Crimée", *Le Figaro*, 16 August (2014), http://lefigaro.fr/international/2014/08/15/01003-20140815ARTFIG00097-un-puy-du-fou-russe-va-ouvrir-en-crimee.php
273 Charles Bremner, "Le Pen's Party Asks Russia for €27m Loan", *The Times*, 19 February (2016), http://thetimes.co.uk/tto/news/world/europe/article4693936.ece
274 Darya Borysyak, Tatyana Voronova, "Rossiyskie problemy cheshskogo banka", *Vedomosti*, No. 43, 14 March (2016), p. 14.
275 "Rossiyskiy bank-kreditor Marin Le Pen priznan bakrotom", *Republic*, 20 September (2016), https://republic.ru/posts/73717
276 Sanita Jemberga, "Latvian Financier Said to Act as a Go-between to Get Russian Loan for Le Pen", *Re:Baltica*, 2 May (2017), http://en.rebaltica.lv/2017/05/latvian-financier-said-to-act-as-a-go-between-to-get-russian-loan-for-le-pen/. See also Duparc, "Le Front national a traité avec des banques mafieuses russes".
277 "PAO 'Aktsionerny Komercheskiy Bank "Strategiya' ", *Banki.ru*, 29 February (2016), http://banki.ru/banks/memory/bank/?id=9088422
278 "Decision du Bureau Executif du Front National", 15 June (2016), https://drive.google.com/file/d/0B7aNf14k01iZcm5YNmpXcm56M0E/view

279 "Bank of Russia Cancels Bank Strategia and ABB Licenses", *Banki.ru*, 21 July (2016), http://banki.ru/news/engnews/?id=9089141
280 "Bank of Russia Withdraws NCB License", *Banki.ru*, 29 December (2016), http://banki.ru/news/engnews/?id=9463868
281 "A Republican Primary Upset Knocks Nicolas Sarkozy out of France's Presidential Race", *The Economist*, 20 November (2016), http://economist.com/news/europe/21710616-fran-ois-fillon-former-pm-takes-lead-over-favourite-alain-jupp-republican-primary
282 See, for example, "Présidentielle 2017: les rapports de force électoraux à cinq mois du scrutiny", *IFOP*, 6 December (2016), http://ifop.com/media/poll/3576-1-study_file.pdf
283 See, for example, "'Il n'y a pas une culture française': Macron s'attire les foudres de la droite", RT, 6 February (2017), https://francais.rt.com/france/33569-il-n-a-pas-culture-francaise-macron-attire-foudres-droite; "Dupont-Aignan soupçonne Macron de conflits d'intérêts et veut qu'il clarifie 'ses financements'", RT, 11 February (2017), https://francais.rt.com/france/33829-dupont-aignan-soupconne-macron-conflit-interets-clarifie-financements
284 On the anti-Semitic myth of Jewish economic dominance related to the Rothschild banking dynasty see the chapter "The Economic Root", in William I. Brustein, *Roots of Hate: Anti-Semitism in Europe Before the Holocaust* (Cambridge: Cambridge University Press, 2003), pp. 177–264.
285 "Ex-French Economy Minister Macron Could Be 'US Agent' Lobbying Banks' Interests", *Sputnik*, 4 February (2017), https://sputniknews.com/analysis/201702041050340451-macron-us-agent-dhuicq/
286 "Meeting with Marine Le Pen", *President of Russia*, 24 March (2017), http://en.kremlin.ru/events/president/news/54102
287 Ibid.
288 Turchi, Destal, "Le Pen-Putin Friendship Goes back a Long Way".

7

THE MOSCOW-STRASBOURG-BRUSSELS AXIS

Introduction

Since 2013, a number of Western far-right organisations, movements and individual activists have manifestly orientated themselves to Putin's Russia. This consistent support for Russian domestic and foreign policies suggests the existence of 'a black international', that is transnational far-right movement controlled or, at least, coordinated by the Kremlin. As the previous chapters have shown, however, the Kremlin does not exert direct control of Russia's relations with Western far-right actors. Unlike the KGB's centralised collaboration with particular elements of the far-right scene in Western Europe during the Cold War, contemporary relations between various Western far right and Russian actors have a decentralised character and are a result of a wide range of partly overlapping, partly convergent initiatives that have been coming from different sources, rather than only one – the Kremlin.

This situation reflects the structure of power relations in Putin's Russia in general. As Yevgeniy Minchenko, an expert on the Russian ruling elites, argues,

> The rule in Russia is [not] a rigid vertical structure managed by one person. . . . The rule in Russia is a conglomerate of clans and groups that compete with each other for resources. And the role of Vladimir Putin in this system [is] the role of an arbiter and moderator.[1]

Rather than being a top-down demand from Putin, the cooperation and engagement with Western far-right politicians and activists is a bottom-up offer to the Kremlin made by those Russian actors who want to consolidate their own positions in a competitive market of many offers to Russia's highest quarters of power in the hope of receiving an advantage in the allocation of resources. This situation contrasts not only with the Soviet Union's KGB-coordinated collaboration with particular Western far-right organisations during the Cold War, but also with relations between Western and Russian ultranationalists, as the latter – by engaging in these relations – have pursued their own political goals without any prospect to be able to 'sell' them to those in power, as discussed in Chapter 2. The only exception was Russian ultranationalist leader Vladimir Zhirinovsky who in 2003 suggested that Moscow could 'have [additional] leverage in world politics' through the European far-right parties that Zhirinovsky cooperated with.[2] At that time Putin's regime was not interested, while Zhirinovsky, in any circumstance, failed to build a pro-Russian far-right coalition.

Still, discussing contemporary relations between Western far right and Russian actors, who have presented this cooperation as being beneficial to the state, one can distinguish between two periods.

In 2005–2012, the peripheral, yet unambiguously pro-Kremlin, Russian actors increasingly cooperated with Western far-right politicians and activists in the areas of electoral monitoring and the media.

Starting from 2013, the prominence of these relations dramatically increased as signified by the rising status of the representatives of the Russian establishment engaged in these relations. This implied a growing perception of Western far-right organisations and individuals as political allies of Putin's Russia. This change was the result of two major, largely overlapping developments:

1   The ongoing process of the anti-Western and anti-American radicalisation of Putin's regime that started in 2004–2005 as a response to the 'colour revolutions' in the post-Soviet space (seen by Moscow as a Western attempt to undermine Russia and its 'sphere of influence'). This process was deepened by – among other factors – Moscow's negative reaction to the wave of protests, riots and regime changes in the Arab world in 2010–2012 (collectively known as the 'Arab Spring'), as well as by the anti-Putin protests in Moscow and other Russian cities in 2011–2013.

2   The growing criticism of domestic and foreign policies of Putin's Russia coming from Western mainstream politicians and state officials was an additional factor. This criticism related, in particular, to (a) the failure of the Russian authorities to investigate the death of imprisoned corporate lawyer Sergei Magnitsky in a Moscow prison in 2009; (b) the Kremlin's crackdown on the anti-Putin protests and the polarising measures employed by the Kremlin to divide the opposition (most importantly, the criminal case against Pussy Riot, the 'Dima Yakovlev Law' and the 'anti-LGBT propaganda law'); and (c) Putin's unwavering support for Syrian President Bashar al-Assad whose suppression of the anti-government protests resulted in the outbreak of the Syrian civil war in 2011. As mainstream politicians and officials in Western countries gradually withdrew their political support for Putin's regime, the latter started looking for non-mainstream political allies in the West.

The meetings of the high-ranking members of the ruling 'Yedinaya Rossiya' party, Russian diplomats and state officials such as Sergey Naryshkin or Aleksey Pushkov, as well as President Vladimir Putin himself, with the leaders of the European far-right parties implied a qualitatively new type of relations between Russian actors and Western far-right politicians. This turn was crowned by Putin's declaration, in April 2014, that the electoral victory of Viktor Orbán's Fidesz and electoral successes of Jobbik and the FN pointed to a 'rethinking of values in European countries' along the lines promoted by Moscow, that is 'conservative values'.[3]

This new type of relations between the Russian actors and Western far-right politicians implied the deliberate integration of the activities of the latter into the broader framework of the Kremlin's levers of influence in domestic and international environments. Apart from the pro-Russian efforts of the European far right discussed in the previous chapters, these activities also included 'collective performances' of particular European ultranationalists in two important settings that this final chapter focuses on: (1) high profile discussion platforms initiated by the then Chairman of the Russian State Duma Sergey Naryshkin and held in Moscow in 2014–2015, and (2) certain sessions of the European Parliament debating Russia-related resolutions in the same period.

'Collective counselling' in Moscow

In 2009, Russian lawyer Sergei Magnitsky, who worked as a legal advisor for the London-based investment fund Hermitage Capital Management, died in custody awaiting trial on suspicion of aiding tax evasion. He had been arrested a year before his death after discovering and reporting to the authorities what he said was a state-sanctioned €130 million tax fraud by Russian tax officials, police officers, the judiciary, bankers and organised criminals. He was 'said to have died of acute heart failure and toxic shock, caused by untreated pancreatitis'.[4] Human rights monitors, including Russia's Presidential Human Rights Council, announced that 'Magnitsky had been beaten and intentionally deprived of medical help'.[5] The Russian authorities ordered an investigation, but it was eventually dropped. Nobody was punished for his death, and the Russian officials denied that Magnitsky had been beaten and/or tortured while in custody.[6]

In June 2012, the US Senate's Foreign Relations Committee adopted the Sergei Magnitsky Rule of Law Accountability Act that imposed visa bans and assets freezes on Russian officials suspected of involvement in Magnitsky's detention, abuse and death.[7] In October the same year, the European Parliament adopted a resolution recommending to the European Council to impose and implement an EU-wide visa ban on, as well as freezing any financial assets of, Russian officials 'responsible for the death of Sergei Magnitsky, for the subsequent judicial cover-up and for the ongoing and sustained harassment of his mother and widow'.[8] These measures, as Nicholas Redman argued, 'highlighted the vulnerability of Russia to pressure on its globalised elite. Putin responded in mid-2013 with initiatives to "nationalise" all state officials: they were obliged to declare all of their family's foreign property, which they could keep; and to bring all of their assets back to Russia'.[9]

Apparently also in response to the measures taken by the United States and EU in relation to Magnitsky's death, Sergey Naryshkin initiated the International Parliamentary Forum, the first meeting of which – titled 'Contemporary Parliamentarianism and the Future of Democracy' – was held in the Imperial Hall of the Moscow State University on 10 December 2012. The forum hosted more than 200 participants: Russian high-ranking officials, ministers, leaders of all the establishment parties, diplomats, as well as a number of foreign parliamentarians and experts.[10] Officially, the forum 'discussed the issues of strengthening . . . institutions of representative democracy, their engagement with the civil society, improving law-making and law-enforcement practices, as well as problems of Eurasian integration and development of parliamentarianism in the CIS space'.[11] In fact, however, the forum was used to promote the Kremlin's view on the international relations and, in particular, to lambast the Magnitsky-related sanctions and the alleged 'double standards' in the West's approaches towards Russia. Naryshkin, Foreign Minister Sergey Lavrov, KPRF leader Gennadiy Zyuganov and some other leading officials and politicians promised to take action in response to the sanctions, and their criticism of the 'Magnitsky Act' was joined by Richard Sakwa, Professor of Russian and European Politics at the University of Kent and a member of the Valdai Discussion Club.

The FN's Marion Maréchal-Le Pen attended the forum as a guest, but not in a speaking capacity. It was not until the Third International Parliamentary Forum – titled 'New Dimensions of the Parliamentary Dialogue in the Contemporary Period' and held on 26 June 2014 – that European far-right politicians became regular speakers at this discussion platform initiated by Naryshkin. The third meeting seemed to be urgent: unlike the first and second forums, which were held in late autumn – early winter in the previous 2 years, the Russian officials decided to move the Third International Parliamentary Forum to June, apparently due to the introduction of Crimea-related sanctions against Russia and the PACE's decision to suspend, from 10 April 2014, the voting rights of the Russian delegation and exclude it from the leading bodies.[12] In this international environment, Moscow needed all the international support it could garner, and the composition of the plenary session of the third meeting reflected this need. It featured, among others, Moscow-friendly high-ranking officials from Algeria, Argentina, Bolivia, Indonesia, Moldova, and Serbia, as well as two former PACE presidents, namely Jean-Claude Mignon and René van der Linden who had been known for their pro-Russian positions.[13] The radical element at the plenary session was represented by the ECAG's Mateusz Piskorski and Wolfgang Gehrcke, a German MP and one of the leaders of Die Linke, some members of which had been involved in pro-Kremlin 'election observation' activities.

The anti-US sentiments, as well as pro-Moscow narratives on the 'Ukrainian question' and the Western sanctions dominated the Third International Parliamentary Forum. Piskorski talked of 'the most violent geopolitical struggle waged for Ukraine against Russia and Eurasian integration, against the Eurasian integration bloc as an idea that [was] being turned into reality, but also against Europe and the European integration, and against the European Union'.[14] In another speech, Piskorski discussed the 'geopolitical plans' of the unnamed ominous forces that wanted to configure 'social historical conscience' and create 'new artificial identities', but expressed his hope that Russia, together with anti-American forces in Europe, would be able to ruin these plans:

> . . . At the recent elections to the European Parliament, we have observed that strong support goes to those political forces in the EU that do not share the views of the pro-American, Atlanticist mainstream.
>
> I am glad that the events such as the one we have today, as well as the position of the Russian authorities, including the State Duma, facilitate a dialogue with – among others – the European forces that are currently in the opposition, but already understand perfectly what is going on on a global scale, that geopolitical game that I talked about. I hope . . . that we will be meeting more often in Moscow which is an island of freedom – freedom of speech, thought and exchange of ideas.[15]

The FPÖ's Johann Gudenus, who spoke at the forum two days after Putin's official visit to Vienna, praised Russia for maintaining freedom of speech, in contrast to 'many countries of the EU'.[16] Like Piskorski, Gudenus articulated an idea that the United States had employed the 'divide and rule' tactic in Ukraine in order to weaken Russia and Europe and, thus, enforce its 'geopolitical interests'. At the same time, Gudenus unequivocally positioned the FPÖ as defending the Russian interests:

> Unfortunately, the European Union, many countries of the European Union are hostages of NATO and the Council of Europe that seem to have only one aim: to present Russia as 'a bad guy', to exclude Russia from the game. They appear to pursue this aim, but we, our party, in alliance with other democratic forces of Europe, strive to counter this.[17]

Gudenus argued that a 'multipolar world' would be able to ensure 'geopolitical balance and lasting peace', and insisted that Europe and 'Russia as part of Europe' needed to show to the United States that Europe was not an American 'zone of responsibility' and essentially drive the United States out of Europe.[18] Discussing these issues, Gudenus used the geopolitical narratives popular among the historical and contemporary pan-European fascists. For example, he claimed that the FPÖ was against the Transatlantic Trade and Investment Partnership, that is a trade agreement between the EU and United States, because the party supported the idea of trans-European and Eurasian space *'from the Atlantic to Vladivostok'*.[19] In a piece that he contributed to the neo-Eurasianist *Journal of Eurasian Affairs*, Gudenus used a similar argument: 'The powers-that-be in Europe must finally realise that the important axis required by Europe is not Brussels-Washington but *Paris-Berlin-Moscow*'.[20] The phrase 'Paris-Berlin-Moscow axis' has been popularised by the neo-Eurasianists since the 1990s.

The LN's Claudio D'Amico, who also delivered his address at the Third International Parliamentary Forum, largely focused on the 'legitimacy' of the 'Crimean referendum' that he observed, and criticised – in concordance with Moscow's line – international organisations such as the OSCE that had not recognised the 'referendum' as they allegedly applied 'double standards towards Russia'.[21] In conclusion, D'Amico expressed his hope that Europe and Russia would be together 'fighting against the current and future challenges, rather than against each other'.[22]

In July-September 2014, in response to the escalation of Russia's war in Ukraine and the downing of Malaysia Airlines Flight 17, Western societies – the EU, United States, Norway, Switzerland, Canada, Australia and Japan – introduced tougher anti-Russian sanctions. Speaking at the OSCE Parliamentary Conference that took place in Switzerland in October 2014 and was titled 'New Security Challenges: The Role of Parliaments', Naryshkin fired a broadside at Western sanctions, the Ukrainian authorities and the United States. He also touched upon the 'faults' of European integration that manifested themselves, in his view, in 'the aspiration of a range of European regions for independence'. Furthermore, he attacked 'the shift towards a complete rejection of Europe's self-dependence in foreign policy', claiming that the United States seemed to deny the EU political agency that would allow the Union to address 'geopolitical issues' independently.[23]

Shortly upon his return back to Moscow, Naryshkin convened an international roundtable titled 'Ways of overcoming a crisis of trust in Europe' on 25 November 2014. One Russian journalist commented that, 'judging from the speeches, only those politicians, who were on the same page with [Russia] in its relations with the EU, came to Moscow' for the meeting.[24] The far-right participants of the meeting were among the most pro-Kremlin speakers. The FPÖ's leader Heinz-Christian Strache's address echoed Gudenus' statements at the Third International Parliamentary Forum and was almost entirely congruent with Naryshkin's talk at the OSCE Parliamentary Conference in October that year. According to Strache,

> We consider the events on Maidan in Kyiv . . . as a result of policies pursued in Ukraine by, in particular, the US. With respect to geopolitical strategy, they are aimed against . . . Russia and provoke retaliatory measures from Russia.
>
> In recent years, the European Union has not been adopting a position of its own. The European Union is now practically equal to NATO and has joined the sanctions regime against Russia automatically, following American interests. . . .
>
> We are in favour of people in the continental part of Europe creating their own history, rather than following the interests of the Americans.[25]

The FN's Aymeric Chauprade, who spoke right after Strache, repeated these arguments: 'the coup on Maidan had been elaborated in Washington with the unfortunate assistance from the German government'; the United States forced Europe to adopt anti-Russian sanctions; 'the restoration of trust . . . should be carried out through a rejection of the American dictate'.[26] The narrative of US control over Europe, popular among the far right since the 1950s, was particularly prominent in Chauprade's speech:

> Through the enlargement of the European Union by means of joining East European, Baltic states, the governments of which are . . . set against Russia, the US has tightened control over the European Union. Through economic leverage, by subjecting the elites of the European countries to the values of money, the US has managed to increase its influence in Europe.[27]

Gudenus, who also took part in the roundtable, went along with what had been said previously: the United States pursued their own interests in Europe and 'ordered' the EU to impose anti-Russian sanctions detrimental to Austria and Europe in general.[28]

On 1 October 2015, the State Duma, together with Russia's MFA, held the Fourth International Parliamentary Forum again presided over by Naryshkin. This time, none of the foreign far-right politicians participated in the plenary session of the forum, but other sections of the conference hosted D'Amico, Chauprade and Marion Maréchal-Le Pen, the FPÖ's Johannes Hübner, and Ataka's Volen Siderov.

Speaking during the section on 'strengthening the rule of international law and security', Siderov attacked national parliaments in the EU, as well as the European Parliament, dominated by 'parties adhering to globalisation and supranational companies, and opposing conservative values and national economies'.[29] In particular, he criticised the Bulgarian parliament for supporting the Bulgarian military involvement in the US-led invasion of Iraq, deployment of foreign military bases in Bulgaria, 'suicidal sanctions against Russia', and abandoning the South Stream project. For Siderov, the situation in Europe looked critical and only 'anti-globalist parties supporting conservative values and national sovereignty' could save it:

> It is now an historical moment for Europe: if there is no large-scale ideological shift, no change of the politics of the continent, no rupture in the puppet-like dependence on the United States, Europe will perish as a civilisation and parliamentarianism will be the last thing that the Europeans will be thinking about while fleeing from the Islamic invasion, and Russia will look like an island of refuge for the Christian world.[30]

In the course of the forum, Siderov also had a personal meeting with Naryshkin, during which the Bulgarian far-right politician repeated the main theses of his speech.

Other far-right politicians participated in the session on 'the challenges of migration in the contemporary world', apparently in order to corroborate – from a right-wing perspective – Moscow's narratives about the EU's inability to tackle migration problems, the EU's general decadence, and the West's responsibility for the refugee crisis.

Maréchal-Le Pen attempted to persuade the audience that the migration problems were 'the result of our historical mistakes including France's politics in Libya, Syria, [and] Iraq'. At the same time, France could not deal with the migration problem, because the country 'transferred much of its competence' to the EU.[31]

Chauprade saw the roots of 'the migration crisis' in two factors: (1) the lack of control of migration from the EU guided by 'the ideology that opposed national identity' and paved the way for 'the migration flow to the countries of the EU'; (2) the violation of sovereignty of the states like Iraq and Libya by Western countries and, especially, the United States that resulted in the current crisis.[32] If the EU wanted to solve the crisis, it should, in Chauprade's view, look to Russia for inspiration:

> Russia consolidates in itself the notion of 'nation-state'. Defending the interests of peace, it strives to support the sovereignty of Iraq and Syria, and this is exactly the politics that should now be advocated, because it will help save the nation-states thus leading to stability and peace in the world.
> . . .
> National parliaments should cling to the policy of realism that consists in supporting the actions of the Russian Federation, because these actions are pragmatic, absolutely realistic.[33]

During the same session, D'Amico described his experience of working at the OSCE and expounded particular points – largely congruent with the conservative agenda – in the OSCE resolutions that he had helped elaborate.[34]

In his turn, Hübner insisted that national parliaments in the EU had to serve the interests of the people who elected them, rather than the interests of the international organisations that urged the EU societies to be humanistic and accept refugees. In particular, he blamed the politics of the EU, especially the governments of Austria, Germany and Sweden, for 'the huge wave of migration' to Europe, and criticised 'the taboo' on discussing the migration problem.[35]

Considering the narratives that the politicians from the FPÖ, FN, LN, Ataka and other far-right organisations articulated at the conferences convened by Sergey Naryshkin, they served the purpose of legitimising Russia's foreign policy and endorsing Moscow's views of the West in general and the United States in particular against the background of growing international criticism of Russia. In this sense, the functions of these activities were similar to those of the far right's electoral observation and engagement with Russian media. However, the audiences in each case were different. Notably, none of the events discussed in this section was covered widely in Russian domestic or international media, let alone foreign media. Thus, apparently, the targeted audience of these events were their participants themselves, while the meetings could be described as 'sessions of collective counselling'. Representatives of the Russian political class could gladly listen to the praise of Moscow's policies from foreign politicians and convey to them other pro-Kremlin narratives that could be used in their home countries. Foreign politicians coming from diverse political and ideological backgrounds could consolidate their pro-Moscow, or at least Russia-friendly, views while listening to speeches of other foreign participants. Representatives of the unrecognised 'states' (Abkhazia, South Ossetia, Transnistria) could reassure themselves of the 'legitimacy' of their pseudo-republics.

The parliamentary battlefield in Strasbourg and Brussels

In his study of the behaviour of the far right in the European Parliament during its seventh term (2009–2014), Marley Morris noted a fundamental conflict in their work as MEPs: 'in most cases their ideology commits them to being fiercely critical of the EU', but at the same time 'they benefit from the EU – obtaining money, representation, legitimacy and contacts'.[36] Morris argues that this conflict is manifested in several ways: they are marginalised within the European Parliament, they find it difficult to build alliances because of conflicting nationalisms and heterogeneous ideology, and they have little impact on the EU's policies. Thus, they seem to have little choice but 'to use the opportunities of giving speeches and asking questions at the plenary as a platform for promoting their (regularly Eurosceptic) worldviews, in the hope they will be picked up by the national and international media',[37] and, therefore, gain publicity.

The EU member states use several different voting systems to elect MEPs, but, according to the EU laws, they are all obliged to elect them on the basis of proportional representation using the list system or the single transferable vote.[38] In several EU member states, the European voting rules largely favour small, marginal or new parties. For example, France's two-round system used for national parliamentary elections is unfavourable for the parties that do not obtain at least 12.5 per cent of the vote in the first round. In the European parliamentary elections, however, French parties simply need to pass the 5 per cent threshold per constituency to have its representatives be elected in the European Parliament. Since 1989 and, at least, until the time of writing – because of the differences between the voting systems used in the national and European elections – there have always been more FN's MEPs than FN's members of the National Assembly. Another example is the United Kingdom: its restrictive first-past-the-post system never allowed members of the BNP to be elected in the House of Commons, but after the 2009 European parliamentary elections, two members of the BNP were elected MEPs after the party had obtained 6.2 per cent of the vote.

While the national parliaments seem to be more prominent, in terms of publicity in domestic contexts, than the European Parliament, the latter is still a significant platform that far-right MEPs use to promote their messages in the hope they reach national audiences and media. Therefore, 'when it comes to making speeches and asking questions' in the European Parliament, the far right even tend 'to outdo other MEPs'.[39] Discussions in the European Parliament concerning the issues of Russian domestic and international policies have not been an exception.

Over the years, the European Parliament has adopted a number of resolutions directly and indirectly related to Moscow's political and geopolitical interests. Despite the non-legislative procedure of their adoption, these resolutions represent important lines of communicating messages from the European Parliament to the Russian authorities. As Stefano Braghiroli explains, unlike the European Commission or the Council of the EU, the European Parliament 'is the only directly elected supranational institution of the EU', and hence its positions generally reflect the views of the EU citizens, including those on EU-Russia relationships.[40] Moreover, after the enactment of the Treaty of Lisbon, the European Parliament 'has gained power exponentially vis-à-vis the other EU institutions, while showing greater activism within the sphere of external relations', and has been 'inclined to adopt value-oriented stances' enshrined in the resolutions.[41] Because of the European Parliament's value-based approach to the Russia-related resolutions, they were mostly critical of developments in Russia, which elicited disgruntled response from Russian officials.

Nowhere has the pro-Russian 'collective performance' of many European ultranationalists been demonstrated more clearly than during the debates over, as well as voting on, the Russia-related resolutions in the European Parliament in 2014–2016. The phenomenon of some far-right MEPs voting against critical Russia-related resolutions is not a new one, but it had been less homogeneous and consistent before 2014. One example is the approach towards Georgia after the war with Russia in August 2008. When the European Parliament adopted, during its sixth term, a resolution on the situation in Georgia that, in particular, 'called on Russia to respect the sovereignty, territorial integrity and inviolability of the internationally recognised borders of the Republic of Georgia',[42] three MEPs from the far-right VB supported it, while Forza Nuova's Roberto Fiore, Fiamma Tricolore's Luca Romagnoli and the FN's MEPs voted against it. When, during its seventh term, the European Parliament adopted a resolution on 'providing macro-financial assistance to Georgia',[43] which was not beneficial to Russia in geopolitical terms, all the LN's MEPs, who then belonged to the right-wing Europe of Freedom and Democracy (EFD) group, as well as the FN's Jean-Marie Le Pen and Bruno Gollnisch, the FPÖ's Andreas Mölzer and Franz Obermayr, and the PRM's Claudiu Ciprian Tănăsescu[44] supported the resolution. The nine far-right MEPs who voted against it were members of Ataka, BNP, VB, and PVV.

Until 2014–2015, during the debates at the European Parliament, many far-right MEPs demonstrated a relatively balanced approach towards Russia-related issues, which was often marked by four argumentative patterns: (1) Russia is an important economic partner of the EU; (2) the EU cannot judge Russia because it lacks moral authority to do so; (3) democratic transition is still an ongoing process in Russia which is a result of the previous authoritarian rule; and (4) the EU should adopt a realistic, rather than confrontational, policy towards Russia.

One of the most typical combinations of these argumentative patterns can be found in the FPÖ's MEP Franz Obermayr's speech during the debate on a motion for the resolution 'On the situation in Russia'[45] that, in particular, expressed the European Parliament's 'profound disappointment with the conduct of the 4 December [2011] Duma elections, marred with frequent violations' and strongly condemned 'mass arrests and beatings by the police during peaceful demonstrations in Moscow, St Petersburg and other Russian cities against Duma elections violations':

> Democracy in Russia is undoubtedly still in its infancy and this was made clear once again during the last elections. It also goes without saying that 70 years of Soviet rule have left their mark. Russia is constantly being reprimanded by the EU, without the EU itself setting a good example. . . . Patriotic movements which try to go against the Brussels mainstream regularly become victims of hate campaigns in the political arena and the media. We should not therefore be pointing the finger at others. Because of our mutual interests in the field of energy, the EU should ensure that large companies like Gazprom comply with the competition rules on the energy market. On the other hand, we should not be disregarding Moscow's interests in the post-Soviet market.[46]

Criticism of the developments in Russia – ranging from apologetic or indulgent to principled – was not uncommon among far-right MEPs during the debates in the European Parliament. The BZÖ's MEP Ewald Stadler was arguably the most apologetic towards Russia, condoning the undemocratic practices of Putin's regime with reference to different speeds of democratic development in Russia and the West. While debating on the resolution 'Political Use of Justice in Russia',[47] Stadler argued that 'the Russian people [were] capable of themselves developing a state under the rule of law and at a speed and with the focuses that they themselves cho[se]'.[48] Implicit or explicit references to 'speed' could be observed in other speeches too. For example, according to Jaroslav Paška of the ultranationalist Slovenská národná strana (Slovak National Party, SNS), Russia was 'still getting used to democratic rule',[49] while the FPÖ's Andreas Mölzer insisted that Russia had 'a great deal of catching up to do when it [came] to democracy and human rights'.[50]

Some MEPs from far-right parties were more critical. During a debate on the detention of Greenpeace activists by the Russian authorities in 2013,[51] the PVV's Daniël van der Stoep complained that, in the Netherlands, they faced 'enough of the arrogance of the Russian state' noting that Russian diplomats refused to pay parking fines and could always rely on their international immunity if they mistreat their children.[52] Nikolaos Salavrakos from the Greek far-right Laikós Orthódoxos Synagermós (Popular Orthodox Rally, LAOS), who supported the resolution 'Political Use of Justice in Russia' in 2012, explained his decision by saying that 'the human rights situation in Russia ha[d] deteriorated drastically over recent months and measures need[ed] to be taken to protect civil society and freedom of expression and assembly'.[53] However, harsh, principled criticism of Putin's Russia was, in general, scarce among the far-right MEPs.

Apart from the references to Russia 'still getting used to democratic rule', another popular rhetorical 'way out' of criticism of the developments in Russia was guided by a 'whataboutist' tactic shifting the focus of the discussion from Russia to the EU. The FN's Bruno Gollnisch disputed the right of the European Parliament and, apparently, of the EU to 'lecture Russia on human rights', because 'Julian Assange, a dissident publicist and founder of the WikiLeaks site [had] been detained for weeks in the United Kingdom because of a totally outrageous and ridiculous extradition request from Sweden'.[54] In his turn, Andreas Mölzer asserted that 'the EU should refrain from trying to teach Russia lessons in democratic politics and should instead work on its own democratic deficit, putting an end to the leftist authoritarian pressure on Hungary'.[55]

Often, the focus of the debates on Russia-related resolutions shifted from Russia to individual member states, as far-right MEPs used the platform of the European Parliament to criticise the phenomena related to their own countries. According to Jobbik's Krisztina Morvai, the EU could not call the relevant Russian state agencies 'for an immediate, thorough investigation' into the murder of human rights activists, because the EU did not 'have the confidence and moral authority to do this'. The EU, Morvai maintained, should better investigate 'human rights violations in Hungary'.[56] Discussing the same resolution on the murder of human rights activists in Russia, Morvai's fellow party member Zoltán Balczó argued that the EU was right to speak out against human rights violations, but he questioned whether the EU had 'the moral basis for doing this after it acquired [Czech President] Václav Klaus's signature on the Treaty of Lisbon by letting the Beneš Decrees continue to apply'.[57] Ewald Stadler's counterargument to the claim that 'indirect campaigning [had been] carried out on television in Russia by government reporting' during the 2012 presidential campaign was a request to explain 'the Austrian Government's coverage, where three quarters of all reports on [sic] the Austrian broadcaster ORF [had been] devoted to the government under [Austrian] Chancellor [Werner] Faymann'.[58] During a debate on another Russia-related resolution, Ataka's Slavi Binev said that he 'support[ed] the visa restrictions for all individuals implicated in the Sergei Magnitsky case', but he could not support the resolution because

> Everything that has been said on the Magnitsky case – abuse of power, lawsuits to remove political and economic rivals, arrests, torture, impunity of human rights abusers – applies to the current situation in Bulgaria. Despite numerous reports on my part, the European institutions remain silent, and no such measures or proposals have been made to the Council.[59]

Some far-right MEPs also suggested that, instead of 'lecturing' Russia, the EU could pursue a realistic policy towards Russia. This argument was perhaps best articulated by Jaroslav Paška:

It is good to have proper discussions with our Russian friends on all of the issues that concern us regarding the running of the country by the Russian authorities. However, this dialogue must be businesslike, in a spirit of partnership, and motivated by an effort to improve the functioning of the democratic system in Russia, rather than by the lecturing of a self-styled custodian of global democracy. Let us negotiate with Russia as with a friend, in a correct manner, openly and decently.[60]

Niki Tzavela, then a member of the LAOS, also thought that denouncing 'everything that [was] happening in Russia' was 'not productive or creative'. Tzavela believed that rapprochement between the EU and Russia could be achieved, first of all, through 'multi-faceted cooperation in the trade, energy, culture and education sectors, before moving on to the human rights sector'.[61] The LN's Fiorello Provera, speaking on behalf of the EFD group, held that 'a general feeling of aversion towards and mistrust of Russia' did not 'represent a sound basis for the cooperation', and that 'support and trust [were] needed more than criticism'.[62]

However, for the FPÖ's MEPs Mölzer and Obermayr, a realistic policy towards Russia, especially in terms of international relations, implied acknowledging a Russian sphere of influence, or, as Mölzer put it, showing 'respect for Russia's historical sensitivities with regard to geopolitical matters'.[63] This narrative became especially prominent after Russia started exercising economic and political pressure on several non-EU East European countries and particularly Ukraine, in the run-up to the Vilnius Eastern Partnership Summit in the second half of 2013. During the debates on the resolution 'on the pressure exerted by Russia on Eastern Partnership countries' that called on Russia to respect fully the sovereign right of those countries 'to pursue their own political choices',[64] Mölzer explicitly stated that the EU had to accept that those East European countries, which were not members of the EU and were previously Soviet republics, were 'in the sphere of influence or interest of the Russians'.[65]

In the vote on the last Russia-related resolution adopted during the seventh term of the European Parliament and after the beginning of the Russian-Ukrainian war, the overwhelming majority of far-right MEPs refused to support a resolution, which condemned 'in the strongest possible terms the escalating destabilisation and provocations in eastern and southern Ukraine'; rejected 'any preparation for illegal "Crimea-like" referendums'; and urged Russia 'to immediately withdraw its presence in support of violent separatists and armed militias' and 'to remove troops from the eastern border of Ukraine'.[66] Out of 27 far-right MEPs who took part in the vote, only four supported the resolution: Sampo Terho of the Perussuomalaiset (The Finns, PS), the PRM's Vadim Tudor and Dan Dumitru Zamfirescu, and the DF's Morten Messerschmidt;[67] 3 MEPs abstained: Jaroslav Paška of the SNS, Nikolaos Salavrakos of the LAOS, and VB's Frank Vanhecke.

The eighth election to the European Parliament held in May 2014 saw a rise of support for far-right parties such as the FPÖ, FN, DF, SD and PS which had 'been able to capitalise upon popular discontent associated and a general feeling of disillusionment with democratic politics at the national level'.[68] For the first time in their political histories, representatives of the far-right AfD, NPD, XA, Anexartitoi Ellines (Independent Greeks), Nacionālā apvienība (National Alliance, NA)[69] and Tvarka ir teisingumas (Order and Justice, TT) became MEPs. Electoral support declined for Jobbik, PVV, LN and VB, yet they remained represented in the European Parliament, while members of Ataka, BZÖ, BNP, LAOS, SNS and PRM failed to get re-elected.

Because of the Russian-Ukrainian war and internal developments in Russia characterised by increasing pressure on opposition leaders (including the assassination of prominent member of the Russian opposition Boris Nemtsov in Moscow on 27 February 2015), the European Parliament discussed and adopted even more Russia-related resolutions compared to the previous term. Among those MEPs who generally declined to support the resolutions that criticised Russia, the following argumentative patterns were prevalent and were largely congruent with messages promoted by official Moscow, Russian pro-Kremlin expert circles and Russian state-funded media: (1) sanctions imposed by the EU on Russia for the annexation of Crimea and invasion of Eastern Ukraine are harmful or useless; (2) Russia-related resolutions are driven by Cold War mentality on the part of the EU and/or anti-Russian sentiments; (3) only the US benefits from the confrontation between the EU and Russia; (4) rather than being at enmity with Russia, the EU should engage with this country and jointly respond to various international challenges. Whereas these patterns are, to a certain extent, similar to those characterising the far-right MEPs' arguments during the previous term of the European Parliament, references to the idea that democratic transition was still an ongoing process in Russia were almost absent in the eighth term.

The debates and results of the vote on two particular resolutions of the European Parliament (see Table 7.1) provide insights into the attitudes towards Russia presented by far-right MEPs and into the interplay of the above-mentioned argumentative patterns: 'The state of EU-Russia relations'[70] (Vote 1) and 'The strategic military situation in the Black Sea Basin following the illegal annexation of Crimea by Russia'[71] (Vote 2).

The resolution 'The state of EU-Russia relations' was very critical of Moscow's actions in the international and domestic domains. In particular, it stated that:

> Russia's direct and indirect involvement in the armed conflict in Ukraine and its illegal annexation of Crimea, together with its violation of the territorial integrity of Georgia, and economic coercion and political destabilisation of its European neighbours constitute a deliberate violation of democratic principles and fundamental values and of international law.[72]

Moreover, the resolution argued that Russia could no longer be 'treated as, or considered, a "strategic partner"' of the EU and that the EU had 'to conduct a critical re-assessment of its relations with Russia'.[73] The resolution was adopted by 494 votes in favour, 135 against and 69 abstentions. It was supported by five political

TABLE 7.1 Far-right MEPs' votes on the European Parliament resolutions 'The state of EU-Russia relations' (Vote 1) and 'The strategic military situation in the Black Sea Basin following the illegal annexation of Crimea by Russia' (Vote 2)

"+" – for the resolution, "−" against the resolution, "A" – abstained, "X" – absent or did not vote.

Country/MEP	Party	Group	Vote 1	Vote 2
Austria				
Barbara Kappel	FPÖ	NI	−	−
Georg Mayer	FPÖ	NI	−	−
Franz Obermayr	FPÖ	NI	−	−
Harald Vilimsky	FPÖ	NI	−	−
Belgium				
Gerolf Annemans	VB	NI	A	−
Denmark				
Jørn Dohrmann	DF	ECR	A	A
Rikke Karlsson	DF[1]	ECR	A	A
Morten Messerschmidt	DF	ECR	X	X
Anders Primdahl Vistisen	DF	ECR	A	X
Finland				
Jussi Halla-aho	PS	ECR	+	+
Pirkko Ruohonen-Lerner	PS	ECR	+	+
France				
Louis Aliot	FN	NI	−	−
Marie-Christine Arnautu	FN	NI	−	−
Nicolas Bay	FN	NI	−	−
Dominique Bilde	FN	NI	−	−
Marie-Christine Boutonnet	FN	NI	−	−
Steeve Briois	FN	NI	−	−
Aymeric Chauprade	FN[2]	NI	−	−
Mireille d'Ornano	FN	NI	−	−
Édouard Ferrand	FN	NI	−	−
Sylvie Goddyn	FN	NI	−	−
Bruno Gollnisch	FN	NI	−	−
Jean-François Jalkh	FN	NI	−	−
Jean-Marie Le Pen	FN	NI	X	X
Marine Le Pen	FN	NI	−	−
Gilles Lebreton	FN	NI	−	−
Philippe Loiseau	FN	NI	−	−
Dominique Martin	FN	NI	−	−
Joëlle Mélin	FN	NI	−	−
Bernard Monot	FN	NI	−	−
Sophie Montel	FN	NI	−	−
Florian Philippot	FN	NI	−	−
Jean-Luc Schaffhauser	RBM	NI	−	−
Mylène Troszczynski	FN	NI	−	−

continued . . .

TABLE 7.1 Continued

Country/MEP	Party	Group	Vote 1	Vote 2
Germany				
Hans–Olaf Henkel	AfD[3]	ECR	+	A
Bernd Kölmel	AfD[4]	ECR	A	A
Bernd Lucke	AfD[5]	ECR	A	A
Marcus Pretzell	AfD	ECR	–	–
Joachim Starbatty	AfD[6]	ECR	A	A
Beatrix von Storch	AfD	ECR	–	–
Ulrike Trebesius	AfD[7]	ECR	A	A
Udo Voigt	NPD	NI	–	–
Greece				
Georgios Epitideios	XA	NI	–	–
Lampros Fountoulis	XA	NI	X	X
Eleftherios Synadinos	XA	NI	–	X
Hungary				
Zoltán Balczó	Jobbik	NI	–	–
Béla Kovács	Jobbik	NI	–	–
Krisztina Morvai	Jobbik	NI	–	–
Italy				
Mara Bizzotto	LN	NI	–	–
Mario Borghezio	LN	NI	–	–
Gianluca Buonanno	LN	NI	–	–
Lorenzo Fontana	LN	NI	–	–
Matteo Salvini	LN	NI	–	X
Latvia				
Roberts Zīle	NA	ECR	+	+
Lithuania				
Rolandas Paksas	TT	EFDD	A	A
Netherlands				
Marcel de Graaff	PVV	NI	X	–
Vicky Maeijer	PVV	NI	–	–
Olaf Stuger	PVV	NI	–	–
Sweden				
Peter Lundgren	SD	EFDD	A	A
Kristina Winberg	SD	EFDD	A	A

1 Rikke Karlsson left the DF on 16 October 2015.
2 Aymeric Chauprade left the FN on 9 November 2015.
3 Hans–Olaf Henkel left the AfD on 7 July 2015.
4 Bernd Kölmel left the AfD on 7 July 2015.
5 Bernd Lucke left the AfD on 7 July 2015.
6 Joachim Starbatty left the AfD on 7 July 2015.
7 Ulrike Trebesius left the AfD on 7 July 2015.

groups in the European Parliament: European People's Party (EPP), Progressive Alliance of Socialists and Democrats (S&D), Alliance of Liberals and Democrats for Europe Group (ALDE/ADLE), The Greens – European Free Alliance (Greens/ EFA), and European Conservatives and Reformists (ECR); while the generally right-wing and Eurosceptic Europe of Freedom and Direct Democracy (EFDD), the left-wing European United Left/Nordic Green Left (GUE-NGL), as well as the majority of independent MEPs, or Non-Inscrits (NI), rejected it.

In its turn, the resolution 'The strategic military situation in the Black Sea Basin following the illegal annexation of Crimea by Russia', in particular, supported 'the non-recognition of Russia's annexation of Crimea', reiterated 'its commitment to the independence, sovereignty and territorial integrity of Ukraine', noted 'with concern that the illegal annexation of Crimea ha[d] precipitated a significant change in the strategic landscape of the Black Sea Basin and the adjacent area', and warned 'that the illegal annexation of Crimea offer[ed] Russia a "southern Kaliningrad", another outpost directly bordering on NATO'.[74] The resolution was adopted by 356 votes in favour, 183 against and 96 abstentions. It was supported by the EPP, ALDE/ADLE and ECR, while EFDD, Greens/EFA, GUE-NGL, as well as the overwhelming majority of NI, decided not to support it. The S&D group seemed to be divided, but the majority still voted in its favour.

As seen from Table 7.1, far-right MEPs largely voted against the two above-mentioned resolutions, with the majority of the negative votes coming from the FPÖ, FN, XA, Jobbik, LN and PVV. The smallest group of far-right MEPs mostly representing the PS and NA supported the resolutions. Their vote can be explained both by the troubled historical (and, in Latvia's case, contemporary) relations between their countries and Russia, as well as by the PS's and NA's MEPs affiliation with the ECR that largely supported both resolutions.

The TT's Rolandas Paksas's abstentions can also be partly explained by his group affiliation. Lithuania, too, has troubled historical and contemporary relations with Russia; yet the EFDD rejected the resolution and, by abstaining, Paksas rebelled against his group. Despite his abstention, it seemed during the debates that Paksas would have rather supported the resolution if not for the position of his group. For example, discussing the resolution 'The state of EU-Russia relations', he stated that the EU could not cooperate with Russia 'at the expense of international principles and European values, norms and international obligations'. Paksas also argued that it was 'necessary to respect the territorial integrity and sovereignty of Ukraine' and that cooperation with Russia could only be renewed 'upon full implementation of the Minsk agreements'.[75]

The SD's MEPs Kristina Winberg and Peter Lundgren also abstained during both votes and rebelled against the EFDD's decision. Their abstentions were, to a certain extent, determined by their nuanced approach towards Russian domestic and foreign policy. Previously, both of them supported the resolution titled 'Murder of the Russian opposition leader Boris Nemtsov and the state of democracy in Russia' that, in particular called 'on the Russian authorities to stop all pressure, repressive acts and intimidation – both political and judicial – against opposition leaders, civil society representatives and independent media',[76] despite the fact that they believed that the EU had 'no right to call for any other countries to make any changes to their domestic policies whatsoever': they supported the resolution to express their 'condolences to the family, friends and supporters of Mr. Nemtsov'.[77] Debating on the resolution 'The state of EU-Russia relations', Lundgren noted that the annexation of Crimea and the war against Ukraine created a situation where the EU had to take action and impose sanctions on Russia, and asserted that re-establishing cooperation with Russia would only be possible in case the Russian authorities complied 'with their international and legal obligations'.[78] While Lundgren's position concerning the EU-Russia relations might be considered – his abstention notwithstanding – as critical of Russia's actions, it was most likely the SD's sceptical attitude towards NATO that informed Winberg and Lundgren to abstain during Vote 2. The resolution stressed 'that modernising and enhancing the military capabilities of those Black Sea littoral states that [were] members of EU and NATO [was] of key importance to ensuring security and stability in the region',[79] and Winberg considered this as a step towards 'the escalation of the conflict between Russia and the Western democracies' and the idea of moving NATO forces to the Black Sea Basin – as 'an ill-advised and confrontational suggestion'.[80]

The VB's Gerolf Annemans's abstention during Vote 1 could be seen as a result of him being more distrustful towards the EU's actions rather than those of Russia. While he seemed to agree that Russia's actions in Crimea should be strongly condemned, he criticised the process of rapprochement between the EU and Ukraine, as well as claiming that the VB advocated re-establishing diplomatic relations with Russia and contested mutual economic sanctions and a trade boycott.[81]

The contradictory vote on both resolutions on the part of the AfD's MEPs seemed to reflect an internal conflict within the party. The AfD was formed in 2013 by several disaffected members of the CDU and was considered as a non-radical, Eurosceptic or even only softly Eurosceptic party.[82] However, a conflict between AfD's leading members Bernd Lucke and Frauke Petry, who represented the neo-liberal and national-conservative factions in the party correspondingly, eventually led to Petry taking control over the party in the beginning of July 2015 and radicalising the AfD in a more clearly right-wing direction. On 7 July 2015, Lucke and four other MEPs from his own faction left the party. Lucke referred to rising xenophobic, anti-Western and pro-Russian leanings in the party as the reason for his departure.[83] Out of seven original AfD's MEPs,[84] only two remained in the party: Marcus Pretzell and Beatrix von Storch, who belonged to Petry's faction. In 2016, von Storch left the ECR and joined the EFDD, while Pretzell was expelled from the ECR and joined the more radical Europe of Nations and Freedom group in the European Parliament.

MEPs from Lucke's faction, while still members of the AfD in June 2015, largely abstained during the votes on both resolutions (Henkel supported Vote 1), while Pretzell and von Storch rejected them. However, these differences – most likely reflecting the disputes within the party – did not imply any radical contrast between the two groups' positions towards the Russian-Ukrainian conflict. In the final analysis, the two groups – with the exception of Henkel in relation to Vote 1 – rebelled against the ECR's decision to support both resolutions. Debates on other Russia-related resolutions also demonstrated certain affinities between the two factions' positions. For example, Lucke condemned 'the illegal annexation of Crimea and any covert or overt support of violent attempts at secession', but at the same time criticised the idea of ending strategic security partnership with Russia.[85] Pretzell called Russia's annexation of Crimea an obvious breach of international law, yet contested the rapprochement between the EU and Ukraine, as well as criticising the EU's alleged meddling in Russia's internal affairs.[86] Debating on Vote 1, Ulrike Trebesius and von Storch blamed *both* Russia and the EU for the cooling off in relations between them.[87]

The idea that the European Parliament's Russia-related resolutions were contributing to the escalation of the conflict between the EU and Russia underpinned the FPÖ's MEPs' negative vote on both resolutions. During the debates regarding Vote 1, they submitted written and almost identical explanations of their decisions to reject the resolution, with the underlying message that the report on the state of EU-Russia relations was unbalanced and biased, and that proposals featured in the resolution did not help improve relations between the EU and Russia. Barbara Kappel added to this main message that it was time that the EU started seeking a dialogue and came to a compromise with Russia.[88] The FPÖ's MEPs presented a similar message during Vote 2: in their identical written statements, Harald Vilimsky and Georg Mayer argued that the Crimea-related resolution was 'totally unbalanced and one-sided' and would only result in the 'escalation of the conflict'.[89] Kappel built on this argument, adding that she was opposed to the NATO military build-up in the Black Sea. Scepticism about enhancing the role of NATO in the Black Sea Basin was present in Vilimsky's oral statement too.[90]

Opposition to the European Parliament's allegedly confrontational Russia-related resolutions, criticism of the sanctions against Russia, and conspiracy theories about the involvement of the United States were used by the LN's MEPs to justify their rejection of both resolutions. For example, for Gianluca Buonanno, the resolution on the state of EU-Russia relations was 'biased and full of anti-Russian prejudices', while the Crimea-related resolution was 'excessively anti-Russian'. For him, the EU policies towards Russia were inspired by the United States and had to be reversed, as Russia was an important partner for Italian companies, and he would like to see Moscow more involved in European development policies.[91]

Jobbik's MEPs followed a similar argumentative line: Zoltán Balczó and Béla Kovács claimed that the sanctions were damaging to European economies and served as evidence that the EU pursued policies inspired by the United States. Krisztina Morvai turned to a 'whataboutist' tactic questioning the validity of the Western criticism of Russia's behaviour with references to allegedly equally ambiguous practices in the West. The NPD's Udo Voigt largely adopted this 'whataboutist' tactic too.

The analysis of the FN's MEPs' explanations of their negative votes on both resolutions suggests that they followed guidelines distributed among them – otherwise it seems impossible to understand why some explanations coming from different FN's MEPs were identical, while some others were reworded but still contained identical phrases. Comparing written statements of different FN's MEPs during the debates on Vote 1, it is possible to distinguish a set of theses most likely featured in these hypothetical guidelines: (1) anti-Russian sentiment, or so-called 'Russophobia', is the main motivation behind the resolution; (2) Georgia was responsible for the Russian-Georgian war in 2008; (3) the Crimean 'referendum' in 2014 was legitimate; (4) Russia is a key partner of the EU; (5) the resolution only serves the US interests; and (6) one can witness 'the advent of a multipolar world' in which neither France nor Europe 'would be subject to any great foreign power'.[92] The FN's MEPs' statements during the debates on Vote 2 reiterated the third and fourth theses, as well as featuring a modified fifth argument: Europe should reject submission to the United States and NATO.

The explanations provided by the XA's MEPs for their negatives votes were arguably the most straightforward among the far-right MEPs. For the debates on Vote 1, Georgios Epitideios and Eleftherios Synadinos submitted two almost identical statements that argued: 'The movement [i.e. XA] is geopolitically oriented towards Russia. Europe serves the interests of the system controlled by the United States, especially regarding the issues related to the EU-Russia cooperation'.[93] Indeed, the XA's thesis on the need of Greece's 'geostrategical turn' reads as follows:

> It is required to immediately reverse our geopolitical orientation and re-examine our alliances that have contributed nothing to our national interests. We should turn, for investments and energy at first, to Russia. A trade and defence agreement with the Russians would rid our country from the deadly embrace of the USA and their allies.[94]

Conclusion

The 'Arab Spring', anti-Putin protests in 2011–2013, intensifying criticism of Russia's domestic and international actions coming from mainstream Western politicians and officials, as well as the introduction of Magnitsky-related sanctions by the EU and United States, amplified pre-existing anti-Western and, especially, anti-American sentiments of the Russian authorities, for whom external legitimation of Putin's regime became of even greater concern. The perceived gradual loss of established foreign allies made Moscow dependent on some remaining mainstream pro-Russian figures in the West, and, increasingly, led to rapprochement with anti-establishment actors, including far-right parties and organisations.

In order to consolidate the pro-Russian Western camp consisting of both mainstream and anti-establishment figures, Chairman of the Russian State Duma Sergey Naryshkin launched, in 2012, the International Parliamentary Forum that became a major platform for pro-Russian Westerners to exchange views and reassure themselves of their soundness. The far-right element of the International Parliamentary Forums built on the existing network of pro-Russian far-right politicians who had previously been engaged in electoral observation to the benefit of Russia's foreign policy, undermining Western political narratives in Russian media, and implementing pro-Russian projects in their home countries. However, the meetings within the framework of the International Parliamentary Forum featured only select representatives of the far-right pro-Russian camp, namely politicians from the FPÖ, FN, LN, Ataka, and ECAG. At the meetings in Moscow, they essentially reproduced the Kremlin's narratives that, at the same time, complied with their own ideas about Russia and the West: (1) the revolution in Ukraine was inspired by Washington to undermine Russia's sphere of influence in the post-Soviet space; (2) the Crimean 'referendum' was legitimate; (3) the United States and/or NATO forced the submissive EU to impose sanctions on Russia; (4) Europe should get rid of American influence; (5) Europe and Russia should build a common geopolitical structure on the Eurasian continent. Some far-right participants clearly positioned themselves as Russia's allies in Europe.

One could hear similar narratives in Strasbourg and Brussels during the debates on the European Parliament's Russia-related resolutions, especially since the beginning of the European Parliament's eighth term in July 2014. However, the far-right voices in the European Parliament were not always friendly or sympathetic towards Putin's Russia. Moscow's actions in the domestic and international spheres found little appreciation from MEPs representing the PS, NA, TT, DF, SD, and Bernd Lucke's faction of the AfD. Nevertheless, the majority of far-right MEPs did support Moscow's actions, and the staunchest far-right supporters of the Kremlin's policies could be found among the members of the FPÖ, FN, Jobbik, LN, PVV, NPD, VB, XA, and Frauke Petry's faction of the AfD. The critics of the European Parliament's Russia-related resolutions insisted that they were driven by anti-Russian and pro-American sentiments, and hindered cooperation between the EU and Russia considered as a key partner of Europe. Thus, it would be no exaggeration to say that, when MEPs from the FPÖ, FN, LN, PVV, VB, as well as the AfD's Marcus Pretzell and individual right-wing MEPs from Poland, Romania and the United Kingdom formed the Europe of Nations and Freedom group on 15 June 2015, Moscow secured a predominantly loyal political structure at the heart of European democracy.

Notes

1 Yevgeniy Minchenko, "Bol'shoe pravitel'stvo Vladimira Putina i 'Politbyuro 2.0'", *Minchenko Consulting*, 21 August (2012), http://stratagema.org/netcat_files/File/Политбюро и большое правительство-2-2(1).pdf
2 "V. Zhirinovsky: Vsemirny Kongress patriotov".
3 "Direct Line with Vladimir Putin".
4 "Q&A: The Magnitsky Affair", *BBC*, 11 July (2013), www.bbc.com/news/world-europe-20626960

5   "Magnitsky Death Reminiscent of Worst Russian Abuses of the Past", *Euronews*, 11 July (2013), http://euronews.com/2013/07/11/magnitsky-death-reminiscent-of-worst-russian-abuses-of-the-past/; "Q&A: The Magnitsky Affair".

6   A detailed discussion of the Magnitsky Affair, from the point of view of the CEO and co-founder of Hermitage Capital Management Bill Browder, can be found in: Bill Browder, *Red Notice: A True Story of High Finance, Murder, and One Man's Fight for Justice* (New York: Simon & Schuster, 2015).

7   "Text of the Russia and Moldova Jackson-Vanik Repeal and Sergei Magnitsky Rule of Law Accountability Act of 2012", *GovTrack*, 7 December (2012), https://govtrack.us/congress/bills/112/hr6156/text/enr

8   "Common Visa Restrictions for Russian Officials Involved in the Sergei Magnitsky Case", *European Parliament*, 23 October (2012), http://europarl.europa.eu/sides/getDoc.do?type=TA&reference=P7-TA-2012-0369&language=EN

9   Nicholas Redman, "Russia's Breaking Point", *Survival*, Vol. 56, No. 2 (2014), pp. 235–244 (240).

10 Naryshkin (ed.), *Sovremenny parlamentarizm i budushchee demokratii*, p. 6.

11 Ibid.

12 "Citing Crimea, PACE Suspends Voting Rights of Russian Delegation and Excludes It from Leading Bodies", *Parliamentary Assembly*, 10 April (2014), http://assembly.coe.int/nw/xml/News/News-View-EN.asp?newsid=4982&cat=8

13 Mignon voted against the PACE's decision to suspend the voting rights of the Russian delegation; van der Linden adopted a clear pro-Moscow line in Russia's conflict with Estonia, see Vladimir Socor, "PACE Chairman Bending to the Kremlin Wind against Estonia", *Eurasia Daily Monitor*, 3 August (2007), http://jamestown.org/single/?tx_ttnews[tt_news]=32919

14 Naryshkin (ed.), *Novye izmereniya parlamentskogo dialoga*, p. 57.

15 Ibid., pp. 148–149.

16 Ibid., p. 135.

17 Ibid., pp. 135–136.

18 Ibid., p. 136.

19 Ibid., p. 137. My emphasis.

20 Johann Gudenus, "The FPÖ Is against Centralism in the EU and Advocates a Europe of Fatherlands", *Journal of Eurasian Affairs*, Vol. 3, No. 1 (2015), pp. 30–31 (30). My emphasis.

21 Naryshkin (ed.), *Novye izmereniya parlamentskogo dialoga*, p. 161.

22 Ibid., p. 162.

23 "Vystuplenie Predsedatelya Gosudarstvennoy Dumy Federal'nogo Sobraniya Rossiyskoy Federatsii S.E. Naryshkina na Parlamentskoy konferentsii 'Novye vyzovy bezopasnosti: rol' parlamentov' v ramkakh sessii 1: Voenno-politicheskie izmereniya – diskussiya po voprosam krizisa v Ukraine, Zheneva, 3 oktyabrya 2014 goda", *Ministerstvo inostrannykh del Rossiyskoy Federatsii*, 4 October (2014), http://mid.ru/pravozasitnye-social-no-ekonomiceskie-gumanitarnye-voprosy-deatel-nosti-oon/-/asset_publisher/Z02tOD8Nkusz/content/id/668290

24 Viktor Khamraev, "Sergey Naryshkin nashel svoikh v Evroparlamente", *Kommersant. Daily*, No. 214, 26 November (2014), p. 2.

25 Andrey Petrov (ed.), *Puti preodoleniya krizisa doveriya v Evrope. Materialy Mezhdunarodnogo "kruglogo stola"* (Moscow: Izdanie Gosudarstvennoy Dumy, 2015), pp. 15–16.

26 Ibid., pp. 17–18.

27 Ibid., pp. 16–17.

28 Ibid., p. 58.

29 Andrey Petrov (ed.), *Rol' parlamentov v obespechenii mezhdunarodnoy bezopasnosti v sovremennykh usloviyakh. Materialy chetvertogo Mezhdunarodnogo parlamentskogo foruma* (Moscow: Izdanie Gosudarstvennoy Dumy, 2015), p. 69.

30   Ibid., p. 70.
31   Ibid., p. 99.
32   Ibid., p. 117.
33   Ibid., pp. 117–118.
34   Ibid., pp. 121–123.
35   Ibid., p. 127.
36   Marley Morris, *Conflicted Politicians: The Populist Radical Right in the European Parliament* (London: Counterpoint, 2013), p. 5.
37   Ibid., p. 70.
38   Kai-Friederike Oelbermann, Antonio Palomares, Friedrich Pukelsheim, "The 2009 European Parliament Elections: From Votes to Seats in 27 Ways", *European Electoral Studies*, Vol. 5, No. 1 (2010), pp. 148–182.
39   Morris, *Conflicted Politicians*, p. 7.
40   Stefano Braghiroli, "Voting on Russia in the European Parliament: The Role of National and Party Group Affiliations", *Journal of Contemporary European Studies*, Vol. 23, No. 1 (2015), pp. 58–81 (60).
41   Ibid.
42   "European Parliament Resolution of 3 September 2008 on the Situation in Georgia", *European Parliament*, 3 September (2008), http://europarl.europa.eu/sides/getDoc.do?type=TA&reference=P6-TA-2008-0396&language=EN
43   "European Parliament Legislative Resolution of 24 November 2009 on the Proposal for a Council Decision Providing Macro-financial Assistance to Georgia", *European Parliament*, 24 November (2009), http://europarl.europa.eu/sides/getDoc.do?type=TA&reference=P7-TA-2009-0071&language=EN
44   In 2010, Tănăsescu joined the Romanian centre-left Partidul Social Democrat (Social Democratic Party).
45   "European Parliament Resolution on the Situation in Russia", *European Parliament*, 8 February (2012), http://europarl.europa.eu/sides/getDoc.do?type=MOTION&reference=B7-2012-0057&language=EN
46   "Situation in Russia (Debate)", *European Parliament*, 1 February (2012), http://europarl.europa.eu/sides/getDoc.do?pubRef=-//EP//TEXT+CRE+20120201+ITEM-015+DOC+XML+V0//EN&language=EN
47   "European Parliament Resolution of 13 September 2012 on the Political Use of Justice in Russia", *European Parliament*, 13 September (2012), http://europarl.europa.eu/sides/getDoc.do?type=TA&reference=P7-TA-2012-0352&language=EN
48   "Debates", *European Parliament*, 13 September (2012), http://europarl.europa.eu/sides/getDoc.do?type=CRE&reference=20120913&secondRef=ITEM-012&language=EN&ring=P7-RC-2012-0427#4-181-000
49   "Rule of Law in Russia (Debate)", *European Parliament*, 15 February (2011), http://europarl.europa.eu/sides/getDoc.do?pubRef=-//EP//TEXT+CRE+20110215+ITEM-005+DOC+XML+V0//EN&language=EN
50   "Situation in Russia (Debate)".
51   On the detention of the Greenpeace activists by Russia see Alex G. Oude Elferink, "The Arctic Sunrise Incident: A Multi-faceted Law of the Sea Case with a Human Rights Dimension", *The International Journal of Marine and Coastal Law*, Vol. 29, No. 2 (2014), pp. 244–289.
52   "Detention of Greenpeace Activists in Russia (Debate)", *European Parliament*, 23 October (2013), http://europarl.europa.eu/sides/getDoc.do?pubRef=-//EP//TEXT+CRE+20131023+ITEM-017+DOC+XML+V0//EN&language=EN
53   "Debates".
54   "Rule of Law in Russia (Debate)". Assange was not detained in the UK, but applied for, and was eventually granted, political asylum at the Ecuadorian Embassy in London.

55 "Explanations of Vote", *European Parliament*, 15 March (2012), http://europarl.europa.
eu/sides/getDoc.do?pubRef=-//EP//TEXT+CRE+20120315+ITEM-012+DOC+
XML+V0//EN&language=EN

56 "Murder of Human Rights Activists in Russia", *European Parliament*, 17 September
(2009), http://europarl.europa.eu/sides/getDoc.do?pubRef=-//EP//TEXT+CRE+
20090917+ITEM-009-01+DOC+XML+V0//EN&language=EN

57 Ibid. The Decrees of the President of the Republic and the Constitutional Decrees of
the President of the Republic, also known as the Beneš Decrees, were a series of laws
passed by the government of Czechoslovakia after the Second World War that
ordered the expulsion of the German and Hungarian minorities and confiscation of
their property.

58 "Outcome of the Presidential Elections in Russia (Debate)", *European Parliament*,
14 March (2012), http://europarl.europa.eu/sides/getDoc.do?pubRef=-//EP//
TEXT+CRE+20120314+ITEM-013+DOC+XML+V0//EN&language=EN

59 "Common Visa Restrictions for Russian Officials Involved in the Sergei Magnitsky
Case (Short Presentation)", *European Parliament*, 22 October (2012), http://europarl.
europa.eu/sides/getDoc.do?pubRef=-//EP//TEXT+CRE+20121022+ITEM-024+
DOC+XML+V0//EN&language=EN

60 "Rule of Law in Russia (Debate)".

61 "Outcome of the Presidential Elections in Russia (Debate)".

62 "EU-Russia Summit on 18 November 2009 in Stockholm (Debate)", *European
Parliament*, 11 November (2009), http://europarl.europa.eu/sides/getDoc.do?pubRef
=-//EP//TEXT+CRE+20091111+ITEM-016+DOC+XML+V0//EN&language
=EN

63 Ibid.

64 "European Parliament Resolution of 12 September 2013 on the Pressure Exerted by
Russia on Eastern Partnership Countries (in the Context of the Upcoming Eastern
Partnership Summit in Vilnius)", *European Parliament*, 12 September (2013), http://
europarl.europa.eu/sides/getDoc.do?type=TA&reference=P7-TA-2013-0383&lang
uage=EN

65 "Pressure Exercised by Russia on Countries of the Eastern Partnership (in the
Context of the Upcoming Eastern Partnership Summit in Vilnius)", *European
Parliament*, 12 September (2013), http://europarl.europa.eu/sides/getDoc.do?pubRef=
-//EP//TEXT+CRE+20130912+ITEM-014-21+DOC+XML+V0//EN&language
=EN

66 "European Parliament Resolution of 17 April 2014 on Russian Pressure on Eastern
Partnership Countries and in Particular Destabilisation of Eastern Ukraine", *European
Parliament*, 17 April (2014), http://europarl.europa.eu/sides/getDoc.do?type=TA&
reference=P7-TA-2014-0457&language=EN

67 A Hungarian MEP Csanád Szegedi, who was elected to the European Parliament as
a member of the far-right Jobbik party, supported the resolution, but he resigned from
all the posts he held in Jobbik in 2012, shortly after revealing that he had Jewish roots.

68 Daphne Halikiopoulou, Sofia Vasilopoulou, "Support for the Far Right in the 2014
European Parliament Elections: A Comparative Perspective", *The Political Quarterly*,
Vol. 85, No. 3 (2014), pp. 285–288 (285).

69 The full name of this Latvian party is Nacionālā apvienība "Visu Latvijai!" –
"Tēvzemei un Brīvībai/LNNK" (National Alliance "All For Latvia!" – "For Fatherland
and Freedom/LNNK").

70 "European Parliament Resolution of 10 June 2015 on the State of EU-Russia
Relations", *European Parliament*, 10 June (2015), http://europarl.europa.eu/sides/
getDoc.do?type=TA&reference=P8-TA-2015-0225&language=EN

71 "European Parliament Resolution of 11 June 2015 on the Strategic Military Situation
in the Black Sea Basin Following the Illegal Annexation of Crimea by Russia", *European*

Parliament, 11 June (2015), http://europarl.europa.eu/sides/getDoc.do?type=TA&reference=P8-TA-2015-0232&language=EN

72   "European Parliament Resolution of 10 June 2015".

73   Ibid.

74   "European Parliament Resolution of 11 June 2015".

75   "State of EU-Russia Relations", *European Parliament*, 10 June (2015), http://europarl.europa.eu/sides/getDoc.do?pubRef=-//EP//TEXT+CRE+20150610+ITEM-009-05+DOC+XML+V0//EN&language=EN

76   "European Parliament Resolution of 12 March 2015 on the Murder of the Russian Opposition Leader Boris Nemtsov and the State of Democracy in Russia", *European Parliament*, 12 March (2015), http://europarl.europa.eu/sides/getDoc.do?type=TA&language=EN&reference=P8-TA-2015-0074

77   "Murder of the Russian Opposition Leader Boris Nemtsov and the State of Democracy in Russia", *European Parliament*, 12 March (2015), http://europarl.europa.eu/sides/getDoc.do?pubRef=-//EP//TEXT+CRE+20150312+ITEM-011-04+DOC+XML+V0//EN&language=EN

78   "State of EU-Russia Relations (Debate)", *European Parliament*, 9 June (2015), http://europarl.europa.eu/sides/getDoc.do?pubRef=-//EP//TEXT+CRE+20150609+ITEM-003+DOC+XML+V0//EN&language=EN

79   "European Parliament Resolution of 11 June 2015".

80   "Strategic Military Situation in the Black Sea Basin Following the Illegal Annexation of Crimea by Russia", *European Parliament*, 11 June (2015), http://europarl.europa.eu/sides/getDoc.do?pubRef=-//EP//TEXT+CRE+20150611+ITEM-006-01+DOC+XML+V0//EN&language=EN

81   "State of EU-Russia Relations".

82   See Kai Arzheimer, "The AfD: Finally a Successful Right-Wing Populist Eurosceptic Party for Germany?", *West European Politics*, Vol. 38, No. 3 (2015), pp. 535–556; Robert Grimm, "The Rise of the German Eurosceptic Party Alternative für Deutschland, between Ordoliberal Critique and Popular Anxiety", *International Political Science Review*, Vol. 36, No. 3 (2015), pp. 264–278.

83   Noah Barkin, "German AfD Founder Leaves Party Decrying Xenophobic Shift", *Reuters*, 8 July (2015), http://reuters.com/article/us-germany-politics-eurosceptics-idUSKCN0PI25720150708

84   For brief political portraits of these seven MEPs see chapter "Repräsentanz: Entstehungsgeschichte und Flügel der AfD", In David Bebnowski, *Die Alternative für Deutschland. Aufstieg und gesellschaftliche Repräsentanz einer rechten populistischen Partei* (Wiesbaden: Springer Fachmedien, 2015), pp. 19–31.

85   "Situation in Ukraine and State of Play of EU-Russia Relations (Debate)", *European Parliament*, 16 September (2014), http://europarl.europa.eu/sides/getDoc.do?pubRef=-//EP//TEXT+CRE+20140916+ITEM-004+DOC+XML+V0//EN&language=EN

86   "Situation in Ukraine (Debate)", European Parliament, 14 January (2015), http://europarl.europa.eu/sides/getDoc.do?pubRef=-//EP//TEXT+CRE+20150114+ITEM-007+DOC+XML+V0//EN&language=EN. Note, however, that despite his earlier belief that Russia's annexation of Crimea was against the international law, Pretzell took part in the Second Yalta International Economic Forum that was held in Crimea in April 2016, see Chapter 6.

87   "State of EU-Russia Relations".

88   Ibid.

89   "Strategic Military Situation in the Black Sea Basin Following the Illegal Annexation of Crimea by Russia".

90   "Strategic Military Situation in the Black Sea Basin Following the Illegal Annexation of Crimea by Russia (Debate)", *European Parliament*, 10 June (2015), http://europarl.

europa.eu/sides/getDoc.do?pubRef=-//EP//TEXT+CRE+20150610+ITEM-013+DOC+XML+V0//EN&language=EN

91 "State of EU-Russia Relations"; "Strategic Military Situation in the Black Sea Basin Following the Illegal Annexation of Crimea by Russia".
92 "State of EU-Russia Relations".
93 Ibid.
94 "Πολιτικές Θέσεις", *Χρυσή Αυγή*, http://xryshaygh.com/kinima/thesis

CONCLUSION

Almost 100 years ago, particular ultranationalist circles in Germany envisaged an alliance with Soviet Russia that would help liberate their country from 'predatory' English and French capitalists, and secure truly German rule over Germany. The Soviets, while formally promoting communism worldwide, were ready to collaborate with German fascists not only to break up Western isolation of Soviet Russia but also to inflict damage on the Entente capitalists that allegedly endeavoured to enslave the German and Soviet peoples.

Today, one can hear echoes of the interwar reciprocities between the Soviets and German ultranationalists in a post-Cold War international setting. The actors have changed, but some correlations remain similar. The 'Entente' of today is the liberal-democratic West in general and the United States and NATO in particular. Certain far-right forces in Europe, North America and elsewhere embrace Putin's Russia as an ally in their struggle against Western liberal democracy and multiculturalism hoping that a (geo)political alliance with Moscow will help them reconstruct the mythologised and romanticised nation-state and 'take our country back'. In their turn, Russian officials, leading politicians and loyalists are using the Western far right not only to consolidate the authoritarian kleptocratic regime at home and impose Moscow's geopolitical objectives in the post-Soviet space, but also to counteract the growing isolation of Russia in the Europeanised world and, in particular cases, to disrupt the liberal-democratic consensus in Western societies and, thus, destabilise them.

In terms of ideology, contemporary far-right authors, movements and organisations, which consciously align themselves with Putin's Russia, draw on a vast repository of historical right-wing extremist discourses. The major ideological inspiration for the rapprochement with Russia originating from the interwar period was National Bolshevism that combined commitments to class struggle, nationalisation of the means of production and ultranationalism. Minor inspirations from the same period included the Conservative Revolution and Strasserite left-wing Nazism. The Cold War era brought new incentives for cooperation with Russia, namely particular neutralist strands in post-war pan-European fascism that initially saw both the United States and USSR as tantamount enemies of Europe, but increasingly shifted to a pro-Soviet position considering the United States a much more sinister force eroding the ethnic, cultural and psychological fabric of European nations. The pro-Soviet far-right neutralists' dream centred around a common geopolitical space imagined as 'a European Imperium' that would unite Europe and Russia in a geopolitical symbiosis, or the 'Euro-Soviet Empire' from Vladivostok to Dublin – an idea that could be traced back to the interwar National Bolshevik concept of the 'Germanic-Slavonic bloc' from Vladivostok to Vlissingen.

Despite the readiness of some far-right activists and politicians to cooperate with the Soviet Union with the aim of creating an anti-American geopolitical bloc, Moscow seemed to be reluctant to fully engage in this sort of cooperation. Yet the Soviet security services readily exploited the Western far right in the field of subversive operations, or active measures, against the West.

The closed nature of the Soviet Union impeded Western far-right activists' communication with their potential political allies in the Soviet Union, but the latter's demise opened a wide window of opportunity for cooperation. In the 1990s, during the rule of Russia's President Boris Yeltsin, representatives of various Western far-right movements and organisations rushed to Russia to build contacts with people they thought were close to taking power in the country. However, they soon appeared to be disappointed because the only contacts they had managed to establish were those with Russian ultranationalist activists and politicians whose chances to come to power were slim. Russian ultranationalists were eager to develop relations with the Western far right too, albeit for a different reason: for them, international contacts offered a prospect of consolidating their positions among other Russian 'patriots'.

This situation changed little during Vladimir Putin's first presidential term. Despite the already growing authoritarianism of his kleptocratic regime and rapidly deteriorating state of human rights in Russia, Moscow aspired to maintain relations with mainstream Western politicians, who, in their turn, embraced and welcomed friendship with Putin's Russia. This situation started to change after a series of 'colour revolutions' in the post-Soviet space in 2003–2005 which the Kremlin interpreted as a US-led Western attempt to undermine Russia's 'legitimate' sphere of influence and to orchestrate a regime change in Russia itself. This interpretation resulted in Moscow's ever intensifying rethinking of its relationship with the United States and EU. As Putin's regime felt threatened, pro-Western politicians and officials within the Russian ruling elite became gradually marginalised, while the representatives of the force institutions, or *siloviki*, with their Cold War mentality came to the fore of the debate on the relations between Russia and the West. Since then, Putin's Russia was no longer simply an authoritarian kleptocracy, because – due to Moscow's reactions to the 'colour revolutions' and rethinking of its relations with the West – it now mainstreamed, legitimized and sanctioned radically conservative, anti-Western and, especially, anti-American discourses' that, in the period between 1991 and 2004, existed largely on the peripheries of socio-political life.

These developments did not automatically result in the Kremlin's partnership with the Western far right. However, in 2005–2006, as a response to the work of independent electoral observation missions, whose critical assessment of fraudulent electoral practices contributed to the outbreaks of 'colour revolutions' against stolen elections, there emerged a political project that enabled some minor Russian actors and European far-right activists to join forces in a cause that directly benefited Putin's regime. This project involved politically biased observation of legitimate and illegitimate electoral processes in the post-Soviet space, or – in Moscow's understanding – Russia's sphere of influence. The Russian side of this project was represented by the formally independent, but intrinsically pro-Kremlin electoral monitoring organisation CIS-EMO. The other side was represented by the Belgian Eurasian Observatory for Democracy and Elections and the Polish European Centre for Geopolitical Analysis led and staffed by right-wing radicals. The three organisations invited far-right and far-left politicians and activists for international election observation missions, and, since 2005–2006, have been engaged in legitimising practices of electoral authoritarianism in the post-Soviet space while remaining loyal to general objectives of Russia's foreign and domestic policies. Since 2011, CIS-EMO gradually receded into the background; the organisation Civic Control managed by figures closely associated with the State Duma and the Civic Chamber of the Russian Federation took over CIS-EMO's contacts with Western far-right politicians and activists involved in electoral observation.

Russia's five-day war with Georgia in August 2008 became yet another important milestone in the development of relations between Russian pro-Kremlin actors and Western far-right activists. Immediately after the war, the Kremlin understood that it might have won the war easily, but had eventually failed to convince Western societies in the allegedly justified nature of Russia's aggression against Georgia. As Moscow was facing criticism from the West, the Russian state-controlled media changed the tactics. Previously, they relied solely on promoting the argument that Moscow's international and domestic activities were driven by good intentions, but since 2008–2009 the Russian media also started pushing the message that the West could not appreciate Russia's actions because Western liberal-democratic societies were decadent, plagued by same-sex marriages, moral crisis, failing multiculturalism and disrespect for the rights of the majority. To promote this message, Russian media, especially RT, have started engaging more intensely with far-right activists and politicians, as well as various conspiracy theorists and isolationists, who were willing to corroborate Moscow's message for ideological reasons. The narratives produced by the Russian state-controlled media with the help of Western far-right elements had two distinct audiences: a Western audience, whom the Russian media tried to convince that their ruling elites were failing them (in those areas where Putin's Russia succeeded); and a Russian audience, for whom the main message was that the presumed deficiencies of the EU and United States demonstrated the failure of liberal democracy as such and the unacceptability of Western models of development for Russia.

The anti-Western turn of Putin's regime and aggressive foreign policy moves inspired hope among particular Western far-right movements and organisations that have increasingly started operating, since 2006–2009, as pro-Kremlin front organisations promoting Moscow's geopolitical interests in their respective societies and internationally. Their cooperation with Russian stakeholders and institutions was facilitated by several types of operators. The first type of these operators is 'Russophile' far-right politicians who made substantial contribution to pro-Kremlin turns of their parties. The second type is Russian ultranationalists who encouraged pro-Kremlin efforts of a number of radical right-wing parties in Europe. The third type is Russian soft power institutions such as Rossotrudnichestvo and Fond 'Russkiy Mir' that generally aim to influence public opinion outside Russia. The fourth type is Russian ultraconservative activists, who – similar to the second type of operators – encouraged pro-Kremlin efforts of the European far right, but, unlike Russian ultranationalists, were actually able to help European far-right leaders reach politically significant Russian officials through their personal contacts. The fifth type is Russian diplomats who helped formalise relations between leaders of radical right-wing parties and representatives of Putin's regime. Finally, the sixth type is high-profile members of the Russian ruling 'Yedinaya Rossiya' party who became the most important point of contact between certain far-right politicians and the Russian ruling elites.

In 2010–2014, several major developments gave further incentive to cooperation between Russian actors and Western far-right politicians. On the one hand, Moscow's reaction to the 'Arab Spring' in 2010–2012 and the anti-Putin protests in 2012–2013 intensified the anti-Western and anti-American radicalisation of Putin's regime. On the other hand, many Western mainstream politicians and officials gradually withdrew their support for Putin's regime over its crackdown on the anti-Putin protests, show trials and dubious laws violating human rights, Moscow's backing of Bashar al-Assad's regime, and, most importantly, the annexation of Crimea and covert invasion of Eastern Ukraine.

To be sure, more than ever Putin's regime wanted to pursue relations with influential politicians in the West. But it seems that in 2012–2014 – against the background of the dramatic deterioration of relations with the West and, especially, after the EU, the United States and some other countries imposed sanctions against Russia – Putin and his inner circle convinced themselves that the West was waging a 'war' on Russia and that it was hardly possible to return to the political honeymoon with the West that Putin's kleptocracy had enjoyed in 2000–2004. As a result, Putin's regime – drawing on a disparate range of its grievances, concerns and complaints over the perceived Western approaches towards Russia – formulated its long-term objective: to conclude with the West a 'new Yalta agreement' that would fix a Russian geopolitical sphere of influence and legitimise the indefinite rule of the authoritarian kleptocratic regime in Russia. In order to achieve this objective, Moscow would ideally cooperate with Western mainstream politicians and officials who, for whatever reason, would be ready to agree to the Kremlin's conditions, return to business as usual and build what Putin called 'a harmonious economic community stretching from Lisbon to Vladivostok'.[1] In Germany, the mainstream apologists of Putin's regime received the name *Putin-Versteher* (Putin understanders).

The problem for Moscow is that a 'new Yalta agreement' is opposed by those Western politicians who understand the deeply illiberal and undemocratic nature of the Kremlin's proposal, and the threat that this 'agreement' poses to the EU and the international order. The accomplishment of Putin's objective, as Timothy Snyder notes, will ultimately lead to the destruction of the EU as a liberal-democratic project.[2] Even more problematic for the Kremlin is that Western opposition to a 'new Yalta agreement' is relatively united and, so far, has prevailed over the *Putin-Versteher*. Beyond all doubt, this unity is neither ideal nor seamless – the institutions, traditions, and practices of Western liberal democracies themselves render them vulnerable to Russia's active measures. But it is based on the workings of powerful alliances such as the EU, NATO and transatlantic partnerships that are difficult to undermine.

These circumstances triggered an upsurge of Moscow's cooperation with Western far-right forces, some of which had already proven their unwavering loyalty to Moscow by that time. Moreover, Russian ultranationalist, ultraconservative and other operators involved in building and developing contacts with the Western far right in favour of the Kremlin's foreign policy objectives, actively promoted this cooperation as it would help them consolidate their position inside Putin's regime.

Russian ultranationalist and ultraconservative operators of Western far-right contacts are open about their ideological aversion of the West and their sincere commitment to the destruction of the EU. One Dugin's associate makes this point clear:

> Acknowledging the civilisational nature of the conflict between Russia and the West, we aim at destroying the West in its current form as a civilisation. Therefore, having recourse to the use of existing networks, we should give priority to those that are themselves directed at the destruction of modern European civilisational identity.
>
> Groups that can act in this capacity include totalitarian sects, separatist movements, neo-Nazi and racist movements, anarchists and anti-globalists, radical ecologists, Eurosceptics, isolationists, illegal migrants, etc. This is exactly how the West operates, using [against Russia] liberal and human rights non-governmental organisations whose ideology is destructive and pernicious for the Russian civilisation.[3]

Naturally, this openness about the willingness to destroy the liberal-democratic West is intrinsic only to the most extreme Russian operators of Western far-right contacts. However, apart from its ostentatiously radical anti-Westernist message, the above-mentioned quote contains another important narrative that can also be found in the rhetoric of Russian high-ranking circles: Russia's actions, no matter how aggressive they are, are justified by what is perceived by Moscow as aggressive actions of the West. Or, as Ivan Krastev puts it, the Kremlin is engaged in 'reverse engineering' Western foreign policy, that is 'trying to reconstruct and imitate what they believe the West is doing',[4] and the Kremlin believes that the West is waging a war on Russia.

This context is key to understanding the so-called 'Gerasimov's Doctrine', an article on the recent past, present and expected future of warfare written by the Chief of the General Staff of Russia's Armed Forces Valery Gerasimov[5] and most likely addressed to Russia's senior political leadership.[6] Discussing the role of non-military methods in the resolution of interstate conflicts, Gerasimov argued that the primary phases of conflict development involved such non-military measures employed by an aggressor-nation as 'the formation of coalitions and alliances' and 'formation of the political opposition' in a victim-nation.[7] As Keir Giles asserts, what Gerasimov described 'was the Russian perception of how the US-led West intervenes in the internal affairs of states, exacerbating instability by engendering "colour revolutions" in those that resist US hegemony, and financing and supplying weapons to rebel groups and mercenaries'.[8]

Following the 'reverse engineering' pattern mentioned above, for Moscow, 'formation of coalitions and alliances' with the Western far right constitutes one of several types of active measures aimed at achieving the Kremlin's major foreign policy objectives, in case other, softer active measures do not work. In other words, Moscow's cooperation with the far right is dependent on the level and quality of contacts with the *Putin-Versteher* in Western national contexts, and Moscow always considers these two scenarios. The first scenario, or Plan A, is that if Putin's regime still has – or finds new – influential mainstream allies in a Western country, it will prefer to work with them to advance its interests. In the majority of cases Moscow will not directly support those far-right groups that are in opposition to the *Putin-Versteher* in fear of compromising relations with the latter. Indeed, why, for example, bid welcome to Jobbik when Putin's regime is already benefiting from the illiberal-democratic policies of Hungary's Prime Minister Viktor Orbán to whom Jobbik is opposed? Nevertheless, even in cases such as this, Moscow will strive to maintain *medium-level* contacts with the anti-EU, anti-NATO, anti-American and generally anti-systemic forces through various operators. Thus, the second scenario, or Plan B, is that if the *Putin-Versteher* in a particular Western country become either too few or of little authority, then Moscow will activate and play the far-right card and directly support the anti-systemic forces to subvert the liberal-democratic order with the aim of undermining the unity of the Western opposition to Moscow's illiberal vision of a 'new Yalta agreement'. This is demonstrated, in particular, by the case of the FPÖ: official Moscow is on good terms with the Austrian mainstream political forces, but they were considered to be in decline in mid-term perspective; therefore, the Kremlin became interested in building stronger contacts with the FPÖ in the hope that this far-right party comes to power in

Austria. However, a reversal of the second scenario is possible too, as the case of the FN showed: Moscow provided support to the FN in 2013–2015, but François Fillon, the candidate of the centre-right Les Républicains for the 2017 presidential election, was seen by the Kremlin as a mainstream *Putin-Versteher* and – according to public opinion polls conducted until the end of January 2017 – was more popular than the FN's presidential candidate Marine Le Pen; thus, the Kremlin limited (but did not entirely end) its cooperation with the FN in order not to sour relations with Fillon. However, with the decline of Fillon's popularity in February 2017, the Kremlin, again, returned to the second scenario and supported Le Pen.

In the second scenario, the question of how far Moscow is prepared to go in using or exploiting the Western far right against the EU, NATO and the liberal-democratic consensus needs further exploration. May Russia go as far as building a modern version of the Schwarze Reichswehr that would imply cooperation with Western right-wing paramilitaries willing to wage a real war on the modern 'Entente'? Could Moscow eventually fulfil a dream of Jean Thiriart and provide European national-revolutionaries with an 'outside lung' which fascists can use to prepare for the destruction of the EU and liberation of Europe from 'American influence'?

These questions may sound dramatic or conspirological, but various reports indicate that they are legitimate. Russian Neo-Eurasianists had developed relations with, and trained, pro-Russian separatists in Eastern Ukraine almost 10 years before the latter facilitated the Russian invasion of the region in 2014.[9] The Slovak right-wing paramilitary movement Slovenskí Branci (Slovak Conscripts), which is characterised by pro-Russian and anti-NATO views, was formed in 2012 by a Slovak national who had received training in Russia by former officers of the Spetsnaz, that is Russia's Special Purpose Military Units.[10] A pro-Russian and anti-NATO right-wing paramilitary group Českoslovenští vojáci v záloze (Czechoslovak soldiers in reserve) exists in the Czech Republic too.[11] According to the findings of a German investigative journalist, officers of Russia's Main Intelligence Directorate and Air Landing Troops may be involved in the training of German right-wingers on the basis of a Russian martial arts school connected to the Russian pro-Putin biker gang 'Night Wolves'.[12] In 2014, British right-wing extremists were reported to have received training in Wales from representatives of the Russian neo-Nazi group White Rex.[13] Hungarian investigative journalists András Dezső and Szabolcs Panyi argue that the extreme-right paramilitary movement Magyar Nemzeti Arcvonal, whose leader István Győrkös killed a police officer in October 2016, had Russian connections and that 'Russian diplomats have participated in the airsoft drills' organised by the MNA.[14]

One suspects, like in the case of Russia's covert invasion of Ukraine, that some relevant information remains unrevealed. As Chapter 1 demonstrated, particular historical details of the covert Soviet cooperation with the European far right were discovered dozens of years later. There is little doubt that some information may never come to the surface at all. The situation today may be similar. This should encourage academics to do further research, analysis and clarification of the areas

Conclusion

and aspects of cooperation between various Russian actors and Western far-right activists, movements and organisations discussed or not discussed in this book.

Future investigations, could focus on national case studies and address the issues such as, for example, Russian relations with US far-right figures who supported the election of Donald Trump as a new US president. One especially intriguing connection is the American far-right movement known as Alternative Right (or alt-right). A prominent representative of alt-right is Steve Bannon, a former Executive Chair of the influential far-right website *Breitbart News*, whom President Donald Trump designated as his chief strategist and senior counsellor. Another notable representative of alt-right is Richard Spencer, President of the think-tank National Policy Institute, whom RT approached as a 'political analyst' and expert on the Libyan and Syrian issues already in 2013. Spencer's former wife Nina Kouprianova[15] translated into English the writings of Aleksandr Dugin later published in Spencer's publishing house Washington Summit Publishers.[16]

Further research could also consider the question about the significance of ideological aspects: in which cases is ideology the only motivation that drives certain far-right movements and parties to become pro-Kremlin front organisations in the West? And in which cases do personal biographies, business interests, financial reward or counterintelligence operations possibly play a more prominent role?[17] One also needs to explore, in more detail, the patterns of communication between Western far-right and the highest quarters of political power in Russia: who creates which channels of the communication? What operators are involved in each case? Who makes a decision to increase or decrease the intensity and significance of this or that communication? Another open question is the magnitude of the impact of the far-right parties' engagement with various Russian actors on the socio-political situation in their Western societies. By exploring these issues researchers will contribute not only to the emergent field of studies of the relations between Russia and the Western far right, but will also make a contribution to the information and formation of current Western public affairs, and, eventually, to the strengthening of liberal democracy and consolidation of democratic international institutions.

Notes

1   " 'From Lisbon to Vladivostok': Putin Envisions a Russia-EU Free Trade Zone", *Spiegel Online*, 25 November (2010), http://spiegel.de/international/europe/from-lisbon-to-vladivostok-putin-envisions-a-russia-eu-free-trade-zone-a-731109.html

2   Timothy Snyder, "The Battle in Ukraine Means Everything", *New Republic*, 12 May (2014), https://newrepublic.com/article/117692/fascism-returns-ukraine

3   Aleksandr Bovdunov, "Tsivilizatsionnye razborki", *Evrazia*, 13 January (2015), http://evrazia.org/article/230

4   "Ivan Krastev: Russia Is 'Reverse Engineering' Western Foreign Policy", *Graduate Institute Geneva*, 18 November (2015), http://graduateinstitute.ch/home/relations-publiques/news-at-the-institute/news-archives.html/_/news/corporate/2015/ivan-krastev-russia-is-reverse-e

5   Valery Gerasimov, "Tsennost' nauki – v predvidenii", *Voenno-promyshlenny kur'er*, No. 8 (2013), pp. 1–3. For the English translation of this article see Valery Gerasimov,

"The Value of Science Is in the Foresight", *Military Review*, January-February (2016), pp. 23–29.

6   Charles K. Bartles, "Getting Gerasimov Right", *Military Review*, January-February (2016), pp. 30–38 (31).

7   Gerasimov, "The Value of Science Is in the Foresight", p. 28.

8   Giles, *Russia's "New" Tools for Confronting the West*, p. 10.

9   See Anton Shekhovtsov, "Aleksandr Dugin's Neo-Eurasianism and the Russian-Ukrainian War", in Mark Bassin, Gonzalo Pozo-Martin (eds.), *The Politics of Eurasianism: Identity, Popular Culture and Russia's Foreign Policy* (Lanham: Rowman & Littlefield International, 2017), pp. 185–204.

10 Krekó, Győri, Milo, Marušiak, Széky, Lencsés, *Marching towards Eurasia*, p. 49.

11 Jan Wirnitzer, "V Česku roste proruská polovojenská milice. Chce si 'vzít vlast zpět' ", *iDNES.cz*, 24 November (2015), http://zpravy.idnes.cz/profil-ceskoslovensti-vojaci-v-zaloze-obrtel-foo-/domaci.aspx?c=A151123_123952_domaci_jw

12 Boris Reitschuster, *Putins verdeckter Krieg: Moskaus Allianz gegen Europa* (Berlin: Econ, 2016), pp. 256–264.

13 Scott Hesketh, Colin Cortbus, "Neo-Nazi Nuts Are Training Yobs to Embark on Race War", *The Daily Star*, 9 November (2014), http://dailystar.co.uk/news/latest-news/409339/Neo-Nazi-activists-train-right-wing-Brits-race-war-secret-camps; Gerry Gable, "Not Thugs but Terrorists in the Making", *Searchlight*, 10 November (2014), https://web.archive.org/web/20150818045435/http://searchlightmagazine.com/blogs/searchlight-blog/not-thugs-but-terrorists-in-the-making

14 András Dezső, Szabolcs Panyi, "Russian Diplomats Exercised with Hungarian Cop Killer's Far-right Gang", *Index*, 28 October (2016), http://index.hu/belfold/2016/10/28/russian_diplomats_exercised_with_hungarian_cop_killer_s_far_right_gang/

15 They apparently separated in 2016. Nina Kouprianova also uses a pen name Nina Byzantina.

16 Aleksandr Dugin, *Martin Heidegger: The Philosophy of Another Beginning* (Arlington: Raddix/Washington Summit, 2014).

17 In May 2014, Hungary's Constitution Protection Office accused Jobbik's Béla Kovács of being a Russian spy, see Benjámin Novák, "Jobbik MEP Accused of Spying for Russia", *Budapest Beacon*, 17 May (2014), http://budapestbeacon.com/featured-articles/jobbik-mep-accused-of-spying-for-russia; in May 2016, Polish prosecutors detained Mateusz Piskorski on suspicions of spying for Russia, see "Poland Detains Pro-Kremlin Party Leader for 'Spying' ", *The Guardian*, 19 May (2016), https://the guardian.com/world/2016/may/19/poland-detains-pro-kremlin-party-leader-mateusz-piskorski-spying. If Kovács's and Piskorski's activities are properly investigated, we may know more details about the cooperation with various Russian actors.

INDEX

Page numbers in bold indicate a table, n indicates an endnote